EU Immigration and Asylum Law

(Text and Commentary):

Second Revised Edition

Immigration and Asylum Law and Policy in Europe

Edited by

Jan Niessen
Elspeth Guild

VOLUME 27

The titles published in this series are listed at brill.nl/ialp

EU Immigration and Asylum Law

(Text and Commentary):

Second Revised Edition

Volume 1: Visas and Border Controls

Edited by

Steve Peers, Elspeth Guild and Jonathan Tomkin

MARTINUS
NIJHOFF
PUBLISHERS

LEIDEN • BOSTON
2012

Library of Congress Cataloging-in-Publication Data

Peers, Steve.
  EU immigration and asylum law / edited by Steve Peers, Elspeth Guild, and Jonathan Tomkin. -- 2nd rev. ed.
    p. cm. -- (Immigration and asylum law and policy in Europe ; v. 27)
  Includes index.
  ISBN 978-90-04-22222-9 (hardback : alk. paper) -- ISBN 978-90-04-22237-3 (e-book)
  1. Emigration and immigration law--European Union countries. 2. Asylum, Right of--European Union countries. I. Guild, Elspeth. II. Tomkin, Jonathan. III. Title.

  KJE6044.P44 2012
  342.2408'2--dc23

                                             2012018016

ISSN 1568-2749
ISBN 978-90-04-22222-9 (hardback)
ISBN 978-90-04-22237-3 (e-book)

This book is printed on acid-free paper.

Printed by Printforce, the Netherlands

Contents

Preface vii

Chapter 1   Overview 1

Chapter 2   Institutional Framework 7

Chapter 3   The Schengen Borders Code 33

Chapter 4   Schengen Information System 97

Chapter 5   Frontex 119

Chapter 6   Other Border Control Measures 205

Chapter 7   EU Visa Lists 223

Chapter 8   The Visa Code 251

Chapter 9   Visa Facilitation 315

Chapter 10 Visa Information System 337

Chapter 11 Other Visa Measures 393

Preface

Since the first edition of EU *Immigration and Asylum Law: Text and Commentary* in 2006, much has changed. Not only has the legal framework of the EU been substantially revamped by the Lisbon Treaty, but the development of EU law on border controls, immigration and asylum has mushroomed. The purpose of this second edition is to take into account all these changes and provide a coherent, comprehensive and authoritative work which covers the whole field. As in the first edition, each chapter includes a detailed analysis of each EU measure under discussion as well as the text of the measure. This work is designed primarily for academics and practitioners in the field of asylum, borders and immigration law. Since EU asylum legislation is still being overhauled, it will be addressed in a further future volume: *EU Asylum Law: Text and Commentary*. This book is updated to 1 August 2011.

This work is the result of the hard work of a number of people who have participated in writing the chapters. Thanks must first be expressed to Nicola Rogers, the co-editor of the first edition of the book. While she has not participated in this second edition, her work has been the basis of many of the chapters in this work. While the review of the chapters has been collective, primary responsibility for writing the chapters has fallen on different members of the team. Professor Steve Peers, of the University of Essex, has pulled together the entire work and written the majority of the chapters. These are chapters 1, 2, 4 and 6–11. Some of these chapters are adapted from parts of *EU Justice and Home Affairs Law*, 3rd edition (OUP, 2011), but in each case the material has been updated and expanded.

Professor Elspeth Guild, Radboud University Nijmegen, is primarily responsible for chapter 3, while Jonathan Tomkin, barrister and Director, Irish Centre for European Law, Trinity College Dublin, wrote chapter 5.

Our approach in this book has been to examine EU law in this field from the perspective of the development of the European Union as a lawmaker, rather than the continued legislative role of the Member States. The intention of the Treaty drafters to create a "common" policy on visas and borders, and the initial case law of the Court of Justice, demonstrates that the EU is developing a coherent and complete structure of borders and migration law. In our opinion, such an approach is critical to the enduring value and importance of the work.

We would like to thank a number of other people for their enthusiastic encouragement of this project, not least our editor, Lindy Melman at Brill who has been both sympathetic and demanding – just the right combination to keep authors working on their projects. Thanks are also due to Steve Peers' family – his wife Pamela Chatterjee and children Kiran, Isabella, Serena and Sophia – for their understanding and support.

Chapter 1

Overview

1. *Introduction*

The EU's immigration legislation runs the gamut from highly technical operational matters to broad measures covering basic aspects of immigration law. Between them, the proposed or adopted measures cover most immigration issues. In the particular field of visas and border controls, EU legislation in principle leaves little leeway to Member States to apply different policies.

This volume contains the text of and commentary upon all of the most important measures as regards visas and borders. However, it only includes a briefer summary of the less important measures in this field. The purpose of this chapter is to give an integrated overview of all of the various measures, as well as the overall political context.

2. *Legal Context*

Each of these three volumes take as its starting point the entry into force of the Treaty of Amsterdam on 1 May 1999, because only at that point was it possible for the European Community (as it then was) to adopt measures dealing with most or all aspects of immigration and asylum law. Before that point, the Community's power was limited to measures concerning aspects of visa policy (from 1993 to 1999) and matters largely relating to the free movement (between Member States) of EU citizens and their family members (from the inception of the Community). But the exact scope of these limits of the Community's "classical" powers were a subject of dispute, as analysed further in Chapter 2 of each volume. They potentially remain a subject of dispute, even after the entry into force of the Treaty of Lisbon on 1 December 2009, because the institutional rules relating to other fields of EU law (ie fields of law not related to Justice and Home Affairs issues), are different from the rules governing EU immigration and asylum law, found (after the Treaty of Lisbon) in "Title V" of Part Three of the Treaty on the Functioning of the European

Union (TFEU), as regards possible "opt-outs" from EU law.[1] Chapter 2 provides an analysis of the functioning of the EU institutions in this distinct legal context, as it has evolved over time pursuant to the Treaties of Amsterdam, Nice and Lisbon.

Prior to the Treaty of Amsterdam, there were two distinct phases in the development of EU immigration and asylum law. In the first phase, before the entry into force of the Treaty on European Union in November 1993, there was no formal Treaty context for the adoption of rules on immigration and asylum at all within the European Communities, except for the highly disputed possibility that the regular rules of the "Community method" could be used. In the second phase, the "Maastricht era" from 1993 to 1999, the Community gained its limited initial powers over visas, but the main powers were granted to the "European Union", which was then distinct (as regards substantive law) from the Community, and constituted a "formal intergovernmental" system. But given Member States' reluctance to agree any binding measures during this period, the output of this era consists largely of non-binding measures such as Resolutions and Recommendations.

There are three other important aspects to the legal context. First of all, the Treaty of Amsterdam terminated a parallel development, begun with the 1985 Schengen Agreement and continuing with the 1990 Schengen Convention and a huge number of implementing measures. The Schengen process was a system agreed among most (but not all) Member States to provide for (*inter alia*) abolition of internal border controls between Member States, an integrated system of external border controls and common rules on short-stay visas. There were also flanking rules on aspects of irregular immigration, responsibility for asylum applications, criminal justice and police cooperation, including the creation of a database (the Schengen Information System, or SIS) which *inter alia* contained a list of persons to be denied entry to the entire Schengen area. These rules were integrated into the scope of the European Community and European Union legal system by the Treaty of Amsterdam.[2] Since the Schengen system began operating in March 1995 and resulted in agreement on far more immigration measures than proved possible within the EU before the Treaty of Amsterdam, most chapters in this volume examine what happened to the previous Schengen rules (the "Schengen *acquis*") after it was integrated into the EU legal framework. It will be seen that

---

[1] Arts 67-89 TFEU. The specific provisions on immigration and asylum are set out in Arts 77-80 TFEU (Chapter II of Title V).

[2] See the Decisions in OJ 1999 L 176.

in the area of visas and border controls, the Schengen *acquis* has been almost entirely replaced by EU measures – except in the specific field of the freedom to travel for third-country nationals and (for now) the Schengen Information System.

Secondly, the developments within this field obviously have an important impact on protection of human rights, within the scope of the European Convention on Human Rights (ECHR), the Geneva Convention on the status of refugees and other treaties. This aspect, including the relevant rules set out in the EU's Charter of Rights and forming part of the general principles of EU law, is considered throughout both volumes.

Thirdly, the enlargement of the European Union in 2004 and 2007 had an important impact upon developments in this field. The substantive law in this area has clearly been adapted to accommodate, to some extent, the interests and preferences of the new Member States – just as those Member States had to accommodate themsleves to apply the existing EU rules.

3. *Political Context*

The European Union has consistently attempted to agree on the broad lines of immigration and asylum policy at the summit meetings of heads of state and government ("European Councils"). It is often forgotten that back in December 1991, the Maastricht European Council agreed an initial detailed immigration and asylum policy to be implemented once the new Treaty on European Union entered into force.[3] But in practice, almost no concrete measure to implement this policy was ever actually adopted before the Treaty of Amsterdam entered into force in 1999.

This time around, the EU first of all agreed a detailed Action Plan on the implementation of Justice and Home Affairs (JHA) policy in December 1998, which was ultimately endorsed by the Vienna European Council later that month.[4] But further attention to the issue was deemed necessary, and so a special European Council to that end was held in Tampere, Finland in October 1999. This summit meeting set out broad principles in relation to JHA matters and apparently endorsed a relatively liberal and balanced immigration and asylum policy for the EU.

---

[3] For the text, see Guild and Niessen, *The Developing Immigration and Asylum Policies of the European Union: Adopted Conventions, Resolutions, Recommendations, Decisions and Conclusions* (Kluwer, 1996), 449–491.

[4] OJ 1999 C 19.

Nevertheless, by the time to review the Tampere conclusions at the end of 2001, little had in fact been agreed. However, the Laeken European Council in December that year did nothing to help matters, simply "passing the buck" back to the Commission to come up with revised proposals in several areas where the Council had failed to reach agreement and weighting the balance of EU policy further towards control of external borders and illegal immigration. Shortly afterwards, highly detailed "Action Plans" were agreed on those specific subjects. In the meantime, by the spring of 2002, events took another turn, with a perceived increase in the political sensitivity of immigration and asylum matters following French and Dutch elections. As a result, immigration and asylum policy became the centrepiece of the Seville European Council in June 2002, with a four-part plan adopted. In particular, the agreed detailed plan for control of EU external borders was endorsed and certain aspects of that plan were highlighted for early agreement.[5]

Subsequently, the EU adopted a second multi-year JHA progamme, the Hague Programme, in 2004.[6] A particular feature of this plan was the decision to move away from unanimous voting in the Council and mere consultation of the European Parliament (EP) towards the "co-decision" process,[7] which entails qualified majority voting (QMV) in Council and joint decision-making powers for the EP, for most immigration and asylum law issues, as from the start of 2005.[8] Finally, immediately following the entry into force of the Treaty of Lisbon, the European Council adopted the latest multi-year JHA programme, the Stockholm programme.[9]

4. *Specific Policies*

Since the "Schengen *acquis*" already contained a number of measures on visas and border controls, the Tampere conclusions did not focus much on development of legislation on these issues, despite the detailed Community powers granted by Article 62 EC (now Article 77 TFEU). As regards visas, an early priority was the completion of a fully common list of countries whose

---

[5] For more detailed comment on the summit conclusions, see Peers, "EU Immigration and Asylum Law after Seville", 16 IANL Journal (2002) 176.

[6] OJ 2005 C 53/1.

[7] Now known as the "ordinary legislative procedure" since the entry into force of the Treaty of Lisbon.

[8] See further chapter 2.

[9] OJ 2010 C 115. See the Commission's action plan on implementation of the programme (COM (2010) 171, 20 Apr. 2010).

nationals did or did not require visas to enter the Union.[10] Other visa measures included amendments to the common visa format, creation of new common formats for certain types of visas, adoption of special *ad hoc* visa arrangements (for the Olympics and Kaliningrad) and agreement on rules for the amendment of the Common Consular Instructions and associated manuals.[11] The latter measures were in turn used to amend the EU visa rules to set up a common form for visa applications, to charge a fee for visa applications (rather than for the issue of visas), to harmonise these fees and to adopt common rules on considering collective applications submitted by travel agents. Further development of the Schengen rules on freedom to travel for three months was hindered by complex arguments over whether the EU could or should agree rules permitting an extended stay for non-visa nationals, and if so, how to arrange for such extensions.

Since the extension of QMV to all visas and borders issues in 2004 and 2005, EU action in this area has intensified, with further amendments to the common visa list, the adoption of a "visa code" that brings together almost all rules relating to the visa application process, the development of a policy on visa facilitation for certain countries and the development of a "Visa Information System" to hold extensive amounts of personal data on all applicants for visas.[12]

As for border controls, there was no initiative at all up to the start of 2004 dealing with internal border issues, while from mid-2001 the development of *policy*, and eventually legislation, concerning external borders assumed growing importance. However, from 2004 onwards the EU adopted an extensive corpus of legislation, in particular adopting a "Borders Code" that brings together the rules concerning the crossing of both internal and external borders,[13] establishing an Agency for control of external borders (known as "Frontex"),[14] measures to establish a second-generation SIS,[15] rules on stamping passports and standard rules for Member States' treaties on local border traffic.[16]

---

[10] See chapter 7.
[11] See chapter 11.
[12] See respectively chapters 8–10.
[13] See chapter 3.
[14] See chapter 4.
[15] See chapter 5.
[16] On the latter measure, see chapter 6.

Chapter 2

Institutional Framework

1. *Introduction*

The EU rules concerning visas and border controls have historically been subject to a complex institutional framework, although that framework was simplified before, and as a result of, the entry into force of the Treaty of Lisbon. This chapter looks in turn at the rules in this area on: decision-making and competence; the jurisdiction of the Court of Justice; the territorial scope of EU law; and the application of other areas of EU law, in particular EU free movement law and EU association agreements.

2. *Decision-Making and Competence*

2.1. *Legislative Measures*

The rules concerning decision-making and competence as regards visas and borders were originally set out partly in the European Community (EC) Treaty, as amended by the original Treaty on European Union (TEU), and partly in the TEU itself. On the one hand, Article 100c EC gave the EC the power to adopt a common list of countries whose nationals required a visa to cross the external borders of the Member States and a common visa format, acting by qualified majority voting (QMV) in the Council on the basis of a Commission proposal after consulting the European Parliament (EP).[1] On the other hand, Article K.1 of the TEU stated that the Member States, within the context of the European Union (EU), could adopt measures on the crossing of external borders and related controls, as well as rules on the "conditions of entry and movement" of third-country nationals. This form of intergovernmental cooperation was known in practice as the "third pillar", and it entailed different forms of legal acts than EC law, along with unanimous voting in the

---

[1] QMV was phased in as regards the powers to adopt the visa list legislation, for the Council had to act unanimously on that subject until the end of 1995.

Council, a very limited role for the EP and only a shared power of initiative for the Commission. Unsurprisingly, there were disputes about the correct "legal base" for measures adopted or proposed (EC law, or the "third pillar"?), one of which reached the Court of Justice;[2] the EP also sued to enforce its power of consultation as regards visa list legislation.[3]

The Treaty of Amsterdam fundamentally changed this system by integrating all of the powers concerning the adoption of visa and border control measures into the EC Treaty, namely in Article 62 EC, which provided as follows:

> The Council, acting in accordance with the procedure referred to in Article 67, shall, within a period of five years after the entry into force of the Treaty of Amsterdam, adopt:
>
> 1. measures with a view to ensuring, in compliance with Article 14, the absence of any controls on persons, be they citizens of the Union or nationals of third countries, when crossing internal borders;
> 2. measures on the crossing of the external borders of the Member States which shall establish:
>   (a) standards and procedures to be followed by Member States in carrying out checks on persons at such borders;
>   (b) rules on visas for intended stays of no more than three months, including:
>   (i)   the list of third countries whose nationals must be in possession of visas when crossing the external borders and those whose nationals are exempt from that requirement;
>   (ii) the procedures and conditions for issuing visas by Member States;
>   (iii) a uniform format for visas;
>   (iv) rules on a uniform visa;
> 3. measures setting out the conditions under which nationals of third countries shall have the freedom to travel within the territory of the Member States during a period of no more than three months.

Article 67(3) EC provided for the continued application of the previous decision-making rules applying to the visa list and visa format legislation. However, other visa and border measures would have to be adopted in accordance with the rule in Article 67(1) EC, for a five-year period (until 1 May 2004): unanimity in Council, after consultation of the EP, on a proposal from either the Commission *or* a Member State. After this five-year period, these intergovernmental rules were moderated in that only the Commission could

---

[2] Case C-170/96 *Commission v Council* [1998] ECR I-2763. The Commission lost this case, as the Court of Justice held that the regulation of airport transit visas did not fall within the scope of Art. 100c EC.

[3] Case C-392/95 *EP v Council* [1997] ECR I-3213.

make proposals after this point,[4] and that legislation on the conditions for issuing visas or a uniform visa had to be adopted by means of the co-decision procedure (entailing joint decision-making power for the EP and QMV in Council).[5]

But all decision-making on border control and freedom to travel issues (Articles 62(1), 62(2)(a) and 62(3) EC) would remain subject to unanimous voting in the Council and consultation of the EP, unless the Council decided unanimously to alter these voting rules and apply the co-decision procedure (including QMV).[6] In practice, the Council decided as from 1 January 2005 to apply the co-decision procedure to these areas of law.[7] Emergency measures remained subject to QMV in Council with no EP involvement.[8]

The Treaty of Lisbon extended the co-decision procedure (now known as the "ordinary legislative procedure" to measures on the visa format and the visa list. It also revised the EU's competences in this area. The EU's powers in this field are now set out in Article 77 of the Treaty on the Functioning of the European Union (TFEU), which reads as follows:

1. The Union shall develop a policy with a view to:
   (a) ensuring the absence of any controls on persons, whatever their nationality, when crossing internal borders;
   (b) carrying out checks on persons and efficient monitoring of the crossing of external borders;
   (c) the gradual introduction of an integrated management system for external borders.
2. For the purposes of paragraph 1, the European Parliament and the Council, acting in accordance with the ordinary legislative procedure, shall adopt measures concerning:
   (a) the common policy on visas and other short-stay residence permits;
   (b) the checks to which persons crossing external borders are subject;
   (c) the conditions under which nationals of third countries shall have the freedom to travel within the Union for a short period;
   (d) any measure necessary for the gradual establishment of an integrated management system for external borders;
   (e) the absence of any controls on persons, whatever their nationality, when crossing internal borders.
3. If action by the Union should prove necessary to facilitate the exercise of the right referred to in Article 20(2)(a), and if the Treaties have not provided the necessary powers, the Council, acting in accordance with a special legislative

---

[4] Art. 67(2) EC, first indent.

[5] Art. 67(4) EC.

[6] Art. 67(2) EC, second indent.

[7] OJ 2004 L 396/45. For discussion, see Peers, "Transforming Decision- Making on EC Immigration and Asylum Law" (2005) 30 ELRev. 283.

[8] Art. 64(2) EC.

procedure, may adopt provisions concerning passports, identity cards, residence permits or any other such document. The Council shall act unanimously after consulting the European Parliament.
4. This Article shall not affect the competence of the Member States concerning the geographical demarcation of their borders, in accordance with international law.

It should be noted that in practice the EU institutions have consistently adopted Regulations in this area, although there is no legal requirement to do so. This may reflect the intention to ensure a degree of uniformity in this area, given that Directives afford Member States some flexibility in their application.[9]

A number of issues arise as regards the EU's competence over border controls and visa issues.[10] As regards Article 77(3) TFEU, this provision must be distinguished from the general external borders powers because it is subject to unanimity in Council and consultation of the EP (a "special legislative procedure"), rather than the ordinary legislative procedure. Also, the this legal base and measures adopted pursuant to it have to be interpreted in light of EU citizenship, not the EU's immigration objectives, given the cross-reference in Article 77(3) to facilitating EU citizens' free movement rights in Article 20 TFEU. Such powers can only be used to facilitate those rights to "move and reside freely", and this power can only be applied if other provisions of the Treaty "have not provided the necessary powers". The better view is that the EU's external borders competence is a valid legal base for the adoption of measures concerning the *security features* of EU citizens' passports, identity cards held by EU citizens and residence cards held by EU citizens' family members, since such measures relate to checks at external borders, at least where such borders are also internal borders between Schengen and non-Schengen Member States. Moreover, the harmonisation of such security features would not as such facilitate EU citizens' right to move and reside freely. On the other hand, harmonisation of the format of such documents facilitates free movement of EU citizens and their family members, because a common format ensures the immediate recognition of such documents by border guards when crossing internal EU borders.

The EU has legal powers pursuant to Article 77(2) TFEU as regards the creation of databases and the exchange of information concerning such documents, to the extent that storing, exchanging and accessing such data was

---

[9] See Art. 288 TFEU.
[10] See further Peers, *EU Justice and Home Affairs Law*, 3rd edition (OUP, 2011), 150–157 and 234–236.

linked to checks at the Member States' external borders. On the other hand, the 'passports' legal base does not confer power to establish or regulate such databases or exchange of information, since the development of such policies would not facilitate EU citizens' rights to move and reside freely.

Similarly, neither legal base conferred competence upon the EU to require Member States to introduce identity cards or to harmonise national law on the *internal* use (ie within a Member State's national territory) of such cards, because identity cards are not sufficiently connected to the crossing of external borders *or* the facilitation of EU citizens' free movement rights.

Although the practice of the Council is to adopt measures restricting the entry of specific third-country nationals on foreign policy grounds on the basis of the EU foreign policy powers, this can be questioned since the content of the measures concerned relates to border controls and visas, despite the foreign policy objective.

Finally, it should be noted that while the EU's powers over visas and border control issues are shared with Member States, the EU is not limited to setting minimum standards only in this area and the provisions of the TFEU point the EU towards establishing a "common" policy.[11] The Treaty does, however, reserve Member States' powers as regards the demarcation of their borders.[12]

2.2. *Implementing Measures*

Before the entry into force of the Treaty of Lisbon, this area of EC law (as it then was) was subject to the standard rule in Article 202 EC (as it was then) that the Commission should in principle have power to adopt measures implementing EC legislation at Community level, assisted by various committees of Member States' representatives (known in practice as "comitology committees"). However, Article 202 provided that in special circumstances the power to adopt implementing measures can be conferred upon the Council.[13] The case law of the Court of Justice made clear that basic rules could not be the subject of implementing measures, but must be set out following the full legislative process, and that implementing measures could not be ultra vires the

---

[11] See Arts. 67(2) and 77(2)(a) TFEU.

[12] Art. 77(4) TFEU.

[13] From a large literature, see Andenas and Turk, eds, *Delegated Legislation and the Role of Committees in the EU* (Kluwer, 2000); Joerges and Vos, eds, *EU Committees: Social Regulation, Law and Politics* (Hart, 1999); and Lenaerts and Verhoeven, "Towards a Legal Framework for Executive Rule- Making in the EU? The Contribution of the new Comitology Decision" (2000) 37 CMLRev. 645.

powers delegated by the parent measure.[14] There was a basic decision of the Council setting out the types of committee which assist the Commission (advisory, regulatory and management committees),[15] and the EC legislative process was rife with disputes about the form of committee to be established; sometimes these disputes reached the Court of Justice.[16]

The application of the general rules regarding implementing measures was controversial as regards visas and borders rules, where the Council gave power to itself (and, in part, the individual Member States) to adopt measures amending two key provisions of the Schengen *acquis* which were integrated into EC law: the Common Consular Instructions for visa applications and the Common Manual concerning external borders.[17] However, otherwise the Council was willing to apply the normal rule and confer powers on the Commission in this area (see further below).

Some of these exceptions from the normal rule were challenged. First, the Commission disputed the decision of the Council to confer power upon itself and the Member States to implement the Schengen visas and borders rules before the Court of Justice.[18] Ultimately, the Commission lost this case, as the Court upheld the Council's decision, *inter alia* because in 2001 (when the measures concerned had been adopted) the issues had until recently been dealt with pursuant to the "third pillar", the transitional period for decision-making in this area was still in force, the subject-matter being delegated was clearly circumscribed and the Council had committed itself to review the delegation to itself by 2004. Ultimately, when the Schengen measures were replaced by the border code (in 2006) and the visa code (in 2009), these special powers were replaced by the normal rule that the power to adopt implementing measures is conferred upon the Commission.[19]

The basic rules governing comitology committees were amended in 2006 to establish a new "regulatory procedure with scrutiny" ("RPS"), which gave the EP and the Council extra scrutiny powers where a measure adopted pursuant

---

[14] See particularly Case 25/70 *Koster* [1970] ECR 1161 and Case C- 93/00 *EP v Council* [2001] ECR I-10119.

[15] See initially Decision 87/393 (OJ 1987 L 197/33), replaced by Decision 1999/468 (OJ 1999 L 184/33) as amended in 2006 (OJ 2006 L 200/11).

[16] Cases C-378/00 *Commission v EP and Council* [2003] ECR I-937, C-122/04 *Commission v EP and Council* [2006] ECR I-2001, C-443/05 P *Common Market Fertilizers v Commission* [2007] ECR I-7209 and C-14/06 and C-295/06 *Parliament v Commission* [2008] ECR I-1649.

[17] Regs. 789 and 790/2001 (OJ 2001 L 116/2 and 5).

[18] Case C-257/01 *Commission v Council* [2005] ECR I-345.

[19] See Art. 33 of the borders code (Reg. 562/2006, OJ 2006 L 105/1), and Art. 52 of the visa code (Reg. 810/2009, OJ 2009 L 243/1). The voting rule for implementing measures had anyway shifted from unanimity to QMV from the start of 2005: see OJ 2004 L 396/45.

to the co-decision procedure provided "for the adoption of measures of general scope designed to amend non-essential elements of that instrument, *inter alia* by deleting some of those elements or by supplementing the instrument by the addition of new non-essential elements".[20] The Borders Code was amended to apply these new rules to the adoption of measures implementing that Code,[21] and the subsequent Visas Code also provides for the use of the RPS procedure for the adoption of most measures implementing it.[22] The RPS procedure also applies as regards the adoption of "strategic guidelines" for the EU's Borders Fund.[23]

Following the entry into force of the Treaty of Lisbon, the TFEU also now provides for the adoption of "delegated" acts implementing legislative measures, as follows (Article 290(1) TFEU):

> A legislative act may delegate to the Commission the power to adopt non-legislative acts of general application to supplement or amend certain non-essential elements of the legislative act.
>
> The objectives, content, scope and duration of the delegation of power shall be explicitly defined in the legislative acts. The essential elements of an area shall be reserved for the legislative act and accordingly shall not be the subject of a delegation of power.

The legislation in question must explicitly lay down the conditions for such delegations of power, which "may" be either the revocation of the delegated power by the EP or the Council, and/or a power for the EP or the Council to block the entry into force of the delegated act by objecting to it within a specified period.[24] The RPS procedure cannot be provided for in any new legislation adopted after the entry into force of the Treaty of Lisbon, and the conditions for the application of the delegated powers rule are very similar to those which previously applied to the RPS procedure (see above). However, the *control process* is different, and the delegated powers provision applies to *all* EU legislation, not just legislation adopted by the ordinary legislative procedure (as it is now called).

---

[20] N. 15 above.

[21] Reg. 296/2008, OJ 2008 L 97/60. The amendment of the comitology rules in the Borders Code had been a priority: see the statement in OJ 2006 C 255/1, point (e). A dispute over the adoption of a measure implementing the Borders Code pursuant to the RPS procedure, on the grounds that the implementing measure is *ultra vires* the parent legislation, is pending before the Court of Justice: Case C-355/10 *EP v Council*.

[22] Arts. 50 and 52(3) of the visa Code (n. 19 above).

[23] Art. 24(4) of the Decision establishing the Fund (OJ 2007 L 144/22), referring to Art. 56(3) of the Decision.

[24] Art. 290(2) TFEU.

There are no general rules on the use of the delegated acts procedure, but rather specific provisions in each legislative act which provides for the procedure.[25] So far, no legislation concerning visas or border controls which provides for the adoption of delegated acts has been adopted, but the Commission has proposed that the provisions in the Schengen Borders Code allowing for the use of RPS be amended to allow for the use of delegated acts.[26]

There is still provision for the adoption of implementing measures in other cases,[27] and the general legal framework governing the adoption of implementing measures was replaced with effect from 1 March 2011.[28] The new general rules have replaced the rules which previously governed the adoption of implementing measures (including as regards visa and borders measures), except for the prior rules concerning the use of the RPS procedure for measures adopted before the entry into force of the Treaty of Lisbon.[29] The Commission has stated that it intends to propose legislative amendments in time so that all existing RPS procedures are converted to delegated acts procedures by the end of the current EP term (in mid-2014).[30] In this area of EU law, the conversion of existing RPS procedures to delegated acts procedures will be relevant only as regards the Borders Code, the visa Code and the Borders Fund; as noted above, the relevant changes to the Borders Code have already been proposed.

Leaving aside the RPS and delegated acts procedures, EU law (before the 2011 reforms) provided for an advisory procedure, a management procedure and a regulatory procedure to adopt implementing measures. After the 2011 reforms, the rules provide instead for an advisory procedure and an examination procedure. The prior management and regulatory procedures were converted into the examination procedure as from 1 March 2011, but there is a continuing distinction (explained below) between cases in which the management procedure used to apply and cases in which the regulatory procedure used to apply.

As regards the EU's current visas and borders legislation, the following procedures were/are now applicable:

---

[25] See the Commission communication on the use of the procedure (COM (2009) 673, 9 Dec. 2009).

[26] COM (2011) 118, 10 Mar. 2011.

[27] See Art. 291 TFEU, which amended the prior Art. 202 EC.

[28] Reg. 182/2011, OJ 2011 L 55/13.

[29] Art. 12, Reg. 182/2011 (ibid).

[30] See Commission statement on Reg. 182/2011 (ibid).

a) visa code: operational instructions regarding the code: examination procedure (ex-regulatory procedure);[31]
b) Schengen Information System, project management: examination procedure (ex-regulatory procedure);[32]
c) Schengen Information System, operations: examination procedure (ex-regulatory procedure);[33]
d) Visa Information System ("VIS"), project management: examination procedure – ex-regulatory procedure as regards key issues; ex-management procedure as regards other implementing measures;[34]
e) VIS operations: examination procedure – ex-regulatory procedure as regards selection of VIS regions for roll-out and use of the VIS at external crossing points; ex-management procedure as regards other implementing measures;[35]
f) visa format: examination procedure (ex-regulatory procedure);[36]
g) passport formats: examination procedure (ex-regulatory procedure);[37] and
h) the EU borders fund: examination procedure (ex-management procedure) for most implementing measures.[38]

As regards legislation proposed (but not yet adopted) before the new general rules on implementing measures entered into force, the Commission had proposed the use of an advisory procedure as regards measures implementing the proposed Decision concerning a manual of travel documents,[39] and a management procedure as regards the proposed Regulation revising the Schengen evaluation procedure.[40]

The examination procedure provides that the committees of Member States' representatives which scrutinise draft implementing measures to be adopted

---

[31] Arts. 51 and 52(2) of the Code (n. 19 above).
[32] Art. 17 of Reg. 1103/2008 (OJ 2008 L 299/4).
[33] Art. 51 of Reg. 1987/2006 (OJ 2006 L 381/4). The same rule applies to the Commission's adoption of the Sirene manual for the current SIS: Art. 3 of Reg. 378/2004, OJ 2004 L 64/5.
[34] Arts. 3-5 of the VIS Decision (OJ 2004 L 213/5).
[35] Arts. 18(3), 45(2), 48(4) and 49 of Reg. 767/2008 (OJ 2008 L 218/60).
[36] Art. 6 of Reg. 1683/95 (OJ 1995 L 164/1), as amended by Reg. 334/2002 (OJ 2002 L 53/7). See also Art. 6 of Reg. 333/2002 (OJ 2002 L 53/4) and Art. 4 of Reg. 694/2003 (OJ 2003 L 99/15).
[37] Art. 5(2), Reg. 2252/2004 (OJ 2004 L 385/1).
[38] Arts. 7(3), 19(3), 21(5), 22(2) and 27(4) of the Borders Fund Decision, referring to Art. 56(2) of the Decision (n. 23 above). The exception concerns the application of the RPS procedure in one case (idem).
[39] Art. 7 of the proposed Decision (COM (2010) 662, 12 Nov. 2010).
[40] Art. 15 of the proposed Reg. (COM (2010) 624, 16 Nov. 2010).

by the Commission always vote by QMV.[41] If the committee in question votes in favour of the draft measure by QMV, the Commission can adopt it; if that committee votes against the draft measure by QMV, the Commission cannot adopt it. If there is no opinion (ie no QMV for or against the draft measure), the Commission can adopt the draft measure, except where a simple majority of committee members opposes it, or where the basic act which has conferred the implementing powers provides that the draft implementing act cannot be adopted where no opinion is adopted. On the latter point, the distinction between acts which previously provided for the management procedure and acts which previously provided for the regulatory procedure is crucial, because the general rules on implementing measures provide that acts which previously provided for the regulatory procedure must automatically be regarded as basic acts which rule out the adoption of a draft implementing act where no opinion is delivered. Also, acts which previously provided for the management procedure are not subject to the rule that a simple majority of the committee members can block the proposed measure.[42]

In the event that the Commission is blocked from adopting a measure, it can submit a revised proposal to that same committee or can make a proposal to an appeal committee of Member States' representatives, which also votes by QMV. In the event that the Commission seizes this appeal committee, it *must* adopt the measure if the appeal committee is in favour; it *may* adopt the measure if no opinion is delivered; and it *cannot* adopt the measure if the appeal committee votes against it.[43] The appeal committee procedure is new, and replaces the possibility under the previous rules that if the Commission's draft implementing measure was rejected by a committee, the Commission could request the Council to adopt the measure concerned. This process was used as regards the adoption of rules concerning tests related to the development of the second-generation Schengen Information System.[44] The possibility of asking the Council to break a deadlock still exists as regards the RPS procedure, and this process applied as regards the adoption of rules concerning the coordination of maritime surveillance by Frontex, the EU's border control agency.[45]

The examination procedure will likely apply in future to the adoption of measures implementing most visas and borders legislation, since the general

---

[41] For the details of this procedure, see Art. 5 of Reg. 182/2011 (n. 28 above).
[42] Art. 13(1)(b) and (c), Reg. 182/2011 (ibid).
[43] Art. 6, Reg. 182/2011 (ibid).
[44] Council Reg. 189/2008 (OJ 2008 OJ L 57/1).
[45] Decision 2010/252 (OJ 2010 L 111/20).

rules adopted in 2011 specify that it should normally be used where implementing acts have general scope, or where they concern "programmes with substantial implications" or "security and safety".[46] However, as noted above, the Commission has proposed the use of advisory procedure as regards measures implementing the proposed Decision concerning a manual of travel documents.[47] And where the examination procedure will apply to new measures adopted in future, there will still be a choice (and a possible argument) as to whether the basic act will rule out the adoption of an implementation measure by the Commission where the committee has delivered no opinion.[48]

In practice, following the entry into force of the general rules, the Council and the EP have agreed to use the advisory procedure for measures implementing the agreed Decision concerning a manual of travel documents.[49] The Commission has also proposed to use the examination procedure when it exercises a power to decide to re-impose visas for a limited period on countries which were previously on the EU's visa white-list.[50] It might be argued that such a measure should take the form of a delegated act (since it would amend the Annex to a legislative act, although only temporarily), or even that the legislative procedure must always be used to amend the Annexes to the Regulation, since the list of countries whose nationals are subject to a visa requirement (or not) is an "essential element" of that legislation.[51]

Finally, it must be noted that the Court of Justice ruled before the Treaty of Lisbon that the Council cannot confer some form of secondary legislative power upon itself. It must either confer implementing powers upon the Commission or upon itself (in duly justified situations) or use a fully-fledged legislative procedure to amend existing rules.[52] This case law presumably applies *mutatis mutandis* (taking account of the creation of the delegated acts procedure) after the entry into force of the Treaty of Lisbon. It must follow

---

[46] Art. 2(2), Reg. 182/2011 (n. 28 above). However, the advisory procedure could possibly be used instead in "duly justified cases" (Art. 2(3), Reg. 182/2011). On the choice of procedure, see by analogy Cases C-378/00 and C-122/04, n. 16 above.

[47] N. 39 above.

[48] Art. 5(4)(b) of Reg. 182/2011 (n. 28 above). Note, however, that in any case the opposition of a simple majority of committee members will be able to block the adoption of the proposal (Art. 5(4)(c)); this is a more stringent rule than previously applied as regards measures adopted by management committees (Art. 13(1)(b)).

[49] Art. 7(2) of the agreed text, in Council doc. 12058/11, 27 June 2011. This Decision has not yet been formally adopted.

[50] Proposed new Art. 4a of the visa list Reg., in COM (2011) 290, 24 May 2011. See further chapter 7.

[51] See the Advocate-General's opinion in Case C-392/95 *EP v Council* [1997] ECR I-3213.

[52] Case C-133/06 *EP v Council* [2008] ECR I-3189.

that the provision in the visa list Regulation which apparently confers upon the Council a secondary legislative power to re-impose visas in the event of non-reciprocity is legally dubious.[53] In fact, the Commission has proposed to amend this provision, instead providing for the ordinary legislative procedure.[54]

2.3. *The Schengen Acquis*

A vital feature of the development of EU law in this area is the development of a body of legal rules initially outside the EC (now EU) legal order, in the form of the Schengen Convention and measures implementing it. These measures (known as the "Schengen *acquis*") were integrated into the EU and EC legal order as from 1 May 1999 when the Treaty of Amsterdam entered into force,[55] subject to temporary delays for some current or future Member States, permanent exceptions for the UK and Ireland and special rules on the association of certain third States.[56]

Almost every measure discussed in this book either formed part of this Schengen *acquis* integrated into the EC and EU legal order in 1999, amended or replaced parts of this *acquis*, or "built upon" this *acquis* without actually amending it.[57] The main exception is the visa facilitation and visa waiver treaties between the EU and third countries,[58] and even those treaties have a very close link with the *acquis*. By summer 2011, nearly the entire Schengen *acquis* in this area had been replaced by subsequent EU measures, except for Articles 18-22, 25 and 136 of the Schengen Convention (which have, however, been amended by EU measures) and a small number of Decisions of the Schengen Executive Committee.[59]

---

[53] See generally chapter 7.

[54] Proposed amendment of Art. 1(4)(c) of the visa list Reg., in COM (2011) 290, 24 May 2011.

[55] See the Protocol on the Schengen *acquis*, Council Decision 1999/435 defining the Schengen *acquis* (OJ 1999 L 176/1) and Council Decision 1999/436 (OJ 1999 L 176/17) allocating the *acquis*. The *acquis* was mostly published in OJ 2000 L 239. For more on this process, see Thym, "Schengen Law: A Challenge for Legal Accountability in the European Union", (2002) 8 ELJ 218 and Peers, "*Caveat Emptor*? Integrating the Schengen *Acquis* into the European Union Legal Order", (2000) 2 CYELS 87.

[56] See further section 4 below.

[57] On the concept of "building on" the *acquis*, see Cases C-77/05 *UK v Council* [2007] ECR I-11459 and C-137/05 *UK v Council* [2007] ECR I-11593.

[58] See chapters 7 and 9.

[59] On these remaining measures, see chapters 6 and 11. The repealed measures have been replaced by the EU's border code, visa code and visa list legislation: see chapters 3, 7 and 8.

3. *Jurisdiction of the Court of Justice*

The initial period of EU involvement in this area, before the entry into force of the Treaty of Amsterdam in 1999, entailed the jurisdiction of the Court of Justice only as regards the EC legislation on the visa list and visa format. Otherwise the Court lacked jurisdiction over measures adopted within the Schengen framework (since they were not yet integrated into the EU and EC legal order) and within the "third pillar" framework, since the Court of Justice could only have jurisdiction over third pillar Conventions, and no Conventions were adopted in this area of law. During this period, no references were made to the Court of Justice from national courts on visa or borders issues, but two annulment actions were decided by the Court.[60]

The Treaty of Amsterdam gave the Court of Justice its regular jurisdiction over this area, subject to the proviso that only final courts could send references for a preliminary ruling to the Court, that the Court did not "have jurisdiction to rule on any measure or decision taken pursuant to Article 62(1) [regarding the crossing of internal borders] relating to the maintenance of law and order and the safeguarding of internal security" and that the Commission, the Council or a Member State could lodge a special request for interpretation of measures in this area with the Court of Justice if desired.[61]

During the Amsterdam era, the Court of Justice received three cases referred from national courts on the interpretation of EU law in this area, concerning in particular the rules on freedom to travel, on transit procedures and on the Schengen Borders Code.[62] The Court also received further annulment actions,[63] but no infringement procedures were brought in this area, presumably because Regulations (which do not entail national transposition) are used in this area of law. Furthermore, the cross-over between the Court's limited jurisdiction in this area and its wider jurisdiction in other fields raised

---

The Commission has proposed further repeals or amendments to Arts. 21, 22 and 136 of the Convention: see COM (2011) 118, 10 Mar. 2011.

[60] Cases C-392/95 *EP v Council* [1997] ECR I-3213 and C-170/96 *Commission v Council* [1998] ECR I-2763.

[61] Art. 68 EC.

[62] Respectively Case C-241/05 *Bot* [2006] ECR I-9627, Case C-139/08 *Kqiku* [2009] ECR I-2887 and Joined Cases C-261/08 *Zurita Garcia* and C-348/08 *Choque Cabrera* [2009] ECR I-10143. On the substance of these cases, see chapters 3, 6 and 11. One case concerning visas was ruled inadmissible, as it was referred from a lower court: Case C-51/03 *Georgescu* [2004] ECR I-3203.

[63] Cases C-257/01, *Commission v Council* [2005] ECR I-345, C-77/05 (n. 57 above), C-137/05 (n. 57 above) and C-482/08 *UK v Council*, judgment of 26 Oct. 2010, not yet reported.

complex questions of "mixed jurisdiction", which the Court touched on in its jurisprudence.[64]

Finally, with the entry into force of the Treaty of Lisbon, there are no longer any restrictions on the Court's jurisdiction over immigration and asylum matters, including visa and border control matters. The lifting of these restrictions even applied retroactively, to cases referred to the Court before the entry into force of the Treaty of Lisbon.[65]

In practice, the Court of Justice received four references from national courts on visa and border control issues in the first twenty months after the Treaty of Lisbon entered into force, according to the information available as of 1 August 2011.[66] This is as many cases as the Court received on this issue in the previous eleven years. It should be noted that one of these cases was referred from a lower court, while another would perhaps have been inadmissible on grounds of the "internal borders" exception in the previous Article 68 EC.[67] The Court has already received a further annulment action in this area,[68] but as before there have been no infringement actions in this area of law.

The Treaty of Lisbon has also revised the rules regarding references from national courts to provide that if a question regarding the interpretation or validity of EU law "is raised in a case pending before a court or tribunal of a Member State with regard to a person in custody, the Court of Justice of the European Union shall act with the minimum of delay".[69] This provision has already been applied to accelerate proceedings in one case in this area.[70]

---

[64] See Case C-228/06 *Soysal* [2009] ECR I-1031.

[65] See the judgment of 17 Feb. 2011 in Case C-283/09 *Werynski*, not yet reported.

[66] Joined Cases C-188/10 and C-189/10 *Melki and Abdeli*, judgment of 22 June 2010, not yet reported; Case C-430/10 *Gaydarov*, pending; Case C-606/10 *Association Nationale d'Assistance aux Frontières pour les Etrangers*, pending; and C-254/11 *Shomodi*, pending. All of these cases concern the EU's Borders Code, except *Shomodi*, which concerns the border traffic Regulation; but the *Gaydorov* case largely focusses on the position of a Member State's own citizens.

[67] See respectively *Gaydorov* and *Melki and Abdeli*, although note that the *Gaydorov* case also concerns EU free movement legislation. This case whould therefore have raised a "mixed jurisdiction" issue prior to the entry into force of the Treaty of Lisbon.

[68] Case C-355/10 *EP v Council*, pending.

[69] Art. 267 TFEU.

[70] *Melki and Abdeli*, n. 66 above. Note that procedures to this effect were already put in place before the entry into force of the Treaty of Lisbon, in the form of amendments to the Court's Statute and Rules of Procedure, and a related statement (OJ 2008 L 24/42, 39 and 44). On this procedure in practice, see Barnard, "The PPU: Is it worth the candle? An early assessment" (2009) 34 ELRev. 281.

4. *Territorial Scope of EU Law*

An essential feature of EU law in this area is its complex territorial scope, as regards a number of its Member States on the one hand and four countries closely associated with the Schengen rules (the "Schengen associates" on the other).

First of all, the UK and Ireland are covered by a Protocol exempting them from the abolition of border controls, and another specific Protocol regulating their relationship with the Schengen *acquis*. The latter Protocol gave the UK and Ireland the possibility of applying to participate in only part of the Schengen *acquis*, subject to a decision in favour by the Council, acting with the unanimous approval of the Schengen States (ie the other Member States).[71] The Council accepted the UK's application for partial participation in Schengen in 2000, and the parallel Irish application in 2002,[72] although the partial participation of these Member States in the Schengen rules only took effect (for the UK) or will take effect (for Ireland) when the Council approved or later approves it separately.[73] However, neither Member State participates (or will participate) in the Schengen rules relating to visas, border controls or freedom to travel.

As regards measures building on the Schengen *acquis*, the Schengen *acquis* Protocol states that "[p]roposals and initiatives to build upon the Schengen *acquis* shall be subject to the relevant provisions of the Treaties".[74] The meaning of this provision was disputed between the UK and the Council, as regards whether the UK needed the Council's approval to opt in to such measures or whether it could opt in to them whenever it chose, pursuant to a different Protocol on the UK's and Ireland's relationship with EU immigration and asylum law. Ultimately, the UK challenged its exclusion from the EU legislation on security features for EU passports and the creation of Frontex, the EU borders agency, and subsequently challenged the restriction on its law enforcement officials' access to the Visa Information System.[75]

The Court of Justice ruled that to ensure the "effectiveness" of the rules on the UK and Ireland's participation in the Schengen *acquis*, there was a necessary link between the question of their participation in the original *acquis* and

---

[71] Art. 4, Schengen *acquis* Protocol.

[72] Decisions 2000/365/EC (OJ 2000 L 131/43) and 2002/192/EC (OJ 2002 L 64/20).

[73] See Art. 6 of Decision 2000/365/EC and Art. 4 of Decision 2002/192/EC (both ibid), and the Decision on UK participation from 1 Jan. 2005 (OJ 2004 L 395/70).

[74] Art. 5(1), Schengen *acquis* Protocol.

[75] Cases C-77/05 *UK v Council*, C-137/05 *UK v Council* and C-482/08 *UK v Council* (n. 57 and 63 above).

their participation in measures building upon it. Therefore those Member States would need the unanimous support of the Council if they wished to participate in measures building upon that *acquis*. Moreover, the Court adopted in these cases a broad interpretation of measures building upon the *acquis*, ruling that all three measures *built* upon the *acquis* even though they did not actually *amend* it, because they were sufficiently linked to the control of external borders and the issuing of visas. The Treaty of Lisbon did not amend the provisions of the Schengen *acquis* Protocol dealing with this issue, so presumably the Court's prior case law continues to apply.

Next, Denmark also has a special position as regards the issues discussed in this volume. Originally, the rules governing this issue were split between the Schengen *acquis* Protocol[76] and a particular Protocol relating to Denmark (the "Danish Protocol"). Following the entry into force of the Treaty of Lisbon, all of the special rules relating to Denmark as regards the Schengen *acquis* appear in the Danish Protocol. According to the Danish Protocol in its original form, Denmark was exempted from *almost* all measures in this area,[77] except for measures determining a list of third countries whose nationals require visas to cross the external borders of the Member States, or of measures determining a common visa format,[78] as both of these issues were already within EC competence prior to the Treaty of Amsterdam.

As for measures which build upon the Schengen *acquis*, Denmark has six months to decide whether to apply each such measures within its national law.[79] If it does so, this decision creates "an obligation under international law" between Denmark and the other Member States participating in the measure. If Denmark fails to apply such a measure, the other Schengen States and Denmark "will consider appropriate measures to be taken".[80] In practice, Denmark has consistently opted into all measures building upon the Schengen *acquis*.

Denmark has two options open if it wishes to change its position: either it can denounce "all or part" of the Danish Protocol, in which case it has to apply immediately all measures adopted in the relevant field without any need for the Commission or Council to approve its intention to apply those measures,[81]

---

[76] Art 3, Schengen *acquis* Protocol, before amendment by the Treaty of Lisbon. All further references as regards Denmark are to the Danish Protocol unless otherwise indicated.
[77] Arts. 1–3.
[78] Art. 4, which was renumbered Art. 6 (but not amended) by the Treaty of Lisbon.
[79] Art. 4(1).
[80] Art. 4(2).
[81] Art. 7.

or (since the Treaty of Lisbon) it may decide to replace the rules concerning its general opt-out from EU Justice and Home Affairs measures with a new set of opt-out rules, which are almost identical to the relevant opt-outs for the UK and Ireland.[82] But crucially, if Denmark chooses this latter option, the previous Schengen *acquis* and prior acts building upon the Schengen *acquis* will apply fully to Denmark as EU law, rather than international law, six months after the Danish decision takes effect,[83] and Denmark would have to opt in to any future measures that build upon the Schengen *acquis*.[84] In practice, Denmark has not yet denounced all or part of its Protocol or applied the new opt-out rules.

Next, new Member States which join the EU are obliged to join the Schengen *acquis*, but not all at once.[85] To this end, the 2003 Accession Treaty, specified that the ten new Member States which joined the EU pursuant to that Treaty applied as from the date of accession (1 May 2004) the measures in the *acquis* as integrated into the EC and EU Treaties "and acts building on it or otherwise related to it", as referred to in Article 3(1) of the Act of Accession and listed in Annex 1 to the Act, along with other such measures adopted between agreement of the Accession Treaty and the date of accession.[86] However, there was a delay in applying the remaining provisions of the Schengen *acquis* (or measures building upon it).[87] Those measures were *binding* on the new Member States as from 1 May 2004, but did not *apply* until a unanimous Council decision by the representatives of the Member States fully applying the Schengen *acquis* at that time and the Member State(s) seeking to participate fully.

More precisely, the provisions of the Schengen *acquis* and the measures building upon it which applied as from 1 May 2004 in the new Member States as regards visas and border controls were the rules on external border controls (except for checks in the SIS) and the visa list and visa format. On the other hand, the rules on abolition of internal border controls, the other aspects of the common visa policy and the freedom to travel did not apply until the later Council decision. As for measures building upon the Schengen *acquis* adopted after agreement on the Accession Treaty, and subsequently adopted after accession, each measure indicated whether it applied immediately or after a delay to the new Member States.

---

[82] Art. 8(1) and the Annex to the Protocol.
[83] Art. 8(2).
[84] Art. 6(2) of the Annex.
[85] Art. 7, Schengen *acquis* Protocol.
[86] OJ 2003 L 236/33 (Act of Accession).
[87] Art. 3(2), Act of Accession, ibid.

Ultimately nine of the ten Member States which joined the EU in 2004 participated in the full Schengen system as from December 2007, and from March 2008 as regards air borders.[88] Only Cyprus was left out of the extension of the Schengen zone, because of the practical difficulties controlling the borders as long as the country is divided. However, Cyprus has expressed an intention of applying the provisions of the Schengen *acquis* relating to visas;[89] the Council has not yet acted on this request.

The model set out in the 2003 Treaty of Accession was largely copied in the 2005 Treaty of Accession with Romania and Bulgaria, in force from 1 January 2007.[90] To date, the Council has not yet decided to apply the full Schengen *acquis* to these countries. It is understood that the same provisions have been agreed as regards the planned accession of Croatia to the EU; the accession of this State is likely to be agreed by mid-2011, with an accession treaty signed later in 2011 and accession by 2013.

Finally, the position of the EU's Schengen associates (Norway, Iceland, Switzerland and Liechtenstein) is governed (as regards Norway and Iceland) by two association agreements agreed in 1999.[91] Pursuant to these treaties, the Schengen area was extended to Norway and Iceland in March 2001, at the same time it was extended to Nordic EU Member States.[92]

The Schengen association treaty requires Norway and Iceland to apply the Schengen *acquis*, including EU measures related to the *acquis*, as it existed in spring 1999, as well as to accept (in principle) measures building upon the *acquis*. In practice, the treaty has entailed Norwegian and Icelandic acceptance of most measures concerning visas and border control. Also, the EU has agreed with those States further treaties associating them with the EU's borders agency (Frontex),[93] the EU's borders funds legislation[94] and participation in comitology committees connected to the Schengen *acquis*.[95]

---

[88] OJ 2007 L 323/34.

[89] See the Council statement in the summary of Council acts for June 2008 (Council doc. 12750/08, 8–9 Sep. 2008).

[90] Art 3 and Annex I to Act of Accession (OJ 2005 L 157/203).

[91] OJ 1999 L 176/35 and OJ 2000 L 15/1. Both treaties entered into force on 26 June 2000 (OJ 2000 L 149/36).

[92] OJ 2000 L 309/24.

[93] OJ 2007 L 188/19. The treaty has not yet entered into force, but is being applied provisionally.

[94] OJ 2010 L 169/22. The treaty entered into force on 1 April 2011.

[95] COM (2009) 605 and 606, 30 Oct. 2009. The Council has agreed to sign this treaty, but it has not yet entered into force.

As for Switzerland, it agreed a treaty associating itself with the Schengen *acquis* in 2004; this treaty entered into force on 1 March 2008,[96] and was applied as from 12 December 2008 (29 March 2009 as regards Schengen air borders).[97] This treaty is essentially identical to the Schengen agreements with Norway and Iceland, except that (*inter alia*) Liechtenstein may accede to it. Indeed, a Protocol concerning accession of Liechtenstein to this treaty was agreed in 2006, and entered into force in April 2011.[98] Also, Switzerland and Liechtenstein have agreed a treaty with the EU concerning their relationship with Frontex (paralleling the agreement with Norway and Iceland on this subject),[99] and are also parties to the treaties concerning association with the Borders Funds and comitology committees.[100]

5. *Other Provisions of EU Law*

Following the entry into force of the Treaty of Lisbon, the distinction between EU measures relating to visas and border controls and other (non-Justice and Home Affairs) EU measures is not quite as significant as it once was, since the jurisdiction of the Court of Justice is the same regardless of which measures apply. Also, the original distinctions concerning the form and legal effect of EU acts and the decision-making process had disappeared even before the Treaty of Lisbon entered into force. However, the distinction still matters as regards the territorial scope of the legislation concerned (see section 4 above) and the difference in the relevant substantive rules.

The principal areas of EU law which must be distinguished from EU law on visas and border controls are EU free movement law on the one hand and the EU's association agreements on the other. The Court of Justice has also established that even EU citizens who have not moved within the EU, and their family members, can derive rights from EU citizenship.[101] In the event of any conflict between the visas and border control rules and the other two sets of rules, the latter rules prevail. In any case, most measures building upon the

---

[96] OJ 2008 L 53/13 and 52. On the date of entry into force, see OJ 2008 L 53/18.

[97] OJ 2008 L 327/15.

[98] The Protocol was signed in 2008 (OJ 2008 L 83/3 and 5), and concluded by the Council in March 2011 (OJ 2011 L 160/1). A separate decision will still have to be taken to apply the full Schengen *acquis* to Liechtenstein, but the SIS provisions already apply (OJ 2011 L 160/84).

[99] COM (2009) 255, 4 June 2009. The treaty entered into force between the EU and Switzerland on 1 Aug. 2010, but has not yet entered into force between the EU and Liechtenstein.

[100] OJ 2010 L 169/22 and COM (2009) 605 and 606 (ns. 94 and 95 above).

[101] See the discussion in volume 2, chapter 2.

Schengen *acquis* provide in some form expressly for priority for EU free movement law.[102]

5.1. *EU Free Movement Law*

Article 26 TFEU (originally Article 7a EEC/EC, subsequently Article 14 EC) requires the abolition of internal border checks between Member States. According to the Court of Justice's judgment in *Wijsenbeek*, Article 26 TFEU (as it now is) did not have the automatic effect of abolishing internal border checks between Member States, because such abolition could only result from the harmonisation of national law on visas, external border checks, asylum and immigration.[103] Similarly, the right of EU citizens to "move and reside freely" within the EU, pursuant to Article 21 TFEU (originally Article 8a EC, subsequently Article 18 EC) did not preclude Member States from checking whether persons were indeed citizens of the Union who could benefit from that right. But the punishment imposed by the authorities for unauthorised crossing of internal borders had to be "comparable to those which apply to similar national infringements", and "Member States may not lay down a penalty so disproportionate as to create an obstacle to the free movement of persons, such as a term of imprisonment."

The free movement rights of EU citizens and their family members are elaborated upon in other provisions of the TFEU and in secondary EU legislation, which was amended and consolidated in 2004 in the form of Directive 2004/38, which Member States had to apply by 30 April 2006 (the "EU citizens' Directive").[104] The rules on visas and border controls in this Directive[105] are the same as the previous rules,[106] which had provided (as regards exit)[107] that Member States had to allow EU citizens and their family the right to leave the territory to enter another Member State, "on production of a valid identity card or passport", and could not demand exit visas or any equivalent

---

[102] See particularly the borders code, the visas code and the legislation governing SIS II, as discussed in chapters 3, 4 and 8.

[103] Case C-378/97 [1999] ECR I-6207.

[104] OJ 2004 L 229/35.

[105] Arts. 4 and 5 of the Directive (ibid).

[106] Directive 68/360 (OJ Spec Ed 1968, L 257/13, p. 485) as regards workers, and Directive 73/148 (OJ 1973 L 172/14) as regards self- employed persons and service providers and recipients. Art. 2(2) of each of Directives 90/364 (OJ 1990 L 180/26), 90/365 (OJ 1990 L 180/28) and 93/96 (OJ 1993 L 317/59) extended the relevant provisions of Directive 68/360 to other groups of EU citizens.

[107] Art. 2 of Directives 68/360 and 73/148.

document from their citizens. Member States had to issue such documents to their nationals "in accordance with their laws". As for entry, Member States had to allow entry merely "on production of a valid identity card or passport".[108] Member States could not demand entry visas or an equivalent document, except for family members who were non-EU nationals. In that case, "Member States [had to] afford to such persons every facility for obtaining any necessary visas". These visas had to be free of charge.[109]

The only changes from the previous rules are that (as regards borders) the right of entry and exit is "without prejudice to the provisions on travel documents applicable to national border controls", passports of third-country national family members cannot be stamped if they present the a residence card, EU citizens and family members without the required documents must be given the chance to obtain them or corroborate their identity before being turned back.[110] As regards visas, the legislation now refers to the EU's visa list legislation "or, where appropriate … national law" as regards family members' visa requirements,[111] third- country national family members are exempt from the visa requirement where they hold a residence card issued to third- country national family members of an EU citizen who resides in a different Member State, and visas must be issued "as soon as possible and on the basis of an accelerated procedure".[112]

The case law on the prior rules, which must be considered as incorporated into the EU citizens' Directive,[113] had specified that a policy of imposing an entry clearance stamp in an EU citizen's passport upon entry is an equivalent measure to requiring a visa, and was therefore banned.[114] It was not permissible for border guards to ask EU citizens questions about the intended purpose of their visit, or their financial means.[115] On the other hand, the Court of

---

[108] Art. 3 of Directives 68/360 and 73/148.

[109] Art. 9(2) of Directive 68/360 and Art. 7(2) of Directive 73/148.

[110] The Commission report on the application of the Directive (COM (2008) 840, 10 Dec. 2008) stated that six Member States did not apply this provision (Art. 5(4)) at all, and three of them applied it incorrectly.

[111] Presumably the reference to national law is only relevant to the UK and Ireland: see section 4 above.

[112] Art. 5(2), Directive 2004/38. The Commission's report on the application of the Directive (n. 110 above) indicates that there are significant failings applying these rules in practice. See also the later Commission guidance on the application of the Directive (COM (2009) 313, 2 July 2009).

[113] See Case C-127/08 *Metock* [2008] ECR I-6241 and recitals 3 and 5 in the preamble to Directive 2004/38.

[114] Case 157/79 *Pieck* [1980] ECR 2171.

[115] Case C-68/89 *Commission v Netherlands* [1991] ECR I-2637.

Justice had ruled that unsystematic and sporadic checks on EU citizens, on occasion at the border, to see if they are carrying the correct permits, did not violate EU law if similar checks are carried out on that State's own nationals, unless those checks were "carried out in a systematic, arbitrary or unnecessarily restrictive manner".[116]

As for third-country national family members of EU citizens, the Court had ruled that they could be turned back at the border if they lacked an identity card or passport, or (if necessary) a visa, but not if they were able to prove their identity and conjugal ties and if there were no evidence that they were a risk to public policy, public security or public health.[117] In order to give the free movement Directives "their full effect, a visa [where it is required] must be issued without delay and, as far as possible, on the place of entry into national territory".[118] Third-country national family members were covered by the separate legislation setting out substantive limits to Member States' power to expel or deny entry to citizens of other EU Member States on grounds of public policy, public security and public health, as well as procedural protection for those affected.[119]

The Court of Justice has ruled that third-country national family members of EU citizens who have moved within the Community have a right of entry in order to stay on the territory of the host Member State with that EU citizen— even if those family members are entering directly from a non-Member State, and thereby crossing the EU's external border.[120] This judgment also confirms that the competence to address the issue of the entry across the external borders of the family members of EU citizens who have moved within the EU derives from EU free movement law, not the EU competences concerning visas and border controls, et al. There is no reason to doubt that this judgment is still good law following the entry into force of the Treaty of Lisbon.

The relationship between EU free movement rules and the criteria for including a person on the SIS list of persons to be banned entry into the entire EU has also been a matter of some controversy. On this point, the Court of Justice has ruled that the Spanish government wrongly refused a visa and entry at the border to family members of EU citizens solely because their

---

[116] Case 321/87 *Commission v Belgium* [1989] ECR I-997, para 15.

[117] Case C-459/99 *MRAX* [2002] ECR I-6591, paras 53–62.

[118] Ibid, para. 60.

[119] Directive 64/221 (OJ 1964 Spec Ed L 850/64, p 117). Art. 1(2) of that Directive expressly extended its scope to family members. Directive 64/221 was also incorporated, with amendments, into Directive 2004/38.

[120] *Metock*, n. 113 above.

names were listed in the SIS by another Member State, without first using the mechanisms established (the Sirene system) to ensure that such persons actually were a sufficiently serious threat to a requirement of public policy affecting one of the fundamental interests of society—a far higher threshold than established by the Convention.[121] This interpretation is now reflected in the legislation establishing the second-generation Schengen Information System (SIS II),[122] and the Schengen Borders Code and visa code also provide expressly for the primacy of EU free movement law.[123]

Finally, the right of EU companies to send their third- country national employees to other Member States, as part of the corporate provision of services,[124] has implications for border controls. It must follow from the Court of Justice's case law that the employees have a right of entry to another Member State, otherwise their employers' right to provide services would be entirely nugatory.[125]

5.2. *EU Association Agreements*

The European Economic Area (EEA) agreement with Norway, Iceland and Liechtenstein,[126] and a further agreement with Switzerland on free movement of persons,[127] extend EU free movement law to these third States. The EU citizens' Directive applies as between EU Member States and EEA States,[128] while

---

[121] Case C-503/03 *Commission v Spain* [2006] ECR I-1097; compare to Art. 96 of the Convention (OJ 2000 L 239). See further the Commission Communication on the derogations from EU free movement l aw (COM (1999) 372, 19 July 1999), p 19, and the Declaration of the Schengen Executive Committee on this issue (SCH/Com-ex (96) decl. 5, OJ 2000 L 239/458).

[122] Art. 25, Reg. 1987/2006 (OJ 2006 L 381/4). See further chapter 4.

[123] Art. 3(a), Reg. 562/2006 (n. 19 above) and Art. 1(2), Reg. 810/2009 (n. 19 above). See also the definition of beneficiaries of free movement in Art. 2(5) of the borders Code, and the specific rules in Arts 7(2) and 10(2) of that code; and the specific rules in Arts. 3(5)(d) and 24(2)(a) and Art. 4 of Annex XI of the visa code. See further chapters 3 and 8.

[124] Cases: C-43/93 *Van der Elst* [1994] ECR I-3803; C-445/03 *Commission v Luxembourg* [2004] ECR I-10191; C-244/04 *Commission v Germany* [2006] ECR I-885; C-168/04 *Commission v Austria* [2006] ECR I-9041; and C-219/08 *Commission v Belgium* [2009] ECR I-9213.

[125] In the *Commission v Austria* judgment (ibid), the Court confirmed that a refusal to issue an entry permit to a worker who had entered without prior authorisation and lacked a required visa was a breach of Art. 49 EC (now Art. 56 TFEU). This suggests strongly that there is an underlying right of entry for such workers.

[126] OJ 1994 L 1/1.

[127] OJ 2002 L 114/6.

[128] Pursuant to EEA Joint Committee Decision 158/2007 (OJ 2008 L 124/20), Dir. 2004/38 applied to EEA States as from 4 Dec. 2007 (Art. 4).

a distinct set of free movement rules, similar to the EU's previous legislation on free movement of persons, applies as between the EU and Switzerland.[129] To that extent, the rules concerning borders applicable to EU citizens and their family members are equally applicable to citizens of the EEA States and Switzerland and their family members.

As regards the EU's Association Agreement with Turkey,[130] the Court of Justice has confirmed that the initial admission of Turkish workers and their family members is a matter for Member States, although such admission has become subject in part also to the EU's internal law.[131] However, once such persons have acquired rights pursuant to the EU–Turkey association agreement and its implementing rules, they have a right to *return* to the Member State where they acquired those rights.[132] As for Turkish service providers (and possibly service recipients) and self-employed Turks, there is a directly effective standstill on national rules which make the provision (and possibly the receipt) of services or the exercise of establishment more restrictive.[133] The Court of Justice has confirmed that this standstill applies to rules on entry control and visas.[134] Therefore national rules on entry control and visas for Turkish persons providing (or possibly also receiving) services or exercising establishment cannot become any more stringent than they were at the date when the relevant Protocol entered into force for the Member State concerned.[135] This equally applies to *EU* rules concerning border control

---

[129] See Annex I to the EU-Swiss treaty (n. 127 above).

[130] OJ 1977 L 261/60.

[131] See the legislation discussed in volume 2 of this book.

[132] See Cases C-351/95 *Kadiman* [1997] ECR I-2133, C-329/97 *Ergat* [2000] ECR I-1487 and C-188/00 *Kurz* [2002] ECR I-10691.

[133] Case C-37/98 *Savas* [2000] ECR I-2927 (self-employed persons); Joined Cases C-317/01 and C-369/01 *Abatay and others* [2003] ECR I-12301 (services). See also Case C-186/10 *Oguz*, judgment of 21 July 2011, not yet reported. By analogy with the standstill on Turkish workers, the standstill on restrictions on establishment and services is dynamic, ie if a Member State or the EU liberalises the entry control or visa rules after the entry into force of the standstill, it cannot renege on such liberalisation: see Joined Cases C-300/09 and C-301/09 *Toprak and Oguz*, judgment of 9 Dec. 2010, not yet reported.

[134] As regards border controls, see Case C-16/05 *Tum and Dari* [2007] ECR I-7415; as regards visas, see *Soysal* (n. 64 above). For more on the question of visa requirements for Turkish nationals following the *Soysal* judgment, see: Peers "EC Immigration Law and EC Association Agreements: Fragmentation or Integration?" (2009) 34 ELRev. 628 and Groenendijk and Guild, *Visa policy of Member States and the EU towards Turkish nationals after Soysal*, online at: <http://cmr.jur.ru.nl/cmr/docs/Soysal.Report.pdf>.

[135] For the first nine Member States, this date was 1 Jan. 1973. However, for other Member States, the relevant date is not clear, because no Protocols extending the EU–Turkey agreements to other Member States have yet entered into force. In practice the Court of Justice

and visas.[136] The Court of Justice has been asked to clarify whether the stand-still prohibits the imposition of new visa requirements on *any* Turkish visitors after the entry into force of the Protocol for each Member State.[137]

Finally, as regards the rules on freedom of establishment under the Stabilisation and Association Agreements (SAAs) with Western Balkan countries, once those rules are applied,[138] they must presumably be interpreted by analogy with the case law on the Europe Agreements with ten Central and East European States that have now joined the EU. As regards the latter agreements, the Court of Justice ruled that Member States could impose prior entry clearance requirements before nationals of the EU's associate members could enter and take up their right to establish themselves,[139] and that nationals of associated States who had legally entered on a short-term visa or for a short period without being subject to a visa obligation did not have the right to make an in-country application for establishment.[140]

---

and the national courts of Austria and Spain have assumed that the EU–Turkey agreement is applicable there: see (for Austria) Cases: C- 65/98 *Eyup* [2000] ECR I-4747; C-171/01 *Birlite* [2003] ECR I-4301; C-465/01 *Commission v Austria* [2004] ECR I-8291; C-373/02 *Ozturk* [2004] ECR I-3605; C-136/03 *Dorr* [2005] ECR I-4759; and C-383/03 *Dogan* [2005] ECR I-6237, and (for Spain) Case C-152/08 *Kahveci* [2008] ECR I-6291.

[136] See *Soysal* (n. 64 above).

[137] Case C-221/11 *Demirkan*, pending.

[138] OJ 2004 L 84 (Former Yugoslav Republic of Macedonia (FYROM)), OJ 2005 L 26 (Croatia), OJ 2009 L 107 (Albania) and OJ 2010 L 108 (Montenegro). SAAs have also been signed with Bosnia- Herzegovina (COM (2008) 182, 8 Apr. 2008), and Serbia (COM (2007) 743, 20 Nov. 2007), but these two SAAs are not yet in force. No SAA has been agreed with Kosovo yet. The SAA with FYROM provides that a decision will be made five years after entry into force of the agreement "whether" to extend the establishment rules to self-employed persons (Art. 48(4), FYROM SAA), while the other SAAs state that after four or five years, the "modalities" of extending the establishment rules to self- employed persons will be adopted (Art. 49(4), Croatia SAA; Art. 50(4), Albania SAA; Art. 53(4), Montenegro SAA; Art. 51(3), Bosnia SAA; and Art. 53(4), Serbia SAA). No decisions on this issue have been adopted or proposed.

[139] See judgments in Cases: C-63/99 *Gloszczuk* [2001] ECR I-6369; C-235/99 *Kondova* [2001] ECR I-6427; C-257/99 *Barkoci and Malik* [2001] ECR I-6557; and C-268/99 *Jany* [2001] ECR I-8615.

[140] Case C-327/02 *Panayotova* [2004] ECR I-11055.

Chapter 3

The Schengen Borders Code

1. *Introduction*

The Schengen Borders Code (the "Code"), adopted on 15 March 2006, came into force on 13 October 2006.[1] As a Regulation, it has direct applicability in the Member States and does not require transposition. Indeed, in some Member States when the Code took effect, the relevant sections of national law were repealed and nothing put in their place as the Regulation was immediately applicable.[2] This caused consternation among practitioners looking for the relevant rules on the crossing of EU borders.

The Code provides the rules for two situations:

- The absence of border controls of persons crossing the internal borders between the Member States of the EU;
- The rules governing border control of persons crossing the external borders of the Member States.

As for the territorial scope of the Code,[3] not all EU Member States participate, but nor is the Code limited to EU Member States. Ireland and the UK do not participate in the Code, since it builds upon the Schengen *acquis*; Bulgaria, Cyprus and Romania do not yet apply the provisions of the Code concerning internal borders and the use of the Schengen Information System, as they have not been admitted to the area without internal frontiers; Denmark participates through national legislation and as an extension of the Schengen *acquis* to which it is bound. Iceland and Norway apply the Code as an extension of the Schengen *acquis* and since Switzerland's admission to the Schengen border control free area, it too applies the Code. Liechtenstein will apply the Code once it joins the Schengen *acquis*. As further countries join the EU, they too will be obliged to participate in the Schengen Borders Code.

---

[1] Reg. 562/2006, OJ 2006 L 105/1.
[2] For instance in the Netherlands.
[3] See further chapter 2.

Finally, the legal basis of the Code is Article 77(2)(e) TFEU[4] in so far as ensuring the absence of any controls on persons crossing internal borders forms part of the Union's objective of establishing an area without internal borders in which free movement of persons is ensured. In this regard the Code is also intimately tied to Article 14 EC (now Article 26 TFEU) as regards the completion of the internal market. As for the crossing of external frontiers, the legal basis of the Code is Article 62(2)EC (now Article 77(2)(b) TFEU), the common policy on the crossing of external borders as a flanking measure to the area without internal borders.

2. *Background*

The lifting of internal borders (and the parallel strengthening of external border controls) initially took place among five Member States (with some reservations) on 25 March 1995,[5] pursuant to the Schengen Implementing Agreement (the "Schengen Convention") 1990.[6] The Schengen area has been gradually extended until it has taken on its current configuration: five Member States outside, three non Member States inside. It has proven popular, evidenced by the importance of the possibility of control-free travel in accession discussions and the efforts made by the 2004 Member States to fulfill the requirements placed upon them by the existing participating Member States to join the space.[7] Nine of the ten Member States which joined the EU in 2004 enjoyed the lifting of controls on land borders with the other Schengen states on 21 December 2007 and the lifting of controls at air borders on 30 March 2008.[8] Cyprus was left out of this process as its own external borders are not entirely under its control as a result of the divided nature of the island. Bulgaria and Romania will join the Schengen system fully as soon as the existing participating states consider that their border management systems are adequate for the purposes. At the time of writing it is not known when this will take place.

---

[4] Formerly Art. 62(1) EC.
[5] Groenendijk, "New Borders inside Old Ones?", in Groenendijk, Guild and Minderhoud, eds., *In Search of Europe's Borders* (Kluwer, 2003) p. 131.
[6] Arts. 2-8 of the Convention (OJ 2000 L 239/1). For more detail on the measures concerning external border controls in force before the adoption of the Schengen Borders Code, see chapter 6.
[7] See the JHA Council conclusions of 8–9 Nov. 2007.
[8] OJ 2007 L 323/34.

The provisions of the Schengen Convention concerning borders had been supplemented by measures adopted by the Schengen Executive Committee, particularly a Common Manual for use by border control authorities, and other Decisions of the Schengen Executive Committee.[9]

Following the integration of the Schengen *acquis* into the EC and EU legal order, in accordance with the Treaty of Amsterdam,[10] these measures were supplemented by EC acts, in particular a Decision concerning border signs and a Regulation on the stamping of documents.[11] Furthermore, the Council adopted in 2001 a Regulation which conferred upon itself (and Member States) the power to amend the Common Manual.[12] A challenge to this measure by the Commission before the Court of Justice (on the grounds that the Council had not adequately explained why it conferred those implementing powers upon itself, whereas the normal rule is to confer them on the Commission) was unsuccessful.[13] This Regulation was used to amend the Common Manual on several occasions, in particular to add a standard form for refusing entry and the border.[14] The Manual was also amended on several other occasions: by the EC's borders legislation,[15] by legislative acts concerning visas,[16] as well as incidentally when the Council amended the basic rules

---

[9] These were Sch/Com-ex (94) 1 on adjustments regarding traffic flows at internal borders, Sch/Com-ex (94) 17 on introducing the Schengen system, Sch/Com-ex (98) 1 on the activities of a task force and SCH/Com-ex (95) 20 rev 2 on the procedures for the reintroduction of internal border checks (OJ 2000 L 239/157, 168, 191 and 133).

[10] Arts. 2-8 of the Convention and Schengen Executive Committee Decisions Sch/Com-ex (94) 17 and Sch/Com-ex (98) 1 were allocated to Art. 77(2)(b) TFEU, except for Art. 7 of the Convention, which was allocated to Art. 74. TFEU, and Art. 4 of the Convention, which was not allocated at all due to obsolescence. SCH/Com- ex (95) 20 rev 2 was allocated to Art. 77(2)(e) TFEU. The Common Manual was allocated to Arts. 77-79 TFEU. See the Council Decisions on the definition and allocation of the *acquis* (1999/436 and 1999/436, OJ 1999 L 176/1 and 17).

[11] See respectively OJ 2004 L 261/119 and Reg. 2133/2004, OJ 2004 L 369/5. The Reg. *inter alia* inserted two new provisions into the Schengen Convention (Arts. 6a and 6b) and amended Art. 6(2)(e) of the Convention, while the Decision *inter alia* amended Sch/Com-ex (94)17.

[12] Reg. 790/2001, OJ 2001 L 116/5.

[13] Case C-257/01 *Commission v Council* [2005] ECR I-345.

[14] The first two amendments (OJ 2002 L 123/47 and OJ 2002 L 187/50) made "housekeeping" changes; the third amendment increased checks on minors (OJ 2004 L 157/36); and the fourth amendment introduced a common form to be used when refusing entry at the border (OJ 2004 L 261/36).

[15] Art. 3 of Reg. 2133/2004.

[16] Art. 7(2) of Reg. 539/2001 (OJ 2001 L 81/3); Art. 2 of Reg. 334/2002 (OJ 2002 L 53/7); Art. 5(2) and (3) of Reg. 415/2003 ([2003] OJ L 64/1); and Art. 11(2) of Reg. 693/2003 (OJ 2003 L 99/8). On the substance of these measures, see chapters 7 and 11.

governing the procedure for visa applications (the Common Consular Instructions).[17]

In 2006, the various measures setting out the basic rules governing border controls were all integrated into and amended by the Regulation establishing the Schengen Borders Code.[18] The Code, which applied from 13 October 2006,[19] repealed the relevant provisions of the Schengen Convention, three Schengen Executive Committee Decision on borders, the Common Manual (as amended by EU measures) and the EU legislation on border signs, the stamping of documents and the power to amend the Common Manual.[20]

The Borders Code has been amended on four occasions.[21] As for the future, the Commission proposed a number of amendments to the Code in March 2011 (the "March 2011 proposal");[22] these amendments are noted throughout this chapter. The Commission may propose legislation on an entry-exit system and a registered traveller system which would require amendment of the Code. Furthermore, the European Council (EU leaders) has asked the Commission

---

[17] Art. 1(2), 1(4) and 1(5) of Decision 2001/329 (OJ 2001 L 116/32); Art 3 of Decision 2001/420 (OJ 2001 L 150/47); Art 2 of Decision 2002/44 (OJ 2002 L 20/5); the Decision on fees for considering visa applications (OJ 2003 L 152/82); Decisions 2003/585 and 2003/586 on transit visa requirements (OJ 2003 L 198/13 and 15); Art. 2 of Decision 2004/17 on travel medical insurance requirements (OJ 2004 L 5/79); and the 2006 Decision on visa fees (OJ 2006 L 175/77).

[18] Reg. 562/2006, n. 1 above. All further references in this chapter are to the Borders Code Reg., unless otherwise indicated. See further Commission Communication, "Towards an integrated management of the external borders of the Member States of the European Union" (COM (2002) 233, 7 May 2002); the objective was also found in the "Plan for the management of the external borders of the Member States of the European Union" approved by the Council on 13 June 2002 and endorsed by the Seville European Council of 21 and 22 June 2002, then again by the Thessaloniki European Council of 19 and 20 June 2003.

[19] Art. 40.

[20] Art. 39. More precisely, Sch/Com-ex (94) 1, (94) 17 and (95) 20 were repealed, but Sch/Com-ex (98) 1 remained in force. The latter Decision has not been amended or repealed. Also, the Code deleted Annex 7 to the Common Consular Instructions (on which, see chapter 11 below).

[21] The first amendment was Reg. 296/2008 (OJ 2008 L 97/60), which amended the rules in the Code regarding "comitology" (Arts. 12, 32 and 33), in line with broader changes to those rules introduced in 2006 (see further chapter 2). The second amendment was Reg. 81/2009, regarding the use of the Visa Information System at borders (OJ 2009 L 35/56), which amended Art. 7(3) of the Code. The third amendment was set out in the visa code (Art. 55 of that code: Reg. 810/2009, OJ 2009 L 234/1), which amended Annex V. The fourth amendment was set out in Reg. 265/2010 on long-stay visas (OJ 2010 L 85/1), which amended Arts. 5(1)(b) and 5(4)(a). The Code has not been officially codified by the EU, but an informally codified version appears as an Annex to this Chapter.

[22] COM (2011) 118, 10 Mar. 2011.

in September 2011 to make a proposal which would permit the further re-introduction of internal border controls as a "last resort" in the event of certain problems; this proposal, if adopted, might entail amendments of the Borders Code.[23]

The Code confers powers upon the Commission to adopt implementing measures as regards three of its eight attached Annexes; the Commission can also adopt implementing measures as regards border surveillance.[24] All these measures are currently subject to the "regulatory procedure with scrutiny", which entails greater scrutiny power for the European Parliament (EP), but the March 2011 proposal would replace this by the "delegated acts" procedure introduced by the Treaty of Lisbon.[25] To date, one implementing measure has been adopted, regarding maritime surveillance.[26]

Certain decisions relating to external border crossing (such as the penalties for crossing at unauthorised points or times) have been left to the Member States' discretion, but there is nevertheless an obligation for Member States to inform the Commission of these decisions; the Commission must then inform the public.[27] The Commission has also drawn up a Recommendation containing practical information for border guards.[28]

3. *Text of the Borders Code*

3.1. *The Objectives as Set Out in the Preamble*

Since the Court of Justice of the European Union (CJEU) takes seriously preambles to EU legislation in order to determine the intention of the legislation,[29] it is important for scholars and practitioners too, to be aware of the objectives. It is in light of these objectives that the Court of Justice will interpret the provisions where there is any doubt. The most important objective of

---

[23] On both of these issues, see further chapter 6.

[24] Arts 12(5), 32 and 33, as amended by Reg. 296/2008 (n. 22 above). The implementing powers concern Annexes III, IV and VIII, which concern signs for separate lanes at border crossings, stamping of travel documents and proof that the border has been crossed without travel documents being stamped.

[25] See further chapter 2.

[26] OJ 2010 L 111/20. See further chapter 5. This measure has been challenged by the EP: Case C-355/10 *EP v Council*, pending.

[27] Arts 34 and 37, which would be amended by the March 2011 proposal.

[28] C (2006) 5186, reproduced in Council doc. 15010/06, 9 Nov. 2006, amended by C(2008) 2976, reproduced in Council doc. 11253/08, 30 June 2008 and by C(2010) 5559, 15 Aug. 2010.

[29] See, for instance, Case C-127/08 *Metock* [2008] ECR I-6241.

the Code is to complete the internal market and the area without internal border controls on the movement of persons (preambles (1) and (2)). It is important to note, and stated in the preambles, that the Code does not call into question nor affect the rights of free movement enjoyed by citizens of the Union and members of their families (of any nationality) nor third country nationals and members of their families who under agreements between the EU and the Member States and the third country(ies) enjoy rights of free movement equivalent to Union citizens (preamble 5). This confirms the priority of Directive 2004/38 on the right to move and reside of citizens of the Union and their family members over the Code. It also preserves the position of nationals of Iceland, Norway and Switzerland as assimilated to that of EU citizens, as stated in the main text.

This is important as, for instance, the Code requires third country nationals whose state of nationality is on the visa black list to have a visa to enter the EU for a stay of three months (Article 5).[30] However, Directive 2004/38 provides that family members as defined in the directive, of any nationality, of a citizen of the Union who is moving to or residing in a Member State other than that of his or her nationality, have the right to present themselves at the border of the host Member State and seek admission, whether or not they have a visa.

The preamble states that border control is in the interest of all Member States which have abolished border controls at internal borders. It also states that border control "should help to combat illegal immigration and trafficking in human beings and to prevent any threat to the Member States' internal security, public policy, public health and international relations" (preamble para 6). Further, border checks should be carried out in such a way as to fully respect human dignity, according to preamble para 7. This is repeated in Article 6(1) of the Regulation, but the preamble adds that the checks will be carried out in a professional and respectful manner and be proportionate to the objectives pursued. Thus the EU principle of proportionality is incorporated into the objectives of the Regulation. Should border checks be so invasive as to be disproportionate to the objectives of the Regulation, then they will not be in accordance with it.

The preamble goes farther than the text of the Regulation in setting the scope of the meaning of border controls. While these are defined in Article 2(9) as "the activity carried out at a border, in accordance with and for the purposes of the Regulation, in response exclusively to an intention to cross or the act of crossing that border, regardless of any other consideration, consisting of border checks and border surveillance" which in turn are defined,

---

[30] On the content of the black list, see chapter 7.

the preamble states that "border control comprises not only checks on persons at border crossing points, but also an analysis of the risks for internal security and analysis of the threats that may affect the security of external borders." It is on this basis that the Regulation sets out the conditions, criteria and detailed rules governing checks at crossing points and surveillance. The preamble also takes into account trade needs in respect of border crossing. It states that "Member States should ensure that control procedures at external borders do not constitute a major barrier to trade and social and cultural interchange" (preamble para 11). In order to achieve this, the preamble recommends the deployment of adequate resources.

An issue, which arises more than once in the Regulation, is the capacity for Member States authorities to carry out checks under general police powers.[31] The preamble already signals this concern stating that it is without prejudice to security checks on persons identical to those carried out for domestic flights, the possibility of exceptional baggage checks, national law on carrying travel or identity documents and national law on notification of presence on the territory (preamble para 14). The temporary re-introduction of inter Member State border controls was also a matter of some discussion. The preamble reflects this at paragraph 15 where it states that Member States should have this possibility on the basis of a serious threat to public policy or internal security but in accordance with conditions and procedures set out in the regulation. Reference is made to the need for an exceptional circumstance and respect for the principle of proportionality.

Finally, the preamble states that the Regulation respects fundamental rights and observes the principles set out in the EU Charter of Fundamental Rights. Further, the application of the Regulation should be in accordance with Member States' international protection obligations (para 20). This is also stated in the main text of the Regulation. These obligations arise primarily out of the UN Convention relating to the status of refugees (ie the Geneva Convention), the International Covenant on Civil and Political Rights, the UN Convention against Torture and the European Convention on Human Rights. The difficulty of implementing protection-friendly border procedures has dogged many Member States and is now also a headache for the EU institutions. This problem is most acute for FRONTEX, the EU external borders agency, which has yet to devise a system of policing the external borders with the objective of fighting irregular migration while at the same time providing

---

[31] See Guild, "Citizens without a Constitution, Borders without a State: EU Free Movement of Persons" in Baldaccini, Guild and Toner, eds., *Whose Freedom, Security and Justice? EU Immigration and Asylum Law and Policy* (Hart, 2007) pp 25–56.

the opportunity for persons seeking international protection to make their claims and to enjoy protection while their claims are being processed (as required by all the above international conventions – see chapter 5). However, it also arises in the context of this regulation. EU external border controls must be compatible not only with the EU Directive on asylum procedures (Directive 2005/85), but also with the Member States' international obligations not to send anyone who claims a well founded fear of persecution or torture or inhuman or degrading treatment back to a country where he or she is likely to suffer that treatment.[32]

3.2. *Territorial Scope*

Regarding the territorial scope of the Regulation, preamble 21 provides that only the territories of France and the Netherlands which are in Europe are covered by it. This means that the Code does not apply to French overseas territories or the Dutch Antilles. The Spanish enclaves of Ceuta and Melilla are also subject to special arrangements contained in the agreement on Spain's accession to the Schengen Agreement. Basically, the declaration to that accession treaty regarding Ceuta and Melilla provides that goods and persons traveling from the enclaves to the EU (including Spain) will continue to be subject to border controls, the preexisting visa exemption for border traffic between the enclaves and the bordering Moroccan provinces will continue and the simplified visa system for Moroccan residents in the region will continue.[33]

3.3. *General Provisions*

The subject matter and principles of the Regulation are clear and unambiguous – it provides for the absence of border controls on persons crossing internal borders between the Member States and establishes the rules governing border control of persons crossing the external border (Article 1). As for the definitions (Article 2),[34] first of all, the definition of "internal" and "external" borders bears some attention. Internal borders are defined as the common land borders, including river and lake borders of the Member States, airports for internal (ie inter Member State) flights and ports for internal ferry

---

[32] For a fuller analysis of international asylum law, see Goodwin-Gill & McAdam, *International Refugee Law*, 3rd ed. (OUP, 2008). On Directive 2005/85, see *EU Asylum Law: Text and Commentary* (forthcoming).

[33] OJ 2000 L 239/69.

[34] The 2011 proposal would amend a number of the definitions and add one new one.

connections. External borders are all other borders which do not come within the definition of internal borders. Thus the external border is defined as a negative – anything that is not internal. However, as will become apparent later, the key definition for the external border is that of a "border crossing point", as these are the places in respect of which the Regulation provides the most detail. These points are defined as any crossing-point authorised by the competent authorities for the crossing of external borders. It is for the Member States to notify the Commission in accordance with Article 34(1)(b) their external border crossing points. In theory, if a Member State failed to notify a single external border crossing point, then arguably none of the provisions regarding the crossing of external borders set out in the Regulation would apply to that border point. At the very least, the Member State concerned would be in breach of its obligation to notify its crossing points.

Border control is defined as an activity carried out at a border (not elsewhere). It must be in response exclusively to an intention to cross or the act of crossing a border without regard to other considerations and it consists of border checks and border surveillance. Border checks are checks carried out at border crossing points to ensure that persons (and their objects) may be authorised to enter a Member State's territory or leave it and border surveillance is defined as surveillance of borders between crossing points or outside fixed border crossing point opening hours which are intended to prevent people from circumventing checks. The concept of "second line checks" is introduced in the definitions as checks which are carried out away from the location at which all persons are checked. Border guards are defined quite widely to cover a fairly substantial number of different agencies. It is for the Member States to notify the Commission under Article 34 which bodies are border guards for the purpose of the Regulation. The categories include any public official assigned under national law to a border crossing point or along a border or in the immediate vicinity of a border who carries out under the Regulation and national law border control tasks. This wide definition may be important, as the obligations on border guards to respect the dignity of travellers and the prohibition on discrimination thus applies to the whole class (see below on Article 6).

The Regulation provides a detailed definition of a residence permit, as this is crucial to the operation of external border checks. It provides that residence permits include those issued in accordance with Regulation 1030/2002, which lays down a uniform format for residence permits for third country nationals.[35] But the term also includes all other documents issued by a Member

---

[35] OJ 2002 L 157. On this Reg., see further volume 2 of this book, chapter 1.

State to third country nationals authorising stay in or re-entry into the territory but excludes temporary permits issued to cover the period during which an application for a residence permit is being undertaken. Three important definitions relate to cruise ships, pleasure boating and coastal fisheries – cruise ships must have a specific itinerary and tourist programme, pleasure boating is the use of boats for sports or tourism and coastal fisheries are defined as fishing carried out with vessels which return every day or 36 hours to an EU port without stopping at a non-EU port. Finally, the term "threat to public health" is defined as any disease with epidemic potential according to the WHO International Health Regulations and other infectious diseases or contagious parasitic diseases if they are the subject of protection provisions applying to nationals of the Member States. This is effectively the same definition which applies to public health limitations on the free movement of EU citizens contained in Article 29 of Directive 2004/38.

3.4. *Personal Scope*

Article 3 provides that the Regulation does not apply to persons enjoying the EU right of free movement.[36] This backs up the preamble's objective that the Regulation is subordinate to the right of free movement of EU citizens and their third country national family members. The control of their external and internal border crossing is covered by Directive 2004/38 which gives effect to the EU law right of free movement of persons which is much wider than the Regulation's provisions. Articles 6 and 7 of Directive 2004/38 provide a right of entry and residence for EU citizens and their third country national family members the former for periods of less than three months and without formalities and the second for periods of more than three months with formalities. The relationship of the two measures is important not least as the Directive applies also to Denmark, Ireland and the UK as EU law while the Regulation does not (though Denmark applies it).

The definition of persons enjoying the EU right of free movement includes all EU citizens (defined in Article 20 TFEU), their third country family members as defined in Directive 2004/38 and third country nationals and their family members who under agreements between the EU and their country of nationality enjoy rights equivalent to free movement of EU citizens. As noted above, this is EU code for referring to Icelanders, Norwegians and Swiss nationals.

---

[36] The March 2011 proposal would replace the reference to "Community" free movement rights in Art. 3 with a reference to "Union" rights.

The scope of the Regulation is also without prejudice to the rights of refugees and persons requesting international protection, in particular as regards non-refoulement. None of these concepts are defined in the Regulation but Directive 2011/95 (the refugee qualification directive) does define these terms.[37] According to that Directive, which in its pre-amendment form predates the Regulation, ""«refugee» means a third country national who, owing to a well-founded fear of being persecuted for reasons of race, religion, nationality, political opinion or membership of a particular social group, is outside the country of nationality and is unable or, owing to such fear, is unwilling to avail himself or herself of the protection of that country, or a stateless person, who, being outside of the country of former habitual residence for the same reasons as mentioned above, is unable or, owing to such fear, unwilling to return to it, and to whom [the exclusion provision] does not apply" (Article 2(c)). Similarly, the Directive states that "«international protection» means the refugee and subsidiary protection status as defined in (d) and (f);" (Article 2(a)). The Asylum Procedures Directive (Directive 2005/85)[38] uses the concept of non-refoulement extensively but recognises the priority of the Geneva Convention relating to the status of refugees 1951 and its Protocol of 1967 in defining the concept.[39] According to Article 33(1) of the Geneva Convention signatory states must not "expel or return ("refouler") a refugee in any manner whatsoever to the frontiers of territories where his life or freedom would be threatened on account of his race, religion, nationality, membership of a particular social group or political opinion". For the purposes of the Convention, the prohibition on refoulement applies to everyone who claims to be a refugee until such time as the claim is rejected definitively by the state (subject to the exclusions). It is arguable that the EU asylum legislation must be used to interpret the Regulation, where relevant.

3.5. *Crossing the EU's External Border*

Title II of the Code, which contains three Chapters,[40] sets out the main rules concerning external borders. Chapter I comprises two Articles, which set out in turn out the rules concerning crossing external borders and the conditions

---

[37] OJ 2004 L 304/12. On this Directive, see further *EU Asylum Law: Text and Commentary* (forthcoming).

[38] OJ 2005 L 326/13. On this Directive, see further *EU Asylum Law: Text and Commentary* (ibid).

[39] See particularly Arts. 27(1)(b), 36(4) and Annex of Dir. 2005/85 (ibid).

[40] Arts. 4-19.

for entry at the external borders.[41] Borders must be crossed at official points during official hours,[42] and notice of opening hours must be provided. Derogations may be permitted for pleasure shipping or coastal fishing,[43] seamen under certain conditions, individuals or groups where there is a "requirement of a special nature" (subject to certain conditions), or individuals or groups in an unforeseen emergency.[44] Penalties must be imposed by Member States for breach of the obligation to cross at official points; these penalties shall be "effective, proportionate and dissuasive",[45] and this obligation is "without prejudice to … [Member States'] international protection obligations".[46] These two express provisions respectively reflect the underlying effective sanctions principles of EU law and the exemption of refugees from penalties for irregular entry as set out in Article 31 of the Geneva Convention on refugee status.[47]

The key provision of the Schengen Borders Code is Article 5, which sets out the conditions for entry for short-term stays (three months within a six-month period). These conditions "shall be the following":

a) possession of valid documents necessary to cross the border;[48]
b) possession of a visa if required by the EU visa list legislation,[49] although a residence permit is equivalent to a visa for this purpose;[50] a long-stay visa also fulfils this criterion.[51]
c) justification of the purpose and conditions of the stay, and possession of sufficient means of subsistence (subject of a notification requirement for the Member States under Article 34);

---

[41] Arts. 4 and 5.

[42] Member States must notify their border crossing points to the Commission (Art. 34(1)(b)).

[43] For definitions of these concepts, see Art. 2(17) and (18).

[44] Art. 4(2). The March 2011 proposal would amend Art. 4(2).

[45] Member States must notify these penalties to the Commission (Art. 37).

[46] Art 4(3).

[47] On the first point, see Case 68/88 *Commission v Greece* (Greek maize) [1989] ECR 2685.

[48] The relevant documents are listed in a Manual of travel documents, established by Schengen Executive Committee Decisions Sch/com-ex (98) 56 and (99) 14 (OJ 2000 L 239/207 and 298), since updated pursuant to Reg. 789/2001 (OJ 2001 L 116/2). The Commission has proposed to replace this Manual by an EU Decision: COM (2010) 664, 12 Nov. 2010; the Council and European Parliament have agreed in principle on this Decision (see the agreed text in Council doc. 12058/11, 27 June 2011, not yet formally adopted). The March 2011 proposal would amend Art. 5(1).

[49] On the content of the visa list, see chapter 7.

[50] Art. 2(15) defines "residence permit".

[51] Reg. 265/2010 on long-stay visas (OJ 2010 L 85/1) – applicable from 5 April 2010.

d) absence from the list of persons banned from entry set up within the Schengen Information System ("SIS");[52] and

e) absence of a "threat to public policy, national security or the international relations" of *any* of the Member States, "in particular" where there is no alert in Member States' national databases refusing entry on such grounds.

The final provision could be interpreted as a requirement to check *all* Member States' national databases, but this is not practical on grounds of technical difficulties and cost. A "non-exhaustive" list of documents providing justification of the stay is set out in Annex I to the Code, which is a straightforward list of documents which can serve as evidence of travel for business, studies, tourism or private reasons or for political, scientific, cultural, sports, religious or other reasons.[53] The subsistence requirement "shall be assessed in accordance with the duration and the purpose of the stay and by reference to average prices for board and lodging",[54] and Member States' reference amounts for subsistence are to be notified to the Commission.[55] The possession of sufficient subsistence "may" be verified, "for example", by "the cash, travellers' cheques and credit cards in the third-country national's possession" as well as sponsorship declarations, where a Member State's law recognises such declarations, and guarantees from hosts, as defined by national law.[56]

There are three exceptions to the rules concerning entry conditions:[57]

a) persons with a residence permit, a long stay visa[58] or a re-entry visa from a Member State who wish to cross the external borders in transit back to the State which issued the permit shall be admitted across the border, unless they are listed on the watch-list of the Member State they wish to cross, along with instructions to refuse entry or transit;

---

[52] See further the definition in Art. 2(7), which refers to Art. 96 of the Schengen Convention, which concerns the grounds for issuing "alerts" in the SIS for persons to be refused entry. There is also an express requirement to check the SIS upon entry (Art. 7 of the Code, discussed below).

[53] Art. 5(2).

[54] Art. 5(3), first sub-paragraph.

[55] Art. 34(1)(c).

[56] Art. 5(3), second sub-paragraph.

[57] Art. 5(4). On the interpretation of the first exception, see Case C-606/10, *Association nationale d'assistance aux frontières pour les étrangers (Anafé)*, pending. The March 2011 proposal would amend Art. 5(4)(a) and (b).

[58] Art. 2 of Reg. 265/2010, OJ 2010 L 85/1.

b) persons who do not meet the visa requirement, but who satisfy the criteria for obtaining a visa at the border set out in EU visa legislation, may be authorised to enter if a visa is issued at the border pursuant to those rules;[59] and

c) a person may be permitted to enter if a Member State "considers it necessary" to derogate from the criteria for entry on humanitarian grounds, national interest or international obligations; but in such a case the permission to enter should be limited to the territory of that Member State, and other Member States must be informed of such decisions, if the person concerned is listed on the Schengen Information System ("SIS").[60]

The first exception is mandatory ("shall be authorised to enter"); the permits concerned must be notified to the Commission.[61] The consequence of these rules is that persons who do not meet the criteria for entry must be denied entry, unless they fall into one of the three special categories listed above. However, the obligation to refuse entry is "without prejudice to the application of special provisions concerning the right of asylum and to international protection or the issue of long-stay visas."[62] The special provisions on the right to asylum and international protection are not further defined, and as noted above, it could be argued that this is a reference to the EU's asylum procedures Directive. Alternatively, it is arguably a reference to national law, to a uniform EU concept which could be defined by the Court of Justice or to a minimum EU standard which could again be defined by the Court.[63]

Next, Chapter II of Title II of the Code concerns border checks and refusal of entry.[64] As regards the conduct of border checks, border guards must respect human dignity, act proportionately and not discriminate on any listed grounds while carrying out border checks.[65]

---

[59] This initially referred to Reg. 415/2003, but this Reg. has now been replaced by Arts. 35 and 36 of the visa code (Reg. 810/2009 OJ 2009 L 243/1: see chapter 8).

[60] Cf the provisions for visas with "limited territorial validity", set out in Art. 25 of the visa code (ibid).

[61] Art. 34(1)(a).

[62] Art. 13(1).

[63] However, it should be recalled that the Schengen associates and Denmark do not apply the procedures Directive. On the substance of that Directive, see *EU Asylum Law: Text and Commentary* (forthcoming).

[64] Arts. 6–13.

[65] Art. 6.

The Code then addresses the crucial issue of the checks that must be carried out at external borders on entry and on exit.[66] In particular, the "minimum checks" to be carried out on all persons at external borders must entail a "rapid and straightforward verification" of the validity of the documents carried, including an examination for signs of counterfeiting or falsification, using technical devices and consulting databases on lost or stolen documents "where appropriate".[67] Presumably it cannot seriously be intended that the documentation of every single traveller will be fully checked in all possible databases.

It is specified that while such checks are the "rule" for persons exercising EU free movement rights, it is possible for border guards to check databases on a "non-systematic basis" in order to determine that such persons "do not represent a genuine, present and sufficiently serious threat to the internal security, public policy, international relations of the Member States or a threat to the public health".[68] There is no cross-reference as regards these grounds to EU free movement law, and this proviso differs from EU free movement law because it refers to "internal security" rather than "public security" and also to "international relations".[69] However, it is specified that such checks "shall not jeopardise" the right of entry set out in free movement legislation,[70] and further that checks on persons with free movement rights must be carried out "in accordance with" EU free movement law.[71]

Although these safeguards (and the general safeguard for free movement law set out in the Code),[72] in conjunction with EU free movement rights, should be interpreted to prevent any restriction on free movement rights as a result of checking databases, it is possible in practice that a border guard might apply these conflicting provisions more restrictively. In particular, it is objectionable that the border checks provision of the Code does not fully reflect free movement rules and refers to more extensive grounds than free movement law provides for.

---

[66] Art. 7. The March 2011 proposal would amend several paragraphs of Art. 7, and add a new Art. 7(8).

[67] Art. 7(2), first sub-paragraph.

[68] Art. 7(2), second sub-paragraph.

[69] Moreover, compared to Art. 28(2) of Directive 2004/38 on EU citizens' free movement rights (OJ 2004 L 229/35), there is no reference to "personal conduct" or to threatening the "fundamental interests of society". But at least, as noted above, the definition of "public health" is identical (Art. 29(1) of the Directive and Art. 2(19) of the Code).

[70] Art. 7(2), third sub-paragraph.

[71] Art. 7(6).

[72] Art 3(a).

The Code then specifies the "thorough checks" to be carried out on third-country nationals (other than those with EU free movement rights). On entry, such persons shall be checked as regards their documents, the purpose and period of stay including subsistence requirements, along with checks in national databases and the SIS.[73]

Furthermore, once the Visa Information System ("VIS") becomes fully operational, third-country nationals shall also (if they hold a visa) be checked in the VIS on entry for the purposes of verification (a "one-to-one" search), using fingerprints and the visa sticker number.[74] Due to doubts about the practicality of this obligation, particularly as regards land borders, it will be subject to a derogation, concerning the checking of fingerprints, for a transitional period of three years, beginning three years after the VIS has started operations.[75] The Commission must evaluate the application of the derogation and report on its implementation to the EP and the Council within two years of the start of the derogation. Either the EP or the Council may then suggest that the Commission table a proposal to amend the legislation.[76]

As for the substance of the derogation, it will apply where intense traffic results in excessive delay at border crossing points, all resources have been exhausted as regards staff, facilities, and organization, and "on the basis of an assessment there is no risk related to internal security and illegal immigration".[77] The first two criteria match the criteria applicable to the decision to relax border controls in the Borders Code,[78] but the third criterion (risk assessment) does not. Also, as compared to the rules on the relaxation of border controls, a Member State will not have to show (as regards the derogation from the obligation to check fingerprints in the VIS) that there were "exceptional and unforeseeable circumstances", which "shall be deemed to be those

---

[73] Art. 7(3)(a).

[74] Art. 7(3)(aa), as inserted by Reg. 81/2009 (n. 22 above). For the details of the VIS, see chapter 10. It should be noted that the VIS Reg. (Reg. 767/2008, OJ 2008 L 218/60) does not lay down a requirement for border guards to use the VIS; the amendment to the Schengen Borders Code did that.

[75] Art. 7(3)(ae), as inserted by Reg. 81/2009. Presumably the transitional period does not begin for three years because of the three-year delay, after the VIS begins operations, before the VIS Reg. permits the use of fingerprints to search the VIS at all borders (Art. 18(2) of the VIS Reg.). Art. 18(2) of the VIS Reg. permits that date to be brought forward as regards air borders; the Borders Code does not make any special provision for this situation.

[76] Ibid. See also Art. 50(5) of the VIS Reg. (ibid), which provides for evaluation of the provisions regarding fingerprint searches in the VIS by external border guards, one year and three years after the VIS starts operations.

[77] Art. 7(3)(ab), as inserted by Reg. 81/2009.

[78] Art. 8(1), discussed further below.

where unforeseeable events" lead to the intense traffic in question.[79] It follows that in principle, the decision to relax border controls and the derogation from full use of the VIS on entry will not always apply simultaneously, although in practice it is likely that this will often be the case.

If the derogation applies, the VIS must still be searched in all cases using the visa sticker, and in random cases using fingerprints as well.[80] The VIS will also have to be searched using visa sticker and fingerprints in "all cases where there is doubt as to the identity of the holder of the visa and/or the authenticity of the visa". Decisions to apply the derogation will have to be taken by the border guard in command at the border post or at a higher level, and notified immediately to the other Member States and to the Commission.[81] Member States must report annually on the use of the derogation to the Commission, including providing information on "the number of third-country nationals who were checked in the VIS using the number of the visa sticker only and the length of the waiting time" which justified the derogation.[82]

A statement was adopted by the Council and Commission when the relevant Regulation amending the borders code was adopted, asserting that "the Council and the Commission stress that the derogation...should not be applied for a total period of more than 5 days or 120 hours per year at any border crossing point". Also, the statement provides that the "evaluation carried out by the Commission...will consider the infrastructure of the border crossing points, including recent and planned developments, as well as any factor that may have an influence on passenger flows, and may contain suggestions for improvements accordingly".[83] It should be recalled that according to the Court of Justice, "such a declaration cannot be used for the purpose of interpreting a provision of secondary legislation where...no reference is made to the content of the declaration in the wording of the provision in question". The declaration therefore has no legal significance.[84]

---

[79] Art. 8(1).

[80] It should also be noted that passports also still have to be stamped, even where border controls are relaxed: see Art. 8(3), discussed below.

[81] Art. 7(3)(ac) of the Borders Code, inserted by Reg. 81/2009. Note that the border guard on command at the border post also decides on whether to relax border controls in the first place: Art. 8(2), discussed below. However, as compared to the VIS derogation, the Borders Code does not require the notification of each decision to relax border controls.

[82] Art. 7(3)(ad), inserted by Reg. 81/2009. Note that Member States must also report annually on the relaxation of border checks generally (Art. 8(4)).

[83] Council doc. 15501/08 add 1, 20 Nov. 2008.

[84] Case C-292/89 *Antonissen* [1991] ECR I-745, para. 18.

It should be noted that neither the obligation nor the option to check the VIS at external borders will apply to third-country national family members of EU citizens, since they are not subject to the relevant provisions of the Borders Code.[85] The point is important, because information on the persons concerned will nevertheless be stored in the VIS.

Moving to controls on exit, checks must include a check on the validity and genuineness of travel documents and "whenever possible" a verification that the person is not a threat to "public policy, internal security, or the international relations of any of the Member States".[86] Exit checks *may* also involve verification of a visa, checks as to whether a person overstayed and checks in the SIS or national databases[87] – although of course the *required* check "wherever possible" on whether the person is a threat to public policy et al would seem to entail a mandatory SIS check. Member States will also have an option, once the VIS becomes operational, to check persons on exit in the VIS for the purposes of verification.[88] When the VIS becomes fully operational, Member States will have an option to search the VIS, presumably either on entry or exit, to check persons in the VIS for the purposes of *identification* (a "one-to-many" search).[89]

Through checks will take place, if possible, in a non-public area, at the request of the person concerned.[90] Persons must be given information about the purpose of the check and the procedures applicable, and may request the name or service number of the border guard(s) carrying out the check and the location and the date of crossing.[91] Both these provisions should contribute to the objective of ensuring fair treatment during border checks. Finally, the information which must be registered at the borders is listed in Annex II to the Code:[92] the names of the border guards; any relaxation of checks; the issuing of documents at the borders; persons apprehended and complaints; persons refused entry (grounds for refusal and nationalities); information on the security stamps used and the guards using them; complaints from persons subject to checks; police or judicial action; and particular occurrences.

---

[85] Art. 7(2) and (3), along with the definitions in Art. 2(5) and (6).
[86] Art. 7(3)(b).
[87] Art. 7(3)(c).
[88] Art. 7(3)(c)(i), as amended by Reg. 81/2009. There is no derogation permitted.
[89] Art. 7(3)(d), inserted by Reg. 81/2009 (ibid). There is no derogation permitted.
[90] Art. 7(4).
[91] Art. 7(5).
[92] See Art. 7(7).

These provisions should make a useful contribution respectively to ensuring reasonable behaviour by border guards and to combating corruption or other criminal activity regarding falsified documents.

Member States are obliged to provide for separate lanes at airports for EU and EEA citizens and their family members, on the one hand, and for all (other) third-country nationals, on the other hand. They have an option as to whether to provide for separate lanes at sea and land borders.[93]

As noted already, the Code provides for the possible relaxation of checks in limited circumstances, "as a result of exceptional and unforeseen circumstances", which are "deemed to be those where unforeseeable events lead to traffic of such intensity that the waiting time at the border crossing point becomes excessive, and all resources have been exhausted as regards staff, facilities and organisation."[94] In that case, entry checks must take priority over exit checks, and there is anyway an obligation to stamp each travel document on entry and exit.[95] Member States must submit an annual report on the relaxation of border checks to the EP and Commission,[96] but there is no information available on these reports.

Next, travel documents (usually passports) must be stamped when all third-country nationals cross the border, both on entry and exit, regardless of whether the travellers are subject to a visa obligation or not.[97] There is an exemption for third-country national family members of EU citizens if they hold residence cards, in accordance with EU free movement law.[98] There are also express exemptions for heads of state and dignitaries, certain transport workers and to nationals of Andorra, San Marino and Monaco. The obligation might also "[e]xceptionally" be waived where stamping a travel document "might cause serious difficulties" for an individual; in such cases, a separate sheet has to be stamped to record entry and exit.[99]

If a travel document is not stamped on entry, Member States may presume that the person concerned does not fulfil the conditions for the duration of

---

[93] Art. 9, which took over the provisions of the 2004 Decision on this issue. The March 2011 proposal would amend Art. 9 and Annex III of the Code on this issue, in order to allow for an optional "visa free" lane at border crossings.

[94] Art..8(1). Arts 8, 10, and 11 took over the provisions of Reg. 2133/2004.

[95] Art. 8(2) and (3) respectively; on stamping of documents, see below.

[96] Art. 8(4).

[97] Art. 10(1). The detailed arrangements for stamping are set out in Annex IV (Art 10(4)).

[98] Art. 10(2), interpreted *a contrario*. The March 2011 proposal would amend Art. 10(2).

[99] Art. 10(3). The March 2011 proposal would amend Art. 10(3).

stay in the Member State concerned.[100] This presumption can be rebutted by the traveller,[101] but if he or she cannot rebut it, they may be expelled.[102]

The Commission reported on the application of the provisions on stamping of documents and presumptions of irregular stay in 2009.[103] According to this report, there have been no problems applying the stamping obligations fully; in particular the obligations have not caused long waiting times at borders. Difficulties have arisen where a passport was full, where the stamping was confusing or illegible (due to stamping on top of a previous stamp), where children did not have a separate passport and as regards whether the passport of a third-country national with a residence permit from a Schengen State should be stamped. In the latter case, the Commission took the view that the passport need not be stamped, because a risk of exceeding the authorised period of short stay does not arise. While this is a sensible argument, nevertheless there is no express exception to this end in the Code.[104] Equally the Commission did not see the need to create an exception to the stamping obligation for lorry drivers, who are the main group affected by stamps filling up a passport early, due to the risk of illegal immigration; it argued that an entry-exit system will eventually address their position.[105] The Commission did intend, on the other hand, to propose an express exception from the stamping obligation for railway workers who regularly travel in and out of the EU. Also,

---

[100] Art. 11(1).

[101] Art. 11(2) and Annex VIII.

[102] Art. 11(3).

[103] COM (2009) 489, 21 Sep. 2009, pursuant to Art. 10(6). The March 2011 proposal does not suggest repealing Art. 10(6), even though it is now obsolete.

[104] The same point could be made where the person concerned holds a long-stay visa, but the Commission does not mention this. The Commission's argument raises the question whether the list of exceptions from the stamping obligation set out in Art. 10(2) and (3) is exhaustive or non-exhaustive. The text of the Code does not make this clear, although the exclusion of third-country national family members of EU citizens with residence cards from the stamping obligation is not expressly set out – it follows from an *a contrario* reading of Art. 10(2) along with Art. 3(a). It might be possible to argue (although the Commission does not) that the stamping obligation does not apply to such persons because the Code only applies to persons admitted for a short stay in the first place (see Art. 5(1)). But if that where the case, why does the Code contain references to persons with long-stay visas and residence permits in other provisions (Art. 5(1)(b) and 5(4)(a), for instance)?

[105] Note, however, that an entry-exit system is not forecast to be operational until 2015, so this would not alleviate the position of the lorry drivers in the meantime. The Commission seems unwilling to consider any special solution for this category of persons (the creation of a special permit, a system of employers' liability, reciprocal agreements with states of origin on special travel documents or the development of a *sui generis* entry-exit system for the meantime).

the Commission took the view that a stamping obligation cannot be applied at internal borders, even where border checks are re-instated pursuant to the applicable provisions of the Code, given that the re-introduction of those checks cannot alter the total length of authorised stay. This is again undoubtedly a sound argument, but not expressly set out in the wording of the Code.[106] The March 2011 proposal to amend the Code would introduce further express exceptions from the stamping requirement only for train crews and passengers and for third-country national family members of EU citizens.

As for the presumption of illegality, most Member States do not collect statistics on the numbers of persons who are found on the territory or detected while exiting without an entry stamp, or who are able or not able to rebut any presumption of irregular stay, although in fact the Code does not require them to do so.[107] The Commission rightly pointed out that this information would obviously be useful in order to assess the effect of the provisions on stamping, but the fault here lies with the legislation, which failed to set out an obligation in this respect. Equally, most Member States have not informed the Commission about their practices on the presumption of illegal stay, although on this point the Code does set out an obligation.[108] It was not clear from the information supplied to the Commission whether or not Member States always presume that the absence of an entry stamp indicates an irregular stay. Ultimately, the Commission drew no conclusions about the rules in the Code on the presumption of an illegal stay, and did not mention the issue of the link between these rules and the Returns Directive (see the discussion above).

The Court of Justice has interpreted these rules in the case of *Zurita Garcia and Cabrera*[109] in which the Court considered the situation of third country nationals who had been irregularly present in Spain for an unspecified period of time. The Spanish authorities sought to expel Ms Zurita Garcia and Mr Cabrera and place re-entry bans on them. The Court found that as both Ms Zurita Garcia and Mr Cabrera were present on the territory when the expulsion orders were made the Regulation did not apply to them. However, taking into account both the Schengen Convention and the Regulation, the Court of Justice found that there was no *requirement* on a Member State to

---

[106] Art. 28 provides that: "[w]here border control at internal borders is reintroduced, the relevant provisions of Title II shall apply *mutatis mutandis*." It might be deduced that Art. 10(1) is not a "relevant provision" for this purpose, but it might be better to specify exactly what these "relevant provisions" are, in the interests of legal certainty.

[107] This is a distinct issue from the obligation to provide statistics on *refusal of entry* decisions (Art. 13(5)).

[108] Art. 11(2), final sub-paragraph.

[109] Joined Cases C-261/08 and C-348/08 [2009] ECR I-10143.

expel someone who no longer fulfils the conditions of Article 5 of the Regulation.[110] Arguably the position in such a case is now affected by the application of the Returns Directive.[111] In fact, the March 2011 proposal would amend the Code to refer to the Returns Directive expressly.[112]

Next, the Code contains basic rules on border surveillance, addressing the purposes of surveillance, the types of units to be used, the numbers of border guards to be used and their methods and the requirement to survey sensitive areas in particular.[113] Further measures concerning surveillance may be adopted in accordance with a "comitology" procedure, involving participation of the EP,[114] or (in future, pursuant to the March 2011 proposal) in accordance with a "delegated acts" procedure. As noted above, an implementing measure relating to maritime border surveillance has been adopted.[115]

The Code then sets out rules concerning refusal of entry, which are obviously among its most important provisions. As noted above, the general rule is that persons who do not meet the criteria for admission must be denied entry, subject to certain exceptions;[116] more detailed rules on the procedure for

---

[110] Although the Spanish text of the Code states that the person "must" be expelled, the Court gave priority to the wording in all of the other language versions, which indicate that there is an option to expel. With respect, it is not clear from the facts of these cases whether or not there was a failure to stamp the documents of the persons concerned; the Court (and Advocate-General) simply assumed that Art. 11 of the Code was applicable. The judgment also interpreted Art. 23 of the Convention, which has been replaced by the Returns Directive (Dir. 2008/115 ([2008] OJ L 348/98) as from 24 Dec. 2010 (Arts. 20 and 21 of the Dir.).

[111] Dir. 2008/115, which has been applicable from 24 Dec. 2010 (ibid). The Dir did not amend the Borders Code and there is no express provision in the Dir. indicating how the *prima facie* mandatory expulsion set out in Art. 6 of the Dir relates to the optional expulsion referred to in Art. 11(3) of the Code. However, the Dir. does specify that it is "without prejudice" to "more favourable provisions" in the "Community acquis relating to immigration and asylum" (Art. 4(2) of the Dir). This must surely mean that the optional expulsion in the Code must take precedence over the mandatory expulsion in the Dir., where the two rules overlap. It should also be noted that Art. 11(1) of the Code only provides for an option, not an obligation, to presume in the first place that the conditions for stay have been breached in the event of that the documents in questions are not stamped. On the relationship between the Code and the Dir on this point, see also the opinion in *Zurita Garcia*, note 23, which, with respect, fails to take Art. 4(2) of the Dir into account.

[112] Proposed amendment to Art. 11(3). The March 2011 proposal would also add a new Art. 11(4).

[113] Art. 12(1) to (4).

[114] Art. 12(5), as amended by Reg. 296/2008.

[115] N. 27 above.

[116] Art. 13(1); see the discussion of Art. 5 above and also Case C-606/10, *Association nationale d'assistance aux frontières pour les étrangers (Anafé)*, pending.

refusing entry are set out in an Annex to the Code.[117] This Part of the Annex sets out rules on: filling out the standard entry form and giving it to the third-country national to sign; cancelling a visa and inserting a cancelled entry stamp in the travel document; registering the details of the refusal; obligations of carriers, in accordance with Article 26 of the Schengen Convention and the carrier sanctions Directive and the possible arrest of the third-country national pursuant to criminal law.

There are also procedural rights for persons denied entry. Entry may only be refused "by a substantiated decision stating the precise reasons for the refusal", which is given by means of a standard form annexed to the Code. The decision must be taken by a legally empowered authority, must take effect immediately, and the decision form must be given to the person concerned, who "shall acknowledge receipt".[118] Persons refused entry have "the right to appeal"; the appeal "shall be conducted in accordance with national law". Member States must give the person concerned a written list of contact points who could provide information on persons who could represent him or her. But appeals "shall not have suspensive effect". If successful, an appeal must entail that the cancelled entry stamp is corrected; this is "[w]ithout prejudice to any compensation granted in accordance with national law".[119]

Unsurprisingly, the Code specifies that border guards must ensure that persons refused entry shall not enter the territory of the Member States.[120] Member States must collect statistics on the numbers refused entry, their nationality, the grounds for refusal of entry and the type of border where entry was refused. This information must be transmitted annually to the Commission, which must publish it every two years.[121]

Compared to the previous rules in the Common Manual, the procedural rights in the Code are substantially more developed. The Manual provided for a possible delay in entry into force of the refusal decision (if national law provides for this), and an obligation to "state the procedures for appeal *where these exist*" (emphasis added). There were no provisions on representation during appeals, the effect of pending appeals or the consequences of a successful appeal. Also, there was previously no requirement to compile statistics and

---

[117] Art. 13(6), referring to Annex V, Part A, since amended by Art. 55 of the visa code. Point 3 of this Annex refers to the Schengen and EU rules on carrier sanctions.

[118] Art. 13(2) and Annex V, Part B.

[119] Art. 13(3).

[120] Art. 13(4).

[121] Art. 13(5). Some of this information is available online at: <http://ec.europa.eu/home -affairs/policies/borders/borders_maps_en.htm>. The March 2011 proposal would amend Art. 13(5), to refer to the EU legislation on immigration statistics.

transmit them to the Commission for publication. The obligation to use a standard form for refusals, which contains an exhaustive list of grounds for refusal, was previously part of the Common Manual, pursuant to an implementing measure adopted by the Council in 2004, although the Code amended the form to provide for a new ground for refusal, and the person concerned was not previously required to acknowledge or sign the form as such (although he or she had to acknowledge receipt of the decision).

It is possible that these provisions overlap with the scope of the Returns Directive, which gives Member States an option (but not an obligation) to exclude persons refused entry in accordance with the Borders Code from the scope of that Directive, which contains its own specific rules on procedural rights and related issues such as detention. Member States may also exclude from the scope of that Directive those persons "who are apprehended or intercepted by the competent authorities in connection with the irregular crossing by land, sea or air of the external border of a Member State and who have not subsequently obtained an authorisation or a right to stay in that Member State".[122] If Member States take up these options, the former category of persons will at least benefit from the procedural rights set out in the Borders Code.[123] But more problematically, the latter category of persons will not benefit from any procedural rights whatsoever as a matter of EU law; this position is impossible to defend. Arguably this category of persons falls sufficiently within the scope of EU law to be covered by the EU Charter of Fundamental Rights and the general principles of EU law, and can therefore derive procedural rights in that connection. In any event, the Returns Directive requires that for both categories of persons, Member States must "ensure that their treatment and level of protection are no less favourable than" the rules in that Directive regarding limitations on use of coercive measures, postponement of removal, emergency health care, the needs of vulnerable persons, and detention conditions, and must also "respect the principle of non-refoulement".[124]

---

[122] Art. 2(2)(a) of Dir. 2008/115. Member States had to apply this Dir. by 24 Dec. 2010 (Art. 20).

[123] Conversely, of course, if a Member State does not invoke the exclusion, persons refused entry at the border will benefit from the provisions in both the Returns Directive and the Borders Code. Presumably, in the event of overlap, the rule setting the highest standards will apply.

[124] Art. 4(4), Dir. 2008/115. The obligation to respect the principle of non-refoulement is not further defined (cf also Art. 5 of the Dir), although note that in any event the Directive is subject to more favourable provisions in other EU immigration and asylum measures (Art. 4(2)).

Next, Chapter III of Title II concerns cooperation between national authorities, as well as staff and resources for border controls.[125] Member States must deploy "appropriate staff and resources" in order to carry out border checks as provided for in Chapter II, "to ensure an efficient, high and uniform level of control at their external borders".[126] Checks must be carried out by border guards in conformity with national law; the guards must be sufficiently specialised and trained, and encouraged to learn relevant languages. Member States must ensure effective coordination of all relevant national services, and notify the Commission of the services responsible for border guard duties.[127]

As for cooperation between Member States, there is a general requirement of assistance and cooperation in accordance with other provisions of the Code. Member States must also exchange relevant information. The Code furthermore refers to the role of Frontex in coordinating border operations, as well as Member States' role as regards operational coordination, including the exchange of liaison officers, as long as this does not interfere with the work of the Agency. Member States must also provide for training of border guards on border control and fundamental rights, taking account of the standards developed by the Agency.[128] There is also a special rule concerning joint control of the common land borders of those Member States not yet fully applying the Schengen rules. Until the Schengen *acquis* is fully applicable to them, those States can jointly control their borders, without prejudice to Member States' individual responsibility. To this end, Member States may conclude bilateral agreements, of which they must inform the Commission.[129]

3.6. *Specific Rules on Border Checks*

Finally, Chapter IV of Title II of the Code sets out specific rules for border checks in certain cases, concerning respectively different types of borders and different categories of persons.[130] For instance, the rules on crossing by road in particular permit drivers usually to stay in their vehicles during checks, while the rules for checking trains en route to or from third countries have been

---

[125] Arts. 14–17.

[126] Art. 14.

[127] Art. 15; see Art. 34(1)(d) on notification. The March 2011 proposal would amend Art. 15(1).

[128] Art. 16.

[129] Art. 17; see Art. 37 on notification.

[130] Arts. 18–19. The detailed rules appear in Annexes VI and VII. The March 2011 proposal would amend Arts. 18 and 19, and both Annexes.

amended to allow for "juxtaposed control" in third States, and to delete a specific rule about checking sleeper carriages. The rules on air travel essentially set out when checks should be carried out given the different stops that some flights make inside and outside the Schengen States; these were amended to provide for possible checks on the aircraft or in transit areas. Special rules on aerodromes (which exempt Member States from having to provide border guards permanently) were maintained, with an additional reference to legislation on EU civil aviation security, and an entirely new section was added on private flights, ensuring that border checks are carried out and advance passenger information is provided. The rules on sea borders were amended in particular to strengthen the rules on control of cruise ships and pleasure boats and to tighten the definition of fishing vessels which will not generally be checked (confining this exemption to boats which dock at least every 36 hours in a Member State's ports without docking in non-EU ports). Finally, the relatively detailed rules on the process of checking ferries (which do not provide for any derogations from the general rules) and brief provisions on inland waterway traffic (which essentially apply the general sea borders rules) were not amended.

As for checks on particular categories of persons (see Annex VII of the Code), there are six categories of persons subject to special treatment: heads of state; pilots and other aircraft crew; seamen; holders of diplomatic, official or service passports and of documents issued by international organisations; cross-border workers; and minors. For example, the special rules for Heads of State and their delegation exempt them entirely from border checks. Pilots and aircraft crew can enter airports without having to meet the entry conditions set out in Article 5 of the Code. Seamen may visit ports and adjacent municipalities without being checked or passing through an official crossing point.

Holders of diplomatic, official or service passports and documents issued by international organisations are exempt from subsistence requirements, must be given priority when crossing and cannot be refused entry by border guards unless the guards first check with foreign ministries, even in the case of a SIS alert. However, they may still be subject to a visa, except for accredited diplomats and their families who hold special permits issued by foreign ministries. Cross-border workers need not be subject to a check every time they cross the border, if they are "well known" to the border guards due to their "frequent crossing" and they were not listed in the SIS when an initial check was carried out; this exemption may be extended to other categories of regular cross-border commuters. Finally, minors must be the subject of "particular attention" from border guards, to ensure that accompanied minors are with persons entitled to exercise parental care and that unaccompanied minors are not leaving the territory against the wishes of the person with parental care of them.

4. *Internal Borders*

4.1. *Title III of the Code*

Title III (Articles 20–31) concerns internal border controls, and Chapter I of this Title (Articles 20–22) concerns the abolition of such controls. Article 20 repeats the basic rule at the core of the Schengen Convention, that "internal borders can be crossed at any point without any checks on persons being carried out". Article 21 provides for four types of such checks which are permitted despite the abolition of internal border controls: the exercise of police powers; security checks at ports and airports (if such checks also apply to movement within a Member State); the possibility to impose an obligation to hold or carry documents; or the registration requirement set out in Article 22 of the Schengen Convention. The March 2011 proposal would amend the fourth possible requirement (along with Article 22 of the Convention).

This leaves the provision concerning police powers, which was amended as compared to the Schengen Convention rule and which was moreover the subject of difficult negotiations between the EU institutions. Previously, the Convention provided that it did not affect "the exercise of police powers throughout a [Member State's] territory by the competent authorities under [national] law". But there was evidence that at least some Member States simply replaced border checks with police patrols just inside the territory.[131] The final Code sets out four cases "in particular" where the exercise of police powers shall not be considered equivalent to border checks: the checks do not have border control as an objective; they are based on general police information and experience and aim "in particular" at combating "cross-border crime"; they are devised and executed differently from systematic checks at the external borders; and they do not entail spot-checks. These provisions are vague and subjective, the list of indications is non-exhaustive (as is the second indication) and this provision provides for a subjective test (the "intention" of checks) in order to ascertain whether an *objective* rule has been broken (the "effect" of checks). Also, there is no notification or transparency requirement which would assist in an assessment of whether the rules are being applied correctly.

---

[131] See Groenendijk, n. 6 above.

One key question is whether police checks would infringe the Code if they are carried out at or near the borders for the purposes of migration control. It is striking that there is no direct reference to this issue in Article 21(a) of the Code. In light of this, and since any checks carried out at or near borders for the main purpose or with the main effect of migration control must surely be considered as having the prohibited objective of border control, it must follow that such checks would violate the Code. Finally, it should be noted that the police checks permitted by Article 21 are not covered by the ban on discriminatory conduct set out in Article 7, which only applies to border checks; but surely it can be argued that a police check within the scope of Article 21 which is mainly aimed at non-white people falls nonetheless within the scope of the principle of equality, which is protected as a general principle of EU law and by the EU Charter of Fundamental Rights.

Article 21 was the subject of a judgment of the Court of Justice in June 2010, which answered questions posed to it only on 16 April 2010 by a French court. The accelerated procedure was used in order to deal with a number of procedural issues of some importance to the French system of judicial review but beyond the scope of this chapter. In this case two third country nationals, Mr Melki and Mr Abdeli, were subject to a police control within a 20 kilometer radius of the Franco-Belgian border on their identity and then detained as irregularly present in France.[132] Under the Schengen Convention the 20 kilometers radius was relevant as there was something of a fudge regarding how far into the territory controls could be carried out, to be determined by national authorities. The question which the Court of Justice had to address was whether Article 67 TFEU (the Treaty provision which sets out the general objectives of the EU's Justice and Home Affairs policies) permits national police authorities to check the identity of any person in order to ascertain whether he or she fulfills national law regarding the carrying and production of identity documents.

The Court's judgment began by affirming that the relevant law is the Regulation, not the TFEU or the Schengen Convention. Thus the 20 kilometer radius is irrelevant as it only applied under the Schengen Convention. Therefore the question was whether the police identity checks fulfilled the requirements of Article 21(a) of the Regulation, in that they were police checks unrelated to border controls and which do not have equivalent effect to border controls. Notwithstanding the fact that the national legislation permits identity checks only within a 20 kilometer radius of the French border, the Court of Justice found that they were not necessarily the equivalent of border

---

[132] Joined Cases C-188/10 and C-189/10, judgment of 22 June 2010, not yet reported.

controls. However, the fact that national legislation on checks lays down specific rules on board international trains or on toll motorways (unlike the 20 kilometer radius on roads) regarding the territorial scope the Court left open the possibility that the challenged checks might have an equivalent effect to border controls. It went on to examine the checks by reference to their purpose and found that as the checks are authorised irrespective of the behavior of the individual or on the specific circumstance for instance a public order threat, they fail a legal certainty requirement inherent in Articles 20 and 21(a) of the Regulation. The Court stated that where checks are authorised in a border zone with other Member States and do not depend on the behavior of the individual, they must be in a framework which guides the exercise of discretion by the police in their use. That framework must guarantee that the practical exercise of the powers cannot have an effect equivalent to border checks. This is something of a mouthful but it is clearly an indication that the Court will take seriously checks which are put forward as the exercise of police powers but are carried out with the kind of unlimited discretion which is normally associated only with border controls.

Article 22 provides for the removal of road-traffic obstacles at the internal borders, but nonetheless requires Member States to retain facilities to reintroduce internal border checks if necessary. Chapter II of this Title (Articles 23–31) concerns the reintroduction of controls by a Member State. Article 23(1) sets out the basic rule: a Member State can "exceptionally" reintroduce border controls for up to 30 days, or for a longer period if the duration of the relevant event is foreseeable, in the "event of a serious threat to public policy or to internal security". But the "scope and duration" of the reintroduced checks "shall not exceed what is strictly necessary to respond to the reintroduced checks". Article 23(2) permits the reintroduction of controls to be continued for further renewable periods of up to 30 days, "taking into account any new elements". This compares to the previous Article 2(2) of the Schengen Convention, which permitted the reintroduction of checks for a "limited period" if "public policy or national security so require"; these checks had to be "appropriate to the situation". It can clearly be seen that under the Code, the threshold for reintroduction of checks is higher, the time period is more precisely specified and the necessity rule is stricter.

The procedure for reintroducing controls for foreseeable events is set out in Article 24. Member States must inform "as soon as possible" the Commission and other Member States, and provide information "as soon as available" on the reasons for and the scope of the reintroduction of controls, the authorised crossing points, the date and duration of the introduction and (if relevant) the measures to be taken by other Member States. The Commission may issue an opinion on the planned reintroduction, and there shall be consultation on the planned controls between the Member States and the Commission in order to discuss the proportionality of the controls and possibly also "mutual cooperation between the Member States".

In the event that "urgent action" is required, Article 25 permits Member States to reintroduce controls without prior notification, provided that the relevant information is sent to the Commission and other Member States later. The procedure for prolonging controls is set out in Article 26; it simply requires the application of the procedure for reintroducing controls.

Finally, Title III contains provisions on: informing the EP of decisions on reintroduced controls (and reporting to the EP following the third consecutive extension of reintroduced controls); clarifying that the external borders rules will apply when internal border checks are reintroduced; requiring a report when internal border controls are lifted, outlining the operation of the internal checks and their effectiveness; requiring information to the public about reintroduced controls unless there are overriding security reasons to the contrary; and requiring the EU institutions and other Member States to respect the confidentiality of information submitted by a Member State at its request.

4.2. *Commission Report*

The Commission was obliged by the Code to report on the implementation by the Member States of the abolition of intra Member State controls on persons under Title III by 13 October 2009. On 13 October 2010 the report was released.[133] The Commission's assessment of the criteria on the basis of which Title III is implemented in the Member States is somewhat ambiguous. The report rarely identifies a Member State by name, generally only commenting on problem areas. It is clear that the Member States provided scant information on a number of key subjects of concern to the Commission (indeed, two Member States provided no information at all – Hungary and Malta). The Commission is particularly concerned about controls in border zones which appears to give rise to substantial numbers of complaints. It confirms that where Member States carry out controls in such areas they must be targeted and based on concrete and factual police information and experience as regards threats to public security and must not be systematic. Further, they must be constantly reassessed. Most Member States, according to the report,

---

[133] Report from the Commission on the Application of Title III (Internal Borders) of Regulation (EC) No 562/2006 establishing a Community Code on the rules governing the movement of persons across borders (Schengen Borders Code): COM (2010) 554, 13 Oct. 2010.

confirm that they carry out non-systematic random police checks on the basis of risk assessments of the security situation. The specific grounds are irregular migration, breaches of criminal law, security or traffic law. In the opinion of the Commission it is easy to determine whether a check is carried out for traffic law purposes but much less clear when the ground is to enforce immigration law.

Another element of concern to the Commission is the objective of the check – goods or persons? The Commission is not so concerned regarding the identity of the national authority which carries out the control as it seems Member States assign different responsibilities to different authorities according to highly divergent rationales (if indeed rationales are accessible). The frequency of checks carried out in the internal border zones is a matter of great interest to the Commission as indicative of whether the checks are systematic or not but little or no information was forthcoming from the Member States on this issue.

In order to obtain more information the Commission plans to carry out unannounced on-site visits to verify the application of the Code. This is an interesting development and it moves the role of the Commission into an operational mode which it does not often take in this field.

Checks at airports on intra-Schengen flights are also something of a bugbear from the Commission according to the report. The Commission accepts that identity checks by airline staff are security checks but confirms that the airlines are free to accept documents other than passports or identity cards if they so wish. Further, carriers must not enter into investigations of whether third country nationals have visas or residence permits in a Member State. The Commission insists that identity checks at airports must be limited to exactly that, identity checks, not immigration checks.

Member States are entitled to require third country nationals entering their territory from within the Schengen area to register their presence. Seven Schengen States do not do so (SE, EE, DE, FI, LT, DK and NO). The Commission does not like the requirement which it considers difficult to implement and of little or no value. It therefore recommended its removal in its March 2011 proposal.

Road traffic is also a subject of some concern in the report. It seems this is an issue, in particular, on roads between pre 2004 Member States and post 2004 ones. The Code requires all obstacles to fluid traffic flow at internal borders to be removed, including speed limits. It seems the Commission has received many complaints regarding road traffic obstacles – these include buildings, control booths, roofs over the road, mobile equipment such as plastic cones, barriers, reduction of the number of lanes, traffic lights or road signs. Some Member States have kept the old infrastructure at road crossing points (PT, CZ, EL, EE, FR, AT, FI, LT, LV, SI and LU). Most Member States claim their obstacles to free flow of traffic are necessary for road safety considerations. The Commission is not convinced and wants more action on their dismantlement.

There is an exceptional provision in the Code which permits the reintroduction of intra Member State border controls. Since the Code was adopted in 2006 this exception has been used by 12 Schengen States (FR, ES, DE, AT, IT, DK, FI, EE, LV, MT, NO and IS). The controls have all been temporary. A Member State planning to introduce a temporary exceptional control is required to notify the Commission, as noted above. The Commission is particularly unimpressed with the quality of the notifications which are too vague, too late and generally inadequate. Further, on such reintroduction of border controls, the Commission is concerned that citizens of the Union are being refused passage on grounds outside those permitted in Directive 2004/38 on citizens of the Union which limits such refusal to grounds of public policy, public security and public health. The report contains a most interesting table of the Member States which have reintroduced temporary border controls and why. The majority of cases are around meetings of heads of state. The next most common ground is around Basque demonstrations (exclusively of interest to France and Spain), Iceland has twice used the provision around Hells Angels visits to Icelandic motorcycle meetings, Norway introduced border controls form the Nobel Peace Prize though Sweden never introduced controls for any of the other Nobel prizes which are given out in Stockholm.

In general it appears that there are indeed teething troubles attendant on the introduction and correct application of the Code. The Commission may consider further action justified.

5. Final Provisions

Title IV (Articles 32–40) sets out general and final provisions. Article 32 provides that three of the Annexes to the Regulation may be amended by a "comitology" procedure, entailing amendments by the Commission after the involvement of a committee made up of Member States' officials, and the scrutiny of the EP. Implicitly the other five Annexes can only be amended by a full legislative process. The particular rules for the "comitology" process are set out in Article 33; the Regulation also provides for the Commission to adopt detailed rules on surveillance by use of this process.[134] As noted already, the

---

[134] On this process, see further chapter 2.

March 2011 proposal would amend Articles 32 and 33 of the Code to provide for the use of "delegated acts" instead of the "comitology" process.

Article 34 provides that Member States shall inform the Commission of their national rules concerning five issues: the list of residence permits; the list of border crossing points; the reference amounts for subsistence applied to persons crossing the external border; the list of national border control services; and the specimen cards issued by foreign ministers. The March 2011 proposal would amend Article 34 of the Code, requiring more precise information as regards types of residence permits.

Article 35 provides that the entire Code is without prejudice to EU rules on border traffic and to existing bilateral agreements on this subject. The regulation on local border traffic was adopted in 2006 after the Code.[135] Article 36 concerns the territorial scope (exclusion of Ceuta and Melilla); the preamble also points out that the Code only applies to the European territories of France and the Netherlands. Article 37 requires Member States to inform the Commission of their national rules concerning penalties for crossing borders, agreements on joint border controls and the rules on requirements to hold documents and register when crossing internal borders. The March 2011 proposal would amend Article 37.

Article 38 required the Commission to report on the application of Title III (internal border controls) by October 2009, in particular examining any difficulties arising from the reintroduction of internal border controls no other reviews of the Code are provided for.[136] Finally, Articles 39 and 40 set out rules regarding repeals and the entry into force of the Regulation; these provisions were discussed above.

---

[135] Reg. 1931/2006 on local border traffic - OJ 2006 L 405/1. See further chapter 6.
[136] On this report, see section 4 above. The March 2011 proposal would not repeal Art. 38, even though it is now obsolete.

Annex

REGULATION (EC) No 562/2006 OF THE EUROPEAN PARLIAMENT AND OF THE COUNCIL

of 15 March 2006

establishing a Community Code on the rules governing the movement of persons across borders (Schengen Borders Code)

(OJ L 105, 13.4.2006, p. 1)

[informal consolidation of text]
[original footnotes omitted]

THE EUROPEAN PARLIAMENT AND THE COUNCIL OF THE EUROPEAN UNION,

Having regard to the Treaty establishing the European Community, and in particular Articles 62(1) and (2)(a) thereof,

Having regard to the proposal from the Commission,

Acting in accordance with the procedure laid down in Article 251 of the Treaty,

Whereas:

(1) The adoption of measures under Article 62(1) of the Treaty with a view to ensuring the absence of any controls on persons crossing internal borders forms part of the Union's objective of establishing an area without internal borders in which the free movement of persons is ensured, as set out in Article 14 of the Treaty.

(2) In accordance with Article 61 of the Treaty, the creation of an area in which persons may move freely is to be flanked by other measures. The common policy on the crossing of external borders, as provided for by Article 62(2) of the Treaty, is such a measure.

(3) The adoption of common measures on the crossing of internal borders by persons and border control at external borders should reflect the Schengen *acquis* incorporated in the European Union framework, and in particular the relevant provisions of the Convention implementing the Schengen Agreement of 14 June 1985 between the Governments of the States of the Benelux Economic Union, the Federal Republic of Germany and the French Republic on the gradual abolition of checks at their common borders and the Common Manual.

(4) As regards border control at external borders, the establishment of a 'common corpus' of legislation, particularly via consolidation and development of the *acquis*, is one of the fundamental components of the common policy on the management of the external borders, as defined in the Commission Communication of 7 May 2002 'Towards integrated management of the external borders of the Member States of the European Union'. This objective was included in the 'Plan for the management of the external borders of the Member States of the European Union', approved by the Council on 13 June 2002 and endorsed by the Seville European Council on 21 and 22 June 2002 and by the Thessaloniki European Council on 19 and 20 June 2003.

(5) The definition of common rules on the movement of persons across borders neither calls into question nor affects the rights of free movement enjoyed by Union citizens and members of their families and by third-country nationals and members of their families who, under agreements between the Community and its Member States, on the one hand, and those third countries, on the other hand, enjoy rights of free movement equivalent to those of Union citizens.

(6) Border control is in the interest not only of the Member State at whose external borders it is carried out but of all Member States which have abolished internal border control. Border control should help to combat illegal immigration and trafficking in human beings and to prevent any threat to the Member States' internal security, public policy, public health and international relations.

(7) Border checks should be carried out in such a way as to fully respect human dignity. Border control should be carried out in a professional and respectful manner and be proportionate to the objectives pursued.

(8) Border control comprises not only checks on persons at border crossing points and surveillance between these border crossing points, but also an analysis of the risks for internal security and analysis of the threats that may affect the security of external borders. It is therefore necessary to lay down the conditions, criteria and detailed rules governing checks at border crossing points and surveillance.

(9) Provision should be made for relaxing checks at external borders in the event of exceptional and unforeseeable circumstances in order to avoid excessive waiting time at borders crossing-points. The systematic stamping of the documents of third-country nationals remains an obligation in the event of border checks being relaxed. Stamping makes it possible to establish, with certainty, the date on which, and where, the border was

crossed, without establishing in all cases that all required travel document control measures have been carried out.

(10) In order to reduce the waiting times of persons enjoying the Community right of free movement, separate lanes, indicated by uniform signs in all Member States, should, where circumstances allow, be provided at border crossing points. Separate lanes should be provided in international airports. Where it is deemed appropriate and if local circumstances so allow, Member States should consider installing separate lanes at sea and land border crossing points.

(11) Member States should ensure that control procedures at external borders do not constitute a major barrier to trade and social and cultural interchange. To that end, they should deploy appropriate numbers of staff and resources.

(12) Member States should designate the national service or services responsible for border-control tasks in accordance with their national law. Where more than one service is responsible in the same Member State, there should be close and constant cooperation between them.

(13) Operational cooperation and assistance between Member States in relation to border control should be managed and coordinated by the European Agency for the Management of Operational Cooperation at the External Borders of the Member States established by Regulation (EC) No 2007/2004.

(14) This Regulation is without prejudice to checks carried out under general police powers and security checks on persons identical to those carried out for domestic flights, to the possibilities for Member States to carry out exceptional checks on baggage in accordance with Council Regulation (EEC) No 3925/91 of 19 December 1991 concerning the elimination of controls and formalities applicable to the cabin and hold baggage of persons taking an intra-Community flight and the baggage of persons making an intra-Community sea crossing, and to national law on carrying travel or identity documents or to the requirement that persons notify the authorities of their presence on the territory of the Member State in question.

(15) Member States should also have the possibility of temporarily reintroducing border control at internal borders in the event of a serious threat to their public policy or internal security. The conditions and procedures for doing so should be laid down, so as to ensure that any such measure is exceptional and that the principle of proportionality is respected. The scope and duration of any temporary reintroduction of border control at

internal borders should be restricted to the bare minimum needed to respond to that threat.

(16) In an area where persons may move freely, the reintroduction of border control at internal borders should remain an exception. Border control should not be carried out or formalities imposed solely because such a border is crossed.

(17) Provision should be made for a procedure enabling the Commission to adapt certain detailed practical rules governing border control. In such cases, the measures needed to implement this Regulation should be taken pursuant to Council Decision 1999/468/EC of 28 June 1999 laying down the procedures for the exercise of implementing powers conferred on the Commission.

(18) Provision should also be made for a procedure enabling the Member States to notify the Commission of changes to other detailed practical rules governing border control.

(19) Since the objective of this Regulation, namely the establishment of rules applicable to the movement of persons across borders cannot be sufficiently achieved by the Member States and can therefore be better achieved at Community level, the Community may adopt measures, in accordance with the principle of subsidiarity as set out in Article 5 of the Treaty. In accordance with the principle of proportionality, as set out in that Article, this Regulation does not go beyond what is necessary in order to achieve that objective.

(20) This Regulation respects fundamental rights and observes the principles recognised in particular by the Charter of Fundamental Rights of the European Union. It should be applied in accordance with the Member States' obligations as regards international protection and non-refoulement.

(21) By way of derogation from Article 299 of the Treaty, the only territories of France and the Netherlands to which this Regulation applies are those in Europe. It does not affect the specific arrangements applied in Ceuta and Melilla, as defined in the Agreement on the Accession of the Kingdom of Spain to the Convention implementing the Schengen Agreement of 14 June 1985.

(22) In accordance with Articles 1 and 2 of the Protocol on the Position of Denmark annexed to the Treaty on European Union and to the Treaty establishing the European Community, Denmark is not taking part in the adoption of this Regulation and is not bound by it or subject to its application. Given that this Regulation builds upon the Schengen *acquis*

under the provisions of Title IV of Part Three of the Treaty establishing the European Community, Denmark should, in accordance with Article 5 of the said Protocol, decide within a period of six months after the date of adoption of this Regulation whether it will implement it in its national law or not.

(23) As regards Iceland and Norway, this Regulation constitutes a development of provisions of the Schengen *acquis* within the meaning of the Agreement concluded by the Council of the European Union and the Republic of Iceland and the Kingdom of Norway concerning the latters' association with the implementation, application and development of the Schengen *acquis* which fall within the area referred to in Article 1, point A, of Council Decision 1999/437/EC on certain arrangements for the application of that Agreement.

(24) An arrangement has to be made to allow representatives of Iceland and Norway to be associated with the work of committees assisting the Commission in the exercise of its implementing powers. Such an arrangement has been contemplated in the Exchanges of Letters between the Council of the European Union and the Republic of Iceland and the Kingdom of Norway concerning committees which assist the European Commission in the exercise of its executive powers, annexed to the abovementioned Agreement.

(25) As regards Switzerland, this Regulation constitutes a development of provisions of the Schengen *acquis* within the meaning of the Agreement signed between the European Union, the European Community and the Swiss Confederation concerning the association of the Swiss Confederation with the implementation, application and development of the Schengen *acquis*, which fall within the area referred to in Article 1, point A, of Decision 1999/437/EC read in conjunction with Article 4(1) of Council Decisions 2004/849/EC and 2004/860/EC.

(26) An arrangement has to be made to allow representatives of Switzerland to be associated with the work of committees assisting the Commission in the exercise of its implementing powers. Such an arrangement has been contemplated in the Exchange of Letters between the Community and Switzerland, annexed to the abovementioned Agreement.

(27) This Regulation constitutes a development of provisions of the Schengen *acquis* in which the United Kingdom does not take part, in accordance with Council Decision 2000/365/EC of 29 May 2000 concerning the request of the United Kingdom of Great Britain and Northern Ireland to take part in some of the provisions of the Schengen *acquis*. The United Kingdom is therefore not taking part in its adoption and is not bound by it or subject to its application.

(28) This Regulation constitutes a development of provisions of the Schengen *acquis* in which Ireland does not take part, in accordance with Council Decision 2002/192/EC of 28 February 2002 concerning Ireland's request to take part in some of the provisions of the Schengen *acquis*. Ireland is therefore not taking part in its adoption and is not bound by it or subject to its application.

(29) In this Regulation, the first sentence of Article 1, Article 5(4)(a), Title III and the provisions of Title II and the annexes thereto referring to the Schengen Information System (SIS) constitute provisions building on the Schengen *acquis* or otherwise related to it within the meaning of Article 3(2) of the 2003 Act of Accession,

HAVE ADOPTED THIS REGULATION:

TITLE I
GENERAL PROVISIONS

Article 1
Subject matter and principles

This Regulation provides for the absence of border control of persons crossing the internal borders between the Member States of the European Union.

It establishes rules governing border control of persons crossing the external borders of the Member States of the European Union.

Article 2
Definitions

For the purposes of this Regulation the following definitions shall apply:

1. 'internal borders' means:
   (a) the common land borders, including river and lake borders, of the Member States;
   (b) the airports of the Member States for internal flights;
   (c) sea, river and lake ports of the Member States for regular ferry connections;
2. 'external borders' means the Member States' land borders, including river and lake borders, sea borders and their airports, river ports, sea ports and lake ports, provided that they are not internal borders;
3. 'internal flight' means any flight exclusively to or from the territories of the Member States and not landing in the territory of a third country;

4. 'regular ferry connection' means any ferry connection between the same two or more ports situated in the territory of the Member States, not calling at any ports outside the territory of the Member States and consisting of the transport of passengers and vehicles according to a published timetable;

5. 'persons enjoying the Community right of free movement' means:
   (a) Union citizens within the meaning of Article 17(1) of the Treaty, and third-country nationals who are members of the family of a Union citizen exercising his or her right to free movement to whom Directive 2004/38/EC of the European Parliament and of the Council of 29 April 2004 on the right of citizens of the Union and their family members to move and reside freely within the territory of the Member States applies;
   (b) third-country nationals and their family members, whatever their nationality, who, under agreements between the Community and its Member States, on the one hand, and those third countries, on the other hand, enjoy rights of free movement equivalent to those of Union citizens;

6. 'third-country national' means any person who is not a Union citizen within the meaning of Article 17(1) of the Treaty and who is not covered by point 5 of this Article;

7. 'persons for whom an alert has been issued for the purposes of refusing entry' means any third-country national for whom an alert has been issued in the Schengen Information System (SIS) in accordance with and for the purposes laid down in Article 96 of the Schengen Convention;

8. 'border crossing point' means any crossing-point authorised by the competent authorities for the crossing of external borders;

9. 'border control' means the activity carried out at a border, in accordance with and for the purposes of this Regulation, in response exclusively to an intention to cross or the act of crossing that border, regardless of any other consideration, consisting of border checks and border surveillance;

10. 'border checks' means the checks carried out at border crossing points, to ensure that persons, including their means of transport and the objects in their possession, may be authorised to enter the territory of the Member States or authorised to leave it;

11. 'border surveillance' means the surveillance of borders between border crossing points and the surveillance of border crossing points outside the fixed opening hours, in order to prevent persons from circumventing border checks;

12. 'second line check' means a further check which may be carried out in a special location away from the location at which all persons are checked (first line);
13. 'border guard' means any public official assigned, in accordance with national law, to a border crossing point or along the border or the immediate vicinity of that border who carries out, in accordance with this Regulation and national law, border control tasks;
14. 'carrier' means any natural or legal person whose profession it is to provide transport of persons;
15. 'residence permit' means:
    (a) all residence permits issued by the Member States according to the uniform format laid down by Council Regulation (EC) No 1030/2002 of 13 June 2002 laying down a uniform format for residence permits for third-country nationals;
    (b) all other documents issued by a Member State to third-country nationals authorising a stay in, or re-entry into, its territory, with the exception of temporary permits issued pending examination of a first application for a residence permit as referred to in point (a) or an application for asylum;
16. 'cruise ship' means a ship which follows a given itinerary in accordance with a predetermined programme, which includes a programme of tourist activities in the various ports, and which normally neither takes passengers on nor allows passengers to disembark during the voyage;
17. 'pleasure boating' means the use of pleasure boats for sporting or tourism purposes;
18. 'coastal fisheries' means fishing carried out with the aid of vessels which return every day or within 36 hours to a port situated in the territory of a Member State without calling at a port situated in a third country;
19. 'threat to public health' means any disease with epidemic potential as defined by the International Health Regulations of the World Health Organisation and other infectious diseases or contagious parasitic diseases if they are the subject of protection provisions applying to nationals of the Member States.

Article 3
Scope

This Regulation shall apply to any person crossing the internal or external borders of Member States, without prejudice to:
(a) the rights of persons enjoying the Community right of free movement;

(b) the rights of refugees and persons requesting international protection, in particular as regards non-refoulement.

TITLE II
EXTERNAL BORDERS

CHAPTER I
Crossing of external borders and conditions for entry

Article 4
Crossing of external borders

1. External borders may be crossed only at border crossing points and during the fixed opening hours. The opening hours shall be clearly indicated at border crossing points which are not open 24 hours a day.

    Member States shall notify the list of their border crossing points to the Commission in accordance with Article 34.

2. By way of derogation from paragraph 1, exceptions to the obligation to cross external borders only at border crossing points and during the fixed opening hours may be allowed:
    (a) in connection with pleasure boating or coastal fishing;
    (b) for seamen going ashore to stay in the area of the port where their ships call or in the adjacent municipalities;
    (c) for individuals or groups of persons, where there is a requirement of a special nature, provided that they are in possession of the permits required by national law and that there is no conflict with the interests of public policy and the internal security of the Member States;
    (d) for individuals or groups of persons in the event of an unforeseen emergency situation.

3. Without prejudice to the exceptions provided for in paragraph 2 or to their international protection obligations, Member States shall introduce penalties, in accordance with their national law, for the unauthorised crossing of external borders at places other than border crossing points or at times other than the fixed opening hours. These penalties shall be effective, proportionate and dissuasive.

Article 5
Entry conditions for third-country nationals

1. For stays not exceeding three months per six-month period, the entry conditions for third-country nationals shall be the following:

(a) they are in possession of a valid travel document or documents authorising them to cross the border;

(b) they are in possession of a valid visa, if required pursuant to Council Regulation (EC) No 539/2001 of 15 March 2001 listing the third countries whose nationals must be in possession of visas when crossing the external borders and those whose nationals are exempt from that requirement, except where they hold a valid residence permit or a valid long-stay visa;[137]

(c) they justify the purpose and conditions of the intended stay, and they have sufficient means of subsistence, both for the duration of the intended stay and for the return to their country of origin or transit to a third country into which they are certain to be admitted, or are in a position to acquire such means lawfully;

(d) they are not persons for whom an alert has been issued in the SIS for the purposes of refusing entry;

(e) they are not considered to be a threat to public policy, internal security, public health or the international relations of any of the Member States, in particular where no alert has been issued in Member States' national data bases for the purposes of refusing entry on the same grounds.

2. A non-exhaustive list of supporting documents which the border guard may request from the third-country national in order to verify the fulfilment of the conditions set out in paragraph 1, point c, is included in Annex I.

3. Means of subsistence shall be assessed in accordance with the duration and the purpose of the stay and by reference to average prices in the Member State(s) concerned for board and lodging in budget accommodation, multiplied by the number of days stayed.

Reference amounts set by the Member States shall be notified to the Commission in accordance with Article 34.

The assessment of sufficient means of subsistence may be based on the cash, travellers' cheques and credit cards in the third-country national's possession. Declarations of sponsorship, where such declarations are provided for by national law and letters of guarantee from hosts, as defined by

---

[137] The reference to a long-stay visa was added by Reg. 265/2010 (OJ 2010 L 85/1), which entered into force on 5 Apr. 2010 (Art. 6, Reg. 265/2010).

national law, where the third-country national is staying with a host, may also constitute evidence of sufficient means of subsistence.

4. By way of derogation from paragraph 1:

    a) third-country nationals who do not fulfil all the conditions laid down in paragraph 1 but who hold a residence permit, a long-stay visa or a re-entry visa issued by one of the Member States or, where required, a residence permit or a long-stay visa and a re-entry visa, shall be authorised to enter the territories of the other Member States for transit purposes so that they may reach the territory of the Member State which issued the residence permit, long-stay visa or re-entry visa, unless their names are on the national list of alerts of the Member State whose external borders they are seeking to cross and the alert is accompanied by instructions to refuse entry or transit;[138]

    (b) third-country nationals who fulfil the conditions laid down in paragraph 1, except for that laid down in point (b), and who present themselves at the border may be authorised to enter the territories of the Member States, if a visa is issued at the border in accordance with Council Regulation (EC) No 415/2003 of 27 February 2003 on the issue of visas at the border, including the issue of such visas to seamen in transit.

    Visas issued at the border shall be recorded on a list.

    If it is not possible to affix a visa in the document, it shall, exceptionally, be affixed on a separate sheet inserted in the document. In such a case, the uniform format for forms for affixing the visa, laid down by Council Regulation (EC) No 333/2002 of 18 February 2002 on a uniform format for forms for affixing the visa issued by Member States to persons holding travel documents not recognised by the Member State drawing up the form, shall be used;

    (c) third-country nationals who do not fulfil one or more of the conditions laid down in paragraph 1 may be authorised by a Member State to enter its territory on humanitarian grounds, on grounds of national interest or because of international obligations.

Where the third-country national concerned is the subject of an alert as referred to in paragraph 1(d), the Member State authorising him or her to enter its territory shall inform the other Member States accordingly.

---

[138] The reference to a long-stay visa was added by Reg. 265/2010 (OJ 2010 L 85/1), which entered into force on 5 Apr. 2010 (Art. 6, Reg. 265/2010).

CHAPTER II
Control of external borders and refusal of entry

Article 6
Conduct of border checks

1. Border guards shall, in the performance of their duties, fully respect human dignity.

   Any measures taken in the performance of their duties shall be proportionate to the objectives pursued by such measures.
2. While carrying out border checks, border guards shall not discriminate against persons on grounds of sex, racial or ethnic origin, religion or belief, disability, age or sexual orientation.

Article 7
Border checks on persons

1. Cross-border movement at external borders shall be subject to checks by border guards. Checks shall be carried out in accordance with this chapter.

   The checks may also cover the means of transport and objects in the possession of the persons crossing the border. The law of the Member State concerned shall apply to any searches which are carried out.
2. All persons shall undergo a minimum check in order to establish their identities on the basis of the production or presentation of their travel documents. Such a minimum check shall consist of a rapid and straightforward verification, where appropriate by using technical devices and by consulting, in the relevant databases, information exclusively on stolen, misappropriated, lost and invalidated documents, of the validity of the document authorising the legitimate holder to cross the border and of the presence of signs of falsification or counterfeiting.

   The minimum check referred to in the first subparagraph shall be the rule for persons enjoying the Community right of free movement.

   However, on a non-systematic basis, when carrying out minimum checks on persons enjoying the Community right of free movement, border guards may consult national and European databases in order to ensure that such persons do not represent a genuine, present and sufficiently serious threat to the internal security, public policy, international relations of the Member States or a threat to the public health.

The consequences of such consultations shall not jeopardise the right of entry of persons enjoying the Community right of free movement into the territory of the Member State concerned as laid down in Directive 2004/38/EC.

3. On entry and exit, third-country nationals shall be subject to thorough checks.

   (a) thorough checks on entry shall comprise verification of the conditions governing entry laid down in Article 5(1) and, where applicable, of documents authorising residence and the pursuit of a professional activity. This shall include a detailed examination covering the following aspects:

   (i) verification that the third-country national is in possession of a document which is valid for crossing the border and which has not expired, and that the document is accompanied, where applicable, by the requisite visa or residence permit;

   (ii) thorough scrutiny of the travel document for signs of falsification or counterfeiting;

   (iii) examination of the entry and exit stamps on the travel document of the third-country national concerned, in order to verify, by comparing the dates of entry and exit, that the person has not already exceeded the maximum duration of authorised stay in the territory of the Member States;

   (iv) verification regarding the point of departure and the destination of the third-country national concerned and the purpose of the intended stay, checking if necessary, the corresponding supporting documents;

   (v) verification that the third-country national concerned has sufficient means of subsistence for the duration and purpose of the intended stay, for his or her return to the country of origin or transit to a third country into which he or she is certain to be admitted, or that he or she is in a position to acquire such means lawfully;

   (vi) verification that the third-country national concerned, his or her means of transport and the objects he or she is transporting are not likely to jeopardise the public policy, internal security, public health or international relations of any of the Member States. Such verification shall include direct consultation of the data and alerts on persons and, where necessary, objects included in the SIS and in national data files and the action to be performed, if any, as a result of an alert;

[139](aa) if the third country national holds a visa referred to in Article 5(1) (b), the thorough checks on entry shall also comprise verification of the identity of the holder of the visa and of the authenticity of the visa, by consulting the Visa Information System (VIS) in accordance with Article 18 of Regulation (EC) No 767/2008 of the European Parliament and of the Council of 9 July 2008 concerning the Visa Information System (VIS) and the exchange of data between Member States on short-stay visas (VIS Regulation);

(ab) by way of derogation, where:

    (i)   traffic of such intensity arises that the waiting time at the border crossing point becomes excessive;

    (ii) all resources have already been exhausted as regards staff, facilities and organisation; and

    (iii) on the basis of an assessment there is no risk related to internal security and illegal immigration;

the VIS may be consulted using the number of the visa sticker in all cases and, on a random basis, the number of the visa sticker in combination with the verification of fingerprints.

However, in all cases where there is doubt as to the identity of the holder of the visa and/or the authenticity of the visa, the VIS shall be consulted systematically using the number of the visa sticker in combination with the verification of fingerprints.

This derogation may be applied only at the border crossing point concerned for as long as the above conditions are met;

(ac) the decision to consult the VIS in accordance with point (ab) shall be taken by the border guard in command at the border crossing point or at a higher level.

The Member State concerned shall immediately notify the other Member States and the Commission of anysuch decision;

(ad) each Member State shall transmit once a year a report on the application of point (ab) to the European Parliament and the Commission, which shall include the number of third-country nationals who were checked in the VIS using the number of the visa sticker only and the length of the waiting time referred to in point (ab)(i);

---

[139] Art. 7(3)(aa) to (ae) was inserted by Reg. 81/2009 (OJ 2009 L 35/56), in force as from 24 Feb. 2009 (Art. 2, Reg. 81/2009), and applicable as from 20 days from the start of operations of the VIS.

(ae) points (ab) and (ac) shall apply for a maximum period of three years, beginning three years after the VIS has started operations. The Commission shall, before the end of the second year of application of points (ab) and (ac), transmit to the European Parliament and to the Council an evaluation of their implementation. On the basis of that evaluation, the European Parliament or the Council may invite the Commission to propose appropriate amendments to this Regulation.

(b) thorough checks on exit shall comprise:
  (i)   verification that the third-country national is in possession of a document valid for crossing the border;
  (ii) verification of the travel document for signs of falsification or counterfeiting;
  (iii) whenever possible, verification that the third-country national is not considered to be a threat to public policy, internal security or the international relations of any of the Member States;

(c) In addition to the checks referred to in point (b) thorough checks on exit may also comprise:
  (i)   verification that the person is in possession of a valid visa, if required pursuant to Regulation (EC) No 539/2001, except where he or she holds a valid residence permit; such verification may comprise consultation of the VIS in accordance with Article 18 of Regulation (EC) No 767/2008;[140]
  (ii) verification that the person did not exceed the maximum duration of authorised stay in the territory of the Member States;
  (iii) consultation of alerts on persons and objects included in the SIS and reports in national data files.

(d) for the purpose of identification of any person who may not fulfil, or who may no longer fulfil, the conditions for entry, stay or residence on the territory of the Member States, the VIS may be consulted in accordance with Article 20 of Regulation (EC) No 767/2008.[141]

4. Where facilities exist and if requested by the third-country national, such thorough checks shall be carried out in a private area.

---

[140] The second part of Art. 7(3)(c)(i) was inserted by Reg. 81/2009 (ibid), in force as from 24 Feb. 2009 (Art. 2, Reg. 81/2009), and applicable as from 20 days from the start of operations of the VIS.

[141] Art. 7(3)(d) was inserted by Reg. 81/2009 (ibid), in force as from 24 Feb. 2009 (Art. 2, Reg. 81/2009), and applicable as from 20 days from the start of operations of the VIS.

5. Third-country nationals subject to a thorough second line check shall be given information on the purpose of, and procedure for, such a check.

   This information shall be available in all the official languages of the Union and in the language(s) of the country or countries bordering the Member State concerned and shall indicate that the third-country national may request the name or service identification number of the border guards carrying out the thorough second line check, the name of the border crossing point and the date on which the border was crossed.

6. Checks on a person enjoying the Community right on free movement shall be carried out in accordance with Directive 2004/38/EC.

7. Detailed rules governing the information to be registered are laid down in Annex II.

Article 8
Relaxation of border checks

1. Border checks at external borders may be relaxed as a result of exceptional and unforeseen circumstances. Such exceptional and unforeseen circumstances shall be deemed to be those where unforeseeable events lead to traffic of such intensity that the waiting time at the border crossing point becomes excessive, and all resources have been exhausted as regards staff, facilities and organisation.

2. Where border checks are relaxed in accordance with paragraph 1, border checks on entry movements shall in principle take priority over border checks on exit movements.

   The decision to relax checks shall be taken by the border guard in command at the border crossing point.

   Such relaxation of checks shall be temporary, adapted to the circumstances justifying it and introduced gradually.

3. Even in the event that checks are relaxed, the border guard shall stamp the travel documents of third-country nationals both on entry and exit, in accordance with Article 10.

4. Each Member State shall transmit once a year a report on the application of this Article to the European Parliament and the Commission.

Article 9
Separate lanes and information on signs

1. Member States shall provide separate lanes, in particular at air border crossing points in order to carry out checks on persons, in accordance with Article 7. Such lanes shall be differentiated by means of the signs bearing the indications set out in the Annex III.

Member States may provide separate lanes at their sea and land border crossing points and at borders between Member States not applying Article 20 at their common borders. The signs bearing the indications set out in the Annex III shall be used if Member States provide separate lanes at those borders.

Member States shall ensure that such lanes are clearly signposted, including where the rules relating to the use of the different lanes are waived as provided for in paragraph 4, in order to ensure optimal flow levels of persons crossing the border.

2. (a) Persons enjoying the Community right of free movement are entitled to use the lanes indicated by the sign in part A of Annex III. They may also use the lanes indicated by the sign in part B of Annex III.

   (b) All other persons shall use the lanes indicated by the sign in part B of Annex III.

   The indications on the signs referred to in points (a) and (b) may be displayed in such language or languages as each Member State considers appropriate.

3. At sea and land border crossing points, Member States may separate vehicle traffic into different lanes for light and heavy vehicles and buses by using signs as shown in Part C of Annex III.

   Member States may vary the indications on those signs where appropriate in the light of local circumstances.

4. In the event of a temporary imbalance in traffic flows at a particular border crossing point, the rules relating to the use of the different lanes may be waived by the competent authorities for the time necessary to eliminate such imbalance.

5. The adaptation of existing signs to the provisions of paragraphs 1, 2 and 3 shall be completed by 31 May 2009. Where Member States replace existing signs or put up new ones before that date, they shall comply with the indications provided for in those paragraphs.

Article 10
Stamping of the travel documents of third-country nationals

1. The travel documents of third-country nationals shall be systematically stamped on entry and exit. In particular an entry or exit stamp shall be affixed to:

   (a) the documents, bearing a valid visa, enabling third-country nationals to cross the border;

   (b) the documents enabling third-country nationals to whom a visa is issued at the border by a Member State to cross the border;

(c) the documents enabling third-country nationals not subject to a visa requirement to cross the border.

2. The travel documents of nationals of third countries who are members of the family of a Union citizen to whom Directive 2004/38/EC applies, but who do not present the residence card provided for in Article 10 of that Directive, shall be stamped on entry or exit.

   The travel documents of nationals of third countries who are members of the family of nationals of third countries enjoying the Community right of free movement, but who do not present the residence card provided for in Article 10 of Directive 2004/38/EC, shall be stamped on entry or exit.

3. No entry or exit stamp shall be affixed:
   (a) to the travel documents of Heads of State and dignitaries whose arrival has been officially announced in advance through diplomatic channels;
   (b) to pilots' licences or the certificates of aircraft crew members;
   (c) to the travel documents of seamen who are present within the territory of a Member State only when their ship puts in and in the area of the port of call;
   (d) to the travel documents of crew and passengers of cruise ships who are not subject to border checks in accordance with point 3.2.3 of Annex VI;
   (e) to documents enabling nationals of Andorra, Monaco and San Marino to cross the border.

   Exceptionally, at the request of a third-country national, insertion of an entry or exit stamp may be dispensed with if insertion might cause serious difficulties for that person. In that case, entry or exit shall be recorded on a separate sheet indicating the name and passport number.
   That sheet shall be given to the third-country national.

4. The practical arrangements for stamping are set out in Annex IV.

5. Whenever possible, third-country nationals shall be informed of the border guard's obligation to stamp their travel document on entry and exit, even where checks are relaxed in accordance with Article 8.

6. The Commission shall report to the European Parliament and the Council by the end of 2008 on the operation of the provisions on stamping travel documents.

Article 11
Presumption as regards fulfilment of conditions of duration of stay

1. If the travel document of a third-country national does not bear an entry stamp, the competent national authorities may presume that the holder

does not fulfil, or no longer fulfils, the conditions of duration of stay applicable within the Member State concerned.

2. The presumption referred to in paragraph 1 may be rebutted where the third-country national provides, by any means, credible evidence, such as transport tickets or proof of his or her presence outside the territory of the Member States, that he or she has respected the conditions relating to the duration of a short stay.

In such a case:

(a) where the third-country national is found on the territory of a Member State applying the Schengen *acquis* in full, the competent authorities shall indicate, in accordance with national law and practice, in his or her travel document the date on which, and the place where, he or she crossed the external border of one of the Member States applying the Schengen *acquis* in full;

(b) where the third-country national is found on the territory of a Member State in respect of which the decision contemplated in Article 3(2) of the 2003 Act of Accession has not been taken, the competent authorities shall indicate, in accordance with national law and practice, in his or her travel document the date on which, and the place where, he or she crossed the external border of such a Member State.

In addition to the indications referred to in points (a) and (b), a form as shown in Annex VIII may be given to the third-country national.

Member States shall inform each other and the Commission and the Council General Secretariat of their national practices with regard to the indications referred to in this Article.

3. Should the presumption referred to in paragraph 1 not be rebutted, the third-country national may be expelled by the competent authorities from the territory of the Member States concerned.

Article 12
Border surveillance

1. The main purpose of border surveillance shall be to prevent unauthorised border crossings, to counter cross-border criminality and to take measures against persons who have crossed the border illegally.

2. The border guards shall use stationary or mobile units to carry out border surveillance.

That surveillance shall be carried out in such a way as to prevent and discourage persons from circumventing the checks at border crossing points.

3. Surveillance between border crossing points shall be carried out by border guards whose numbers and methods shall be adapted to existing or foreseen risks and threats. It shall involve frequent and sudden changes to surveillance periods, so that unauthorised border crossings are always at risk of being detected.

4. Surveillance shall be carried out by stationary or mobile units which perform their duties by patrolling or stationing themselves at places known or perceived to be sensitive, the aim of such surveillance being to apprehend individuals crossing the border illegally. Surveillance may also be carried out by technical means, including electronic means.

5. Additional measures governing surveillance may be adopted. Those measures, designed to amend non-essential elements of this Regulation by supplementing it, shall be adopted in accordance with the regulatory procedure with scrutiny referred to in Article 33(2).[142]

Article 13
Refusal of entry

1. A third-country national who does not fulfil all the entry conditions laid down in Article 5(1) and does not belong to the categories of persons referred to in Article 5(4) shall be refused entry to the territories of the Member States. This shall be without prejudice to the application of special provisions concerning the right of asylum and to international protection or the issue of long-stay visas.

2. Entry may only be refused by a substantiated decision stating the precise reasons for the refusal. The decision shall be taken by an authority empowered by national law. It shall take effect immediately.

   The substantiated decision stating the precise reasons for the refusal shall be given by means of a standard form, as set out in Annex V, Part B, filled in by the authority empowered by national law to refuse entry. The completed standard form shall be handed to the third-country national concerned, who shall acknowledge receipt of the decision to refuse entry by means of that form.

3. Persons refused entry shall have the right to appeal. Appeals shall be conducted in accordance with national law. A written indication of contact

---

[142] Art. 12(5) was replaced by Reg. 296/2008 (OJ 2008 L 97/60), with effect from 10 Apr. 2008 (Art. 2, Reg. 296/2008). It initially read: "Additional rules governing surveillance may be adopted in accordance with the procedure referred to in Article 33(2)."

points able to provide information on representatives competent to act on behalf of the third-country national in accordance with national law shall also be given to the third-country national.

Lodging such an appeal shall not have suspensive effect on a decision to refuse entry.

Without prejudice to any compensation granted in accordance with national law, the third-country national concerned shall, where the appeal concludes that the decision to refuse entry was ill-founded, be entitled to correction of the cancelled entry stamp, and any other cancellations or additions which have been made, by the Member State which refused entry.

4. The border guards shall ensure that a third-country national refused entry does not enter the territory of the Member State concerned.

5. Member States shall collect statistics on the number of persons refused entry, the grounds for refusal, the nationality of the persons refused and the type of border (land, air or sea) at which they were refused entry. Member States shall transmit those statistics once a year to the Commission. The Commission shall publish every two years a compilation of the statistics provided by the Member States.

6. Detailed rules governing refusal of entry are given in Part A of Annex V.

CHAPTER III
Staff and resources for border control and cooperation between Member States

Article 14
Staff and resources for border control

Member States shall deploy appropriate staff and resources in sufficient numbers to carry out border control at the external borders, in accordance with Articles 6 to 13, in such a way as to ensure an efficient, high and uniform level of control at their external borders.

Article 15
Implementation of controls

1. The border control provided for by Articles 6 to 13 shall be carried out by border guards in accordance with the provisions of this Regulation and with national law.

When carrying out that border control, the powers to instigate criminal proceedings conferred on border guards by national law and falling outside the scope of this Regulation shall remain unaffected.

Member States shall ensure that the border guards are specialised and properly trained professionals. Member States shall encourage border guards to learn languages, in particular those necessary for the carrying-out of their tasks.

2. Member States shall notify to the Commission the list of national services responsible for border control under their national law in accordance with Article 34.

3. To control borders effectively, each Member State shall ensure close and constant cooperation between its national services responsible for border control.

Article 16
Cooperation between Member States

1. The Member States shall assist each other and shall maintain close and constant cooperation with a view to the effective implementation of border control, in accordance with Articles 6 to 15. They shall exchange all relevant information.

2. Operational cooperation between Member States in the field of management of external borders shall be coordinated by the European Agency for the Management of Operational Cooperation at the External Borders of the Member States (hereinafter referred to as the Agency) established by Regulation (EC) No 2007/2004.

3. Without prejudice to the competences of the Agency, Member States may continue operational cooperation with other Member States and/or third countries at external borders, including the exchange of liaison officers, where such cooperation complements the action of the Agency.

Member States shall refrain from any activity which could jeopardise the functioning of the Agency or the attainment of its objectives.

Member States shall report to the Agency on the operational cooperation referred to in the first subparagraph.

4. Member States shall provide for training on the rules for border control and on fundamental rights. In that regard, account shall be taken of the common training standards as established and further developed by the Agency.

Article 17
Joint control

1. Member States which do not apply Article 20 to their common land borders may, up to the date of application of that Article, jointly control

those common borders, in which case a person may be stopped only once for the purpose of carrying out entry and exit checks, without prejudice to the individual responsibility of Member States arising from Articles 6 to 13.

To that end, Member States may conclude bilateral arrangements between themselves.

2. Member States shall inform the Commission of any arrangements concluded in accordance with paragraph 1.

CHAPTER IV
Specific rules for border checks

Article 18
Specific rules for the various types of border and the various means of transport used for crossing the external borders

The specific rules set out in Annex VI shall apply to the checks carried out at the various types of border and on the various means of transport used for crossing border crossing points.

Those specific rules may contain derogations from Articles 5 and 7 to 13.

Article 19
Specific rules for checks on certain categories of persons

1. The specific rules set out in Annex VII shall apply to checks on the following categories of persons:
   (a) Heads of State and the members of their delegation(s);
   (b) pilots of aircraft and other crew members;
   (c) seamen;
   (d) holders of diplomatic, official or service passports and members of international organisations;
   (e) cross-border workers;
   (f) minors.

Those specific rules may contain derogations from Articles 5 and 7 to 13.

2. Member States shall notify to the Commission the model cards issued by their Ministries of Foreign Affairs to accredited members of diplomatic missions and consular representations and members of their families in accordance with Article 34.

TITLE III
INTERNAL BORDERS

CHAPTER I
Abolition of border control at internal borders

Article 20
Crossing internal borders

Internal borders may be crossed at any point without a border check on persons, irrespective of their nationality, being carried out.

Article 21
Checks within the territory

The abolition of border control at internal borders shall not affect:

(a) the exercise of police powers by the competent authorities of the Member States under national law, insofar as the exercise of those powers does not have an effect equivalent to border checks; that shall also apply in border areas. Within the meaning of the first sentence, the exercise of police powers may not, in particular, be considered equivalent to the exercise of border checks when the police measures:

  (i) do not have border control as an objective,

  (ii) are based on general police information and experience regarding possible threats to public security and aim, in particular, to combat cross-border crime,

  (iii) are devised and executed in a manner clearly distinct from systematic checks on persons at the external borders,

  (iv) are carried out on the basis of spot-checks;

(b) security checks on persons carried out at ports and airports by the competent authorities under the law of each Member State, by port or airport officials or carriers, provided that such checks are also carried out on persons travelling within a Member State;

(c) the possibility for a Member State to provide by law for an obligation to hold or carry papers and documents;

(d) the obligation on third-country nationals to report their presence on the territory of any Member State pursuant to the provisions of Article 22 of the Schengen Convention.

Article 22
Removal of obstacles to traffic at road crossing-points at internal borders

Member States shall remove all obstacles to fluid traffic flow at road crossing-points at internal borders, in particular any speed limits not exclusively based on road-safety considerations. At the same time, Member States shall be prepared to provide for facilities for checks in the event that internal border controls are reintroduced.

CHAPTER II
Temporary reintroduction of border control at internal borders

Article 23
Temporary reintroduction of border control at internal borders

1. Where there is a serious threat to public policy or internal security, a Member State may exceptionally reintroduce border control at its internal borders for a limited period of no more than 30 days or for the foreseeable duration of the serious threat if its duration exceeds the period of 30 days, in accordance with the procedure laid down in Article 24 or, in urgent cases, with that laid down in Article 25. The scope and duration of the temporary reintroduction of border control at internal borders shall not exceed what is strictly necessary to respond to the serious threat.

2. If the serious threat to public policy or internal security persists beyond the period provided for in paragraph 1, the Member State may prolong border control on the same grounds as those referred to in paragraph 1 and, taking into account any new elements, for renewable periods of up to 30 days, in accordance with the procedure laid down in Article 26.

Article 24
Procedure for foreseeable events

1. Where a Member State is planning to reintroduce border control at internal borders under Article 23(1), it shall as soon as possible notify the other Member States and the Commission accordingly, and shall supply the following information as soon as available:
   (a) the reasons for the proposed reintroduction, detailing the events that constitute a serious threat to public policy or internal security;
   (b) the scope of the proposed reintroduction, specifying where border control is to be reintroduced;
   (c) the names of the authorised crossing-points;

(d) the date and duration of the proposed reintroduction;
(e) where appropriate, the measures to be taken by the other Member States.

2. Following the notification from the Member State concerned, and with a view to the consultation provided for in paragraph 3, the Commission may issue an opinion without prejudice to Article 64(1) of the Treaty.

3. The information referred to in paragraph 1, as well as the opinion that the Commission may provide in accordance with paragraph 2, shall be the subject of consultations between the Member State planning to reintroduce border control, the other Member States and the Commission, with a view to organising, where appropriate, mutual cooperation between the Member States and to examining the proportionality of the measures to the events giving rise to the reintroduction of border control and the threats to public policy or internal security.

4. The consultation referred to in paragraph 3 shall take place at least fifteen days before the date planned for the reintroduction of border control.

Article 25
Procedure for cases requiring urgent action

1. Where considerations of public policy or internal security in a Member State demand urgent action to be taken, the Member State concerned may exceptionally and immediately reintroduce border control at internal borders.

2. The Member State reintroducing border control at internal borders shall notify the other Member States and the Commission accordingly, without delay, and shall supply the information referred to in Article 24 (1) and the reasons that justify the use of this procedure.

Article 26
Procedure for prolonging border control at internal borders

1. Member States may only prolong border control at internal borders under the provisions of Article 23(2) after having notified the other Member States and the Commission.

2. The Member State planning to prolong border control shall supply the other Member States and the Commission with all relevant information on the reasons for prolonging the border control at internal borders. The provisions of Article 24(2) shall apply.

Article 27
Informing the European Parliament

The Member State concerned or, where appropriate, the Council shall inform the European Parliament as soon as possible of the measures taken under Articles 24, 25 and 26. As of the third consecutive prolongation pursuant to Article 26, the Member State concerned shall, if requested, report to the European Parliament on the need for border control at internal borders.

Article 28
Provisions to be applied where border control is reintroduce at internal borders

Where border control at internal borders is reintroduced, the relevant provisions of Title II shall apply *mutatis mutandis.*

Article 29
Report on the reintroduction of border control at internal borders

The Member State which has reintroduced border control at internal borders under Article 23 shall confirm the date on which that control is lifted and, at the same time or soon afterwards, present a report to the European Parliament, the Council and the Commission on the reintroduction of border control at internal borders, outlining, in particular, the operation of the checks and the effectiveness of the reintroduction of border control.

Article 30
Informing the public

The decision to reintroduce border control at internal borders shall be taken in a transparent manner and the public informed in full thereof, unless there are overriding security reasons for not doing so.

Article 31
Confidentiality

At the request of the Member State concerned, the other Member States, the European Parliament and the Commission shall respect the confidentiality of information supplied in connection with the reintroduction and prolongation of border control and the report drawn up under Article 29.

TITLE IV
FINAL PROVISIONS

Article 32
Amendments to the Annexes

Annexes III, IV and VIII shall be amended in accordance with the regulatory procedure with scrutiny referred to in Article 33(2).[143]

Article 33
Committee

1. The Commission shall be assisted by a committee, hereinafter 'the Committee'.
2. Where reference is made to this paragraph, Article 5a(1) to (4) and Article 7 of Decision 1999/468/EC shall apply, having regard to the provisions of Article 8 thereof.[144]
3. The Committee shall adopt its rules of procedure.

Article 34
Notifications

1. Member States shall notify the Commission of:
   (a) the list of residence permits;
   (b) the list of their border crossing points;
   (c) the reference amounts required for the crossing of their external borders fixed annually by the national authorities;
   (d) the list of national services responsible for border control;
   (e) the specimen of model cards issued by Foreign Ministries.
2. The Commission shall make the information notified in conformity with paragraph 1 available to the Member States and the public through

---

[143] Art. 32 was replaced by Reg. 296/2008, with effect from 10 Apr. 2008 (Art. 2, Reg. 296/2008). It initially read: "Annexes III, IV and VIII shall be amended in accordance with the procedure referred to in Article 33(2)."

[144] Art. 33(2) was replaced by Reg. 296/2008, with effect from 10 Apr. 2008 (Art. 2, Reg. 296/2008). It initially read: "Where reference is made to this paragraph, Articles 5 and 7 of Decision 1999/468/EC shall apply, having regard to the provisions of Article 8 thereof and provided that the implementing measures adopted in accordance with this procedure do not modify the essential provisions of this Regulation. The period laid down in Article 5(6) of Decision 1999/468/EC shall be set at three months." Reg. 296/2008 also repealed the original Art. 33(4), which had set out a "sunset" clause for the application of Art. 33(2), as from the same date.

publication in the *Official Journal of the European Union*, C Series, and by any other appropriate means.

Article 35
Local border traffic

This Regulation shall be without prejudice to Community rules on local border traffic and to existing bilateral agreements on local border traffic.

Article 36
Ceuta and Melilla

The provisions of this Regulation shall not affect the special rules applying to the cities of Ceuta and Melilla, as defined in the Declaration by the Kingdom of Spain on the cities of Ceuta and Melilla in the Final Act to the Agreement on the Accession of the Kingdom of Spain to the Convention implementing the Schengen Agreement of 14 June 1985.

Article 37
Notification of information by the Member States

By 26 October 2006, the Member States shall notify the Commission of national provisions relating to Article 21(c) and (d), the penalties as referred to in Article 4(3) and the bilateral arrangements concluded in accordance with Article 17(1). Subsequent changes to those provisions shall be notified within five working days.

The information notified by the Member States shall be published in the *Official Journal of the European Union*, C Series.

Article 38
Report on the application of Title III

The Commission shall submit to the European Parliament and the Council by 13 October 2009 a report on the application of Title III.

The Commission shall pay particular attention to any difficulties arising from the reintroduction of border control at internal borders. Where appropriate, it shall present proposals aimed at resolving such difficulties.

Article 39
Repeals

1. Articles 2 to 8 of the Convention implementing the Schengen Agreement of 14 June 1985 shall be repealed with effect from 13 October 2006.
2. The following shall be repealed with effect from the date referred to in paragraph 1:

(a) the Common Manual, including its annexes;
(b) the decisions of the Schengen Executive Committee of 26 April 1994 (SCH/Com-ex (94) 1, rev 2), 22 December 1994 (SCH/Com-ex (94)17, rev. 4) and 20 December 1995 (SCH/Com-ex (95) 20, rev. 2);
(c) Annex 7 to the Common Consular Instructions;
(d) Council Regulation (EC) No 790/2001 of 24 April 2001 reserving to the Council implementing powers with regard to certain detailed provisions and practical procedures for carrying out border checks and surveillance;
(e) Council Decision 2004/581/EC of 29 April 2004 determining the minimum indications to be used on signs at external border crossing points;
(f) Council Decision 2004/574/EC of 29 April 2004 amending the Common Manual;
(g) Council Regulation (EC) No 2133/2004 of 13 December 2004 on the requirement for the competent authorities of the Member States to stamp systematically the travel documents of third country nationals when they cross the external borders of the Member States and amending the provisions of the Convention implementing the Schengen agreement and the Common Manual to this end.
3. References to the Articles deleted and instruments repealed shall be construed as references to this Regulation.

Article 40
Entry into force

This Regulation shall enter into force on 13 October 2006. However, Article 34 shall enter into force on the day after its publication in the *Official Journal of the European Union*.

This Regulation shall be binding in its entirety and directly applicable in the Member States in accordance with the Treaty establishing the European Community.

Chapter 4

Schengen Information System

1. *Introduction*

The Schengen Information System ("SIS") is relevant both to border control and the process of issuing visas, since it contains a list of persons who must be banned in principle from entering the States applying the Schengen free movement rules and must be consulted *inter alia* when deciding on a visa application or when a third-country national crosses an external border.

The current rules governing the SIS are still essentially set out in the Schengen Convention,[1] but the EU has planned for some time to establish a revised second-generation Schengen Information System ("SIS II"), and legislation to this end was adopted in 2006.[2] However, there have been technical problems regarding the start of operations of SIS II, and the latest plan is that it will become operational in the first quarter of 2013. This chapter examines in turn the current rules governing the SIS and the rules adopted to govern SIS II, once it becomes operational.

2. *The Current Schengen Information System*

As noted already, the SIS was initially established by Articles 92–119 (Title IV) of the 1990 Schengen Convention, as applied from March 1995. Further rules are set out in various decisions of the Schengen Executive Committee,[3] including the Decision establishing the SIRENE Manual, which governs the procedure for subsequent exchanges of information between national authorities following a "hit" in the SIS.[4] Despite its dual application for immigration purposes on the one hand and criminal law and policing purposes on the other, the SIS remains (from a legal point of view) almost entirely a "third pillar"

---

[1] OJ 2000 L 239.
[2] Reg. 1987/2006 (OJ 2006 L 381/4).
[3] See OJ 2000 L 239.
[4] OJ 2003 L 38.

(ie policing and criminal law) measure due to the failure to allocate the relevant provisions of the Schengen *acquis* to the EC Treaty (as it then was) back in 1999.[5] However, the Schengen Convention SIS rules were amended in 2004 and 2005 to provide for certain changes to the System pending the application of SIS II – the so-called "SIS I+".[6] Furthermore, the procedure for updating the SIRENE Manual was set out in both first and third pillar legislation from 2004.[7]

The immigration provisions of the SIS apply (and the SIS II Regulation will apply in future) to the EU Member States and the Schengen associates which fully apply the Schengen *acquis*.[8]

Article 92 of the Convention (Chapter 1 of Title IV of the Convention) establishes the SIS, setting out its basic structure. In particular, the "technical support function" (what a non-IT specialist would describe as the central computer of the network administering the SIS) is located in Strasbourg, France.[9] Chapter 2 of Title IV (Articles 93–101) concerns the operation and use of the System. Article 93 states the purpose of the SIS: "to maintain public policy and public security, including national security", and to apply the Convention's provisions concerning the movement of persons. Article 94 sets out the list of categories of data which are included in the System, and establishes that the Member State entering data into the System "shall determine whether the case is important enough" to enter into it.

Articles 95–100 then set out the different types of "alert" which can be entered into the System. Of these, only Article 96 relates to immigration law, concerning alerts for the purposes of refusing entry. Such an alert means that a person should in principle be refused entry at the external border or refused a visa,[10] although exceptionally on humanitarian or other grounds a person

---

[5] OJ 1999 L 176/17. On the distinction between third pillar measures and other EU measures, see further chapter 2.

[6] These amendments can be found in Council Reg. 871/2004 (OJ 2004 L 162/29) and a third pillar Decision of 2005 (OJ 2005 L 68/44). Reg. 871/2004, which concerns us here, amended Arts. 94(3), 101(1) and (2), 102(4) and 103 of the Convention and added new Arts. 94(3), 112a and 113a. A separate Regulation adopted in 2005 gave access to some of the existing SIS data to vehicle registration authorities (Reg. 1160/2005, OJ 2005 L 191/18).

[7] The first pillar measure is Reg. 378/2004, OJ 2004 L 64/5; for the text of the updated Manual, following the application of this legislation, see the Commission Decisions in OJ 2006 L 317, subsequently amended by the Commission Decision in OJ 2011 L 186/1.

[8] On the territorial scope of EU legislation on borders and visas, see further chapter 2.

[9] Art. 92(3) of the Convention.

[10] Arts. 5(1)(d) and 15 of the Convention; the former Article has since been replaced by Art. 5(1)(d) of the Schengen Borders Code (Reg. 562/2006, OJ 2006 L 105/1), and the latter Article has been replaced by the visa code (Reg. 843/2009, OJ 2009 L 243/1). See chapters 3

listed in the SIS can be permitted to enter or receive a visa for a single Member State only.[11]

Article 96 sets out the following substantive grounds for entering an alert for the purposes of refusing entry:

1. Data on aliens for whom an alert has been issued for the purposes of refusing entry shall be entered on the basis of a national alert resulting from decisions taken by the competent administrative authorities or courts in accordance with the rules of procedure laid down by national law.

2. Decisions may be based on a threat to public policy or public security or to national security which the presence of an alien in national territory may pose.
   This situation may arise in particular in the case of:
   (a) an alien who has been convicted of an offence carrying a penalty involving deprivation of liberty of at least one year;
   (b) an alien in respect of whom there are serious grounds for believing that he has committed serious criminal offences, including those referred to in Article 71, or in respect of whom there is clear evidence of an intention to commit such offences in the territory of a Contracting Party.

3. Decisions may also be based on the fact that the alien has been subject to measures involving deportation, refusal of entry or removal which have not been rescinded or suspended, including or accompanied by a prohibition on entry or, where applicable, a prohibition on residence, based on a failure to comply with national regulations on the entry or residence of aliens.

The persons with access to SIS data, before the amendments of 2004 and 2005, are the police, customs and border control authorities, along with (for immigration data) the visa and immigration authorities.[12]

Chapter 3 of Title IV of the Convention (Articles 102-118) concerns data protection and data security. The data set out in alerts can only be used for the purposes laid down for each category of alert – in other words, the alerts entered pursuant to Article 96 can only be used for the purposes of refusing entry.[13] Changing a category of alert is only allowed in highly exceptional cases.[14] Every tenth transmission of data has to be recorded.[15] Unless the Convention specifies otherwise, national law applies to alerts, data and the

---

and 8. See also Arts. 18, 19(1), 20(1) and 25 of the Convention (which have also been partly amended: see chapter 11).

[11] Arts. 5(2) and 16 of the Convention; the former Article has since been replaced by Art. 5(4) of the Schengen Borders Code, and the latter Article has been replaced by the visa code (both ibid).

[12] Art. 101 of the Convention.

[13] Art. 102(1).

[14] Art. 102(3).

[15] Art. 103.

action to taken following an alert.[16] The Member State issuing an alert is responsible for ensuring that it is "accurate, up-to-date and lawful",[17] and only that Member State can modify, correct, add to or delete the data which it entered onto the System.[18]

The personal data in the System may only be conserved for the time necessary, with a three-year review period for all Article 96 alerts; Member States may set a shorter review period in their national law. Those alerts are deleted at the end of the review period unless the Member State decides to retain them.[19] There are detailed rules on data security.[20]

As for individual rights, the right of access to data applies in accordance with the national law of the Member State in which a person applies for access to data, and a Member State may decide that a national supervisory authority can take the decision on this issue.[21] Communication of the data may be refused if indispensable for the performance of a task connected to the alert or to protect the rights and freedoms of others.[22] Any person may have factually inaccurate information corrected or unlawfully stored information deleted,[23] but the ability to make arguments on this point is dependent upon successfully invoking the right to access to the information in the first place. Next, any person "in the territory of each [Member State]" may bring an administrative or judicial claim in a Member State to correct or delete information, to gain access to it, or to obtain compensation; Member States agree to recognise the relevant judgments or administrative decisions.[24]

Article 114 obliges Member States to set up national data protection authorities with the power to supervise the national data files of the SIS and to check that the processing and use of the data does not violate individual rights. Any person has the right to request the supervisory authority to check their data in the SIS and the use made of it, but this right is governed by the relevant national law. If the data were entered by another Member State, the relevant supervisory authorities shall work closely together. Article 115 establishes a

---

[16] Art. 104.

[17] Art. 105.

[18] Art. 106.

[19] Art. 112.

[20] Art. 118.

[21] Art. 109(1).

[22] Art. 109(2).

[23] Art. 110.

[24] Art. 111. On the application of these rules in a criminal law context, see Case C-150/05 *Van Straaten* [2006] ECR I-9327.

Joint Supervisory Authority, which shall supervise the technical support function of the SIS. It shall also examine difficulties of interpretation or application regarding the system, or problems that may occur regarding national supervisory authorities' supervision or exercise of the right to access, and for drawing up proposed harmonised solutions to joint problems.

Article 116 allocates liability among Member States for wrongful data or illegal use of data. Finally, Article 117 requires Member States to maintain data protection standards in accordance with the Council of Europe Convention on data protection and a Council of Europe recommendation on the use of data in the police sector. There is no express provision concerning the transfer of data to third states or international organisations.

The final Chapter 4 in Title IV of the Convention (Article 119) apportions the costs of the current SIS.

The amendments to the immigration provisions of the current SIS, as adopted in 2004,[25] are as follows:

a) an amendment to Article 92 provided expressly for the existence of the Sirene system; it has applied from 13 June 2005;[26]
b) an amendment to Article 94 amended the categories of personal data to be included on the SIS to add all forenames (not just the initials of middle names) plus an indication of whether a person has escaped; the date of its entry into force has not yet been fixed;
c) the first amendment to Article 101 allows judicial authorities to have access to SIS data; it has applied from 13 June 2005;[27]
d) the second amendment to Article 101, with a corresponding amendment to Article 102, allowed visa and immigration authorities to access data on stolen travel documents; these provisions have applied from 1 November 2006;[28]
e) an amendment to Article 103 requires all data transmissions to be recorded, not just one-tenth of them; it has applied since 1 January 2006;[29] and
f) new Articles 112a and 113a set out conservation periods for personal Sirene data; they have applied from 11 September 2005.[30]

---

[25] Reg. 871/2004, n. 6 above.
[26] OJ 2005 L 158/26.
[27] Ibid.
[28] OJ 2006 L 256/15.
[29] OJ 2005 L 273/26.
[30] OJ 2005 L 158/26.

3. The Second-Generation Schengen Information System (SIS II)

The object of replacing the SIS with a planned SIS II was initially twofold: to provide for more functions, including more categories of data (notably biometric data), and to permit the expansion of the SIS (and therefore the Schengen free movement zone) to include the new Member States. Back in 2001, first and third pillar legislation was adopted to confer project management powers upon the Commission,[31] and it was agreed that SIS II would be funded from the EU budget.[32]

The Commission proposed three legislative measures to establish the SIS II in May 2005: a Regulation concerning the immigration aspects of the system;[33] a separate Regulation concerning access to the system by vehicle registration authorities;[34] and a third pillar Decision concerning use of the system for policing and criminal law purposes.[35] The separate proposals were necessary due to the different legal bases and decision-making procedures concerned.[36] The three measures were discussed as a package, and the two Regulations were adopted in December 2006,[37] while the third pillar Decision was not formally adopted until June 2007.[38] This analysis examines only the

---

[31] The first-pillar measure is Reg. 2424/2001 (OJ 2001 L 328/4), which was due to expire at the end of 2006, but which was extended for a further two years in light of the delays completing the SIS II project (Reg. 1988/2006, OJ 2006 L 411/1). This Reg. was in turn extended and amended (Regs. 1104/2008, OJ 2008, L 299/1 and 541/2010, OJ 2010 L 155/19). Measures implementing these acts were subsequently adopted: a Commission Decision on the network requirements for SIS II development (OJ 2007 L 79/20); Council Reg. 189/2008 (OJ 2008 L 57/1) on tests of SIS II; and a Commission Decision changing the date of the migration to SIS II (OJ 2009 L 257/26).

[32] The former Article 41(3) TEU provided that third pillar operational measures had to be charged to the EU budget unless there was a unanimous vote in Council to use Member States' budgets, and unanimity on this point was lacking.

[33] COM (2005) 236, 31 May 2005.

[34] COM (2005) 237, 31 May 2005.

[35] COM (2005) 230, 31 May 2005.

[36] Although the two Regulations were both first pillar measures subject to co-decision, the immigration Regulation was subject to the British, Danish and Irish opt-outs applicable to Title IV measures, while the Regulation on access by vehicle registration authorities was not. The third pillar Decision was subject to unanimity in the Council and consultation of the EP, with no opt-outs. The regime for jurisdiction of the Court of Justice was also different. Since the entry into force of the Treaty of Lisbon, the Court's normal jurisdiction applies to the immigration measure, but for a five-year transition period (until 1 Dec. 2014) its old third pillar jurisdiction will apply to the third-pillar Decision. See further chapter 2.

[37] Regs. 1987/2006 (n. 2 above) and 1985/2006 (OJ 2006 L 381/1).

[38] OJ 2007 L 205/63.

immigration Regulation, although there are a number of provisions in common between the immigration Regulation and the third pillar Decision.[39]

The 2006 SIS II immigration Regulation, once it becomes applicable, will entirely replace the current provisions of the Convention and all implementing measures.[40] The Commission has already adopted several measures implementing the Regulation.[41]

Ultimately the delay in implementing the SIS II project, which was due to the delays in proposing and negotiating the legislation and to operational problems,[42] led to a delay in enlarging the Schengen free movement zone to the new Member States. This issue was eventually tackled by adopting a proposal from Portugal for the development of an "SIS One4All", which extended the existing SIS to the new Member States (a solution which had previously been understood to be technically impossible). The JHA Council agreed upon this proposal in December 2006, setting a new date for the enlargement of the Schengen zone between end-2007 and March 2008, and accepting the resulting delay in the development of SIS II.[43]

The following analysis examines the main features of the text of the SIS II immigration Regulation, and compares them to the *status quo* (the current provisions of the Schengen Convention concerning SIS). It does not analyse the details of the negotiations over the proposal.[44]

The focus is on the provisions of the Regulation which are most significant for the institutional framework and for substantive immigration law issues: the management of SIS II; the categories of data included; the substantive grounds for a listing in the SIS and related procedural rights; the relationship between SIS II and EU free movement law; access to SIS II data; data protection rules; and the final provisions.

3.1. *Functioning and Management of SIS II*

Chapter I of the SIS II immigration Regulation (Articles 1–5) sets out general provisions dealing with objectives and scope, definitions, technical architecture, and costs. Chapter II (Articles 6–14) sets out the responsibilities of the

---

[39] On the third pillar measure, see Peers, *EU Justice and Home Affairs Law*, 3rd ed. (OUP, 2011), 907–910.

[40] Art. 52 of Reg. 1987/2006.

[41] OJ 2008 L 123/1 (SIRENE manual), and OJ 2010 L 112/31 (security).

[42] See the 9th report of the House of Lords EU Select Committee (2006–07), para. 23.

[43] See the conclusions of the JHA Council of 2–3 Dec. 2006 on these various issues.

[44] For such an analysis, see Peers, "Key Legislative Developments on Migration in the European Union: SIS II" 10 EJML (2008) 77–104.

Member States, including rules on the exchange of supplementary information (the SIRENE system) and data security and confidentiality.[45] Chapter III
(Articles 15–19) sets out the responsibilities of the "Management Authority",
including data security, confidentiality and a public information campaign.

The issue of managing SIS II proved particularly contentious, as the
Commission had suggested that it should be responsible for the operational
management of the SIS,[46] a role it had already for Eurodac, the EU's database
of asylum-seekers' fingerprints (at the time of the proposal in 2005), and had
at the time also proposed for itself as regards the Visa Information System
(VIS).[47] This would have supplanted the current role of France in administering the system, which was referred to above. Since Member States objected to
the idea of the Commission managing the operation of SIS II, a different solution had to be found.

The final Regulation specifies that in the longer term, SIS II will be administered by a "Management Authority". In the interim transitional period, the
Commission is nominally designated as the manager of SIS II, but in practice
the Commission will in fact delegate this management to France and to
Austria (where the backup site of the SIS II data will be located), who will
nonetheless be held accountable for their management of the system in accordance with EU rules.[48] The same approach will apply to the VIS.[49]

The legislation to establish this Authority (which will take the form of an
EU agency) was proposed in 2009, and this proposal was amended in 2010 to
take account of the entry into force of the Treaty of Lisbon.[50] This proposal
was agreed in summer 2011,[51] and so the agency is likely to become operational in 2012,[52] before SIS II itself becomes operational.

3.2. *Alerts for Refusal of Entry*

Chapter IV of the Regulation (Articles 20–30) sets out the key rules on the
grounds for issuing immigration alerts, the types of data kept, access to those

---

[45] Respectively Arts. 8, 10 and 11 of Reg. 1987/2006.
[46] See Art. 12 of the Commission's original proposal.
[47] On the latter system, see chapter 10; on Eurodac, see *EU Asylum Law: Text and Commentary*
(forthcoming).
[48] Art. 15, Reg. 1987/2006.
[49] See chapter 10.
[50] COM (2009) 293, 24 June 2009; revised: COM (2010) 93, 19 Mar. 2010.
[51] The Regulation establishing the agency had not yet been formally adopted as of 1 August
2011. For the text as agreed in principle between the Council and the European Parliament,
see Council doc. 10827/1/11, 6 June 2011.
[52] See Art. 34(2) of the agreed text of the Regulation (ibid).

alerts by various authorities and the conservation period for data. First of all, as regards the categories of data to be kept, currently the SIS contains only a few lines of "alphanumeric" data (letters and numbers). Further data is then exchanged between Member States after a "hit" in the SIS (ie a consulate finds that an applicant for a visa is apparently listed in the SIS as a person to be refused entry). This is known as the "SIRENE" system, as mentioned above.

The most important change in the SIS II immigration Regulation is to provide for the inclusion of photographs and fingerprints.[53] SIS II will also include data on multiple nationalities (not just a sole nationality), the authority issuing the alert, a reference to the decision giving rise to the alert, and links to other alerts (a new functionality of SIS II).

Next, Article 22 of the Regulation sets out special rules for photographs and fingerprints. This biometric data will only be entered following a "special quality check" in order to ensure data quality.[54] The specifics of this quality check will be established by the Commission pursuant to a "comitology" procedure, which means that the Commission's draft measure will be subject to scrutiny by Member States' representatives.[55] Initially, biometric data will only be used to "confirm the identity" of a person whose name has been found in the SIS following an alphanumeric search, likely meaning in practice that his or her name matches a name in the SIS.[56] But later on, biometrics will be used to "identify" persons "as soon as technically possible".[57] This will entail a "one to many" search (comparing one set of biometric data to much or all of the biometric data in the database), which is technically far less reliable than a "one-to-one" search (which only compares one set of biometric data to the biometric data registered, for example, to the same name, although there might in some cases be a search against more than one name if there are a number of alerts on people with identical or similar names). There will be no further vote before this important functionality is put into practice.

The Regulation also amends the existing rule concerning the right of each Member State to judge whether a case is "important" enough to enter into the SIS, providing more broadly that each Member State must determine whether a case is "adequate, relevant and important enough" to warrant an alert; the Article is headed "proportionality".[58]

---

[53] Art. 20(2).
[54] Art. 22(a), Reg. 1987/2006.
[55] On comitology generally, see chapter 2.
[56] Art. 22(b), Reg. 1987/2006.
[57] Art. 22(c), Reg. 1987/2006.
[58] Art. 21.

The biggest single issue, from the perspective of substantive immigration law, is the grounds for issuing an alert. Article 24(1) of the Regulation, which addresses this issue, starts out by repeating Article 96(1) of the Convention (as set out above) with the additional specification that the decision must be taken "on the basis of an individual assessment", adding the proviso that "[a]ppeals against these decisions shall lie in accordance with national law".

Next, an alert "shall" (not "may") be issued where there is a threat to public policy or public security or national security, which "shall" (not "may") be the case, "in particular" in the two cases which are listed in the current Article 96 of the Schengen Convention (a conviction *in a Member State* for an offence carrying a deprivation of liberty for at least one year, or 'serious grounds' to believe that a person has committed a "serious criminal offence" or "clear *indications*" that the person intends to commit such offences. These grounds differ from the current Article 96(2) of the Convention in that: the issue of an alert on these grounds is mandatory (although it is not clear how the issue of a mandatory alert is compatible with the proportionality rule in the Regulation, discussed above); the threat could materialise in "a Member State", rather than on national territory; a criminal conviction must have taken place in a Member State (although it should be recalled that the criteria remain non-exhaustive, so a Member State still has the option of issuing an alert on a person who was convicted of a crime in a non-Member State); and the current threshold of "clear *evidence*" of an intention to commit offences has been lowered.

Next, Article 24(3) retains the current option of issuing an alert following breaches of immigration law, in wording nearly identical to the current Article 96(3) of the Schengen Convention. Article 24(5) provides for the Commission to review the application of Article 24 (therefore including all grounds for issuing alerts) three years after SIS II starts operations,[59] and then to "make the necessary proposals…to achieve a higher level of harmonisation of the criteria for issuing alerts". In the meantime, the Returns Directive, which *inter alia* regulates the issue of "entry bans" by Member States' authorities, has been adopted.[60]

---

[59] This period matches the point at which all of the pre-existing alerts must have been reviewed for their conformity with the new rules on alerts (see Art. 54(1) of the Regulation, discussed further below), although the review of conformity will not cause much difficulty for Member States since the grounds for issuing alerts have barely been changed.

[60] Directive 2008/115, OJ 2008 L 348/98. Member States had to apply this Directive from Christmas Eve 2010 (Art. 24(1)). For a detailed discussion of the relationship between the SIS II rules and the Directive, see Peers, n. 39 above, 205–208. See also the discussion of the Directive in volume 2 of this book (chapter 17).

Two particular categories of persons are each the subject of specific Articles of the Regulation. First, Article 25 of the Regulation concerns persons who have the right of free movement within the EU. Any alert concerning them "must be in conformity" with the Directive on the rights of EU citizens and their family members. Where there is a "hit" concerning such persons (indicating that they must be denied entry or a visa), the Member State executing the alert must immediately contact the Member State issuing the alert via means of the SIRENE procedure to determine what action to be taken. Under the current Schengen Convention rules on the SIS, there is no specific provision on this category of persons, but the SIS II rules reflect a judgment of the Court of Justice on the relationship between the current SIS rules and EU free movement law.[61]

Second, there is a specific rule in Article 26 of the Regulation concerning persons who are subject to a travel ban established by an EU foreign policy measure, "including" EU measures implementing travel bans established by the UN Security Council. Alerts relating to such persons "shall" be entered into SIS II, and neither Article 23 (concerning the data which must be entered in respect of each alert) nor Article 24 will apply (thereby exempting Member States from the obligation to carry out a specific assessment or to permit appeals in such cases).[62] On the other hand, Article 21 (the rule that an alert can be issued only if the case is "adequate, relevant and important enough") will apply.

It is not clear how alerts on such persons could work without data on them being entered onto the system pursuant to Article 23, although Article 26(1) does specify vaguely that "data-quality requirements" have to be satisfied. It is also specified that this Article is "[w]ithout prejudice to" Article 25 (on the position of third-country national family members of EU citizens), and that the Member State responsible for entering and updating the relevant data shall be decided upon when the foreign policy act is adopted.[63] Alerts on such persons are already being entered into the current SIS on the basis of the current provisions, but the SIS II Regulation provides for an explicit legal basis for such measures.

Next, Article 27 of the Regulation leaves essentially unchanged the list of authorities who have access to SIS II data as compared to the current Convention: authorities responsible for border checks (a cross-reference to the Schengen Borders Code has been added) and other police and customs checks

---

[61] Case C-503/03 *Commission v Spain* [2006] ECR I-1097. See further chapter 2.
[62] See respectively Arts. 26(2) and 24(4) of the Regulation.
[63] Art. 26(1) and (3) respectively.

within the territory and the coordination of such checks, along with judicial authorities (since 2005) and authorities responsible for visas and applying immigration legislation (a reference to EU immigration legislation has been added). The separate Article 28 retains the current rule that users may only search the data necessary to perform their tasks,[64] and the current obligation to notify a list of the authorities with access has been moved into the next Chapter of the Regulation.[65]

The final two provisions of Chapter IV of the Regulation concern the conservation of alerts. Article 29, which largely copies the current Article 112 of the Schengen Convention, provides that alerts must be kept only for the time required. There must be a review after three years at a maximum, although Member States may decide during the three-year period, "following a comprehensive individual assessment", to keep the data in the system, in which case the next review will be due three years after the decision to retain the alert. Statistics must be retained on all early decisions to extend the time period for an alert. The System will delete alerts automatically when the three-year retention period is up, but it will remind Member States about the automatic deletion four months before the deadline. These rules differ from the current Convention only in that the advance notice of automatic deletion has been extended from one month to four, and the obligations for a comprehensive assessment in the event of early extension and to retain statistics have been added.

Article 30, a new express provision as compared to the current Convention, specifies that alerts on persons who obtain EU citizenship should be deleted as soon as the Member State which entered the alert becomes aware of this fact.

3.3. *Data Processing Rules*

Chapter V of the Regulation (Articles 31-39) sets out general data processing rules. First of all, Article 31 sets out a number of general data processing principles,[66] including an obligation to publish a list of all authorities with access to SIS II data in the Official Journal.[67] This is a change from the current Convention.[68] Next, Article 32 contains new rules on copying of data from

---

[64] The rule is currently found in Art. 101(3) of the Convention.

[65] Art. 31(8) of the Regulation, discussed below; this rule is currently found in Art. 101(4) of the Convention.

[66] Compare in particular with the current Arts. 101(4), 102 and 104(2) of the Schengen Convention.

[67] Art. 31(8).

[68] See Art. 101(4) of the Convention.

SIS II, specifying that data can be retained by a Member State if it entered the data itself or took action on the basis of another Member State's alert. Article 33 retains a rule from the existing Convention that if a Member State cannot carry out a requested action following an alert, it must inform the Member state which issued the alert.[69]

Article 34 contains the basic rules on the crucial issue of data quality, specifying first that the Member State which entered an alert is responsible for the accuracy, lawfulness and timeliness of the data.[70] Only the Member State issuing an alert may delete or in any way alter that alert.[71] If another Member State believes an alert is unlawfully stored or factually incorrect, it must inform the Member State which issued the alert, which must then check this point.[72] If a dispute between these Member States on this issue continues for more than two months, the Member State which did not issue the alert must submit the case to the European Data Protection Supervisor and the national data protection supervisors, who will act as mediators.[73] If a person complains that he or she is wrongly identified in an alert, the Member States concerned must exchange supplementary information and inform that person about Article 36 of the Regulation (see further below).[74] If a person is already the subject of an alert issued by a Member State and a second Member State tries to enter a further alert on the person concerned, the two Member States shall reach agreement by means of the exchange of supplementary information.[75]

There is a detailed new procedure, as compared to the current Convention, for distinguishing between persons with similar characteristics.[76] Equally there is an entirely new clause dealing with misused identity, to protect persons whose identity has been stolen by a person who is the subject of an alert.[77] For the first time, links between different types of alerts are permitted,

---

[69] See Art. 104(3), final sentence, of the Convention. The remaining provisions of Art. 104(1) and (3) of the Convention have been dropped.

[70] Art. 34(1), which is taken from Art. 105 of the current Convention.

[71] Art. 34(2), which is taken from Art. 106(1) of the current Convention.

[72] Art. 34(3), which is taken from Art. 106(2) of the current Convention, with the addition of a ten-day deadline to inform the first Member State and a reference to the use of supplementary information.

[73] Art. 34(4). This replaces the current Art. 106(3) of the Convention, which provides for such disputes to be submitted to the Joint Supervisory Authority established by the Convention for an opinion (with no deadline).

[74] Art. 34(5). This important safeguard does not appear in the current Convention.

[75] Art. 34(6). This is taken from Art. 107 of the current Convention, with the addition of the reference to the SIRENE system.

[76] Art. 35 of the Regulation.

[77] Art. 36.

although such links do not alter the retention period or the action to be taken on the basis of each type of alert. Member States which object to the principle of linked alerts may prevent their authorities from having access to the links. Links may only be created where there is an operational need,[78] and the basis for creating a link is national legislation.[79]

Next, there is a new provision governing the use of SIRENE in more detail.[80] Member States must keep a reference to decisions giving rise to a SIRENE alert; personal data kept in SIRENE files must only be kept as long as necessary, and at the latest must be deleted one year after a related SIS II alert is deleted; and each Member State is free to keep SIRENE data for longer if it relates to an alert which that Member State issued or took action upon. This text elaborates considerably upon the brief reference to the SIRENE system in the current Schengen Convention.[81]

Finally, Article 39 bans the transfer of SIS II immigration data to third countries and international organisations. This issue is not expressly addressed in the current Convention.

3.4. *Data Protection*

Chapter VI of the Regulation (Articles 40–47) sets out data protection rules. First of all, Article 40 bans the storage of "sensitive" information such as racial and religious information as defined in EU data protection legislation (and also in the Council of Europe data protection Convention). This proviso is retained from the current Convention.[82]

Next, Article 41 provides that a person's right of access to SIS II data concerning him or her shall be exercised in accordance with the law of the Member State in which that access is invoked. National law may provide that the national supervisory authority will decide on whether the data may be transmitted. A Member State which has not issued the alert in question must first consult the Member State which issued the alert before releasing the data.[83] Communication of the data may be refused if this is indispensable for the performance of a task connected to the alert or to protect the rights and

---

[78] Art. 36(4).

[79] Art. 36(5).

[80] Art. 38.

[81] See the current Art. 92(4), which was inserted into the Convention in 2004 (see Reg. 871/2004, n. 6 above).

[82] Art. 94(3).

[83] Art. 41(1) to (3), essentially identical to the current Art. 109(1) of the Convention.

freedoms of others.[84] An applicant must be informed as soon as possible about his or her application, by 60 days after the application at the latest; this is a new provision, as compared to the current rules.[85]

Any person also has the right to have factually incorrect data corrected or unlawfully stored data deleted.[86] In this case, an applicant must be informed about his or her application within three months at the latest.[87]

There is a wholly new right to information in accordance with the EU's data protection Directive.[88] This means that where data have been obtained from the data subject, the data subject must be informed of the identity of the controller of the data, the purposes of the data processing and any further information such as the recipients of the data, the conditions and consequences of not replying to questions asked, and the existence of the rights of access and rectification, insofar as the further information is necessary in the circumstances "to guarantee fair data processing". The time at which the information must be disclosed is not specified.

Where data is *not* obtained from the data subject, the data subject must be informed of the identity of the controller of the data, the purposes of the data processing and any further information such as the categories of data concerned, the recipients of the data and the existence of the rights of access and rectification, again insofar as the further information is necessary in the circumstances "to guarantee fair data processing". In this case there is a possible exception if "the provision of such information proves impossible or would involve a disproportionate effort or disclosure is expressly laid down by law", although in such cases Member States must provide for "appropriate safeguards". Such information must be given at the time when the data is recorded or if disclosure to a third party is envisaged, no later than the time when the data are first disclosed.

The SIS II Regulation further specifies that this information should be given in writing together with a copy of or a reference to the decision giving rise to the alert. There is no further rule regarding the timing of the notification. The information need not be given in three cases: where the data was not obtained from the data subject *and* where the provision of information would

---

[84] Art. 41(4), essentially identical to the current Art. 109(2) of the Convention.

[85] Art. 41(6).

[86] Art. 41(5), essentially identical to the current Art. 110 of the Convention.

[87] Art. 41(7), which is a new provision as compared to the current rules.

[88] Art. 42(1) of the Regulation, which refers to Arts. 10 and 11 of Directive 95/46 (OJ 1995 L 281/31). It should be noted that the Commission plans to propose amendments to this Directive in 2011 (see the 2011 work programme, COM (2010) 623, 27 Oct. 2010).

be impossible or require disproportionate effort;[89] where the data subject already has the information;[90] or where the disclosure of the information is restricted by national law, "in particular" in relation to national security, defence, public security or criminal law. The final exception is similar to a provision of the data protection Directive,[91] although the Directive provides for a longer (but apparently exhaustive) list of grounds to restrict the provision of information and requires that such restriction must be "necessary".

Article 43 of the Regulation provides for a right of review before the courts or authorities of any Member State as regards the right of access, correction or deletion or as regards obtaining information or compensation. Member States undertake to recognise final decisions of other national authorities in such cases. The rules in this Article were to be reviewed by January 2009 (two years after the Regulation entered into force), but no such review has yet taken place. These provisions are the same as in the current Convention,[92] except for the addition of the right of access, the abolition of an apparent territorial restriction on the right of review and the obligation to review the rules.

The remaining provisions in this Chapter concern supervisory authorities. Article 44 provides that the national supervisory authorities with the powers set out in the EU's data protection Directive shall monitor the lawfulness of the processing of data in and the transmission of data from national territory. There are also provisions on audits by the national authorities and sufficient resources for them. The basic rule is derived from the existing Convention, with amendments,[93] but the rules on audits and resources are new. Article 45 provides for the Management Authority to be checked by the European Data Protection Supervisor ("EDPS"), which shall also arrange for regular audits, while Article 46 provides for cooperation between the EDPS and national supervisory authorities. They shall exchange relevant information, assist each other in carrying out inspections and audits, examine difficulties of interpretation or application, study problems regarding supervision or data subjects'

---

[89] This exception is already set out in Art. 11(2) of the data protection Directive, as noted above; it is not clear whether the obligation in the Directive to provide for "appropriate safeguards" in such cases would apply to SIS II.

[90] Again, this exception is already expressly set out in Arts. 10 and 11 of the data protection Directive.

[91] See Art. 13(1) of the Directive. It is not clear whether this provision would have been applicable in the absence of Art. 42(2)(c) of the SIS II Regulation, or is still applicable despite the specific clause in the Regulation.

[92] Art. 111.

[93] Compare Art. 44(1) of the Regulation to Art. 114(1) of the Convention. Art. 114(2) of the Convention (the right to request supervisory authorities to check data) has been deleted.

rights and promote awareness of data protection rights. Article 47 ensures that the EDPS can monitor the operation of the System by Member States before the Management Authority is established.

These provisions alter the current regime by giving the EDPS the power to supervise the central management of SIS II, a power which is currently held by the Joint Supervisory Authority established by the Schengen Convention.[94] The EDPS and national authorities shall, however, jointly exercise some of the residual functions of the current Joint Supervisory Authority (examining difficulties of interpretation or application, studying problems regarding supervision and the right of access and drawing up harmonised solutions to problems), which have been expanded.

3.5. *Other Rules and Final Provisions*

Chapter VII of the Regulation (Articles 48–49) sets out rules concerning liability and sanctions for breach of the Regulation. Article 48 states that each Member State is liable for damage which results from use of SIS II, including any Member State which enters inaccurate data in an alert or which stores data unlawfully. The Member State which has issued an alert must reimburse other Member States for compensation paid out, unless the use of data by the Member State requesting the compensation infringed the Regulation. If a Member State causes damage to SIS II itself, it is liable for that damage unless the Management Authority or another Member State "failed to take reasonable steps to prevent the damage from occurring or to minimise its impact". This provision is based on the current Convention, with the addition of the rule concerning damage to SIS II by a Member State.[95] Article 49 requires Member States to ensure that any misuse of SIS II data or supplementary information is punishable by "effective, proportionate and dissuasive remedies" in their national law. This provision is new as compared to the current Convention.

As for the final provisions, Chapter VIII of the Regulation (Articles 50–55) contains rules concerning monitoring and statistics, the comitology process, the repeal of all parts of the Schengen *acquis* and EU legislation related to SIS, a transitional period during which alerts are transferred from SIS to SIS II and the decision on when SIS II will begin operations. Article 50, which is entirely new as compared to the current Convention, first of all requires

---

[94] See Art. 115 of the Convention.
[95] See Art. 116 of the Convention.

the Management Authority to establish procedures to ensure the cost-effectiveness, security, output and quality of service of SIS II. The Authority must annually publish statistics relating to the number of records per category of alert, the number of hits per category of alert and how many times SIS II was accessed, in total and for each Member State. There must be a report on the technical functioning of SIS every two years, and a more general evalua-tion report three years after SIS II begins operations and every four years after that.

Next, Article 51 concerns the Commission's power to adopt implementing measures, subject to Member States' control in a "comitology" committee. The Commission had some of these powers already as regards amendment of the SIRENE Manual.[96] The operation of these committees has been affected by general changes to the functioning of "comitology" committees which took effect from 1 March 2011.[97]

The power to adopt implementing measures applies to the following:

a) the adoption of the Sirene Manual (Article 8(4));
b) technical compliance between the national and central databases (Article 9(1));
c) "technical rules" concerning "entering, updating, deleting and searching the data" (Article 20(3));
d) the specifications for a quality check before the uploading of biometric data (Article 22(a));
e) "technical rules" concerning "entering, updating and deleting the data" concerning misused identity (Article 36(4)); and
f) "technical rules" for linking alerts (Article 37(7)).

As noted above, these powers have been used several times to date.[98]

Articles 52 and 53 respectively set out the provisions of the Schengen *acquis* and of EU law which will be repealed once SIS II starts operations. Article 54 sets out transitional rules relating to alerts. Existing SIS data will have to be subject to the new rules in the Regulation at the latest three years after the SIS II begins operations. During this three-year period, any type of amendment made to a pre-existing alert must comply with the Regulation, and a Member State must "examine the compatibility" of an alert with the Regulation in the event of a "hit". But in the latter case, this examination of compatibility will not affect the action to be taken (ie Member States will still refuse to issue the

---

[96] See n. 7 above.
[97] On "comitology" generally, see chapter 2.
[98] N. 41 above.

visa or to allow entry). This Article also contains a rule concerning repayment of the existing SIS budget to the Member States.

Finally, Article 55 provides that SIS II will begin operations once the Council (made up of Member States currently fully participating in Schengen) decides unanimously to launch the new system. Beforehand, the necessary implementing measures must have been adopted, there must be a test of the system,[99] and the Commission and the Member States must have made the necessary technical and legal arrangements.

4. *Analysis*

The Commission's initial proposals were in many respects highly unclear, particularly as regards the key issue of data protection rights and the grounds for inclusion of information on people to be banned from the Schengen area. In part, the Commission suggested that persons could be banned from the Schengen area based on application of EC legislation that had not yet been proposed! There was no impact assessment and many details of the proposals do not seem to have been fully thought through, in light of the very cursory explanation of its proposals offered by the Commission. Above all, the legislative process as regards these proposals was in some respects a sham, as the Council had already decided before May 2005 on the key functions of the next version of the SIS without any democratic consultation (or impact assessment) whatsoever and the Commission had already awarded the tender to set up SIS II, following a controversial tender process.[100]

As for the grounds for a SIS II listing, the obligation to provide for an individual assessment and appeals is very welcome, assuming that the wording of the Regulation is interpreted to mean that there is a *right* to an appeal which is merely subject to more detailed regulation (as regards time limits and competent courts) by national law, rather than a discretion under national law to preclude a right to appeal altogether. It is submitted that the former interpretation is correct, in light of the general principles of EU law, which require an effective remedy for EU law rights, and that furthermore any national regulation of the right of appeal cannot render the right to appeal ineffective. It is unfortunate that SIS II Regulation does not expressly give priority to other EU immigration and asylum legislation was dropped, but it is still arguable that

---

[99] Art. 55(3)(c) and 55(4).
[100] See Case T-447/04 R *Cap Gemini* [2005] ECR II-257.

such legislation takes priority over the SIS II legislation even in the absence of an express rule to that effect, at least where issues of human rights or free movement law are involved (since EU rules on those issues are set out in EU primary law, which takes precedence over secondary law).

However, it is unfortunate that there was not some degree of greater harmonisation of the grounds for issuing an alert, at least to provide that the rather vague grounds set out in the legislation are exhaustive grounds for issuing alerts. The subsequently adopted Returns Directive did little to ensure any further harmonisation on this issue.[101] EU legislation ought to ensure that alerts are only issued when they are genuinely objectively justified in light of the degree of criminality or seriousness of the breach of immigration law committed by a particular third-country national.

There is also a fundamental problem in that there is no obligation to publish the national criteria for issuing alerts in the EU's Official Journal. Without that information it is clearly far more difficult for any person to know if the alert on him or her was correctly or lawfully added to SIS II, or for supervisory authorities to carry out their responsibilities to ensure correct application of the data protection rules more generally. The resulting lack of foreseeability of the circumstances in which data will be collected violates basic principles of data protection law.

In the case of persons subjected to a travel ban pursuant to EU sanction measures, the underlying problem is the inability to attack the "pure" foreign policy acts of the EU directly in the EU courts, although the Treaty of Lisbon has arguably remedied this problem.[102]

As for the use of biometric data, in certain cases it might have the positive effect of ensuring that individuals who are apparently listed in the SIS can "clear their names", and certainly in many cases it will more quickly identify individuals who are genuinely the subject of an alert. But it remains to be seen in practice whether the risk of wrongful identification pointed to by data protection authorities in cases of "one-to-many" searches has been sufficiently addressed.

As for data processing rules, the provisions related to misused identity and the other safeguards for individuals who argue that they are not the subject of alerts can only be welcomed. Also, there is no sufficiently good reason to send SIS immigration to non-EU countries or bodies which do not participate in

---

[101] See Peers, n. 60 above, and the discussion of the Directive in volume 2 of this book (chapter 17).

[102] See Art. 275 of the Treaty on the Functioning of the European Union (TFEU). See, by analogy, Case T-86/11 *Bamba*, judgment of 8 June 2011, not yet reported.

the application of the Schengen free movement zone, so the absolute ban on the transmission of data outside the EU can only be welcomed.

Next, the data protection rules in the Regulation are an improvement on the *status quo* as regards the right to information and the removal of the territorial restriction on access to a review. The Regulation could make clearer its relationship with the EU data protection Directive, in particular as regards restrictions on the right to information; and the content of the right itself as described in the Directive cannot be applied easily to databases like SIS II. The right to information is crucial since it is linked to the right to appeal against a SIS listing; obviously individuals who would be minded to appeal a listing should in principle be given the opportunity to do so as soon as the listing is made, since an appeal right might have expired[103] if the person concerned only finds out about the listing when he or she is subsequently refused a visa or entry at the border. For that reason, it is unfortunate that the timing of the right to information is not made clearer. It would surely be possible to agree on a standard form, like the form given to persons denied entry at external borders, to be given to a person subject to a SIS II alert as soon as the decision to issue the alert is made.

Moreover, it is unfortunate that the restrictions on the right to access data – which is obviously equally crucial to any subsequent review of the correctness and legality of the data held in SIS II – were not limited to highly exceptional circumstances such as national security risks and risks to the effectiveness of ongoing criminal investigations.

As for the final provisions, Article 50 goes well beyond the current requirements for SIS public accountability. However, it could have been better, as it would be useful to have data disaggregated by the specific grounds for the listing and by Member State, and to have more statistics available on actions carried out following alerts and complaints against Member States.

---

[103] Although the expiry of the right to appeal a decision which the person concerned was never informed of could surely be challenged as a breach of the general principles of EU law, and/ or the EU Charter of Fundamental Rights.

Chapter 5

Frontex

1. *Introduction and Overview*

The removal of barriers between Member States, both conceptual and physical, has resulted in the progressive realisation of a European space, referred to in somewhat utopian terms by the Treaties, as an area of Freedom, Security and Justice.[1] An internal space implies an external border and in the case of the EU, that border stretches to 8,826 kilometres of land borders and approximately 42,672 km of external sea borders. It is with a view to facilitating the management of the Union's external borders that the Council established the European Agency for the Management of Operational Cooperation at the External Borders of the Member States of the European Union (referred to in this chapter as "Frontex"[2] or the "Agency").

Since becoming operational on 3 October 2005, Frontex has experienced rapid growth both in terms of its resources and the scope of its activities. The precise workings of Frontex are relatively unknown, however, its interceptions at the borders of EU Member States have been controversial. This chapter will examine the structure and functioning of Frontex in five parts. First, it will provide a brief overview of the background to the adoption of the Regulation establishing Frontex. Second, it will examine the Agency's functions and activities. Third, it will review the Agency's organisational and management structure. Fourth, it will assess the Agency's activities in light of the international protection obligations enshrined in the Union legal order. The final section of this Chapter will consider amendments to the legislative framework governing the Agency that are in the process of being adopted at the time of writing of this Chapter.[3]

---

[1] Art. 67 TFEU and Art. 3 TEU. The European Space in question does not presently coincide exactly with the actual territory of the Member States of the Union, in that the Schengen *acquis* which removes internal borders, extends to certain non EU Member States (Iceland, Norway, Switzerland and Liechtenstein) and excludes certain EU Member States (Denmark, Ireland and the United Kingdom): see further chapter 2.

[2] Derived from the French "*Frontières extérieures*".

[3] 1 August 2011.

1.1. *The Origins of Frontex*

The development of a European Union free of internal borders was a central feature of the Treaty of Amsterdam. The Treaty integrated the Schengen *acquis* into the institutional framework of the European Union and expressly conferred on the Community (now the Union) the task of framing policies on asylum, immigration and external border control.[4]

Soon after the entry into force of the Amsterdam Treaty, the European Parliament, in the context of planning for enlargement of the Union, called for measures to reinforce external border controls.[5] The European Council of Laeken in December 2001 recognised the importance of effective management of the external borders as a means of combating terrorism, illegal immigration and human trafficking. It entrusted the Council and Commission with developing "arrangements for cooperation between services responsible for external border control and to examine the conditions in which a mechanism or common services to control external borders could be created."[6]

In a Communication published in May 2002,[7] the Commission observed that strengthening the EU's external frontiers was of concern to all Member States and required coordination on a European level. The Commission recommended the adoption of a common policy of integrated management of external borders comprised of five mutually interdependent components: (1) Common corpus of legislation (2) Common operational coordination and co-operation mechanism (3) Common integrated risk analysis (4) European dimension to staff training and inter-operational equipment (5) Burden-sharing between Member States and the Union. In order to enhance operational co-ordination between national border services, the Commission proposed establishing an "external borders practitioners' common unit" which would develop from the existing Strategic Committee on Immigration, Frontiers and Asylum (SCIFA) and operate, at least initially, on the basis of the framework for administrative co-operation provided for under what is now Article 74 TFEU. The Commission further proposed establishing a permanent process of exchange and processing of data and information. In the longer

---

[4] Art. 67 TFEU.

[5] See for example, European Parliament resolution of 3 April 1998 on the implications of enlargement of the European Union for cooperation in the field of justice and home affairs (OJ 1998 C 138/214).

[6] European Council Meeting in Laeken, 14 and 15 Dec. 2001 SN/300/1/01 REV 1, Presidency Conclusions, Conclusion No. 42.

[7] "Towards Integrated Management of the External Borders of the Member States of the European Union", Com (2002) 233, 7 May 2002.

term, the Commission envisaged the establishment of a European Corps of Border Guards.

The Commission's recommendations were largely incorporated in the "Plan for the management of the external borders of the European Union", which the Council adopted on 13 June 2002. The Plan was, however, more reticent in endorsing the establishment of a European Border Guard Corps.[8] The Council specified that the external borders practitioners' common unit, meeting within the framework of SCIFA, would include national heads of border control services and be assisted by the Working Party on Frontiers and by other competent working parties of the Council,[9] depending on the nature of the expertise required. The Council envisaged that the common unit could head the common policy on management of external borders, coordinate and control operational projects and act as manager and strategist to ensure greater convergence between the national policies in the field of personnel and equipment. In addition, it was envisaged that the common unit could carry out inspections and increase operational coordination between external border management and other security authorities.[10]

The Seville European Council of 21 and 22 June 2002 welcomed the Commission's Communication and the Council's Plan and called for the prompt introduction of the common unit to coordinate the measures contained in the Plan.[11] The Danish Council Presidency proceeded to create the Common Unit, under the form of SCIFA+ (comprising SCIFA and heads of national border guard services) which met for the first time in July 2002. SCIFA+ approved a number of joint operations and pilot projects.[12] Progress reviews, however, revealed structural limitations of the unit,[13] and consequently the

---

[8] General Affairs Council, 13 June 2002, Council doc. 10019/02, paras 118 to 120. A similarly cautious view was expressed by the Convention on the Future for Europe: see the Final Report of Working Group X, "Freedom, Security and Justice" of the Convention, published on 2 Dec. 2002 (CONV 426/02 WG X 14, p. 17).

[9] For example, Schengen Evaluation, Visa and CIREFI (Centre for Information, Discussion and Exchange on the Crossing of Frontiers and Immigration). See General Affairs Council, 13 June 2002, Council doc. 10019/02, para 45.

[10] General Affairs Council, 13 June 2002, Council doc. 10019/02, para 44.

[11] Presidency Conclusions, Seville, 21 and 22 June 2002, Conclusion No. 31.

[12] Operations included: Ulysses (Jan. and May 2003), Triton (Mar. 2003), Orca and RIO IV (May 2003). See Note from the Greek Presidency, Progress Report for the implementation of the Plan for the management of external borders of the Member States of the European Union and the comprehensive Plan for combating illegal immigration, Council doc. 7504/03, 17 Mar. 2003.

[13] Conclusions of the Council on a more effective management of the external borders of the EU Member States of 5 June 2003, Council doc. 10059/03 FRONT 71 COMIX 355.

Thessaloniki European Council of 19 and 20 June 2003 invited the Commission to examine the necessity of creating new institutional mechanisms, including the possible creation of a Community structure that would promote operational cooperation for the management of external borders.[14] The European Council of 16 and 17 October 2003 subsequently endorsed the establishment of an Agency for the management of external borders and invited the Commission to submit a proposal to this effect.

1.2. *The Adoption of the Frontex Regulation*

On 11 November 2003, the Commission submitted a proposal for a Council Regulation establishing the European Agency for the Management of Operational Cooperation at the External Borders of the Member States of the European Union.[15] The Agency was to be established on a permanent basis with a separate legal personality. Its primary objective was to enhance operational co-operation among Member States in the management of external borders. The proposal set out the tasks of the Agency as well as the management and budgetary framework governing its operation.

In accordance with the procedure set out in Article 67 EC,[16] the Commission, by letter of 8 December 2003, consulted the European Parliament on the proposed Regulation. The President of the Parliament referred the proposal to the Parliamentary Committee on Citizens' Freedoms and Rights, Justice and Home Affairs.[17] In its report of 24 February 2004, the Committee welcomed the establishment of Frontex as an important step in the realisation of the common integrated management of external borders at a European level. The Committee also considered that the Agency's independent status and permanent structure would enhance its effectiveness and transparency.[18] However, it also found the proposed structure of the Agency to be excessively intergovernmental in character and proposed amendments designed to enhance its "Communitarian" attributes through increasing the involvement of the Commission and the Parliament. The Committee opposed entrusting the Agency with co-ordinating or organising joint return operations of Member States in the absence of common legislation on immigration and asylum. In its

---

[14] Presidency Conclusions, Thessaloniki, 19 and 20 June 2003, 11638/08, para. 14.
[15] COM(2003) 687 final/2, Corrigendum in respect of French, English and German language version dated 20 November 2003.
[16] Following the entry into force of the Lisbon Treaty, the legal basis for such legislation is Art. 77 TFEU.
[17] Document no. C5-0613/2003.
[18] Report of the European Parliament, pp. 29–30.

subsequent legislative resolution, the Parliament proposed measures enhancing involvement of Union institutions and deleting references to return-cooperation.[19]

The Council also consulted the European Economic and Social Committee in accordance with what is now Article 304 TFEU. The Committee delivered its Opinion on 29 January 2004.[20] It welcomed the establishment of a European borders agency, but considered that the main tasks of the agency should be expanded to include the humane treatment of individuals and respect for international human rights conventions. The Committee emphasised that effective border controls should not jeopardise the right to asylum. It recommended that tasks of the agency could include co-ordinating rescue services, particularly sea rescue, in light of dangerous practices employed in illegal immigration. The Committee considered that joint return operations must be combined with measures for regularising individuals in irregular situations.

The degree of emphasis on fundamental rights recommended by the Committee, as well as the proposed sea-rescue dimension to the Agency's activities, did not find its way into the final text of Council Regulation (EC) No 2007/2004[21] adopted on 26 October 2004. There was, in particular, no mention of compliance with international protection principles, the prohibition of interdiction, or refoulement. Recital 22 of the Regulation did, however, emphasise, that the Regulation respects fundamental rights, including as enshrined in the Union legal order by what is now Article 6(3) TEU.

By decision dated 26 April 2005, the Council named Warsaw as the seat of the new agency.[22] Frontex became operational as of 3 October 2005.

The United Kingdom had sought to take part in the adoption of the Frontex Regulation, however, it was excluded on the ground that this piece of legislation constituted a development of the Schengen *acquis* in which it had

---

[19] European Parliament legislative resolution on the proposal for a Council regulation establishing a European Agency for the Management of Operational Co-operation at the External Borders P5_TA(2004)0151.

[20] Opinion of the European Economic and Social Committee on the "proposal for a Council Regulation establishing a European Agency for the Management of Operational Co-operation at the External Borders" (OJ 2004 C 108/97).

[21] Reg. 2007/2004 (OJ 2004 L 349/1), as amended by Reg. 863/2007 (OJ 2007 L 199/30), hereinafter "the Frontex Regulation". All references in this chapter are to this Regulation, unless otherwise indicated. For an informally codified text of the Frontex Regulation as amended in 2007, including the text of the amendments agreed in principle in 2011, see the Annex to this chapter.

[22] Council Decision 2005/358/EC of 26 April 2005 designating the seat of the European Agency for the Management of Operational Cooperation at the External Borders of the Member States of the European Union.

not participated.[23] The United Kingdom considered its right of participation was nevertheless assured by opt-in provisions provided for in the Schengen Protocol[24] and consequently sought to have the Regulation annulled. The United Kingdom's exclusion was ultimately upheld, however, by the Court of Justice of the European Union.[25]

The Regulation was amended in 2007,[26] and at the time of writing, the text of a further amending regulation has been agreed by the European Parliament and Council and is in the process of being adopted. The agreed amendments will be considered in section five.[27]

1.3. *States Participating in Frontex*

The Frontex Regulation applies to all Member States, except for the UK, Ireland and Denmark.[28] Nevertheless, the Regulation expressly envisages the possibility for cooperation with the UK and Ireland,[29] and representatives from these Member States are invited to attend meetings of the Management Board.[30]

In addition to 24 EU Member States, the Frontex Regulation applies to certain non-EU Member States associated with the implementation of the Schengen *acquis* (the "Schengen associates"), namely, Iceland, Norway, Switzerland and Liechtenstein.[31]

---

[23] The UK and Ireland opted out of the Schengen *acquis* in accordance with Council Decision 2000/365/EC of 29 May 2000.

[24] In particular, the UK sought to rely on Art. 5(1) of the Protocol integrating the Schengen *acquis* into the framework of the European Union. See also the unilateral statement by the United Kingdom made at the JHA Council of 25 and 26 Oct. 2004.

[25] Case C-77/05 *United Kingdom v. Council* [2007] ECR I-11459.

[26] Reg. 863/2007 of the European Parliament and of the Council of 11 July 2007 establishing a mechanism for the creation of Rapid Border Intervention Teams and amending Council Regulation (EC) No 2007/2004 as regards that mechanism and regulating the tasks and powers of guest officers (the "Border Teams Regulation").

[27] Proposal for a Regulation of the European Parliament and the Council amending Council Regulation (EC) No 2007/2004 establishing a European Agency for the Management of Operational Cooperation at the External Borders of the Member States of the European Union (Frontex), (hereinafter the "agreed amending regulation"), set out in Annex 1 to the Note from Presidency to the Permanent Representatives Committee, (Council doc. 12341/11, 5 July 2011).

[28] Recitals 24, 25 and 26 in the preamble.

[29] Art. 12 tasks the Agency with facilitating operational cooperation of the Member States with Ireland and the United Kingdom in matters covered by its activities and to the extent required for the fulfilment of its tasks.

[30] Art. 23(4).

[31] As regards Iceland and Norway, see recital 23 in the preamble. The modalities of participation of Iceland and Norway in the Agency were adopted pursuant to Council Decision

2. *Functions and Activities of Frontex*

Article 1 of Regulation 2007/2004 formally establishes Frontex with a view to improving the integrated management of the external borders of the Member States of the European Union. While Member States retain primary responsibility for the control and surveillance of borders, Frontex is tasked with facilitating and rendering more effective the application of Union measures relating to external border management.[32] In particular, Frontex is entrusted with:

(a) coordinating operational cooperation between Member States in the field of management of external borders;[33]
(b) assisting Member States in the training of national border guards, including the establishment of common training standards;
(c) carrying out risk analyses;
(d) following up on the development of research relevant for the control and surveillance of external borders;
(e) assisting Member States in circumstances requiring increased technical and operational assistance at external borders;
(f) providing Member States with the necessary support in organising joint return operations; and
(g) deploying Rapid Border Intervention Teams to Member States.[34]

The Frontex Regulation does not preclude Member States from continuing to engage in operational cooperation with other Member States or third countries at external borders where such cooperation complements the action of the Agency.[35] Such cooperation must, however, be notified to the Agency and Member States are required to refrain from engaging in activities that are likely to jeopardise the objectives of the Agency.[36] The exercise of executive power by staff of Frontex on the territory of another Member State is subject to the national law of that Member State.[37]

2007/511/EC (OJ 2007 L 188/15). The modalities of participation of Switzerland and Liechtenstein were adopted pursuant to Council Decision 2010/491/EC of 27 July 2009 (OJ 2010 L 243/66) and Council Decision 2010/490/EU of 26 July 2010 (OJ 2010 L 243/22).

[32] Art. 1(2).
[33] This function is also confirmed in Art. 16(2) of Reg. 562/2006 (OJ 2006 L 105/1, the "Borders Code").
[34] Art. 2(1), as inserted by Art. 12(3) of the Border Teams Regulation.
[35] Art. 16(3) of the Schengen Borders Code.
[36] See Art. 2, second indent, of the Frontex Regulation and also Art. 16(3) of the Schengen Borders Code.
[37] Art. 10.

The Agency's operational model is subject to continuing elaboration and review but centres around a combination of risk analysis, knowledge management, and management of joint operations at the external borders of the Member States.[38] For the purposes of this section, the core activities of Frontex are grouped and considered under four headings: (1) Operational Co-operation (2) Research (3) Training (4) Co-operation with third countries. In particular, section one examines joint operations at external borders, joint return operations, the provision of additional technical and operational assistance, the deployment of Rapid Border Intervention Teams (Border Teams) and Risk analysis. The second section considers the Agency's research activities. The third section considers the role of Frontex in providing training and the development of common training standards. The fourth section examines agreements that Frontex has concluded with third countries.

2.1. *Co-Ordinating Operational Co-Operation*

A primary function of Frontex is co-ordinating operational co-operation by implementing joint operations and pilot projects.

Joint border operations seek to reinforce the monitoring and patrolling of external land, sea and air borders, through the deployment and use of additional human and technical resources. They entail the study of routes used to get to the EU and the interception of illegal immigrants and human traffickers. Joint border operations have taken place both within and beyond the territory of Member States. Frontex has concluded a number of agreements with third States, permitting the patrolling and monitoring of borders beyond territorial waters of the Member States.

In addition, Frontex also assists in co-ordinating the return of individuals subject to removal orders in the territory of the EU and Schengen associated countries. These operations are referred to as joint return operations.

2.1.1. *Legislative Framework Governing Joint Operations at External Borders*
National border guards engaged in the monitoring or surveillance of external borders within the framework of Frontex coordinated operations remain subject to the provisions of the Borders Code.[39] Pursuant to Article 6 of the Borders Code, border guards are obliged to fully respect human dignity in the performance of their duties. They must act proportionately and avoid discrimination.[40] Border guards are required to be specialised and properly

---

[38] Frontex General Report 2009, Foreword by the Executive Director.
[39] N. 32 above. See further chapter 3.
[40] Art. 6(2) of the Borders Code.

trained professionals.[41] Member States are required to encourage border guards to learn languages relevant to the performance of their tasks.[42] Training on the rules for border control and on fundamental rights is also expressly provided for under Article 16, paragraph 4, of the Borders Code.

The Borders Code requires Member States to assist each other and maintain "close and constant cooperation with a view to the effective implementation of border control". The Code expressly recognises the Agency's role in assisting Member States in ensuring such cooperation.[43] Specific rules for external border crossing by land, air and sea are set out in Annex VI of the Borders Code.

The provisions of the Border Code relating to surveillance of the Union's external sea borders are supplemented by Council Decision 2010/252/EU.[44] The Decision, adopted on the basis of Article 12(5) of the Code, sets out in its annex, rules (Part I) and non-binding guidelines (Part II) applicable to the Agency in co-ordinating sea border operations.

Council Decision 2010/252/EU requires the Agency's sea border surveillance operations to be conducted in accordance with fundamental rights and in a manner that does not put at risk the safety of persons intercepted or rescued as well as individuals participating in the operations.[45] The Decision expressly prohibits the transfer of individuals to authorities of another jurisdiction in contravention of the principle of non-refoulement.[46] The prohibition extends to the transfer of individuals to other States from which there may be a risk of onward refoulement. Furthermore, persons intercepted or rescued must be afforded an opportunity to express any reasons for believing that their disembarkation in a particular State would breach the principle of non-refoulement.[47] Frontex is under an obligation to ensure that its maritime operations, in their entirety, take account of the situation of particularly vulnerable individuals, including, children, victims of trafficking, persons in need of urgent medical assistance and persons in need of international protection.[48] The Decision emphasises the requirement for participating border guards to

---

[41] Art. 15 of the Borders Code.
[42] Art. 15(3) of the Borders Code.
[43] See Recital 13 and Art. 16 of the Schengen Borders Code.
[44] Council Decision of 26 April 2010 supplementing the Schengen Borders Code as regards the surveillance of the sea external borders in the context of operational cooperation coordinated by the European Agency for the Management of Operational Cooperation at the External Borders of the Member States of the European Union (OJ 2010 L 111/20).
[45] Decision 2010/252/EU, Part I, Point 1.1.
[46] Decision 2010/252/EU, Part I, Point 1.2.
[47] Decision 2010/252/EU, Part I, Point 1.2.
[48] Decision 2010/252/EU, Part I, Point 1.3.

have been trained on relevant provisions of human rights and refugee law as well as to be familiar with the international regime governing search and rescue.[49]

Once a ship or vessel is detected, the Agency will observe its identity and nationality. Pending further measures, the vessel is to be surveyed from a "prudent distance".[50] Units participating in the Agency's surveillance operation ("participating units") are required to communicate information about the ship immediately to the coordination centre. If the ship is about to enter the waters of a Member State that is not participating in the operation, the participating units are required to inform the co-ordination centre, which will in turn will inform the Member State concerned.[51]

Units participating in the surveillance operation may be authorised to take a number of different interception measures in circumstances where there are reasonable grounds to suspect that a vessel is carrying persons seeking to circumvent border checks.[52] Such measures include requesting information and documentation concerning the ownership and registration of the vessel as well as relating to the voyage, the identity, nationality and other relevant data of persons on board.[53] Agents participating in the surveillance operation may also be authorised to stop, board and search a vessel, including cargo and individuals, and question such individuals on board.[54] They may also be instructed to inform persons on board that they are not authorised to cross the border and that persons directing the craft may face penalties for facilitating the voyage.[55] Additional measures may include seizing the ship and apprehending persons on board.[56] The vessel may be ordered to modify its course outside of or towards a destination other than the territorial waters of the Member State concerned. In such a case, the Frontex units may escort the vessel to ensure compliance with directions.[57] The vessels, or the persons on board, may be brought to the Member State hosting the operation (the "host Member State") or to another Member State participating in the operation[58] or indeed to a third country or to the authorities of a third country.[59]

---

[49] Decision 2010/252/EU, Part I, Point 1.4.
[50] Decision 2010/252/EU, Part I, Point 2.1.
[51] Decision 2010/252/EU, Part I, Point 2.2.
[52] Decision 2010/252/EU, Part I, Point 2.4.
[53] Decision 2010/252/EU, Part I, Point 2.4(a).
[54] Decision 2010/252/EU, Part I, Point 2.4(b).
[55] Decision 2010/252/EU, Part I, Point 2.4(c).
[56] Decision 2010/252/EU, Part I, Point 2.4(d).
[57] Decision 2010/252/EU, Part I, Point 2.4(e).
[58] Decision 2010/252/EU, Part I, Point 2.4(g).
[59] Decision 2010/252/EU, Part I, Point 2.4(f).

Such interception measures may only be exercised on the basis of authorisation expressly granted to the units participating in the surveillance operation. The State entitled to grant such authorisation is determined in accordance with well established principles of the International law of the sea, namely, on the basis of geographical territory and the flag of the vessel concerned.[60] If operational activities take place in the territorial waters or contiguous zones[61] of the host Member State, or a Member State participating in the operation, then interception measures may be authorised on the basis of instructions transmitted by the host Member State to the participating unit via the coordination centre.[62] If the surveillance operation takes place in the territorial waters or contiguous zone of another Member State that is not participating in the operation, then the interception measures may only take place on the basis of authorisation granted from that Member State.[63] In such a case, participating units are required to keep the coordination centre informed of communications with the relevant Member State and of the subsequent action taken.[64] If the master of an intercepted vessel has requested that a diplomatic agent or consular officer of the flag State be notified, Frontex Agents are required to inform the host Member State of that request by way of the coordination centre.[65]

If a surveillance operation is taking place in the high seas beyond the contiguous zone, then the authorisation to take interception measures is determined by the nationality of the vessel, as identified by its flag (the "flag State"). If the detected vessel is flying the flag of a Member State that is participating in the operation, then the national official representing that Member State at the coordination centre may grant or transmit the requisite authorisation.[66]

---

[60] Recital 6 in the preamble to Decision 2010/252/EU states that the Implementation of the Decision does not affect obligations, amongst others, of Member States under the United Nations Convention on the Law of the Sea, the International Convention for the Safety of Life at Sea, the International Convention on Maritime Search and Rescue.

[61] Art. 33 of the United Nations Convention on the Law of the Sea (Montego Bay Convention: OJ 1998 L 179/1) defines the "contiguous zone" as the zone of the high seas adjacent to the territorial seas. It may not extend beyond 24 nautical miles from the baseline. In this zone, the coastal State has the right to exercise the control necessary to: "(a) prevent infringement of its customs, fiscal, immigration or sanitary laws and regulations within its territory or territorial sea; (b) punish infringement of the above laws and regulations within its territory or territorial sea".

[62] Decision 2010/252/EU, Part I, Point 2.5.1.1.

[63] Decision 2010/252/EU, Part I, Point 2.5.1.2.

[64] Decision 2010/252/EU, Part I, Point 2.5.1.2.

[65] Decision 2010/252/EU, Part I, Point 2.5.1.1.

[66] Decision 2010/252/EU, Part I, Point 2.5.2.1.

If a detected vessel is flying the flag of a Member State that is not participating in the operation, or of a third country, then the relevant flag State will be requested to confirm registry of the vessel.[67] Upon receipt of confirmation of nationality, authorisation shall be requested to take interception measures in accordance with the Palermo Protocol against the smuggling of migrants.[68] The coordination centre is to be informed of any communication with the flag State.[69]

Pending or in the absence of authorisation of the flag State, the ship shall be surveyed at a prudent distance. No other measures shall be taken without the express authorisation of the flag State, except those necessary to relieve imminent danger to the lives of persons or those measures which derive from relevant bilateral or multilateral agreements, or unless the ship has entered the contiguous zone.[70]

If there are reasonable grounds for suspecting that a vessel flying a foreign flag is, in reality, of the same nationality as the participating unit, it may dispatch a boat under command of an officer to the suspected vessel for further investigation.[71] Similarly, if there are reasonable grounds for suspecting that the true nationality of a suspected vessel is that of another Member State participating in the operation, then the national representative of the Member State at the coordination centre shall be entitled to authorise further verification.[72] If suspicions prove to be founded, then the interception measures may be taken in accordance with the actual nationality of the vessel.[73]

Where there are reasonable grounds for suspecting that a particular vessel is without nationality,[74] the participating Frontex unit shall proceed to verify the entitlement of the vessel to fly its flag. To this end, a boat under the command of an officer may be dispatched to investigate further. If the suspicion is proven to be founded and there are reasonable grounds to suspect that the ship is engaged in the smuggling of migrants by sea in accordance with the Protocol against the Smuggling of Migrants by Land, Sea and Air,

---

[67] Decision 2010/252/EU, Part I, Point 2.5.2.2.
[68] Decision 2010/252/EU, Part I, Point 2.5.2.2.
[69] Decision 2010/252/EU, Part I, Point 2.5.2.2.
[70] Decision 2010/252/EU, Part I, Point 2.5.2.6.
[71] Decision 2010/252/EU, Part I, Point 2.5.2.3.
[72] Decision 2010/252/EU, Part I, Point 2.5.2.4.
[73] Decision 2010/252/EU, Part I, Point 2.5.2.1.
[74] Defined in Decision 2010/252/EU, Part I, Point 2.5.2.5 as when a vessel has not been granted by any State the right to fly its flag or when it sails under the flags of two or more States, using them according to convenience.

supplementing the United Nations Convention against Transnational Organised Crime, then interception measures will be taken by the Frontex units.[75]

Part II of the Annex sets out non-binding guidelines for search and rescue situations and for disembarkation in the context of sea operations coordinated by Frontex. Section 1 recalls that the obligation to provide assistance to persons in distress at sea shall be carried out in accordance with applicable international law and in accordance with requirements for the respect of fundamental rights. Units participating in Frontex Operations are required to provide assistance to any vessel or person in distress at sea – regardless of the status, nationality of the persons or the circumstances in which they are found.[76]

Where in the context of a border surveillance operation, there is uncertainty or apprehension as to the safety of a ship or of any persons on board, the participating unit is to transmit as soon as possible all information available to the Rescue Coordination Centre responsible for the search and rescue region.[77] In cases where the Rescue Coordination Centre of a third country does not respond to notification, the participating unit should contact the Rescue Coordination Centre of the host Member State. While awaiting instructions from the Rescue Coordination Centre, participating units are to take all appropriate measures to ensure the safety of persons concerned.[78]

Participating units should consider all relevant elements relating to the safety of an intercepted vessel and communicate their assessment to the responsible Rescue Coordination Centre. Factors to consider include, the existence of a request for assistance, the seaworthiness of the vessel and the likelihood that it will not reach its final destination, the number of passengers in relation to the type of vessel, the availability of necessary supplies, the presence of qualified crew and command of the ship, the availability of safety, navigation and communication equipment, the presence of passengers in urgent need of medical assistance, the presence of deceased passengers, the presence of children, pregnant women and the weather and sea conditions.[79]

The guidelines emphasise that the existence of an emergency should not be exclusively dependent on or determined by a request for assistance. Where individuals on board a vessel refuse assistance, the participating unit should inform the Rescue Coordination Centre and continue to fulfil a duty of care,

---

[75] Decision 2010/252/EU, Part I, Point 2.5.2.5.
[76] Decision 2010/252/EU, Part II, Point 1.1.
[77] Decision 2010/252/EU, Part II, Point 1.2.
[78] Decision 2010/252/EU, Part II, Point 1.2.
[79] Decision 2010/252/EU, Part II, Point 1.3.

taking any measure necessary to ensure the safety of the persons concerned, while avoiding taking any action that might aggravate the situation or increase the chances of injury or loss of life.[80] The coordination centre of the operation should be informed as soon as possible of any contact with the Rescue Coordination Centre and the course of action taken.[81] Once the situation of emergency has ceased to exist and the search and rescue operation has been concluded, the participating units should, in consultation with the coordination centre of the operation, resume the operation.[82]

The guidelines recommend that the operational plan set out the modalities for the disembarkation of persons intercepted or rescued, in accordance with international law and applicable bilateral agreements. The operational plan should not, however, impose obligations on Member States that are not participating in the operation. It is further recommended that priority should be given to disembarkation in the third country from which the vessel departed or through the territorial waters or search and rescue region of which that ship transited. If that is not possible, priority should be given to disembarkation in the host Member State unless it is necessary to act otherwise to ensure the safety of these persons.[83]

The coordination centre should be informed of the presence of persons who may be in need of international protection and should convey such information to the competent authorities of the host Member State. Based on the information, the operational plan should determine which follow up-measures may be taken.[84]

The European Parliament has sought the annulment of Decision 2010/252/ EU on the ground that it exceeds the scope of the implementing provision pursuant to which it was adopted.[85] It argues that rules on "interception", "search and rescue" and "disembarkation" do not fall within the meaning of surveillance and modifies the essential elements of the Borders Code. The European Parliament also considers that the Decision modifies the obligations of EU Member States relating to Frontex operations, which are laid down in the Frontex Regulation. Should the Court annul the contested Decision, the

---

[80] Decision 2010/252/EU, Part II, Point 1.4.
[81] Decision 2010/252/EU, Part II, Point 1.5.
[82] Decision 2010/252/EU, Part II, Point 1.6.
[83] Decision 2010/252/EU, Part II, Point 2.1.
[84] Decision 2010/252/EU, Part II, Point 2.2.
[85] Case C-355/10, *EP v. Council*, pending. The European Parliament had voted against the Decision by 336 votes to 253 with 30 abstentions, but failed to obtain the absolute majority (369 votes) required in order to secure rejection.

Parliament nonetheless considers it would be desirable that the Court exercise its discretion to maintain its effects, in accordance with Article 264 (2) TFEU, until such time as it is replaced.

2.1.2. *Procedure for a Joint Operation*

Proposals for joint operations and pilot projects may be initiated by Member States or by Frontex.[86] When the Agency proposes joint operations, such a proposal is submitted on the basis of facts identified through risk analyses undertaken by the Agency's Risk Analysis unit.[87] Proposals submitted by Member States will be evaluated, approved and coordinated by Frontex.[88] Member States confronted with exceptional circumstances may also request Frontex to organise additional technical and operational assistance.[89]

Frontex project proposals for joint operations are formulated in a standard template that clearly identifies the objectives, indicators and expected outcomes of each operation. Following consideration by the Tasking and Coordination Group, the proposal is submitted for approval by the Executive Director. Member States subsequently attend a planning meeting in which the project is outlined. Member States are invited to take part in a hosting or participatory capacity.[90]

A Project Manager is appointed to develop the Operational Plan in consultation with participating Member States. A primary role is reserved to the Member State hosting the operation. The plan provides practical information including information on the legal status and executive powers of guest officers as well as how to deal with media inquiries.[91]

While Frontex co-finances the costs of the joint operation, the salaries of guest officers remain the responsibility of the Member States.[92] The host Member State assumes liability for civil damage caused by guest border guards during their operations.[93] However, where such damage is caused by gross negligence or wilful misconduct, the host Member Sate may seek to recover costs from the State from which the guest officer was deployed.[94] The host

---

[86] Art. 3.
[87] Frontex, External evaluation conducted on the basis of Art. 33 of the Frontex Regulation by COWI, published in January 2008 ("Frontex Evaluation Report"), at p.34.
[88] Art. 3(1), first indent.
[89] Arts. 2(1)(a) and 8.
[90] Frontex Evaluation Report, p.34.
[91] Frontex Evaluation Report. pp. 34 and 36.
[92] Frontex Evaluation Report, p.34.
[93] Art. 10b (1) as inserted by Art. 12(6) of the Border Teams Regulation.
[94] Art. 10b (2) as inserted by Art. 12(6) of the Border Teams Regulation.

Member State's rules of criminal liability will apply if offences are committed by or against guest border guards.[95] Once the Operation Plan has been completed, the relevant Frontex Operations division (sea, land or air) coordinates planning and the gathering of operational and background information.[96]

2.1.3. *Implementation of Joint Operations at External Borders*

Joint border operations are coordinated by the Agency's Operations Division.[97] A Frontex Coordinator is appointed to lead a Project Team at the location of the joint operation. The Frontex Coordinator is charged with monitoring, in conjunction with the local border guard authorities, cooperation between the guest officers and hosting organisations. The Frontex Coordinator is also responsible for keeping Frontex management and the Member States informed on progress of the operation. If difficulties or unexpected problems emerge, the Frontex Coordinator will take immediate action and inform the Frontex Situation Centre.[98]

A Frontex Analyst is assigned to each joint operation in order to facilitate the smooth operation of the reporting system in place. The Analyst collects and processes the daily report and any incident reports. The analyst drafts an analytical assessment at the end of the operation.[99]

The Frontex Situation Centre co-ordinates the exchange of information during land and air border joint operations. It supports and monitors joint operations and manages emergency situations.[100] In sea operations, this function is carried out by the International Coordination Centre.[101]

2.1.4. *Evaluation of Joint Operations*

The results of any joint operations and pilot projects are to be evaluated and analysed with a view to enhancing the quality, coherence and efficiency of future operations and projects.[102]

---

[95] Art. 10c as inserted by Art. 12(6) of the Border Teams Regulation.

[96] Frontex Evaluation Report, p.35.

[97] See section 3 of this chapter for an overview of the Internal Organisation of Frontex.

[98] Frontex Evaluation Report, p.35.

[99] Frontex Evaluation Report, p.35.

[100] Joint Operation Hammer 2008 was the first operation to test and utilise the newly established Frontex Situation Centre over an extended period of time. The Centre provided daily situation reports to National Frontex Points of Contact (NFPOC), airport border authorities and Frontex management. – See "Beyond the Frontiers – Frontex: The first five years", published by Frontex (Warsaw, 2010), p.49.

[101] Frontex Evaluation Report, p.35.

[102] Art. 3. The agreed amending regulation introduces a 60 day time limit for conducting the evaluation.

According to the Frontex evaluation report, there is widespread interest among Member States to participate in joint operations as it is considered to contribute to the development of a uniform approach to border management and the establishment of personal networks across countries, which in turn facilitates official and informal consultation and information exchange.[103]

2.1.5. *Joint Operations at Air, Land and Sea Borders – Developments and Examples*

Frontex has to date co-ordinated a number of joint operations aimed at detecting illegal border crossings into the EU at land, air and sea borders.

Land Border Operations

Recent Land border operations include "Unity 2010", "Focal Points 2009", "Uranus 2009", "Jupiter 2009", "Saturn 2009" (part of the Poseidon Programme), "Neptune 2009", "Good Will 2009" and Northern Light 2009", "Mercury 2009" and "Long Overstayers 2009".[104] "Unity 2010" was hosted by Lithuania and Poland and took place over a fifteen day period in June 2010. The operation involved participation of Austria, Estonia, Finland, Germany, Latvia, Lithuania, Norway and Poland. The objective of the operation is stated to strengthen the security of the eastern EU borders by exchanging operation information between the participating States and the Russian Federation and Republic of Belarus. In addition, border control and surveillance experts were deployed at external EU land borders.[105]

"Euro 2008" took place during the UEFA European Football championship 2008, hosted jointly by Austria and Switzerland in June 2008.[106] The aim of the operation was to prevent illegal immigrants from entering the territory of the Union in the guise of football supporters. The operation also sought to prevent trafficking and to detect forged visas and travel documentation.[107] According to the Frontex Evaluation Report, Operation Euro 2008 was co-hosted by Austria, Switzerland, Slovenia, Hungary, Slovakia and Poland.

---

[103] Frontex Evaluation Report, p. 36.
[104] Examples of accomplished operations are published on the Frontex web-site: http://www .frontex.europa.eu/examples_of_accomplished_operati/page5.html. In relation to each operation, the table specifies the date, duration, objective, host and participating Member States, region, and budget. Land-border operations in 2008 include "Poseidon (Land Borders) 2008", "Lynx 2008", "Kras 2008", "Gordius 2008", "Drive in 2008", "JO Focal Points 2008", "Eurocup 2008", "Herakles 2008", "Five Borders 2008", "Ariadne 2008".
[105] Details available on the Frontex web-site at: http://www.frontex.europa.eu/examples_of _accomplished_operati/art110.html
[106] Frontex Evaluation Report, p. 37.
[107] Frontex Evaluation Report, p. 37.

Twenty-two Member States as well as Croatia, Turkey and Russia participated. As part of the operation guest officers were deployed to the external borders of Austria and Switzerland and selected airports. Documentation experts were deployed to embassies and airports of participating countries. A Frontex Situation Centre co-ordinated activities in cooperation with Headquarters in Vienna and Bern. The operation is claimed to have facilitated the smooth travel of football supporters and eased delays at border crossing points.[108]

Air Border Operations
Examples of recent Air border operations include "Hubble 2010", "Operation Hammer", "Argonauts Pilot Project 2008", "Silence 2008" and "Agelaus". "Operation Hammer" has taken place annually since its introduction in 2008. It is stated to constitute a new approach to combating illegal entry through the external air borders of the Union.[109] Previously operations had been confined to a relatively small number of airports,[110] and experience showed that irregular migrants or traffickers either temporarily suspended travel or operated through different airports. Operation Hammer sought to increase the intensity of air border operations, so that its scope was regional rather than merely local.[111]

Hammer 2008 comprised of five operational phases and took place between August 2008 and March 2009.[112] Each operational phase lasted approximately two weeks and was followed by a period of analysis.[113] As part of Hammer 2008, 233 experts composed of Frontex joint support teams, guest officers and special advisors from 25 States were deployed to 189 different locations selected on the basis of risk analysis.[114] Additionally 115 airports participated in a reporting exercise coordinated by the Frontex Situation Centre. The operation covered 95% to 99% of non Schengen flights at each location.[115]

---

[108] Frontex Evaluation Report, p. 37.
[109] "Beyond the Frontiers – Frontex: The first five years", published by Frontex (Warsaw, 2010), pp. 45–47. See also the Frontex General Report 2008, p. 23.
[110] Prior to Operation Hammer 2008, the maximum number of airports targeted by Frontex had been 27 – "Beyond the Frontiers – Frontex: The first five years", published by Frontex (Warsaw, 2010), p. 49.
[111] "Beyond the Frontiers – Frontex: The first five years", published by Frontex (Warsaw, 2010), p. 46.
[112] Frontex Evaluation Report, p. 39.
[113] http://www.frontex.europa.eu/examples_of_accomplished_operati/art111.html. See also Frontex Evaluation Report, p. 39.
[114] "Beyond the Frontiers – Frontex: The first five years", published by Frontex (Warsaw, 2010), p.48 and the Frontex General Report 2008, p. 23.
[115] "Beyond the Frontiers – Frontex: The first five years", published by Frontex (Warsaw, 2010), p.48 and the Frontex General Report 2008, p. 23.

Through this operation, Frontex claims to have received extensive information on illegal migration which was not previously available for risk analysis –
particularly in relation to illegal migration at smaller European airports and
the involvement of 'low cost' carriers in this field.[116] Frontex reported that in
the first three phases of this operation 762 illegal migrants were detected,
resulting in 695 refusals of entry. Moreover, 71 forged documents were identified.[117] The experience gained through previous operations was used to determine the location of future operational phases.[118]

Other operations include "Hubble 2010", which focused on large third
country national air transport hubs identified by the risk analysis unit.
Operation Agelaus targeted the trafficking of minors in Central Europe.[119]

Sea Border Operations
Recent Sea Operations include "EPN-Hera 2009 (extension) 2010", "Poseidon
2009 (extension 2010)", "Zeus 2009", "Poseidon 2009", "Minerva 2008", "Hera
2008", "Nautilus 2008", "Poseidon (sea part) 2008" and "Hermes 2008".[120]

Operation Hera 2006, the Agency's first major sea operation, was launched
with the aim of preventing illegal immigration across the external sea borders
of the EU from West African countries disembarking in the Canary Islands.[121]
Hera 2006 was the first operation carried out in cooperation with a third
country.[122] As part of the operation's first phase (Hera I), experts were deployed
to the Canary Islands to assist Spanish authorities in interviewing migrants
who had succeeded in reaching the islands. Hera II was launched within a
month and entailed the operation of patrol boats, planes and helicopters off
the shores of West Africa to prevent immigration at source.[123] Senegalese and
Mauritian officials involved in the operation had authority for intercepting
and returning boats. Hera operations have resumed in subsequent years.

The Agency's maritime strategy included the development of a systematic
European network of patrols that would cover the Union's southern maritime

---

[116] Frontex General Report 2008, p. 23.
[117] Frontex General Report 2008, p. 24.
[118] Frontex Evaluation Report, p.40.
[119] "Beyond the Frontiers – Frontex: The first five years", published by Frontex (Warsaw, 2010),
p.45–47. See also the Frontex General Report 2008, p. 51.
[120] Details of accomplished operations are available on the Website of Frontex at: http://www
.frontex.europa.eu/examples_of_accomplished_operati
[121] "Beyond the Frontiers – Frontex: The first five years", published by Frontex (Warsaw, 2010),
pp. 45–47. See also the Frontex General Report 2008, p. 31.
[122] Ibid.
[123] "Beyond the Frontiers – Frontex: The first five years", ibid. See also the Frontex General
Report 2008, p. 33.

border. On the basis of preliminary studies undertaken,[124] Frontex designed a system whereby 8 participating Member States (Portugal, Spain, France, Italy, Slovenia, Malta, Greece and Cyprus) were able to co-ordinate patrol vessels. The European Patrol Network became operational as of May 2007.[125]

2.1.6. *Joint Return Operations*
The tasks conferred on Frontex include providing assistance and support for organising the return of third country nationals who have no legal basis upon which to remain in the territory of the EU.[126] The Agency is required to identify best practices on the implementation of return operations.[127] It may also assist in the financing of such operations.[128]

The return of third country nationals is carried out within the framework of a number of different Union instruments.[129] Member States initiating return flights are able to communicate details of such flights to other Member States through a web-based information network known as "ICO-Net".[130] While overall responsibility for return flights rests with the initiating Member State, the operation may be coordinated by Frontex and the Agency's staff may be present on board the flight. On occasion, the Agency has sent an advance party to the return flight destination.[131]

---

[124] In furtherance of this objective, Frontex launched the "MEDSEA" and "BORTEC" studies to examine the feasibility of improving co-ordinated monitoring of the Mediterraean and to establish a surveillance system covering the entire southern maritime border and the open sea beyond. – "Beyond the Frontiers – Frontex: The first five years", ibid. See also the Frontex General Report 2008, p. 39.

[125] "Beyond the Frontiers – Frontex: The first five years", ibid, pp. 45–47. See also the Frontex General Report 2008, p. 41.

[126] Arts. 2(1)(f) and 9.

[127] Art. 9(2).

[128] Art. 9(2). See also the Frontex General Report 2008, p. 14.

[129] Directive 2008/115 (the "Returns Directive": OJ 2008 L 348/98). See also: Directive 2001/40 on the mutual recognition of decisions on the expulsion of third country nationals (OJ 2001 L 10/75); Directive 2003/110 on assistance in cases of transit for the purposes of removal by air (OJ 2003 L 321/26); Decision 2004/573 on the organisation of joint flights for removals from the territory of two or more Member States, of third-country nationals who are subjects of individual removal orders (OJ 2004 L 261/28); and Decision No 575/2007 establishing the European Return Fund (OJ 2007 L 144/45). On this legislation, see volume 2 of this book.

[130] The Information and Coordination Network for Member States' Migration Management Services (ICOnet) was established by Decision 2005/267/EC (OJ 2005 L 83/48). See Art. 2(2)(d) of the Decision.

[131] Frontex Evaluation Report, p. 58.

As part of the returns operations, task forces from third countries are invited to Member States intending to deport immigrants. Members of the task force interview returnees with a view to establishing their identities.[132] Joint return operations must be carried out in accordance with the Community Returns Policy.[133]

The Agency's budget and operational capacity in relation to return operations has increased significantly in recent years. In 2009, the number of completed joint and co-financed joint returns doubled from 802 to 1622 returnees and from 15 to 32 joint return operations, involving nearly all Member States and Schengen associated countries.[134]

2.1.7. *Technical and Operational Support – Joint Support Team and Rapid Border Intervention Teams*

A further task entrusted to Frontex is the provision of technical and operational assistance in monitoring and protecting external borders.[135] Frontex is able to provide assistance through the provision of Frontex Joint Support Teams (FJSTs), composed of expert border guards deployed during operations coordinated by Frontex.[136] In a situation of urgent and exceptional pressure, Member States may request the deployment of Rapid Border Intervention Teams (RABITs).[137] In addition, the Agency maintains a central record of technical equipment belonging to Member States that is made available for control and surveillance of external borders.[138] The record, referred to as CRATE, specifies the type of equipment available, the authority responsible for such equipment, the time needed to make it available, the time during which the equipment can be used and possible limitations in usage.[139]

Rapid Border Intervention Teams were established by the Border Teams Regulation and are composed of national border guards nominated by Member States.[140] The profile and number of border guards to be made available to form part of such teams is determined by the Agency's Management

---

[132] Frontex Evaluation Report, p. 58.
[133] Recital 11 in the preamble.
[134] Frontex General Report 2009.
[135] Arts. 2(e) and 8.
[136] Frontex Joint Support Teams were established by the Executive Director in May 2008 on the basis of Art. 25(3)(b), which authorises the Director to take all necessary steps, including the adoption of internal administrative instructions and the publication of notices, to ensure the functioning of the Agency in accordance with the provisions of the Regulation.
[137] Art. 8a, inserted by Art. 12(5) of the Border Teams Regulation.
[138] Art. 7.
[139] Frontex Evaluation Report, pp. 53–54.
[140] Art. 8b, inserted by Art. 12(5) of the Border Teams Regulation.

Board by a three-quarters' majority on the basis of a proposal submitted by the Executive Director.[141] According to the Agency's web-site, Border Team members must have several years of border control experience at international airports, external sea borders or external land borders, as well as a working knowledge of English. Core competences include knowledge of surveillance, border checks, second line interviewing, threat and risk analysis and advanced document expertise. Optional skills include, leadership, profiling of risk travellers, detection of stolen cars, dog handling, radar operation, operating infra-red or thermal cameras, operating four wheel cars, knowledge of law of the sea, experience in checking trains and vessels, containers and buses and knowledge of additional languages.[142] Following a request by the Agency, Member States are required to communicate immediately the number, names and profiles of border guards that may be put at the Agency's disposal within five days.[143] Member States may, however, be exempted from this obligation in circumstances where they are experiencing an exceptional situation substantially affecting the discharge of national tasks.[144] Member States retain autonomy over the selection of staff and the duration of deployment.[145]

The Agency's Pooled Resources Unit, part of the Agency's Capacity Building Division, is charged with implementing the Border Teams Regulations.[146] To this end, the Unit established a "Rapid Pool Register" containing the names and skill profiles of individuals nominated by Member States for participation in Rapid Border Teams missions.[147] There are between 500 and 600 specialised border guards available for deployment.[148]

Deployment of Rapid Border Teams is required to take place within the framework of an Operational Plan agreed by the Agency's Executive Director and the Member State requesting assistance.[149] The plan includes the description of the situation and the objectives of the deployment.[150] It is also required to set out the anticipated duration of the deployment, the geographical area of deployment and the tasks and special instructions for team members.

---

[141] Art. 4(2) of the Border Teams Regulation.
[142] The list of basic qualifications, core competencies and optional skills were published by Frontex on their web-site in a "Quick Guide Rabit" at: <http://www.frontex.europa.eu/rabit_2010/background_information/>.
[143] Art. 8b, inserted by Art. 12(5) of the Border Teams Regulation.
[144] Art. 4(3) of the Border Teams Regulation.
[145] Art. 4(3) of the Border Teams Regulation.
[146] Frontex Evaluation Report, p. 52.
[147] Frontex Evaluation Report, p. 52.
[148] "Quick Guide Rabit" at http://www.frontex.europa.eu/rabit_2010/background_information/.
[149] Art. 8e(1), inserted by Art. 12(5) of the Border Teams Regulation.
[150] Art. 8e(1)(a), inserted by Art. 12(5) of the Border Teams Regulation.

Such tasks or instructions may deal with permissible consultation of databases, use of service weapons, ammunition and equipment.[151] The Operational Plan also sets out the composition of the teams, the names and ranks of the host Member State's border teams and technical equipment to be deployed.[152]

Member States are required to establish a national contact point for all communications with the Agency on matters relating to the Rapid Border Teams. They must be contactable at all times.[153] The Executive Director appoints one or more experts from the staff of the Agency to act as coordinating officer, who is required to act as the interface between the Agency and the host Member State as well as between the Agency and members of the teams. The Coordinating officer is tasked with providing assistance on issues relating to the conditions for deployment.[154] The Coordinator may also be called upon to assist with resolving any disagreement on the execution of the operational plan and deployment of the teams.[155] The Coordinator may only receive instructions from the Agency.[156]

During the Operation, Rapid border teams receive instructions from the host Member State in accordance with the Operational Plan.[157] However, the Agency is entitled to express views on instructions issued, and the host Member State is required to take such views into consideration.[158]

In the performance of their duties, members of the Rapid Border Teams are required to wear their national uniform and a blue armband with the insignia of the European Union and the Agency.[159] They must carry an accreditation document specifying their name, nationality, rank and which features a recent digitalised photograph.[160]

Rapid Border Teams are conferred with the requisite capacity to carry out border checks or border surveillance in accordance with the Borders Code.[161] Such tasks must be performed in accordance with instructions received from border guards of the host State and, as a general rule, in their presence.[162]

---

[151] Art. 8e(1)(b) to (d), inserted by Art. 12(5) of the Border Teams Regulation.
[152] Art. 8e(1)(e) to (g), inserted by Art. 12(5) of the Border Teams Regulation.
[153] Art. 8f, inserted by Art. 12(5) of the Border Teams Regulation.
[154] Art. 8g(2)(a) to (d), inserted by Art. 12(5) of the Border Teams Regulation.
[155] Art. 8g(3), inserted by Art. 12(5) of the Border Teams Regulation.
[156] Art. 8g(4), inserted by Art. 12(5) of the Border Teams Regulation.
[157] Art. 5(1) of the Border Teams Regulation.
[158] Art. 5, paras. 1 and 2 of the Border Teams Regulation.
[159] Art. 6(4) of the Border Teams Regulation.
[160] Arts. 6(4) and 8 of the Border Teams Regulation.
[161] Art. 6(1) of the Border Teams Regulation.
[162] Art. 6(3) of the Border Teams Regulation.

Border Team members may carry service weapons and equipment in accordance with the laws applicable to the border service of which they form part.[163] Nevertheless, the host Member State retains a right to prohibit the carrying of arms provided such prohibition applies equally to host State border guards.[164]

Rapid Border Team members may be authorised to use force, including use of service weapons, with consent by the host Member State and the State from which they have been deployed, presumably to be given in advance.[165] Any force, must, however, be exercised in the presence of border guards of the host Member State and in accordance with the national law of that State.[166] Nevertheless, these conditions do not restrict the use of weapons for purposes of legitimate self-defence or for the defence of members of the team or other persons.[167] Rapid Border team members are required at all times to respect human dignity fully, to act proportionately and avoid discrimination.[168]

The Member States hosting Rapid Border Teams may authorise such teams to consult its national and European databases necessary for border checks and surveillance.[169] Only databases required for performing tasks may be consulted. In advance of the deployment of the teams, the Member State shall inform the Agency as to the databases that may be consulted. The Agency subsequently makes this information available to all Member States participating in the deployment.[170] Consultation of databases is subject to Union and national data protection law.[171]

Members of Rapid Border teams remain border guards of their home Member States and their salaries continue to be paid by them.[172] The Agency, however, is required to provide a daily subsistence allowance to team members.[173] In addition, the Agency assumes a number of costs that Member States incurred in making personnel available to serve in Rapid Border Teams. Such costs include travel costs, vaccination costs, insurance and health care and costs related to the Agency's technical equipment.[174] The host State may assume

---

[163] Art. 6(5) of the Border Teams Regulation.
[164] Art. 6(5) of the Border Teams Regulation.
[165] Art. 6(6) of the Border Teams Regulation.
[166] Art. 6(6) of the Border Teams Regulation.
[167] Art. 6(7) of the Border Teams Regulation.
[168] Art. 6(2) of the Border Teams Regulation.
[169] Art. 6(8) of the Border Teams Regulation.
[170] Art. 6(8) of the Border Teams Regulation.
[171] Art. 6(9) of the Border Teams Regulation.
[172] Art. 7(1) of the Border Teams Regulation.
[173] Art. 7(3) of the Border Teams Regulation.
[174] Art. 8h, as inserted by Art. 12(5) of the Border Teams Regulation.

civil liability for damage caused by Rapid Border Teams operating in that Member State.[175] In case of gross negligence or wilful misconduct, the host Member State may seek to recover sums paid from the relevant home Member State. Disputes regarding this provision may be referred to the Court of Justice of the European Union.[176] Damages caused to the Agency's equipment during deployment not caused by gross negligence or wilful misconduct will be assumed by the Agency, without prejudice to any rights it may have against third parties.[177]

Border guards made available to the RAPID pool, are required to participate in advanced training relevant to their functions as well as exercises organised by the Agency. To maintain deployment capability, Frontex organises regular training exercises and simulations based on realistic scenarios.

The first deployment of Rapid Border Teams occurred in October 2010 following a request by the Greek Minister of Citizen Protection. The Border Teams were deployed to the land border between Greece and Turkey. As part of this operation a total of 175 guest officers were deployed from 24 Member States and Schengen associated countries. At the time of the request, Greece accounted for 90% of all illegal border crossings to the European Union. Frontex estimates that by the end of November 2010 there had been an overall decrease of 43.7% in the number of irregular migrants intercepted. By decision dated 3 December 2010, the deployment was extended until March 2011.[178]

2.1.8. *Risk Analysis*

Risk analysis is considered to be the "driver" of the Agency's operational activities and is central to the planning and implementation of joint operations.[179] Data collected by the Risk Analysis Unit is used to determine whether or not the Operations division will proceed to propose a joint operation. If a joint operation is launched, risk analysis will inform the development of the

---

[175] Art. 10 of the Border Teams Regulation.
[176] Art. 10(4) of the Border Teams Regulation.
[177] Art. 10(5) of the Border Teams Regulation.
[178] Frontex Press Releases dated 25 Oct. 2010, 26 Oct. 2010, 30 Nov. 2010 and 7 Dec. 2010, accessed on the Agency's web-site at: http://www.frontex.europa.eu/rabit_2010/news _releases/
[179] See section 2.1.2. above. See also Frontex Evaluation Report p.46 and Frontex General Report 2008, p.18. It has been described as the "inner core of the methodology of Frontex" by the Agency's Executive Director, General Laitinen – see *Frontex: the EU external borders agency*, published by the House of Lords, EU Committee, 9th Report of Session 2007–08, p.25.

operation. Moreover, once the joint operation has been completed and evaluated, the Risk Analysis Unit analyses the evaluation and circulates the results to Member States.[180] The results of risk analyses are to be applied in the development of the common core curriculum for the training of border guards.[181]

In addition to its role in joint operations, the Agency's Risk Analysis Unit is charged with providing strategic analytical products containing threat and risk assessments, developing methods, systems and procedures to achieve higher interoperability in the field of risk analysis, developing systematic collection of human intelligence for risk analysis.[182]

The Risk Analysis Unit produces both long and short term risk analyses, comprising an examination of threats, vulnerabilities and consequences.[183] For the purposes of longer term planning, the Risk Analysis Unit prepares a general annual risk analysis covering a period of 18 months.[184] This analysis constitutes an important basis for the identification of priorities and the development of the annual work programme.[185] It is moreover supplemented by semi-annual risk analysis.[186] Strategic short term risk analysis, is carried out on an interim basis, and is designed to ensure that the annual risk analysis is kept up to date and fit for use during the implementation of the work programme.[187] The Frontex Regulation expressly tasks the Agency with developing and applying a common integrated risk analysis model ("CIRAM").[188] As its title suggests, the CIRAM provides for a common foundation for risk analysis at Member State level. It was initially developed by a Council expert group in 2002. and is subject to continuous development and review.[189]

As part of its task in enhancing interoperability in risk analysis, the Risk Analysis Unit exchanges information with participating States within the framework of the Frontex Risk Analysis Network ("FRAN") composed of the risk analysis units of Member States and Schengen associated countries. It also manages other risk analysis networks such as the Western Balkan Risk Analysis Network ("WB-RAN") and the Eastern Borders Risk Analysis

---

[180] Frontex Evaluation Report, p.46.
[181] Art. 4, third indent.
[182] Frontex Annual Work Programme 2011, pp. 80 to 86.
[183] Frontex General Report 2008, p. 29.
[184] Frontex Evaluation Report, p. 46.
[185] Ibid.
[186] Frontex General Report 2008, p. 18.
[187] Frontex Evaluation Report, p. 46.
[188] Arts. 2(c) and 4.
[189] According to the Frontex Evaluation Report, p. 47, CIRAM was updated by Frontex and Member States in 2007. Moreover, Frontex envisages the rolling out of a 2010 version of the model as part of its 2011 Work Programme.

Network ("EB-RAN"), and has been set the objective of establishing an intelligence community in Africa.[190] In addition, the Risk Analysis Unit has been set the task of maintaining and developing analytical tools, including open source subscriptions, analytical date collection/processing tools and software available for analysts and relevant operational users in Frontex and Member States.[191] To promote the concept of "interoperability", Frontex launched the FronBAC project with the aim of developing a set of overarching analytical standards that will apply to the Agency and analysts from all Member States. The project involves the preparation of structural guidelines and seeks to promote joint training of analysts.[192]

In order to enhance its Risk Analysis capabilities, the Agency launched the "Frontex Intelligence Support Officers" ("FISO") pilot project in September 2008.[193] As part of the project, FISO offices were established in three strategic areas at the external borders of Southern Member States, namely, Madrid, Rome and Athens. The offices constitute a peripheral tool for intelligence gathering and are staffed by analytical experts, intelligence officers and intelligence experts whose tasks include preparing, implementing and evaluating Frontex joint operations.[194]

The challenges in carrying out risk analysis includes the difficulty of estimating unknown numbers, such as the number of undetected illegal crossings in a particular area, referred to in statistics as the dark number problem.[195] According to the Frontex Evaluation Report, 95% of what is discovered during sea operations has already been predicted by the Risk Analysis Unit.[196]

2.2. Research Activities

The Frontex Regulation requires the Agency to follow up on the development of research relevant for the control and surveillance of external borders and to disseminate such research to the Commission and to the Member States.[197] To this end, the Agency has established a Research and Development Unit that forms part of the Capacity Building Division. Research tasks undertaken

---

[190] Frontex Annual Work Programme 2011, p. 85.
[191] Frontex Annual Work Programme 2011, p. 85.
[192] Frontex General Report 2008, p. 31. See also the Frontex Annual Work Programme 2011, p. 86.
[193] Frontex General Report 2008, p. 29.
[194] Frontex General Report 2008, p. 30.
[195] Frontex Evaluation Report, p. 47.
[196] Frontex Evaluation Report, p. 48.
[197] Arts. 2(d) and 6.

include identification and development of best practices in the field of border control and the carrying out cost-benefit analyses on new border surveillance technology.[198] The Unit cooperates with policy makers in the European Commission and Member States, including DG Justice Freedom and Security (now DG Home Affairs) and DG Enterprise and Industry. It also works closely with EU research institutes.[199] In the context of its mandate to disseminate information, the Research and Development Unit organises workshops and seminars with participation from industry, Member States, research institutes and end-users.

2.3. Training Activities

Frontex is tasked with developing and implementing a common core curriculum for the training of border guards. It is also responsible for training, at a European level, instructors of national border guards of Member States.[200] Frontex provides additional specialised training in areas such as air crew training, dog handlers' training, escort leaders for joint returns training, detection of stolen vehicles training, Rapid Border Teams training, training in the field of trafficking of human beings, training in the field of falsified documents training, fundamental rights training and specialised English terminology training.[201] Training sessions for mid-level officers have focussed on leadership, management styles and operational activities including application of the Borders Code.[202] While certain training programmes are developed and implemented by staff at Frontex, most activities are outsourced to partnership academies or external experts.[203]

Frontex also maintains training support networks and developed Virtual Aula ("V-Aula"), an online resource for border guards about border guards, intended to be used for self-training purposes.[204] Access to the tool is limited to law enforcement agencies. It is designed to store relevant information concerning border management systems in the EU, in Schengen associated

---

[198] Frontex Evaluation Report, pp. 49 to 50 and the Frontex Annual Work Programme 2011, p. 92.
[199] Frontex Evaluation Report, p. 49.
[200] Arts. 2(b) 5 of the Frontex Regulation. According to the Frontex General Report 2009, the Agency reached its goal of harmonising national training and education for border guards through 153 specific training courses and seminars as well as through implementing common training tools in Member States via training coordinators.
[201] Annual Work Programme 2011, pp. 95–96 and the Frontex General Report 2008, p. 32.
[202] Frontex General Report 2008, p. 32.
[203] Frontex Evaluation Report, p. 44.
[204] Frontex General Report 2009, p. 29.

countries and in States which have signed working arrangements with Frontex. In particular, details are stored relating to the history, technical equipment, structure, co-operation and contact information of border management agencies.[205]

2.4. *Cooperation with Europol, International Organisations and Third Countries*

Article 13 of the Frontex Regulation authorises the Agency to cooperate with Europol and International organisations competent in matters covered by the Regulation by way of working arrangements concluded with those bodies. Such arrangements must be entered into in accordance with the relevant provisions of the Treaty and the provisions on the competence of those bodies. Pursuant to Article 14 of the Frontex Regulation, the Agency may conclude working arrangements with the authorities of third countries that are competent in matters relevant to the Regulation.

Frontex has entered into working arrangements with a number of international organisations in the area of migration and fundamental rights including Europol, the United Nations High Commissioner for Refugees ("UNHCR"), the International Organisation for Migration ("IOM"), The European Maritime Safety Agency ("EMSA"), Interpol, the International Centre for Migration Policy Development ("ICMPD") and the European Police College ("CEPOL").

The Agency has also concluded working arrangements with the competent authorities of 13 third countries, namely the Russian Federation, Ukraine, Moldova, Georgia, the Former Yugoslav Republic of Macedonia ("FYROM"), Serbia, Albania, Bosnia and Herzegovina, the United States, Montenegro, Belarus and Canada, as well as with the CIS Border Troop Commanders Council and the MARRI Regional Centre in the Western Balkans. As of March 2011, the Agency is in various stages of negotiations with Turkey, Libya, Morocco, Senegal, Mauritania, Egypt, Brazil and Nigeria.[206]

Frontex considers operational co-operation with third countries as an integral part of the Frontex Mission and an indispensable tool for combating illegal migration and cross-border crime. Co-operation agreements with the competent authorities of third countries typically cover areas such as information exchange, risk analysis, training, research and development, joint operations and pilot projects.[207]

---

[205] Ibid.
[206] See Frontex Web-site, "External Relations": <http://www.frontex.europa.eu/external_relations/>.
[207] See ibid.

3. *Overview of Organisational and Management Structure*

Frontex is governed by a Management Board and by an Executive Director, the respective functions of which is set out in the Frontex Regulation.

3.1. *The Management Board*

The Management Board provides strategic direction to the Agency through the adoption of an annual work programme.[208] The Management Board also prepares an annual report that gives an account of the work undertaken by the Agency in the preceding year.[209] The Board carries out various budgetary functions, establishes the organisational structure of Frontex and adopts the Agency's staffing policy. It is responsible for appointing the Executive Director and Deputy Director from candidates proposed by the Commission.

The Management Board is composed of one representative and one alternate of each Member State.[210] Iceland, Norway, Switzerland and Liechtenstein in their capacity as Schengen associates each also have a representative (and an alternate) on the Board with limited voting rights.[211] The Commission has two representatives (each with an alternate) on the Board.[212] The duration of the term of office on the Management Board is four years and a term may be renewed once.[213] Members of the Management Board are appointed on the basis of their degree of high level relevant and expertise in the field of operational cooperation on border management.[214] The Management Board elects a Chairperson and a Deputy Chairperson from among its members. The terms for both officers are two years and the terms are renewable once.

3.2. *The Executive Director*

The Executive Director is responsible for the day to day management of the Agency. The Director is afforded independence in the performance of his or her duties.[215] He develops work programmes and activities for consideration

---

[208] Art. 20(2)(c). In 2009, the Management Board adopted the first multi-annual plan covering activities for the period 2010 to 2013 – Frontex General Report 2009.

[209] Art. 20(2)(b).

[210] Art. 21(1).

[211] Art. 21(3).

[212] Art. 21(1).

[213] Art. 21(1).

[214] Art. 21(2).

[215] Art. 25(1).

and adoption by the Management Board.[216] Once the annual work programme has been adopted by the Board, the Executive Director is responsible for ensuring its implementation within the limits specified by the Regulation, its implementing rules and applicable law.[217] The Executive Director is also authorised to act as appointing authority on behalf of the Agency,[218] and is required to prepare estimates of the Agency's revenue and expenditure for the year ahead.[219] The Executive Director is authorised to take all necessary steps, including the adoption of internal administrative instructions and the publication of notices, to ensure the functioning of the Agency in accordance with the Frontex Regulation.[220] Article 25(f) of the Frontex Regulation provides that the Executive Director may delegate his or her powers to other members of the Agency subject to the provisions of the rules of procedure.

The Executive Director is proposed by the Commission and appointed by the Management Board.[221] The Executive Director is to be appointed on the grounds of merit and documented administrative and management skills as well as his or her relevant experience in managing external borders.[222] The Management Board also appoints a Deputy Executive Director whose function is to assist the Executive Director in the performance of his duties, and to replace the Executive Directive in the event that he or she is absent or indisposed.

3.3. *Organisational Structure*

The Executive Director is assisted by "Executive Support" and "Specialist Support" teams. The Executive Support team is composed of the Directors Aide de Camp and personal assistants.[223] The Specialist Support comprises of special advisors on external relations, strategic development, planning and controlling, quality management, transparency and information.[224]

---

[216] Art. 25(3)(c).
[217] Art. 25(3)(a).
[218] Arts. 25(d) and 17(2). As a result of these provisions, the Executive Director can act as "appointing authority" within the meaning of the Staff Regulations of officials of the European Union.
[219] Art. 29(3).
[220] Art. 25(3)(b).
[221] Art. 20(2)(a).
[222] Art. 26(2).
[223] Frontex Evaluation Report, p. 23.
[224] Ibid.

In addition, the Agency is composed of three divisions: (1) Operations division (2) Capacity Building division and (3) Administration. Each division is headed by a divisional director.[225]

The Operations division comprises three units: the Operations unit, the Risk Analysis Unit and the Frontex Situation Centre. The Capacity Building division comprises three units: the Training unit, the Pooled Resources unit, the Research and Development unit. The Administration Division is composed of the Finance and Procurement, Administrative Services and Legal Affairs units.

3.4. Staff

Since commencing operations in October 2005, Frontex has experienced rapid growth in staff numbers. At the end of its first year of operation, Frontex employed 43 individuals.[226] By the end of 2009, the Agency employed a staff of 226 people.[227] In addition to recruiting staff directly, Frontex hosts a number of national experts on secondment from participating States.[228] The staff of the Agency are employed under the terms of the Staff Regulations for Officials and Temporary Agents of the Union.[229]

3.5. Budget

The Agency's Annual Budget is adopted by the Management Board. Since its establishment, the Agency's budget has increased significantly. In 2006, the Agency's Annual Budget totalled €19.1 million. In 2009, the Agency's budget amounted to €88.2 million.[230]

Frontex receives funding from a number of different sources. Such sources include a subsidy from the Union, contributions from Schengen associated countries and income from fees paid for services provided. Member States may also make voluntary contributions.[231]

In 2009, joint operations accounted for over 70% of the Agency's budget. Within the operational budget, 55% of funds were committed to maritime

---

[225] Published on the Agency's web-site at: <http://www.frontex.europa.eu/structure/>.
[226] Frontex Evaluation Report, p. 24.
[227] Frontex General Report 2009, p. 24.
[228] Frontex General Report 2009, p. 49. See also the Frontex Evaluation Report, p. 24.
[229] Art. 17.
[230] Frontex General Report 2009, p. 22.
[231] Art. 29(1).

operations. Training was allocated 11%. Return co-operation and land border operations were each allocated 9% of the operational budget.[232]

4. *Assessment of Frontex Activities in Light of Member States' International Protection Obligations*

4.1. *International Protection Obligations of EU Member States*

International human rights, refugee law and Union law establish a number of different mechanisms whereby individuals fearing persecution may seek protection in another State. The cornerstone of international protection law is the principle of *non-refoulement*, that is, the prohibition on sending individuals to territories in which they face a real risk of suffering torture, inhuman or degrading treatment or other serious harm. Such prohibition is enshrined in a number of international legal instruments including the 1951 Geneva Convention,[233] the UN Convention against Torture[234] and the International Covenant on Civil and Political Rights.[235] Moreover, the European Court of Human Rights has repeatedly held that contracting States are prohibited from sending individuals into a situation where they would be exposed to violations of fundamental rights.[236] In the context of Article 3 of the European Convention on Human Rights, this prohibition is absolute.[237]

The right to asylum is enshrined in the Union legal order by virtue of Article 18 of the EU Charter of Fundamental Rights, which following the entry into

---

[232] Frontex General Report 2009, p. 22.

[233] Art. 33(1) of the United Nations Convention relating to the Status of Refugees, opened for signature 28 July 1951, 189 UNTS 137 (entered into force 22 April 1954).

[234] Art. 3 of the Convention against torture and other cruel, inhuman or degrading treatment or punishment, opened for signature 10 December 1984, 1465 UNTS 85 (entered into force 26 June 1987).

[235] International Covenant on Civil and Political Rights, opened for signature 16 December 1966, 999 UNTS 172 (entered into force 23 March 1976). See in particular Art. 7 as interpreted by the Human Rights Committee: General Comment No. 20 (forty-forth session, 1992), paragraph 9. For examples of the principle in other instruments, see: Art. 22(8) of the 1969 American Convention on Human Rights; Art. 5 of the 1981 African Charter on the Protection of Human Rights and Peoples' Rights; and 1949 Fourth Geneva Convention relative to the Protection of Civilian Persons in Time of War.

[236] *Soering v. the United Kingdom* (judgment of 7 July 1989, Series A no. 161), *Vilvarajah and Others v. the United Kingdom* (judgment of 30 October 1991, Series A no. 125); *Salah Sheekh v. the Netherlands* (no. 1948/04, § 135, ECHR 2007-I no.1948/04) and *M.S.S. v. Belgium and Greece* (no. 30696/09, judgment of 21 January 2011).

[237] *Saadi v. Italy* (no. 37201/06, judgment of 28 Feb. 2008).

force of the Lisbon Treaty, has the "same legal value" as the Treaties.[238] The Union legislature sought to give effect to the right to asylum through the adoption of the EU asylum *acquis*, including the Qualification Directive,[239] the Procedures Directive[240] and the Reception Conditions Directive.[241] The prohibition on refoulement is expressly referred to in Article 78 TFEU and enshrined in Article 19 of the Charter. The right to asylum and the prohibition of refoulement entails a right to seek or claim international protection. Therefore, international protection law prohibits interdiction, the practice whereby a State may seek to prevent an individual from reaching its territory in order to make a claim for asylum.[242]

The nature and extent to which international protection obligations apply to Frontex operations is not readily apparent. The question arises, for example, as to whether Frontex, as a Union body with a separate legal personality, is subject to international human rights and refugee law treaties to which Member States are party. Moreover, it is not evident whether such treaties would apply to Frontex agents operating outside the territorial jurisdiction of Member States and in areas designated as "high seas" under the International law of the Sea.

To put this question in context, however, it must be recalled that under the framework for the division of competences between the Union and Member States, competence over the control and management of borders remain with the Member States. Frontex plays a co-ordinating role to assist in effective border management. Therefore, the question concerning the nature of international protection obligation applicable to Frontex arises to the extent that acts

---

[238] Article 6(1) TEU Protocol 30 attached to the Treaties by the Lisbon Treaty seeks to limit the effect of the Charter as regards the United Kingdom and Poland. The impact of this Protocol is currently under consideration by the Court of Justice of the European Union in the context of a preliminary reference (Case C-493/10 *N.S*, pending).

[239] Council Directive 2004/83/EC of 29 April 2004 on minimum standards for the qualification and status of third country nationals or stateless persons as refugees or as persons who otherwise need international protection and the content of the protection granted (OJ 2004 L 304/12: the "Qualification Directive").

[240] Council Directive 2005/85/EC of 1 December 2005 on minimum standards on procedures in Member States for granting and withdrawing refugee status (OJ 2005 L 326/13).

[241] Council Directive 2003/9/EC of 27 January 2003 laying down minimum standards for the reception of asylum seekers (OJ 2003 L 31/18).

[242] See for example the 1967 Declaration of Territorial Asylum, A/RES/2312 (XXII) of 14 December 1967 and the OAU Convention Governing the Specific Aspects of Refugee Problems in Africa, UNTS. Vol. 1001 No. 14691. See also UN High Commissioner for Refugees, Executive Committee, Conclusion No. 6 (XXVIII).

relating to the surveillance and control of borders originate from decisions issued by Frontex acting in its own right and independently of Member States.

Pursuant to Article 78(1) TFEU, legislation adopted in furtherance of the asylum *acquis* is required to respect the 1951 Geneva Convention on Refugees and the Protocol of 31 January 1967. In including such a reference, the framers of the Treaty sought to ensure that the Union, although not itself a signatory to that Convention, when adopting measures in the field of borders, immigration and asylum control, would be required to do so in a manner that complies with Convention standards. This requirement may be understood in light of the fact that all Member States are parties to the Geneva Convention, and they would be liable to be in breach of their obligations under that Convention, were they to delegate powers affecting protection obligations imposed by that convention, to an entity that was not itself subject to equivalent standards.[243]

Moreover, it is manifest that following the entry into force of the Charter of Fundamental Rights of the EU, Frontex, as a Union body[244] is subject to its provisions. Therefore agents employed directly by Frontex are, at a minimum, obliged to carry out their functions in a manner that respects rights enshrined in the Charter. Moreover, secondary Union legislation governing the control and surveillance of external borders requires both national border guards and Frontex staff to respect fundamental rights norms in the performance of their duties. The Borders Code requires border guards to respect fully human dignity in the performance of their duties[245] and to undergo training in fundamental rights.[246] The Frontex Regulation asserts that it respects the fundamental rights and observes the principles recognised in what is now Article 6(3) TEU and which are reflected in the Charter of Fundamental Rights.[247] The Border Teams Regulation expressly states that the Regulation should be applied in accordance with the Member States' obligations as regards international protection and non refoulement.[248]

---

[243] See by analogy the judgment of the European Court of Human Rights in *Bosphorus Hava Yolları Turizm ve Ticaret Anonim Şirketi v. Ireland,* Application No. 45036/98, Judgment of 30 June 2005, paras 152 to 159.

[244] Art. 51 of the Charter.

[245] Art. 6(1) of the Borders Code.

[246] Arts. 15 and 16(4) of the Borders Code.

[247] Recital 22 in the preamble.

[248] Recital 17 in the preamble to the Border Teams Regulation. The fundamental rights framework governing Frontex operations is further reinforced in the agreed amending regulation. The principle of non-refoulement is also expressly referred to in the context of return operations, see Art. 5 of the Returns Directive (OJ 2008 L 348/98).

Insofar as geographical location is concerned, operations taking place within the territorial waters and contiguous zones of Member States remain subject to protection obligations under international human rights law and refugee law, as well as Union law.[249] In the zone known as the high seas, jurisdiction over a vessel is determined by the State whose flag the vessel flies and such jurisdiction may only be encroached in limited and exceptional circumstances.[250] However, if a vessel is found to have no flag, and therefore no nationality, it may be boarded and seized. In the event that a Frontex co-ordinated vessel were to take interception measures against such a vessel, there are compelling grounds for considering that, as a matter of international law, the State exercising effective control and authority assumes jurisdiction.[251] In the context of a Frontex operation, the jurisdiction of the Member State hosting the operation would apply,[252] and consequently the actions would be subject to international protection obligations applicable in the Host Member State. The question concerning the nature and extent of international protection obligations in the high seas, is currently the subject of consideration by the European Court of Human Rights in *Hirsi and Others v. Italy*.

From the perspective of Union law, the requirement for Frontex maritime operations to respect international protection obligations has been clarified by Council Decision 2010/252 relating to surveillance operations at the external sea borders of the Union. The Decision regulates operations that take place both within and beyond the territorial seas of Member States. Decision 2010/252 imposes an obligation on units participating in Frontex maritime operations to comply with the principle of non-refoulement and to conduct

---

[249] See Section 1, Art. 2 of the UN Convention on the Law of the Sea. Thus, for example, in *Refugees Without an Asylum Country*, 16 October 1979, No. 15 (XXX) - 1979, available at: http://www.unhcr.org/refworld/docid/3ae68c960.html, the Executive Committee found: "It is the humanitarian obligation of all coastal States to allow vessels in distress to seek haven in their waters and to grant asylum or at least temporary refuge, to persons on board wishing to seek asylum".

[250] See Art. 92 of the United Nations Convention on the Law of the Sea and Art. 11 of the 1958 Convention on the High Seas.

[251] See, for example, UN Human Rights Committee (HRC), General Comment no. 31 [80], The Nature of the General Legal Obligation Imposed on States Parties to the Covenant, 26 May 2004, CCPR/C/21/Rev.1/Add.13, para. 10, http://www.unhcr.org/refworld/pdfid/478b26ae2.pdf, cited in the submissions of the UNHCR in the case of *Hirsi and Others v. Italy* available at: http://www.unhcr.org/refworld/pdfid/4b97778d2.pdf.

[252] On the basis that control and management of borders still remain the competence of Member States, and the competence conferred on Frontex is limited to co-ordinating such control and management.

surveillance operations in a matter that respects fundamental rights,[253] and in doing so makes no distinction as to whether the operations are based within or beyond the territorial waters and contiguous zone of a Member State. The Decision does, however, specify that the asylum *acquis*, and in particular the Procedures Directive, only applies to applications for asylum made in the territory, including at the border, or in the transit zones of Member States.[254]

For the sake of completeness, it is worth recalling that a general obligation to render assistance to persons in distress at sea is imposed on States by a number of international legal instruments governing the law of the sea, including the UN convention on the law of the sea,[255] the International Convention on Safety of life at Sea[256] and the International Convention on Maritime Search and Rescue.[257]

Despite the language of fundamental rights used in EU secondary legislation, a number of non Governmental and International Organisations have expressed concerns that Frontex coordinated operations may put Member States in breach of their protection obligations. In submissions to the Home affairs sub-committee of the Select Committee on the European Union in the UK,[258] the Refugee Council and the European Council on Refugees and Exiles (ECRE) claimed that Frontex failed to demonstrate adequate consideration of international and European asylum and human rights law. They suggested the Agency's extra-territorial operations raised questions regarding jurisdiction, accountability and responsibility towards asylum seekers. It was further submitted that that the interdiction of all potential irregular entrants from physical access to the EU was indiscriminate and that the absence of specific measures to safeguard the rights of individuals potentially in need of protection undermined the right to seek asylum.

The Refugee Council and ECRE have proposed a number of recommendations designed to ensure that Frontex operations comply with international protection obligations. In particular, it is recommended that Frontex, be

---

[253] See Recitals 3 and 10 as well as Section 1 General Principles set out in Part 1 of Annex 1 of the Decision.

[254] See Recital 3 of the preamble to the Decision.

[255] Art. 98(1) of The United Nations Convention on the Law of the Sea, signed in Montego Bay on 10 Dec. 1982 ('UNCLOS'), entered into force on 16 Nov. 1994. It was approved on behalf of the European Community by Council Decision 98/392/EC of 23 March 1998 (OJ 1998 L 179, p. 1).

[256] International Convention on Safety of life at Sea; see Annex A, Chapter V, Regulation 33 of the Convention.

[257] The International Convention on Maritime Search and Rescue, 1979.

[258] *Frontex: the EU external borders agency*, published by the House of Lords, EU Committee, 9th Report of Session 2007–08, pp. 113–119.

required to demonstrate, how its activities comply fully with Member States obligations under International and European Union law. It is recommended that "Asylum Expert Teams" be deployed alongside RABIT officers. The organisations further suggest that a legal framework and mechanisms be established to ensure that Frontex can be held accountable for any breaches of international or European protection obligations. It has been further recommended that Frontex be subject to independent monitoring to ensure compliance with human rights standards.[259]

5. *Future Developments*

5.1. *Amendments to the Frontex Regulation*

On 24 February 2010, the Commission proposed the adoption of a Regulation amending the Frontex Regulation.[260] The proposal sought to clarify the Agency's mandate and adapt the Regulation in light of experience and evaluations carried out on the operation and functioning of the Agency. Following consideration of the Commission's proposal, the text of the amending regulation was agreed, in principle, by the European Parliament and Council in July 2011.[261]

The agreed amending regulation, to be adopted on the basis of Articles 74 and 77(2) (b) and (d) TFEU,[262] contains a number of measures designed to enhance the respect for fundamental rights and international protection obligations. Article 26a provides for the establishment of a Consultative Forum to assist the Agency's Director and Management Board in fundamental rights matters. The Consultative Forum is to comprise representatives of the European Asylum Support Office, the Fundamental Rights Agency, the United Nations High Commissioner for Refugees and other relevant organisations. The Forum is to be consulted on the development and implementation of the Agency's Fundamental Rights Strategy, Code of Conduct and Common Core Curriculum.[263]

The agreed amending regulation confers an overarching duty on the Agency to fulfil its tasks in full compliance with relevant Union law, including the

---

[259] Ibid., p. 115.
[260] COM (2010) 61, 24 Feb. 2010.
[261] Note 27 above.
[262] This represents a modification to the Commission's proposal according to which the Regulation was to be adopted on the basis Articles 74 and 77(1)(b) and (c) TFEU.
[263] Art. 26(a) of the agreed amending regulation.

Charter of Fundamental Rights of the European Union, international law, including the 1951 Geneva Convention, obligations related to access to international protection, in particular the principle of non-refoulement, and fundamental rights. In carrying out its functions, the Agency must also take into account reports prepared by the Consultative Forum.[264] The agreed amending regulation expressly prohibits disembarkation in contravention of the principle of non-refoulement and requires that the special needs of vulnerable persons be addressed in accordance with Union and international law.[265]

Article 2a of the agreed amending regulation provides for the elaboration of a Code of Conduct applicable to all of the Agency's operations and applicable to all persons participating in Frontex operations. The Code of Conduct is to lay down procedures intended to guarantee principles of the rule of law and the respect of fundamental rights with a particular focus on unaccompanied minors and vulnerable persons, as well as persons seeking international protection.[266]

The requirement for the development of the Code of Conduct is supplemented by an obligation on the Agency to ensure all border guards and personnel participating in Frontex operational activities shall, prior to such participation, have received training in relevant Union and international law, including fundamental rights and access to international protection and guidelines for the purpose of identifying persons seeking protection and directing them towards the appropriate facilities.[267] Member States that provide border guards for participation in Frontex operations are required to ensure appropriate disciplinary or other measures in accordance with their law in the event that fundamental rights or international protection obligations are violated in the course of such operations.[268]

In addition to strengthening the protection of fundamental rights, the agreed amending regulation seeks to expand the Agency's role in carrying out risk analyses and research as well as to enhance its systems for border surveillance and information exchange.[269]

Concerning risk analysis, the agreed amending regulation envisages the possibility for the Agency to evaluate the capacity of Member States to face

---

[264] Art. 1(2) of the agreed amending regulation.

[265] Art 2(1b) of the agreed amending regulation. This obligation also arises in the context of sea border surveillance, pursuant to points 1.2 and 1.3 of Council Decision 2010/252/EU referred to in Section 2 of this Chapter.

[266] Art. 2a of the agreed amending regulation.

[267] Art. 5 of the agreed amending regulation.

[268] Art. 3(1a) of the agreed amending regulation.

[269] Arts. 2(c), 2(d), 2(h) and 2(i) of the agreed amending regulation.

present and future threats and pressures at the external borders of the European Union, especially for those Member States facing specific and disproportionate pressures.[270] Moreover, it emphasises the requirement for thorough risk analysis to precede joint operations and pilot projects.[271] The agreed amending regulation also seeks to expand the Agency's research remit to encompass pro-actively monitoring and contributing to research relevant to the control and surveillance of external borders,[272] and charges the Agency with developing and operating information systems that enable swift and reliable exchanges of information regarding emerging risks at the external borders of the Union.[273] It is further envisaged that the Agency would provide assistance in developing and operating a European border surveillance system (to be known as "Eurosur") and developing a common information sharing environment.[274]

A significant innovation in the agreed amending regulation is the establishment of European Border Guard Teams. In addition to replacing Rapid Border Intervention Teams provided for under the Border Teams Regulations, the European Border Guard Teams will be available for deployment in joint operations and pilot projects. The agreed amending regulation specifies the procedure determining composition and deployment of such teams.[275]

The agreed amending regulation provides a legislative basis governing the elaboration of Operational Plans detailing organisational aspects of joint operations and pilot projects. Such plans are to be drawn up by the Executive Director and agreed with the host Member State. Each plan must contain a description of the situation and set out objectives of the deployment, modus operandi and the operation's foreseeable duration. It must also specify the tasks conferred on guest officers and include special instructions to such officers, for example, as regards databases that may be consulted, permissible service weapons, ammunition and equipment in the host Member State. The Operational Plan is also required to specify the composition of the teams of guest officers as well as command and control provisions. It must further outline technical equipment to be deployed, and set out detailed provisions on immediate incident reporting by the Agency to the Management Board and to relevant national public authorities. The Operational Plan is to include a

---

[270] Art. 4 of the agreed amending regulation.
[271] Art. 3(1) of the agreed amending regulation.
[272] Art. 6 of the agreed amending regulation.
[273] Art. (2)(h) and Art. 11 of the agreed amending regulation.
[274] Art. (2)(i) of the agreed amending regulation. For more on Eurosur, see chapter 6.
[275] Art. 3b of the agreed amending regulation.

reporting and evaluation scheme as well as modalities for co-operation with third countries, other European Union agencies and bodies or international organisations. In the context of sea operations, the Plan is required to provide specific information on the relevant jurisdiction and legislation in the geographical area where the joint operation takes place, with references to international and Union law regarding interception, rescue at sea and disembarkation.[276]

Concerning joint return operations, it is proposed that the Agency would, upon request, play a coordinating or organising role, as opposed to a mere supporting role as presently provided for in Article 2(f) of the Frontex Regulation. The agreed amending regulation requires the Agency to develop a specific Code of Conduct applicable to all joint return operations coordinated by the Agency. The Code of Conduct is to describe common standardised procedures with a view to simplifying the organisation of joint return operations and assuring return in a manner that respects fundamental rights, in particular the principles of human dignity, prohibition of torture and of inhuman or degrading treatment or punishment, right to liberty and security, the rights to the protection of personal data and non discrimination. The agreed amending regulation further requires that the Code of Conduct have particular regard to the obligation set out in the Returns Directive to provide for an effective forced-return monitoring system as well as to the contents of the Fundamental Rights Strategy provided for under Article 26a of the Regulation.[277]

Other amendments which will be introduced by the agreed amending regulation include additional and more detailed guidance on the acquisition and management of technical equipment to be deployed during joint operations, pilot projects, rapid interventions, return operations or technical assistance projects in accordance with the financial rules applicable to the Agency.[278] The agreed regulation will also introduce an express provision incorporating rules and principles on security, designed to ensure the protection of classified information as well as of non-classified sensitive information.[279]

Finally, the agreed amending regulation envisages the possibility that Frontex would finance or co-finance joint operations with grants from its budget in accordance with the financial rules applicable to the Agency.[280]

---

[276] Art. 3a of the agreed amending regulation.
[277] Art. 9 of the agreed amending regulation.
[278] Art. 7 of the agreed amending regulation.
[279] Art 11d of the agreed amending regulation.
[280] Art. 3(5) of the agreed amending regulation.

5.2. *Policy Developments*

Frontex operates in a rapidly changing political and legal environment. The Agency's operating structure and activities display a corresponding degree of flexibility and dynamism. The gradual strengthening of the Union's role in co-ordinating the surveillance and control of external borders has been mirrored in the successive augmentation of the Agency's resources and remit. It is likely that this trend will continue into the foreseeable future as amendments introduced by the Lisbon Treaty[281] combined with a number of policy initiatives[282] underscore the political priority afforded to the management and control of the Union's external borders.

It is equally apparent that successive legislative amendments have sought to reinforce the central place that the respect for fundamental rights and international protection norms occupies in Frontex operations. Such enhanced references to fundamental rights are to be welcomed and may even be considered necessary to ensure compliance with Union law. However, the Agency's motto, 'Freedom, Security and Justice' is liable to become imbued with a sense of irony worthy of Orwell, unless the Agency ensures that fundamental rights are afforded a corresponding degree of priority in practice.

---

[281] Art. 77 TFEU.

[282] The Stockholm Programme – An open and secure Europe serving and protecting citizens (OJ 2010 C 115/38). See Paragraphs 1.1, and in particular paragraph 5 of the Programme. See also the European Pact on Immigration and Asylum (Oct. 2008), including the Council conclusions on the follow-up of the Pact (Luxembourg, 3 June 2010). See also the European Council Conclusions of June and October 2009 and the Council Conclusions on 29 measures for reinforcing the protection of the external borders and combating illegal immigration (Justice and Home Affairs Council meeting, 25 and 26 Feb. 2010).

Annex

COUNCIL REGULATION (EC) No 2007/2004

of 26 October 2004

establishing a European Agency for the Management of Operational Cooperation at the External Borders of the Member States of the European Union

(OJ L 349, 25.11.2004, p. 1)

[as amended in 2007; original footnotes omitted]
*[agreed amendments from 2011 in **bold/italics**]*
[existing text that would be deleted by the 2011 amendments in brackets and strike-out][283]

THE COUNCIL OF THE EUROPEAN UNION,

Having regard to the Treaty establishing the European Community, and in particular Articles 62(2)(a) and 66 thereof,

Having regard to the proposal from the Commission,

Having regard to the opinion of the European Parliament,

Having regard to the opinion of the European Economic and Social Committee,

Whereas:

(1) Community policy in the field of the EU external borders aims at an integrated management ensuring a uniform and high level of control and surveillance, which is a necessary corollary to the free movement of persons within the European Union and a fundamental component of an area of freedom, security and justice. To this end, the establishment of common rules on standards and procedures for the control of external borders is foreseen.

(2) The efficient implementation of the common rules calls for increased coordination of the operational cooperation between the Member States.

(3) Taking into account the experiences of the External Borders Practitioners' Common Unit, acting within the Council, a specialised expert body tasked with improving the coordination of operational cooperation between Member States in the field of external border management should therefore be established in the shape of a European Agency for

---

[283] Note that there might be technical changes to the 2011 amendments before their final adoption.

the Management of Operational Cooperation at the External Borders of the Member States of the European Union (hereinafter referred to as the Agency).

(4) The responsibility for the control and surveillance of external borders lies with the Member States. The Agency should facilitate the application of existing and future Community measures relating to the management of external borders by ensuring the coordination of Member States' actions in the implementation of those measures.

(5) Effective control and surveillance of external borders is a matter of the utmost importance to Member States regardless of their geographical position. Accordingly, there is a need for promoting solidarity between Member States in the field of external border management. The establishment of the Agency, assisting Member States with implementing the operational aspects of external border management, including return of third-country nationals illegally present in the Member States, constitutes an important step in this direction.

(6) Based on a common integrated risk analysis model, the Agency should carry out risk analyses in order to provide the Community and the Member States with adequate information to allow for appropriate measures to be taken or to tackle identified threats and risks with a view to improving the integrated management of external borders.

(7) The Agency should provide training at European level for national instructors of border guards and additional training and seminars related to control and surveillance at external borders and removal of third-country nationals illegally present in the Member States for officers of the competent national services. The Agency may organise training activities in cooperation with Member States on their territory.

(8) The Agency should follow up on the developments in scientific research relevant for its field and disseminate this information to the Commission and to the Member States.

(9) The Agency should manage lists of technical equipment provided by the Member States, thereby contributing to the 'pooling' of material resources.

(10) The Agency should also support Member States in circumstances requiring increased technical and operational assistance at external borders.

(11) In most Member States, the operational aspects of return of third-country nationals illegally present in the Member States fall within the competencies of the authorities responsible for controlling external borders. As there is a clear added value in performing these tasks at European level, the Agency should, subject to the Community return policy, accordingly provide the necessary assistance for organising joint

return operations of Member States and identify best practices on the acquisition of travel documents and the removal of third-country nationals illegally present in the territories of the Member States.

(12) For the purpose of fulfilling its mission and to the extent required for the accomplishment of its tasks, the Agency may cooperate with Europol, the competent authorities of third countries and the international organisations competent in matters covered by this Regulation in the framework of working arrangements concluded in accordance with the relevant provisions of the Treaty. The Agency should facilitate the operational cooperation between Member States and third countries in the framework of the external relations policy of the European Union.

(13) Building upon the experiences of the External Borders Practitioners' Common Unit and the operational and training centres specialised in the different aspects of control and surveillance of land, air and maritime borders respectively, which have been set up by Member States, the Agency may itself create specialised branches responsible for dealing with land, air and maritime borders.

(14) The Agency should be independent as regards technical matters and have legal, administrative and financial autonomy. To that end, it is necessary and appropriate that it should be a Community body having legal personality and exercising the implementing powers, which are conferred upon it by this Regulation.

(15) The Commission and the Member States should be represented within a Management Board in order to control effectively the functions of the Agency. The Board should, where possible, consist of the operational heads of the national services responsible for border guard management or their representatives. This Board should be entrusted with the necessary powers to establish the budget, verify its execution, adopt the appropriate financial rules, establish transparent working procedures for decision making by the Agency and appoint the Executive Director and his/her deputy.

(16) In order to guarantee the full autonomy and independence of the Agency, it should be granted an autonomous budget whose revenue comes essentially from a contribution from the Community. The Community budgetary procedure should be applicable as far as the Community contribution and any other subsidies chargeable to the general budget of the European Union are concerned. The auditing of accounts should be undertaken by the Court of Auditors.

(17) Regulation (EC) No 1073/1999 of the European Parliament and of the Council of 25 May 1999 concerning investigations conducted by the European Anti-Fraud Office (OLAF) should apply without restriction to

the Agency, which should accede to the Interinstitutional Agreement of 25 May 1999 between the European Parliament, the Council of the European Union and the Commission of the European Communities concerning internal investigations by the European Anti-Fraud Office (OLAF).

(18) Regulation (EC) No 1049/2001 of the European Parliament and of the Council of 30 May 2001 regarding public access to European Parliament, Council and Commission documents should apply to the Agency.

(19) Regulation (EC) No 45/2001 of the European Parliament and of the Council of 18 December 2000 on the protection of individuals with regard to the processing of personal data by the Community institutions and bodies and on the free movement of such data (4) applies to the processing of personal data by the Agency.

(20) The development of the policy and legislation on external border control and surveillance remains a responsibility of the EU institutions, in particular the Council. Close coordination between the Agency and these institutions should be guaranteed.

(21) Since the objectives of this Regulation, namely the need for creating an integrated management of operational cooperation at the external borders of the Member States of the European Union, cannot be sufficiently achieved by the Member States and can therefore be better achieved at Community level, the Community may adopt measures, in accordance with the principle of subsidiarity as set out in Article 5 of the Treaty. In accordance with the principle of proportionality, as set out in that Article, this Regulation does not go beyond what is necessary in order to achieve those objectives.

(22) This Regulation respects the fundamental rights and observes the principles recognised by Article 6(2) of the Treaty on European Union and reflected in the Charter of Fundamental Rights of the European Union.

(23) As regards Iceland and Norway, this Regulation constitutes a development of the Schengen acquis within the meaning of the Agreement concluded by the Council of the European Union and the Republic of Iceland and the Kingdom of Norway concerning the association of those two States with the implementation, application and development of the Schengen acquis, which fall within the area referred to in Article 1, point A of Council Decision 1999/437/EC (5) on certain arrangements for the application of that Agreement. Consequently, delegations of the Republic of Iceland and the Kingdom of Norway should participate as members of the Management Board of the Agency, albeit with limited voting rights. In order to determine the further modalities allowing for the full

participation of the Republic of Iceland and the Kingdom of Norway in the activities of the Agency, a further arrangement should be concluded between the Community and these States.

(24) In accordance with Articles 1 and 2 of the Protocol on the position of Denmark annexed to the Treaty on European Union and to the Treaty establishing the European Community, Denmark is not taking part in the adoption of this Regulation and is not bound by it, or subject to its application. Given that this Regulation builds upon the Schengen acquis under the provisions of Title IV of Part Three of the Treaty establishing the European Community, Denmark should, in accordance with Article 5 of the said Protocol, decide within a period of six months after the Council has adopted this Regulation whether it will implement it in its national law or not.

(25) This Regulation constitutes a development of provisions of the Schengen acquis in which the United Kingdom does not take part, in accordance with Council Decision 2000/365/EC of 29 May 2000 concerning the request of the United Kingdom of Great Britain and Northern Ireland to take part in some of the provisions of the Schengen acquis. The United Kingdom is therefore not taking part in its adoption and is not bound by it or subject to its application.

(26) This Regulation constitutes a development of provisions of the Schengen acquis in which Ireland does not take part, in accordance with Council Decision 2002/192/EC of 28 February 2002 concerning Ireland's request to take part in some of the provisions of the Schengen acquis. Ireland is therefore not taking part in its adoption and is not bound by it or subject to its application.

(27) The Agency should facilitate the organisation of operational actions in which the Member States may avail themselves of the expertise and facilities which Ireland and the United Kingdom may be willing to offer, in accordance with modalities to be decided on a case-by-case basis by the Management Board. To that end, representatives of Ireland and the United Kingdom should be invited to attend all the meetings of the Management Board in order to allow them to participate fully in the deliberations for the preparation of such operational actions.

(28) A controversy exists between the Kingdom of Spain and the United Kingdom on the demarcation of the borders of Gibraltar.

(29) The suspension of the applicability of this Regulation to the borders of Gibraltar does not imply any change in the respective positions of the States concerned,

HAS ADOPTED THIS REGULATION:

CHAPTER I
SUBJECT MATTER

Article 1
Establishment of the Agency[284]

1. A European Agency for the Management of Operational Cooperation at the External Borders (the Agency) is hereby established with a view to improving the integrated management of the external borders of the Member States of the European Union.
2. While considering that the responsibility for the control and surveillance of external borders lies with the Member States, the Agency *as a body of the Union as defined in Article 15 and in accordance with Article 19 of this Regulation,* shall facilitate and render more effective the application of existing and future [Community] *European Union* measures relating to the management of external borders, *in particular the Schengen Borders Code.* It shall do so by ensuring the coordination of Member States' actions in the implementation of those measures, thereby contributing to an efficient, high and uniform level of control on persons and surveillance of the external borders of the Member States.

   The Agency shall fulfil its tasks in full compliance with the relevant Union law, including the Charter of Fundamental Rights of the European Union, international law, including the Convention Relating to the Status of Refugees of 28 July 1951 ("the Geneva Convention"), obligations related to access to international protection, in particular the principle of non-refoulement, and fundamental rights and taking into account the reports of the Consultative Forum referred to in Article 26a.

3. The Agency shall also provide the Commission and the Member States with the necessary technical support and expertise in the management of the external borders and promote solidarity between Member States, *especially those facing specific and disproportionate pressures.*

Article 1a
Definitions[285]

For the purposes of this Regulation, the following definitions shall apply:

---

[284] The original Art. 1(4) was repealed by Reg. 863/2007. It is now Art. 1a(1).
[285] This Art. was inserted by Reg. 863/2007.

1. 'external borders of the Member States' means the land and sea borders of the Member States and their airports and seaports, to which the provisions of Community law on the crossing of external borders by persons apply;

   1a. *"European Border Guard Teams" means for the purpose of Article 3, Article 3b, Article 3c, Article 8 and Article 17 teams to be deployed during joint operations and pilot projects, for the purpose of Articles 8a to 8g teams to be deployed for the rapid border interventions (hereinafter referred to as "rapid interventions)" within the meaning of Regulation (EC) No 863/2007 and for the purpose of Article 2(1)(ea) and (g) and Article 5 teams to be deployed during joint operations, pilot projects and rapid interventions*

2. 'host Member State' means a Member State [on the territory of] *in* which a [deployment of a Rapid Border Intervention Team or a] joint operation [or] a pilot project *or a rapid intervention* takes place *or from which it is launched*;

3. 'home Member State' means the Member State of which a member of the team or the guest officer is a border guard;

4. 'members of the teams' means border guards of Member States serving with the [Rapid Border Intervention Team] *European Border Guard Teams* other than those of the host Member State;

5. 'requesting Member State' means a Member State whose competent authorities request the Agency to deploy the Rapid Border Intervention Teams on its territory;

6. 'guest officers' means the officers of border guard services of Member States other than the host Member State participating in joint operations and pilot projects.

CHAPTER II
TASKS

Article 2
Main tasks[286]

1. The Agency shall perform the following tasks:

   (a) coordinate operational cooperation between Member States in the field of management of external borders;

   (b) assist Member States on training of national border guards, including the establishment of common training standards;

---

[286] Art. 2(1)(g) was inserted by Reg. 863/2007.

(c) carry out risk analyses, *including the assessment of the capacity of Member States to face threats and pressure at the external borders*;

(d) [~~follow up on~~] *participate in* the development of research relevant for the control and surveillance of external borders;

   (da) assist Member States in circumstances requiring increased technical and operational assistance at the external borders, taking into account that some situations may involve humanitarian emergencies and rescue at sea;

(e) assist Member States in circumstances requiring increased technical and operational assistance at external borders, *especially those Member States facing specific and disproportionate pressures*;

   (ea) set up European Border Guard Teams that are to be deployed during joint operations, pilot projects and rapid interventions;

(f) provide Member States with the necessary support [~~in organising~~] *including, upon request, coordination or organisation of* joint return operations;

(g) deploy [~~Rapid Border Intervention Teams to Member States in accordance with Regulation (EC) No 863/2007 of the European Parliament and of the Council of 11 July 2007 establishing a mechanism for the creation of Rapid Border Intervention Teams and amending Council Regulation (EC) No 2007/2004 as regards that mechanism and regulating the tasks and powers of guest officers~~] *border guards from the European Border Guard Teams to Member States in joint operations, pilot projects or in rapid interventions in accordance with Regulation (EC) No 863/2007.*

(h) develop and operate in accordance with Regulation (EC) No 45/2001 information systems that enable swift and reliable exchanges of information regarding emerging risks at the external borders, including the Information and Coordination Network established by Council Decision 2005/267/EC;

(i) provide the necessary assistance to the development and operation of a European border surveillance system and, as appropriate, to the development of a common information sharing environment, including interoperability of systems.

   1b. In accordance with Union and international law, no person shall be disembarked in, or otherwise handed over to the authorities of, a country in contravention of the principle of non-refoulement, or from which there is a risk of expulsion or return to another country in contravention of that principle. The special needs of children, victims of trafficking, persons in need of medical assistance, persons in need of international protection and other vulnerable persons shall be addressed in accordance with Union and international law.

2. Without prejudice to the competencies of the Agency, Member States may continue cooperation at an operational level with other Member States and/or third countries at external borders, where such cooperation complements the action of the Agency.

Member States shall refrain from any activity which could jeopardise the functioning of the Agency or the attainment of its objectives.

Member States shall report to the Agency on these operational matters at the external borders outside the framework of the Agency. *The Executive Director shall inform the Management Board on these matters on a regular basis and at least once a year.*

Article 2a
Code of Conduct

The Agency shall draw up and further develop a Code of Conduct applicable to all operations coordinated by the Agency. The Code of Conduct shall lay down procedures intended to guarantee the principles of the rule of law and the respect of fundamental rights with particular focus on unaccompanied minors and vulnerable persons, as well as persons seeking international protection, applicable to all persons participating in Frontex activities.

The Code of Conduct shall be developed in cooperation with the consultative forum referred to in Article 26a.

Article 3
Joint operations and pilot projects at *the* external borders

1. The Agency shall evaluate, approve and coordinate proposals for joint operations and pilot projects made by Member States*, including the requests of Member States related to circumstances requiring increased technical and operational assistance, especially in cases of specific and disproportionate pressures*.

   The Agency may itself [, and in agreement] *initiate and carry out joint operations and pilot projects in cooperation* with the Member State(s) concerned [, launch initiatives for joint operations and pilot projects in cooperation with] *and in agreement with the host* Member States.

   It may also decide to put its technical equipment at the disposal of Member States participating in the joint operations or pilot projects.

   Joint operations and pilot projects should be preceded by a thorough risk analysis.

1a. The Agency may also terminate, after informing the Member State concerned, joint operations and pilot projects if the conditions to conduct these initiatives are no longer fulfilled.

Participating Member States may request the Agency to terminate a joint operation or pilot project.

The home Member State shall provide for appropriate disciplinary or other measures in accordance with their law in case of violations of fundamental rights or international protection obligations in the course of such activities.

The Executive Director of the Agency shall suspend or terminate, in whole or in part, joint operations and pilot projects if it considers that violations concerned are of a serious nature or are likely to persist.

2. *The Agency shall constitute a pool of border guards called European Border Guard Teams in accordance with the provisions of Article 3b, for possible deployment during joint operations and pilot projects referred to in paragraph 1. It shall decide on the deployment of human resources and technical equipment in accordance with Articles 3a and 7.*

[2.] **3.** The Agency may operate through its specialised branches provided for in Article 16, for the practical organisation of joint operations and pilot projects.

[3.] **4.** The Agency shall evaluate the results of the joint operations and pilot projects and *transmit the detailed evaluation reports within 60 days following the end of the activity to the Management Board, together with the observations of the Fundamental Rights Officer referred to in Article 26a. The Agency shall* make a comprehensive comparative analysis of those results with a view to enhancing the quality, coherence and efficiency of future operations and projects to be included in its general report provided for in Article 20(2)(b).

[4.] **5.** The Agency [may decide to] *shall finance or* co-finance the operations and projects referred to in paragraph 1, with grants from its budget in accordance with the financial rules applicable to the Agency.

5a.   Paragraphs 1a and 5 shall apply to rapid interventions.

Article 3a
Organisational aspects of joint operations and pilot projects

1. *The Executive Director shall draw up an operational plan for activities referred to in Article 3(1). The Executive Director and the host Member State, in consultation with participating Member States, shall agree on the operational plan detailing the organisational aspects in due time before the envisaged beginning of the activity.*

The operational plan shall cover all aspects considered necessary for carrying out the joint operation or the pilot project, including the following:

(a) a description of the situation, with modus operandi and objectives of the deployment, including the operational aim;

(b) the foreseeable duration of the joint operation or pilot projects;

(c) the geographical area where the joint operation or pilot project will take place;

(d) description of the tasks and special instructions for the guest officers, including on permissible consultation of databases and permissible service weapons, ammunition and equipment in the host Member State;

(e) the composition of the teams of guest officers, as well as the deployment of other relevant staff;

(f) command and control provisions, including the names and ranks of the host Member State's border guards responsible for cooperating with the guest officers and the Agency, in particular those of the border guards who are in command during the period of deployment, and the place of the guest officers in the chain of command;

(g) the technical equipment to be deployed during the joint operation or pilot project, including specific requirements such as conditions for use, requested crew, transport and other logistics, and financial provisions;

(h1) detailed provisions on immediate incident reporting by the Agency to the Management Board and to relevant national public authorities;

(h2) a reporting and evaluation scheme containing benchmarks for the evaluation report and final date of submission of the final evaluation report in accordance with Article 3(4).

(i) regarding sea operations, specific information on the application of the relevant jurisdiction and legislation in the geographical area where the joint operation takes place, including reference to international and Union law regarding interception, rescue at sea and disembarkation;

(j) modalities of cooperation with third countries, other European Union agencies and bodies or international organisations.

2. *Any amendments to or adaptations of the operational plan shall require the agreement of the Executive Director and the host Member State. A copy of the amended or adapted operational plan shall immediately be sent by the Agency to the participating Member States.*

3. *The Agency shall, as part of its coordinating tasks, ensure the operational implementation of all the organisational aspects, including the presence of a staff member of the Agency during joint operations and pilot projects referred to in this Article.*

Article 3b
Composition and deployment of European Border Guard Teams

1. *On a proposal by the Executive Director, the Management Board shall decide by an absolute majority of its members with a right to vote on the profiles and the overall number of border guards to be made available for the European Border Guard Teams. The same procedure shall apply with regard to any subsequent changes in the profiles and the overall numbers. Member States shall contribute to the European Border Guard Teams via a national pool on the basis of the various defined profiles by nominating border guards corresponding to the required profiles.*

2. *The contribution by Member States as regards their border guards to specific operations for the coming year shall be planned on the basis of annual bilateral negotiations and agreements between the Agency and Member States. In accordance with these agreements, Member States shall make the border guards available for deployment at the request of the Agency, unless they are faced with an exceptional situation substantially affecting the discharge of national tasks. Such a request shall be made at least 45 days before the intended deployment. The autonomy of the home Member State in relation to the selection of staff and the duration of their deployment shall remain unaffected.*

3. *The Agency shall also contribute to the European Border Guard Teams with competent border guards seconded by the Member States as national experts pursuant to Article 17(5). The contribution by Member States as regards seconding their border guards to the Agency for the coming year shall be planned on the basis of annual bilateral negotiations and agreements between the Agency and Member States.*

    In accordance with these agreements, Member States shall make the border guards available for secondment, unless this would seriously affect the discharge of national tasks. In such situations Member States may recall their seconded border guards.

    The maximum duration of such secondments shall not exceed six months in a twelve month period. They shall, for the purpose of this Regulation, be considered as guest officers and have the tasks and powers referred to in Article 10. The Member State having seconded the border guards in question shall be considered as "home Member State" as defined in Article 1a(3) for the purpose of applying Articles 3c, 10, and 10b. Other staff employed by the Agency on a temporary basis who are not qualified to perform border control functions shall only be deployed during joint operations and pilot projects for coordination tasks.

4. *Members of the European Border Guard Teams shall, in the performance of their tasks and in the exercise of their powers, fully respect fundamental rights, including access to asylum procedures, and human dignity. Any measures taken in the performance of their tasks and in the exercise of their powers shall be proportionate to the objectives pursued by such measures. While performing their tasks and exercising their powers, they shall not discriminate against persons on grounds of sex, racial or ethnic origin, religion or belief, disability, age or sexual orientation.*

5. *In accordance with Article 8g the Agency will nominate a coordinating officer for each joint operation or pilot project where members of the European Border Guard Teams will be deployed.*

   The role of the coordinating officer shall be to foster cooperation and coordination amongst host and participating Member States.

6. *The Agency shall meet the costs incurred by the Member States in making their border guards available pursuant to paragraph 1 for the European Border Guard Teams in accordance with Article 8h.*

   6a. *The Agency shall inform the EP on an annual basis on the number of border guards that each Member State has committed to the European Border Guard Teams in accordance with this Article.*

Article 3c
Instructions to the European Border Guard Teams

1. *During deployment of European Border Guard Teams instructions to the teams shall be issued by the host Member State in accordance with the operational plan referred to in Article 3a (1).*

2. *The Agency, via its coordinating officer as referred to in Article 3b (5), may communicate its views on those instructions to the host Member State. If it does so, the host Member State shall take those views into consideration.*

3. *In accordance with Article 8g the host Member State shall give the coordinating officer all necessary assistance, including full access to the European Border Guard Teams at all times throughout the deployment.*

4. *Members of the European Border Guard Teams shall, while performing their tasks and exercising their powers, remain subject to the disciplinary measures of their home Member State.*

Article 4
Risk analysis

The Agency shall develop and apply a common integrated risk analysis model.

It shall prepare both general and tailored risk analyses to be submitted to the Council and the Commission.

For the purpose of risk analysis, the Agency may assess, after prior consultation with the Member State(s) concerned, their capacity to face upcoming challenges, including present and future threats and pressures at the external borders of the European Union, especially for those Member States facing specific and disproportionate pressures. To this end the Agency may assess the equipment and the resources of the Member States regarding border control. The assessment shall be based on information given by the Member State(s) concerned, and on the reports and results of joint operations, pilot projects, rapid interventions and other activities of the Agency. These assessments are without prejudice to the Schengen Evaluation Mechanism.

The results of these assessments shall be presented to the Management Board of the Agency. For these purposes Member States shall provide the Agency with all necessary information regarding the situation and possible threats at the external borders.

The Agency shall incorporate the results of a common integrated risk analysis model in its development of the common core curriculum for border guards' training referred to in Article 5.

Article 5
Training

The Agency shall provide border guards who are part of the European Border Guard Teams with advanced training relevant to their tasks and powers and shall conduct regular exercises with those border guards in accordance with the advanced training and exercise schedule referred to in the Agency's annual work programme.

The Agency shall also take the necessary initiatives to ensure that all border guards and other personnel of the Member States who participate in the European Border Guard Teams, as well as the staff of the Agency, shall, prior to their participation in operational activities organised by the Agency, have received training in relevant Union and international law, including fundamental rights and access to international protection and guidelines for the purpose of identifying persons seeking protection and directing them towards the appropriate facilities.

The Agency shall establish and further develop a common core curriculum for border guards' training and provide training at European level for instructors of the national border guards of Member States, *including with regard to fundamental rights and access to international protection and relevant maritime law.*

Training curricula shall be drawn up after consultation of the Consultative Forum referred to in Article 26a.

Member States shall integrate the common core curricula in the training of their national border guards.

The Agency shall also offer additional training courses and seminars on subjects related to the control and surveillance of the external borders and return of third country nationals for officers of the competent national services of Member States.

The Agency may organise training activities in cooperation with Member States on their territory.

The Agency shall establish an exchange programme enabling national border guards participating in the European Border Guard Teams to acquire knowledge or specific know-how from experiences and good practices abroad by working with border guards in a Member State other than their own.

Article 6
[~~Follow-up~~] *Monitor and contribute* to research

The Agency shall [~~follow up on~~] *proactively monitor and contribute to* the developments in research relevant for the control and surveillance of external borders and disseminate this information to the Commission and the Member States.

Article 7
[~~Management of~~] technical equipment

1. *The Agency may acquire, itself or in co-ownership with a Member State, or lease technical equipment for external border control to be deployed during joint operations, pilot projects, rapid interventions, return operations or technical assistance projects in accordance with the financial rules applicable to the Agency. Any acquisition or leasing of equipment entailing significant costs to the Agency shall be preceded by a thorough needs and cost/benefit analysis. Any such expenditure shall be provided for in the Agency's budget as adopted by the Management Board in accordance with Article 29(9). In case the Agency acquires or leases important technical equipment, such as open sea and coastal patrol vessels or vehicles, to be used in joint operations, the following provisions shall apply:*

  – *in case of acquisition and co-ownership, the Agency agrees formally with one Member State that the latter will provide for the registration of the equipment in accordance with the applicable legislation of that Member State;*
  – *in case of leasing, the equipment must be registered in a Member State.*
  Based on a model agreement drawn up by the Agency, the Member State of registration and the Agency shall agree on modalities ensuring the periods of full availability of the co-owned assets for the Agency, as well as on the terms of use of the equipment.

  The Member State of registration or the supplier of technical equipment shall provide the necessary experts and technical crew to operate the technical equipment in a legally sound and safe manner.

2. The Agency shall set up and keep centralised records of [~~technical equipment for control and surveillance of external borders belonging to Member States, which they, on a voluntary basis and upon request from another Member State, are willing to put at the disposal of that Member State for a temporary period following a needs and risks analysis carried out by the Agency~~] *equipment in a technical equipment pool composed of equipment owned either by the Member States or by the Agency and equipment co-owned by the Member States and the Agency for external border control purposes. The technical equipment pool shall contain a minimum number per type of technical equipment defined in accordance with paragraph 5 of this article. The equipment listed in the technical equipment pool shall be deployed during the activities referred to in Articles 3, 8a and 9.*

3. *Member States shall contribute to the technical equipment pool referred to in paragraph 2. The contribution by Member States to the pool and deployment of the technical equipment for specific operations shall be planned on the basis of annual bilateral negotiations and agreements between the Agency and Member States. In accordance with these agreements and to the extent that it forms part of the minimum number of equipment for a given year, Member States shall make their technical equipment available for deployment at the request of the Agency, unless they are faced with an exceptional situation substantially affecting the discharge of national tasks. Such requests shall be made at least 45 days before the intended deployment. The contributions to the technical equipment pool shall be reviewed annually.*

4. *The Agency shall manage the records of the technical equipment pool as follows:*
  (a) classification by type of equipment and by type of operation;
  (b) classification by owner (Member State, Agency, others);
  (c) overall numbers of required equipment;

(d) crew requirements if applicable;

(e) other information such as registration details, transportation and maintenance requirements, national applicable export regimes, technical instructions, or other relevant information to handle the equipment correctly.

5. *The Agency shall finance the deployment of the equipment which forms part of the minimum number of equipment provided by a given Member State for a given year. The deployment of equipment which does not form part of the minimum number of equipment shall be co-financed by the Agency up to a maximum of 100% of the eligible expenses taking into account the particular circumstances of the Member States deploying such equipment.*

The rules including the required overall minimum numbers per type of equipment, the conditions for deployment and reimbursement of costs shall be decided in accordance with Article 24 on a yearly basis by the Management Board on a proposal by the Executive Director. For budgetary purposes this decision should be taken by the Management Board by 31 March.

The minimum number of equipment shall be proposed by the Agency in accordance with its needs, notably be able to carry out joint operations, pilot projects, rapid interventions and return operations, in accordance with the work programme of the Agency for the year in question.

If the minimum number of equipment proves to be insufficient to carry out the operational plan agreed for joint operations, pilot projects, rapid interventions or return operations, it shall be revised by the Agency on the basis of justified needs and of an agreement between the Agency and the Member States.

6. *The Agency shall report on the composition and the deployment of equipment which is part of the technical equipment pool to the Management Board on a monthly basis. In case the minimum number of equipment referred to in paragraph 5 is not reached, the Executive Director shall inform the Management Board without delay. The Management Board shall take a decision on the prioritisation of the deployment of the technical equipment urgently and take the appropriate steps to remedy the identified shortcomings. It shall inform the Commission of the identified shortcomings and the steps taken. The Commission shall subsequently inform the European Parliament and the Council, together with its own assessment.*

6a. *The Agency shall inform the EP on an annual basis on the number of technical equipment that each Member State has committed to the pool in accordance with this Article.*

Article 8
Support to Member States in circumstances requiring increased technical and operational assistance at external borders[287]

1. Without prejudice to Article [64(2)] **78(3)** of the Treaty **on the Functioning of the European Union**, one or more Member States **facing specific and disproportionate pressures and** confronted with circumstances requiring increased technical and operational assistance when implementing their obligations with regard to control and surveillance of external borders may request the Agency for assistance. The Agency [can] **shall in accordance with Article 3** organise the appropriate technical and operational assistance for the requesting Member State(s).

2. Under the circumstances referred to in paragraph 1, the Agency can:
   (a) assist on matters of coordination between two or more Member States with a view to tackling the problems encountered at external borders;
   (b) deploy its experts to support the competent national authorities of the Member State(s) involved for the appropriate duration.
   (ba) deploy border guards from the European Border Guard Teams.

3. The Agency may acquire technical equipment for checks and surveillance of external borders to be used by its experts and within the framework of the [Rapid Border Intervention Teams for the duration of their deployment] **rapid interventions for their duration.**

Article 8a
Rapid [Border Intervention Teams] *Interventions*[288]

At the request of a Member State faced with a situation of urgent and exceptional pressure, especially the arrival at points of the external borders of large numbers of third-country nationals trying to enter the territory of that Member State illegally, the Agency may deploy for a limited period one or more [Rapid Border Intervention] **European Border Guard** Teams (hereinafter referred to as 'team(s)') on the territory of the requesting Member State for the appropriate duration, in accordance with Article 4 of Regulation (EC) No 863/2007.

Article 8b
Composition of teams

1. In the event of a situation as described in Article 8a, Member States shall, at the request of the Agency, immediately communicate the number, names

---

[287] Art. 8(3) was replaced by Reg. 863/2007.
[288] Arts. 8a to 8h were added by Reg. 863/2007.

and profiles of border guards from their national pool which they are able to make available within five days to be members of a team. Member States shall make the border guards available for deployment at the request of the Agency unless they are faced with an exceptional situation substantially affecting the discharge of national tasks.

2. When determining the composition of a team for deployment, the Executive Director shall take into account the particular circumstances which the requesting Member State is facing. The team shall be composed in accordance with the operational plan referred to in Article 8e.

Article 8c
Training and exercises

The Agency shall provide border guards who are part of the Rapid Pool, as referred to in Article 4(2) of Regulation (EC) No 863/2007 with advanced training relevant to their tasks and powers and shall conduct regular exercises with those border guards in accordance with the advanced training and exercise schedule referred to in the Agency's annual working programme.

Article 8d
Procedure for deciding on deployment of the teams

1. A request for deployment of the teams in accordance with Article 8a shall include a description of the situation, possible aims and envisaged needs for the deployment. If required, the Executive Director may send experts from the Agency to assess the situation at the external borders of the requesting Member State.
2. The Executive Director shall immediately inform the Management Board of a Member State's request for deployment of the teams.
3. When deciding on the request of a Member State, the Executive Director shall take into account the findings of the Agency's risk analyses as well as any other relevant information provided by the requesting Member State or another Member State.
4. The Executive Director shall take a decision on the request for deployment of the teams as soon as possible and no later than five working days from the date of the receipt of the request. The Executive Director shall simultaneously notify the requesting Member State and the Management Board in writing of the decision. The decision shall state the main reasons on which it is based.
5. If the Executive Director decides to deploy one or more teams, an operational plan shall immediately, *and in any event no later than 5 working days of the date of the decision,* be drawn up by the Agency and the requesting Member State in accordance with Article 8e.

6. As soon as the operational plan has been agreed, the Executive Director shall inform the Member States of the requested number and profiles of border guards which are to be deployed in the teams. This information shall be provided, in writing, to the national contact points designated under Article 8f and shall indicate the date on which the deployment is to take place. A copy of the operational plan shall also be provided to them.

7. If the Executive Director is absent or indisposed, the decisions related to the deployment of the teams shall be taken by the Deputy Executive Director.

8. Member States shall make the border guards available for deployment at the request of the Agency, unless they are faced with an exceptional situation substantially affecting the discharge of national tasks.

9. Deployment of the teams shall take place no later than five working days after the date on which the operational plan is agreed between the Executive Director and the requesting Member State.

Article 8e
Operational plan

1. The Executive Director and the requesting Member State shall agree on an operational plan detailing the precise conditions for deployment of the teams. The operational plan shall include the following:

   (a) description of the situation, with *modus operandi* and objectives of the deployment, including the operational aim;

   (b) the foreseeable duration of deployment of the teams;

   (c) the geographical area of responsibility in the requesting Member State where the teams will be deployed;

   (d) description of tasks and special instructions for members of the teams, including on permissible consultation of databases and permissible service weapons, ammunition and equipment in the host Member State;

   (e) the composition of the teams;

   (f) **command and control provisions, including** the names and ranks of the host Member State's border guards responsible for cooperating with the teams, in particular those of the border guards who are in command of the teams during the period of deployment, and the place of the teams in the chain of command;

   (g) the technical equipment to be deployed together with the teams [in accordance with Article 8], ***including specific requirements such as conditions for use, requested crew, transport and other logistics, and financial provisions.***

(h1) detailed provisions on immediate incident reporting by the Agency to the Management Board and to relevant national public authorities;

(h2) a reporting and evaluation scheme containing benchmarks for the evaluation report and final date of submission of the final evaluation report in accordance with Article 3(4).

(i) regarding sea operations, information on the application of the relevant jurisdiction and legislation in the geographical area where the joint operation takes place including references to international and Union law regarding interception, rescue at sea and disembarkation;

(j) modalities of cooperation with third countries, other European Union agencies and bodies or international organisations.

2. Any amendments to or adaptations of the operational plan shall require the agreement of both the Executive Director and the requesting Member State. A copy of the amended or adapted operational plan shall immediately be sent by the Agency to the participating Member States.

Article 8f
National contact point

Member States shall designate a national contact point for communication with the Agency on all matters pertaining to the teams. The national contact point shall be reachable at all times.

Article 8g
Coordinating Officer

1. The Executive Director shall appoint one or more experts from the staff of the Agency to be deployed as coordinating officer. The Executive Director shall notify the host Member State of the appointment.

2. The coordinating officer shall act on behalf of the Agency in all aspects of the deployment of the teams. In particular, the coordinating officer shall:

   (a) act as an interface between the Agency and the host Member State;

   (b) act as an interface between the Agency and the members of the teams, providing assistance, on behalf of the Agency, on all issues relating to the conditions for their deployment with the teams;

   (c) monitor the correct implementation of the operational plan;

   (d) report to the Agency on all aspects of the deployment of the teams.

3. In accordance with Article 25(3)f, the Executive Director may authorise the coordinating officer to assist in resolving any disagreement on the execution of the operational plan and deployment of the teams.

4. In discharging his duties, the coordinating officer shall take instructions only from the Agency.

Article 8h
Costs

1. The Agency shall fully meet the following costs incurred by Member States in making available their border guards for the purposes mentioned in Articles *3(2)*, 8a and 8c:
   (a) travel costs from the home Member State to the host Member State and from the host Member State to the home Member State;
   (b) costs related to vaccinations;
   (c) costs related to special insurance needs;
   (d) costs related to health care;
   (e) daily subsistence allowances, including accommodation costs;
   (f) costs related to the Agency's technical equipment.
2. Detailed rules concerning the payment of the daily subsistence allowance of members of the teams shall be established by the Management Board.

Article 9
Return cooperation

1. Subject to the [Community] return policy *of the Union, and in particular Directive 2008/115/EC and without entering into the merits of return decisions,* the Agency shall provide the necessary assistance [for organising] *and upon request of the participating Member States ensure the coordination or the organisation of* joint return operations of Member States, *including through the chartering of aircraft for the purpose of such operations. The Agency shall finance or co-finance the operations and projects referred to in this paragraph, with grants from its budget in accordance with the financial rules applicable to the Agency.* The Agency may *also* use [Community] financial means *of the European Union* available in the field of return. *The Agency shall ensure that in its grant agreements with Member States any financial support is conditional upon the full respect of the Charter of Fundamental Rights.*
2. *The Agency shall develop a Code of Conduct for the return of illegally present third-country nationals which shall apply during all joint return operations coordinated by the Agency, describing common standardized procedures which should simplify the organisation of joint return operations and assure return in a humane manner and in full respect for fundamental rights, in particular the principles of human dignity, prohibition of torture and of inhuman or degrading treatment or punishment, right to liberty and security, the rights to the protection of personal data and non discrimination.*

3. *The Code of Conduct will in particular pay attention to the obligation set out in Article 8(6) of Directive 2008/115/EC to provide for an effective forced-return monitoring system and to the Fundamental Rights strategy referred to in Article 26a(1). The monitoring of joint return operations should be carried out on the basis of objective and transparent criteria and should cover the whole joint return operation from the pre-departure phase until the handover of the returnees in the country of return.*

4. *Member States shall regularly inform the Agency of their needs for the assistance or coordination by the Agency. The Agency shall draw up a rolling operational plan to provide the requesting Member States with the necessary operational support, including technical equipment referred to in Article 7(1). The Management Board shall decide in accordance with Article 24 on a proposal of the Executive Director, on the content and modus operandi of the rolling operational plan.*

[2.] 5. The Agency shall *cooperate with competent authorities of the relevant third countries referred to in Article 14,* identify best practices on the acquisition of travel documents and the removal of illegally present third-country nationals.

Article 10
Tasks and powers of guest officers[289]

1. Guest officers shall have the capacity to perform all tasks and exercise all powers for border checks or border surveillance in accordance with Regulation (EC) No 562/2006 of the European Parliament and of the Council of 15 March 2006 establishing a Community Code on the rules governing the movement of persons across borders (Schengen Borders Code), and that are necessary for the realisation of the objectives of that Regulation.

2. While performing their tasks and exercising their powers guest officers shall comply with [Community] *Union and international* law, *in accordance with fundamental rights,* and the national law of the host Member State.

3. Guest officers may only perform tasks and exercise powers under instructions from and, as a general rule, in the presence of border guards of the host Member State.

4. Guest officers shall wear their own uniform while performing their tasks and exercising their powers. They shall wear a blue armband with the insignia of the European Union and the Agency on their uniforms, identifying

---

[289] Art. 10 was replaced by Reg. 863/2007.

them as participating in a joint operation or pilot project. For the purposes of identification vis-à-vis the national authorities of the host Member State and its citizens, guest officers shall at all times carry an accreditation document, as provided for in Article 10a, which they shall present on request.

5. By way of derogation from paragraph 2, while performing their tasks and exercising their powers, guest officers may carry service weapons, ammunition and equipment as authorised according to the home Member State's national law. However, the host Member State may prohibit the carrying of certain service weapons, ammunition and equipment, provided that its own legislation applies the same prohibition to its own border guards. The host Member State shall, in advance of the deployment of the guest officers, inform the Agency of the permissible service weapons, ammunition and equipment and of the conditions for their use. The Agency shall make this information available to Member States.

6. By way of derogation from paragraph 2, while performing their tasks and exercising their powers, guest officers shall be authorised to use force, including service weapons, ammunition and equipment, with the consent of the home Member State and the host Member State, in the presence of border guards of the host Member State and in accordance with the national law of the host Member State.

7. By way of derogation from paragraph 6, service weapons, ammunition and equipment may be used in legitimate self-defence and in legitimate defence of guest officers or of other persons, in accordance with the national law of the host Member State.

8. For the purpose of this Regulation, the host Member State may authorise guest officers to consult its national and European databases which are necessary for border checks and surveillance. The guest officers shall consult only those data which are required for performing their tasks and exercising their powers. The host Member State shall, in advance of the deployment of the guest officers, inform the Agency of the national and European databases which may be consulted. The Agency shall make this information available to all Member States participating in the deployment.

9. The consultation as referred to in paragraph 8 shall be carried out in accordance with Community law and the national law of the host Member State in the area of data protection.

10. Decisions to refuse entry in accordance with Article 13 of Regulation (EC) No 562/2006 shall be taken only by border guards of the host Member State.

Article 10a
Accreditation document[290]

1. The Agency shall, in cooperation with the host Member State, issue a document in the official language of the host Member State and another official language of the institutions of the European Union to guest officers for the purpose of identifying them and as proof of the holder's rights to perform the tasks and exercise the powers as referred to in Article 10(1). The document shall include the following features of the guest officer:
   (a) name and nationality;
   (b) rank; and
   (c) a recent digitised photograph.
2. The document shall be returned to the Agency at the end of the joint operation or pilot project.

Article 10b
Civil liability

1. Where guest officers are operating in a host Member State, that Member State shall be liable in accordance with its national law for any damage caused by them during their operations.
2. Where such damage is caused by gross negligence or wilful misconduct, the host Member State may approach the home Member State in order to have any sums it has paid to the victims or persons entitled on their behalf reimbursed by the home Member State.
3. Without prejudice to the exercise of its rights vis-à-vis third parties, each Member State shall waive all its claims against the host Member State or any other Member State for any damage it has sustained, except in cases of gross negligence or wilful misconduct.
4. Any dispute between Member States relating to the application of paragraphs 2 and 3 which cannot be resolved by negotiations between them shall be submitted by them to the Court of Justice of the European Communities in accordance with Article 239 of the Treaty.
5. Without prejudice to the exercise of its rights vis-à-vis third parties, the Agency shall meet costs related to damage caused to the Agency's equipment during deployment, except in cases of gross negligence or wilful misconduct.

---

[290] Arts. 10a to 10c were inserted by Reg. 863/2007.

Article 10c
Criminal liability

During the deployment of a joint operation or a pilot project, guest officers shall be treated in the same way as officials of the host Member State with regard to any criminal offences that might be committed against them or by them.

Article 11
Information exchange systems

The Agency may take all necessary measures to facilitate the exchange of information relevant for its tasks with the Commission and the Member States, *and, where appropriate, the European Agencies referred to in Article 13. It shall develop and operate an information system capable of exchanging classified information with these actors, including personal data referred to in Articles 11a, 11b and 11c.*

The Agency may take all necessary measures to facilitate the exchange of information relevant for its tasks with United Kingdom and Ireland if it relates to the activities in which they participate in accordance with Articles 12 and 20(5).

Article 11a
Data protection

Regulation (EC) No 45/2001 shall apply to the processing of personal data by the Agency.

The Management Board shall establish measures for the application of Regulation (EC) No 45/2001 by the Agency, including those concerning the Data Protection Officer of the Agency. These measures shall be established after the consultation of the European Data Protection Supervisor. Without prejudice to Articles 11b and 11c, the Agency may process personal data for administrative purposes.

Article 11b
Processing of personal data in the context of joint return operations

In accordance with the measures referred to in the second paragraph of Article 11a:
1. *In performing its task of the organization and coordination of joint return operations of Member States referred to in Article 9, the Agency may process personal data of persons who are subject to such joint return operations.*

2. *The processing of such personal data shall respect the principles of necessity and proportionality. In particular, it shall be strictly limited to those personal data which are required for the purposes of the joint return operation.*
3. *The personal data shall be deleted as soon as the purpose for which they have been collected has been achieved and no later than 10 days after the joint return operation.*
4. *In case the personal data are not transferred to the carrier by a Member State, the Agency may transfer such data.*

Article 11c
Processing of personal data collected during joint operations, pilot projects and rapid interventions

In accordance with the measures referred to in Article 11a:
1. *Without prejudice to the competence of Member States to collect personal data in the context of joint operations, pilot projects and rapid interventions and subject to the limitations set out in paragraphs 2 and 3, the Agency may further process personal data collected by the Member States during such operational activities and transmitted to the Agency in order to contribute to the security of the external borders of the Member States of the European Union.*
2. *Such further processing of personal data by the Agency shall be limited to personal data regarding persons who are suspected, by the relevant authorities of Member States, on reasonable grounds of involvement in cross-border criminal activities, in facilitation of illegal migration activities or in human trafficking activities as defined in Article 1(1)(a) and (b) of Council Directive 2002/90/EC.*
3. *Personal data referred to in paragraph 2 shall be further processed by the Agency only for the following purposes:*
   (a) Transmission, on a case by case basis, to Europol or other EU law enforcement agencies, subject to Article 13 of this Regulation.
   (b) Use for the preparation of risk analyses referred to in Article 4. In the result of the risk-analyses data shall be depersonalized.
4. *The personal data shall be deleted as soon as they have been transmitted to Europol or other European Agencies or used for the preparation of risk analyses referred to in Article 4. The term of storage shall in any event not exceed three months after the date of the collection of those data.*
5. *The processing of such personal data shall respect the principles of necessity and proportionality. The personal data shall not be used by Frontex*

for the purpose of investigations, which remain under the responsibility of the competent national authorities.

In particular, it shall be strictly limited to those personal data which are required for the purposes referred to in paragraph 3.

6. *Without prejudice to Regulation (EC) No 1049/2001, onward transmission or other communication of such personal data processed by the Agency to third countries or other third parties is prohibited.*

Article 11d
Security rules on the protection of classified information and non-classified sensitive information

1. *The Agency shall apply the Commission's rules on security as set out in the Annex to Commission Decision 2001/844/EC, ECSC, Euratom. This shall cover, inter alia, provisions for the exchange, processing and storage of classified information.*
2. *The Agency shall apply the security principles relating to the processing of non-classified sensitive information as adopted and implemented by the European Commission. The Management Board shall establish measures for the application of these security principles.*

Article 12
Cooperation with Ireland and the United Kingdom

1. The Agency shall facilitate operational cooperation of the Member States with Ireland and the United Kingdom in matters covered by its activities and to the extent required for the fulfilment of its tasks set out in Article 2(1).
2. Support to be provided by the Agency pursuant to Article 2(1)(f) shall cover the organisation of joint return operations of Member States in which Ireland or the United Kingdom, or both, also participate.
3. The application of this Regulation to the borders of Gibraltar shall be suspended until the date on which an agreement is reached on the scope of the measures concerning the crossing by persons of the external borders of the Member States.

Article 13
Cooperation with [Europol] European Union agencies and bodies and international organisations

The Agency may cooperate with Europol, *the European Asylum Support Office, the Fundamental Rights Agency, other European Union agencies and bodies,* and the international organisations competent in matters covered by this Regulation in the framework of working arrangements concluded with those bodies, in accordance with the relevant provisions of the Treaty and the provisions on the competence of those bodies. *In every case the Agency shall inform the European Parliament of any such arrangements.*

Onward transmission or other communication of personal data processed by the Agency to other European Union agencies or bodies shall be subject to specific working arrangements regarding the exchange of personal data and subject to the prior approval of the European Data Protection Supervisor.

The Agency may also, with the agreement of the Member State(s) concerned, invite observers of European Union agencies and bodies or international organisations to participate in its activities referred to in Articles 3, 4 and 5, to the extent that their presence is in accordance with the objectives of these activities, may contribute to the improvement of cooperation and the exchange of best practices, and does not affect the overall safety of the activities. The participation of those observers may take place only with the agreement of the Member States concerned regarding the activities referred to in Articles 4 and 5 and only with the agreement of the host Member State regarding those referred to in Article 3. Detailed rules on the participation of observers shall be included in the operational plan referred to in Article 3a(1). These observers shall receive the appropriate training from the Agency prior to their participation.

Article 14
Facilitation of operational cooperation with third countries and cooperation with competent authorities of third countries

1. In matters covered by its activities and to the extent required for the fulfilment of its tasks, the Agency shall facilitate the operational cooperation between Member States and third countries, in the framework of the European Union external relations policy, *including with regard to human rights.*

The Agency and the Member States shall comply with the norms and standards at least equivalent to those set by the EU legislation also when cooperation with third countries takes place on the territory of those countries.

The establishment of cooperation with third countries shall serve to promote European border management standards, also covering respect for fundamental rights and human dignity.

2. The Agency may cooperate with the authorities of third countries competent in matters covered by this Regulation in the framework of working arrangements concluded with these authorities, in accordance with the relevant provisions of the Treaty. *Those working arrangements shall be purely related to the management of operational cooperation.*

3. *The Agency may deploy its liaison officers, which should enjoy the highest possible protection to carry out their duties, in third countries. They shall form part of the local or regional cooperation networks of Member States' immigration liaison officers set up pursuant to Council Regulation No 377/2004. Liaison officers shall only be deployed to third countries in which border management practices respect minimum human rights standards. Their deployment shall be approved by the Management Board. Within the framework of the European Union external relations policy, priority for deployment should be given to those third countries, which on the basis of risk analysis constitute a country of origin or transit regarding illegal migration. On a reciprocal basis the Agency may receive liaison officers posted by those third countries also, for a limited period of time. The Management Board shall adopt, on a proposal of the Executive Director, the list of priorities on a yearly basis in accordance with the provisions of Article 24.*

4. *The tasks of the Agency's liaison officers shall include, in compliance with European Union law and in accordance with fundamental rights, the establishment and maintaining of contacts with the competent authorities of the third country to which they are assigned to with a view to contribute to the prevention of and fight against illegal immigration and the return of illegal migrants.*

5. *The Agency may benefit from Union funding in accordance with the provisions of the relevant instruments supporting the Union's external relations policy. It may launch and finance technical assistance projects in third countries regarding matters covered by this Regulation.*

6. *The Agency may also with the agreement of the Member State(s) concerned invite observers of third countries to participate in its activities referred to in Articles 3, 4 and 5, to the extent that their presence is in accordance with the objectives of these activities, may contribute to the improvement of cooperation and the exchange of best practices, and does not affect the overall safety of the activities. The participation of those observers may take place only with the agreement of the Member States concerned regarding the activities referred to in Articles 4 and 5 and only with the agreement of the host Member State regarding those referred to in Article 3. Detailed rules on the participation of observers shall be*

included in the operational plan referred to in Article 3a(1). These observ-
ers shall receive the appropriate training from the Agency prior to their
participation.

7. *When concluding bilateral agreements with third countries as referred to*
   in Article 2(2) Member States may include provisions concerning the role
   and competencies of the Agency, in particular regarding the exercise of
   executive powers by members of the teams deployed by the Agency during
   the activities referred to in Article 3.

8. *The activities referred to in paragraphs 2 and 3 shall be subject to receiv-*
   ing a prior opinion of the Commission, and the European Parliament
   shall be fully informed as soon as possible.

CHAPTER III
STRUCTURE

Article 15
Legal status and location

The Agency shall be a body of the [Community] *Union*.

It shall have legal personality.

In each of the Member States, the Agency shall enjoy the most extensive legal capacity accorded to legal persons under their laws. It may, in particular, acquire or dispose of movable and immovable property and may be party to legal proceedings.

The Agency shall be independent in relation to technical matters.

It shall be represented by its Executive Director.

The seat of the Agency shall be decided by unanimity of the Council.

Article 15a
Headquarters Agreement

The necessary arrangements concerning the accommodation to be provided
for the Agency in the Member State in which the Agency has its seat and the
facilities to be made available by that State, as well as the specific rules appli-
cable to the Executive Director, the Deputy Executive Director, the members
of the Management Board, the staff of the Agency and members of their fami-
lies, in that State shall be laid down in a Headquarters Agreement between
the Agency and the Member State in which the Agency has its seat. The
Headquarters Agreement shall be concluded after obtaining the approval of
the Management Board. The Member State in which the Agency has its seat

should provide the best possible conditions to ensure proper functioning of the Agency, including multilingual, European-oriented schooling and appropriate transport connections.

Article 16
Specialised branches

The Management Board of the Agency shall evaluate the need for, and decide upon the setting up of, specialised branches in the Member States, subject to their consent, taking into account that due priority should be given to the operational and training centres already established and specialised in the different aspects of control and surveillance of the land, air and maritime borders respectively.

The specialised branches of the Agency shall develop best practices with regard to the particular types of external borders for which they are responsible. The Agency shall ensure the coherence and uniformity of such best practices.

Each specialised branch shall submit a detailed annual report to the Executive Director of the Agency on its activities and shall provide any other type of information relevant for the coordination of operational cooperation.

Article 17
Staff

1. The Staff Regulations of officials of the European Communities, the Conditions of employment of other servants of the European Communities and the rules adopted jointly by the institutions of the European Communities for the purposes of applying those Regulations and Conditions shall apply to the Agency's staff.
2. The powers conferred on the appointing authority by the Staff Regulations, and by the Conditions of employment of other servants, shall be exercised by the Agency in respect of its own staff.
3. [~~The Agency's staff shall consist of a sufficient number of officials and of national experts in the field of control and surveillance of the external borders seconded by the Member States to carry out management duties. The remaining staff shall consist of other employees recruited by the Agency as necessary to carry out its tasks.~~] *For the purpose of implementing Article 3b(5) only an Agency's staff member subject to the Staff Regulations of Officials and to Title II of the Conditions of employment of other servants of the European Communities employed by the Agency can be designated*

as coordinating officer in accordance with Article 8g. For the purpose of implementing Article 3b(3) only national experts seconded by a Member State to the Agency can be designated to be attached to the European Border Guard Teams. The Agency shall designate those national experts that shall be attached to the European Border Guard Teams in accordance with that Article.

4. *The Management Board shall adopt the necessary implementing measures in agreement with the Commission pursuant to the arrangements provided for in Article 110 of the Staff Regulations of Officials of the Union.*

5. *The Management Board may adopt provisions to allow national experts from Member States to be seconded to the Agency. Those provisions shall take into account the requirements of Article 3b(2), in particular the fact that they are considered as guest officers and have the tasks and powers referred to in Article 10. They shall include provisions on the conditions of deployment.*

Article 18
Privileges and immunities

The Protocol on the privileges and immunities of the European Communities shall apply to the Agency.

Article 19
Liability

1. The contractual liability of the Agency shall be governed by the law applicable to the contract in question.

2. The Court of Justice of the European Communities shall have jurisdiction to give judgment pursuant to any arbitration clause contained in a contract concluded by the Agency.

3. In the case of non-contractual liability, the Agency shall, in accordance with the general principles common to the laws of the Member States, make good any damage caused by its departments or by its servants in the performance of their duties.

4. The Court of Justice shall have jurisdiction in disputes relating to compensation for the damage referred to in paragraph 3.

5. The personal liability of its servants towards the Agency shall be governed by the provisions laid down in the Staff Regulations or Conditions of employment applicable to them.

Article 20
Powers of the Management Board

1. The Agency shall have a Management Board.
2. The Management Board shall:
    (a) appoint the Executive Director on a proposal from the Commission in accordance with Article 26;
    (b) before 31 March each year, adopt the general report of the Agency for the previous year and forward it by 15 June at the latest to the European Parliament, the Council, the Commission, the European Economic and Social Committee and the Court of Auditors. The general report shall be made public;
    (c) before 30 September each year, and after receiving the opinion of the Commission, adopt, by a three-quarters majority of its members with a right to vote, the Agency's programme of work for the coming year and forward it to the European Parliament, the Council and the Commission; this programme of work shall be adopted according to the annual Community budgetary procedure and the Community legislative programme in relevant areas of the management of external borders;
    (d) establish procedures for taking decisions related to the operational tasks of the Agency by the Executive Director;
    (e) carry out its functions relating to the Agency's budget pursuant to Articles 28, 29(5), (9) and (11), Article 30(5) and Article 32;
    (f) exercise disciplinary authority over the Executive Director and over the Deputy Director, in agreement with the Executive Director;
    (g) establish its Rules of Procedure;
    (h) establish the organisational structure of the Agency and adopt the Agency's staffing policy *in particular the multi-annual staff policy plan. In accordance with the relevant provisions of the framework Financial Regulation for the bodies referred to in Article 185 of Council Regulation (EC, Euratom) No 1605/2002 the multi-annual staff policy plan shall be submitted to the Commission and the budgetary authority after receiving a favourable opinion of the Commission;*
    (i) adopt the Agency's Multi Annual Plan aiming at outlining the future long term strategy regarding the activities of the Agency.
3. Proposals for decisions on specific activities to be carried out at, or in the immediate vicinity of, the external border of any particular Member State shall require a vote in favour of their adoption by the Member of the Management Board representing that Member State.

4. The Management Board may advise the Executive Director on any matter strictly related to the development of operational management of the external borders, including [follow-up] *activities related* to research as defined in Article 6.

5. Should Ireland and/or the United Kingdom request to participate in the Agency's activities, the Management Board shall decide thereon.

   The Management Board shall take its decision on a case-by-case basis by an absolute majority of its members with a right to vote. In its decision, the Management Board shall consider if the participation of Ireland and/or the United Kingdom contributes to the achievement of the activity in question. The decision shall set out the financial contribution of Ireland and/or the United Kingdom to the activity for which a request for participation has been made.

6. The Management Board shall forward annually to the budgetary authority any information relevant to the outcome of the evaluation procedures.

7. The Management Board may establish an Executive Bureau to assist it and the Executive Director with regard to the preparation of the decisions, programmes and activities to be adopted by the Management Board and when necessary, because of urgency, to take certain provisional decisions on behalf of the Management Board.

Article 21
Composition of the Management Board

1. Without prejudice to paragraph 3, the Management Board shall be composed of one representative of each Member State and two representatives of the Commission. To this effect, each Member State shall appoint a member of the Management Board as well as an alternate who will represent the member in his/her absence. The Commission shall appoint two members and their alternates. The duration of the terms of office shall be four years. This term of office shall be extendable [once].

2. The Management Board members shall be appointed on the basis of their degree of high level relevant experience and expertise in the field of operational cooperation on border management.

3. Countries associated with the implementation, application and development of the Schengen acquis shall participate in the Agency. They shall have one representative and an alternate each in the Management Board. Under the relevant provisions of their association agreements, arrangements [will be] *have been* developed which [shall, *inter alia*,] specify the nature and extent of, and the detailed rules for, the participation by these countries in the work of the Agency, including provisions on financial contributions and staff.

Article 22
Chairmanship of the Management Board

1. The Management Board shall elect a Chairperson and a Deputy Chairperson from among its members. The Deputy Chairperson shall ex-officio replace the Chairperson in the event of his/her being prevented from attending to his/her duties.
2. The term of office of the Chairperson and Deputy Chairperson shall expire when their respective membership of the Management Board ceases. Subject to this provision, the duration of the terms of office of the Chairperson or Deputy Chairperson shall be two years. These terms of office shall be extendable once.

Article 23
Meetings

1. Meetings of the Management Board shall be convened by its Chairperson.
2. The Executive Director of the Agency shall take part in the deliberations.
3. The Management Board shall hold at least two ordinary meetings a year. In addition, it shall meet at the instance of the Chairperson or at the request of at least one third of its members.
4. Ireland and the United Kingdom shall be invited to attend the meetings of the Management Board.
5. The Management Board may invite any other person whose opinion may be of interest to attend its meetings as an observer.
6. The members of the Management Board may, subject to the provisions of its Rules of Procedure, be assisted by advisers or experts.
7. The secretariat for the Management Board shall be provided by the Agency.

Article 24
Voting

1. Without prejudice to Article 20(2)(c) as well as 26(2) and (4), the Management Board shall take its decisions by an absolute majority of its members with a right to vote.
2. Each member shall have one vote. The Executive Director of the Agency shall not vote. In the absence of a member, his/her alternate shall be entitled to exercise his/her right to vote.
3. The rules of procedure shall establish the more detailed voting arrangements, in particular, the conditions for a member to act on behalf of another member as well as any quorum requirements, where appropriate.

Article 25
Functions and powers of the Executive Director

1. The Agency shall be managed by its Executive Director, who shall be completely independent in the performance of his/her duties. Without prejudice to the respective competencies of the Commission, the Management Board and the Executive Bureau, the Executive Director shall neither seek nor take instructions from any government or from any other body.

2. The European Parliament or the Council may invite the Executive Director of the Agency to report on the carrying out of his/her tasks, *in particular on the implementation and monitoring of the Fundamental Rights Strategy, the general report of the Agency for the previous year, the work programme for the coming year and the Agency's multi-annual plan referred to in Article 20(i).*

3. The Executive Director shall have the following functions and powers:
   (a) to prepare and implement the decisions and programmes and activities adopted by the Agency's Management Board within the limits specified by this Regulation, its implementing rules and any applicable law;
   (b) to take all necessary steps, including the adoption of internal administrative instructions and the publication of notices, to ensure the functioning of the Agency in accordance with the provisions of this Regulation;
   (c) to prepare each year a draft working programme and an activity report and submit them to the Management Board;
   (d) to exercise in respect of the staff the powers laid down in Article 17 (2);
   (e) to draw up estimates of the revenues and expenditure of the Agency pursuant to Article 29, and implement the budget pursuant to Article 30;
   (f) to delegate his/her powers to other members of the Agency's staff subject to rules to be adopted in accordance with the procedure referred to in Article 20(2)(g).
   (g) Ensure the implementation of the operational plan referred to in Articles 3a and 8g.

4. The Executive Director shall be accountable for his activities to the Management Board.

Article 26
Appointment of senior officials

1. The Commission shall propose candidates for the post of the Executive Director based on a list following publication of the post in the *Official*

Journal of the European Union and other press or internet sites as appropriate.

2. The Executive Director of the Agency shall be appointed by the Management Board on the grounds of merit and documented administrative and management skills, as well as his/her relevant experience in the field of management of the external borders. The Management Board shall take its decision by a two-thirds majority of all members with a right to vote.

    Power to dismiss the Executive Director shall lie with the Management Board, according to the same procedure.

3. The Executive Director shall be assisted by a Deputy Executive Director. If the Executive Director is absent or indisposed, the Deputy Executive Director shall take his/her place.

4. The Deputy Executive Director shall be appointed by the Management Board on the grounds of merit and documented administrative and management skills, as well as his/her relevant experience in the field of management of the external borders on the proposal of the Executive Director. The Management Board shall take its decision by a two-thirds majority of all members with a right to vote.

    Power to dismiss the Deputy Executive Director shall be with the Management Board, according to the same procedure.

5. The terms of the offices of the Executive Director and the Deputy Executive Director shall be five years. They may be extended by the Management Board once for another period of up to five years.

Article 26a
Fundamental Rights Strategy

1. *The Agency shall draw up and further develop and implement its Fundamental Rights Strategy. The Agency shall put in place an effective mechanism to monitor the respect for fundamental rights in all the activities of the Agency.*

2. *A Consultative Forum shall be established by the Agency to assist the Director and the Management Board in fundamental rights matters. The Agency shall invite the European Asylum Support Office, the Fundamental Rights Agency, the United Nations High Commissioner for Refugees and other relevant organisation to participate in the Consultative Forum. On the proposal of the Executive Director, the Management Board shall decide on the composition and the working methods of and the modalities of the transmission of information to the Consultative Forum.*

The Consultative Forum shall be consulted on the further development and implementation of the Fundamental Rights Strategy, Code of conduct and Common Core Curriculum.

The Consultative Forum shall prepare an annual report of its activities. Those reports shall be made publically available.

3. *A Fundamental Rights Officer shall be designated by the Management Board of the Agency. He/she shall have the necessary qualifications and experience in the field of fundamental rights. He/she shall be independent in the performance of his/her duties as a Fundamental Rights Officer and shall report directly to the Management Board and the Consultative Forum. He/she shall report on a regular basis and as such contribute to the mechanism for monitoring fundamental rights.*

4. *The Fundamental Rights Officer and the Consultative Forum shall have access to all information concerning respect for fundamental rights, in relation to all the activities of the Agency.*

Article 27
Translation

1. The provisions laid down in Regulation No 1 of 15 April 1958 determining the languages to be used in the European Economic Community (1) shall apply to the Agency.

2. Without prejudice to decisions taken on the basis of Article 290 of the Treaty, the general report and programme of work referred to in Article 20(2)(b) and (c), shall be produced in all official languages of the Community.

3. The translation services required for the functioning of the Agency shall be provided by the Translation Centre for the bodies of the European Union.

Article 28
Transparency and communication

1. Six months after the entry into force of this Regulation, the Agency shall be subject to Regulation (EC) No 1049/2001 when handling applications for access to documents held by it.

2. The Agency may communicate on its own initiative in the fields within its mission. It shall ensure in particular that, in addition to the publication specified in Article 20(2)(b), the public and any interested party are rapidly given objective, reliable and easily understandable information with regard to its work.

3. The Management Board shall lay down the practical arrangements for the application of paragraphs 1 and 2.

4. Any natural or legal person shall be entitled to address himself/herself in writing to the Agency in any of the languages referred to in Article 314 of the Treaty. He/she shall have the right to receive an answer in the same language.

5. Decisions taken by the Agency pursuant to Article 8 of Regulation (EC) No 1049/2001 may give rise to the lodging of a complaint to the Ombudsman or form the subject of an action before the Court of Justice of the European Communities, under the conditions laid down in Articles 195 and 230 of the Treaty respectively.

CHAPTER IV
FINANCIAL REQUIREMENTS

Article 29
Budget

1. The revenue of the Agency shall consist, without prejudice to other types of income, of:
   — a subsidy from the Community entered in the general budget of the European Union (Commission section),
   — a contribution from the countries associated with the implementation, application and development of the Schengen acquis,
   — fees for services provided,
   — any voluntary contribution from the Member States.

2. The expenditure of the Agency shall include the staff, administrative, infrastructure and operational expenses.

3. The Executive Director shall draw up an estimate of the revenue and expenditure of the Agency for the following financial year and shall forward it to the Management Board together with an establishment plan.

4. Revenue and expenditure shall be in balance.

5. The Management Board shall adopt the draft estimate, including the provisional establishment plan accompanied by the preliminary work programme, and forward them by 31 March to the Commission and to the countries associated with the implementation, application and development of the Schengen acquis.

6. The estimate shall be forwarded by the Commission to the European Parliament and the Council (hereinafter referred to as the budgetary authority) together with the preliminary draft budget of the European Union.

7. On the basis of the estimate, the Commission shall enter in the preliminary draft general budget of the European Union the estimates it deems

necessary for the establishment plan and the amount of the subsidy to be charged to the general budget, which it shall place before the budgetary authority in accordance with Article 272 of the Treaty.

8. The budgetary authority shall authorise the appropriations for the subsidy to the Agency.

    The budgetary authority shall adopt the establishment plan for the Agency.

9. The Management Board adopts the Agency's budget. It shall become final following the final adoption of the general budget of the European Union. Where appropriate, it shall be adjusted accordingly.

10. Any modification to the budget, including the establishment plan, shall follow the same procedure.

11. The Management Board shall, as soon as possible, notify the budgetary authority of its intention to implement any project, which may have significant financial implications for the funding of its budget, in particular any projects relating to property such as the rental or purchase of buildings. It shall inform the Commission thereof as well as the countries associated with the implementation, application and development of the Schengen acquis.

    Where a branch of the budgetary authority has notified its intention to deliver an opinion, it shall forward its opinion to the Management Board within a period of six weeks from the date of notification of the project.

Article 30
Implementation and control of the budget

1. The Executive Director shall implement the Agency's budget.

2. By 1 March at the latest following each financial year, the Agency's accounting officer shall communicate the provisional accounts to the Commission's accounting officer together with a report on the budgetary and financial management for that financial year. The Commission's accounting officer shall consolidate the provisional accounts of the institutions and decentralised bodies in accordance with Article 128 of Council Regulation (EC, Euratom) No 1605/2002 of 25 June 2002 on the Financial Regulation applicable to the general budget of the European Communities (1) (hereafter referred to as the general Financial Regulation).

3. By 31 March at the latest following each financial year, the Commission's accounting officer shall forward the Agency's provisional accounts to the Court of Auditors, together with a report on the budgetary and financial management for that financial year. The report on the budgetary and financial management for that financial year shall also be forwarded to the European Parliament and the Council.

4. On receipt of the Court of Auditors' observations on the Agency's provisional accounts, pursuant to Article 129 of the general Financial Regulation, the Director shall draw up the Agency's final accounts under his/her own responsibility and forward them to the Management Board for an opinion.

5. The Management Board shall deliver an opinion on the Agency's final accounts.

6. By 1 July of the following year at the latest, the Executive Director shall send the final accounts, together with the opinion of the Management Board, to the Commission, the Court of Auditors, the European Parliament and the Council as well as the countries associated with the implementation, application and development of the Schengen acquis.

7. The final accounts shall be published.

8. The Director shall send the Court of Auditors a reply to its observations by 30 September at the latest. He shall also send this reply to the Management Board.

9. Upon a recommendation from the Council, the European Parliament shall, before 30 April of the discharge year + 2, give a discharge to the Executive Director of the Agency in respect of the implementation of the budget for the discharge year.

Article 31
Combating fraud

1. In order to combat fraud, corruption and other unlawful activities the provisions of Regulation (EC) No 1073/1999 shall apply without restriction.

2. The Agency shall accede to the Interinstitutional Agreement of 25 May 1999 and shall issue, without delay, the appropriate provisions applicable to all the employees of the Agency.

3. The decisions concerning funding and the implementing agreements and instruments resulting from them shall explicitly stipulate that the Court of Auditors and OLAF may carry out, if necessary, on-the-spot checks among the recipients of the Agency's funding and the agents responsible for allocating it.

Article 32
Financial provision

The financial rules applicable to the Agency shall be adopted by the Management Board after consultation of the Commission. They may not depart from Commission Regulation (EC, Euratom) No 2343/2002 on the framework Financial Regulation for the bodies referred to in Article 185 of the general Financial Regulation, unless specifically required for the Agency's operation and with the Commission's prior consent.

CHAPTER V
FINAL PROVISIONS

Article 33
Evaluation

1. Within three years from the date of the Agency having taken up its responsibilities, and every five years thereafter, the Management Board shall commission an independent external evaluation on the implementation of this Regulation.
2. The evaluation shall examine how effectively the Agency fulfils its mission. It shall also assess the impact of the Agency and its working practices. The evaluation shall take into account the views of stakeholders, at both European and national level.
   2a. *The next evaluation shall also analyse the needs for further increased coordination of the management of the external borders of the Member States, including the feasibility of the creation of a European system of border guards.*
   2b. *The evaluation shall include a specific analysis on the way the Charter of Fundamental Rights was respected pursuant to the application of the Regulation.*
3. The Management Board shall receive the findings of the evaluation and issue recommendations regarding changes to this Regulation, the Agency and its working practices to the Commission, which shall forward them, together with its own opinion as well as appropriate proposals, to the Council. An action plan with a timetable shall be included, if appropriate. Both the findings and the recommendations of the evaluation shall be made public.

Article 34
Entry into force

This Regulation shall enter into force on the day following that of its publication in the *Official Journal of the European Union.*

The Agency shall take up its responsibilities from 1 May 2005. This Regulation shall be binding in its entirety and directly applicable in the Member States in accordance with the Treaty establishing the European Community.

Chapter 6

Other Border Control Measures

1. *Introduction and Overview*

In addition to the key legislation establishing the Schengen Borders Code, Frontex, and the Schengen Information System (SIS),[1] and leaving aside legislation on other matters which impacts upon borders issues,[2] the EU has adopted a number of other legislative measures concerning border controls. This chapter first of all notes those measures which were subsequently integrated into the Schengen Borders Code, and then looks in more detail at the legislation which still remains separate from the code, concerning passport security, local border traffic and other issues. It also examines the EU's plans for future measures in this area.

2. *Measures Integrated into the Schengen Borders Code*

As noted in Chapter 3, the Schengen Borders Code repealed the first EU measures regulating external border controls: the relevant provisions of the Schengen *acquis*, as integrated into the EU legal order when the Treaty of Amsterdam entered into force in 1999. These measures comprised:

a) Chapters 1 and 2 of Title II of the Schengen Convention (Articles 2-8 of the Convention);[3]

b) the "Common Manual" concerning Schengen border checks, which had been adopted in the form of a Decision of the Schengen Executive Committee;[4] and

---

[1] See chapters 3 to 5.

[2] See chapter 2, as regards free movement rules and association agreements.

[3] Art. 39(1) of the code (OJ 2006 L 105/1). The Convention appears in OJ 2000 L 239.

[4] Art. 39(2)(a) of the code (ibid). This Decision (SCH/Com-ex (99) 13) was not published along with most of the rest of the Schengen *acquis* in 2000. However, following its subsequent declassification, the Manual was published in OJ 2002 C 313/97, after certain amendments had been made to it following the entry into force of the Treaty of Amsterdam (see discussion below in this section).

c) three other relevant Decisions of the Schengen Executive Committee.[5]

However, a few of the measures in the Schengen *acquis* concerning border controls were not repealed by the Borders Code, and so still remained in force; these measures are discussed further below.[6]

Furthermore, the Borders Code repealed a number of measures that the EU had adopted in this area in between the entry into force of the Treaty of Amsterdam and the adoption of the Code in 2006, because the content of those measures was integrated into the Borders Code.[7] These measures comprised:

a) Regulation 790/2001 on the procedure for updating the Common Manual on border controls;[8]
b) a Decision on signs at border crossing points;[9] and
c) Regulation 2133/2004 on stamping of travel documents at external borders.[10]

The first of these measures, which conferred power upon the Council (and Member States) to amend the Schengen Executive Committee Decision establishing the Common Manual for border controls, was challenged by the Commission, on the grounds that there was insufficient justification for conferring such powers upon the Council and Member States, instead of upon the Commission. This legal challenge was unsuccessful.[11] This Regulation had been used to amend the Common Manual on four occasions.[12]

3. *Local Border Traffic Rules*

The Schengen Convention originally provided for the Schengen Executive Committee to adopt standardised rules concerning exceptions for local border

---

[5] Art. 39(2)(b) of the code, referring to: SCH/Com-ex (94) 1, rev 2 (OJ 2000 L 239/157), SCH/Com-ex (94)17, rev. 4 (OJ 2000 L 239/168) and SCH/Com-ex (95) 20, rev. 2 (OJ 2000 L 239/133), which concerned respectively the adjustments necessary following the abolition of internal border controls, the introduction of the Schengen system in airports and the procedure for reintroducing border controls in emergencies.

[6] See section 5.

[7] See the content of the code, discussed in chapter 3.

[8] OJ 2001 L 116/5, repealed by Art. 39(2)(d) of the code.

[9] OJ 2004 L 261/119, repealed by Art. 39(2)(e) of the code.

[10] OJ 2004 L 369/5, repealed by Art. 39(2)(g) of the code.

[11] Case C-257/01 *Commission v Council* [2005] ECR I-345.

[12] The first two amendments (OJ 2002 L 123/47 and OJ 2002 L 187/50) made "housekeeping" changes. The third amendment increased checks on minors (OJ 2004 L 157/36). Finally, the

traffic,[13] but this power was never used before the integration of the Schengen *acquis* into the EU legal order. Instead, the Schengen Borders Code, which repealed the relevant provision of the Schengen Convention, provides for the adoption of separate specific rules on local border traffic.[14] The Commission's original proposals on this issue dated from 2003,[15] but it had been difficult to agree these proposals as long as unanimous voting applied to this issue – much as it had not been possible to agree such rules during the Schengen period.[16] However, with the extension of qualified majority voting to borders issues in 2005, the Commission took the opportunity to propose a new version of the Regulation,[17] which was then adopted at the end of 2006.[18] At the same time, there were parallel amendments to the EU's visa list legislation which provided for visa exemptions for persons benefiting from the new border traffic rules.[19] The Commission had to report on the application of the local border traffic Regulation by January 2009, possibly accompanied by legislative proposals.[20] This report was submitted in July 2009 (the "2009 report"),[21] and is discussed further below. The Commission concluded that in light of the limited experience with local border traffic treaties to date (see below), it was too soon to propose changes to the legislation, but it would submit another report in the second half of 2010. This report was in fact released early in 2011 (the "2011 report").[22]

The local border traffic Regulation principally establishes standardised rules for local border traffic, in particular by introducing a standard local border traffic permit.[23] Member States are authorised to agree treaties with neighbouring third countries that are in accordance with the rules of the Regulation.[24]

---

fourth amendment introduced a common form to be used when refusing entry at the border (OJ 2004 L 261/36).

[13] Art. 3 of the Schengen Convention (n. 3 above).

[14] Art. 35 of Reg 562/2006 (n. 3 above).

[15] COM (2003) 502, 14 Aug. 2003.

[16] In particular, Germany, Greece and France objected to the proposals: see Council doc. 8083/04, 1 Apr. 2004.

[17] COM (2005) 56, 23 Feb. 2005.

[18] Reg. 1931/2006 (OJ 2006 L 405/1), which entered into force on 17 Jan. 2007 (Art. 21). All references in this section are to this Reg., unless otherwise indicated. There is case on the interpretation of the Regulation pending before the Court of Justice: Case C-254/11 *Shomodi*.

[19] See chapter 7.

[20] Art. 18. The Commission was not required to produce any subsequent reports on the Reg.

[21] COM (2009) 383, 24 July 2009.

[22] COM (2011) 47, 9 Feb. 2011.

[23] Art. 1(1).

[24] Art. 1(2). For more on EU external relations law in this area, see section 4 below.

According to the 2009 report, a Hungary/Ukraine agreement entered into force in January 2008; a Poland/Ukraine treaty entered into force in July 2009; and a Slovakia/Ukraine treaty applied from September 2008. The 2011 report refers also to a Romania/Moldova treaty, which applied from October 2010. One pre-existing agreement (Slovenia/Croatia) was also examined in both reports. The 2011 report also referred to treaties between Poland/Belarus, Latvia/Belarus, Lithuania/Belarus and Norway/Russia,[25] which were expected to enter into force shortly. Treaties between Latvia/Russia, Lithuania/Russia and Romania/Ukraine had been agreed, but not signed, while draft treaties between Bulgaria/Serbia and Bulgaria/Former Yugoslav Republic of Macedonia (FYROM) had not been taken forward since the 2009 report.

The reports did not mention any local border traffic treaties agreed or under negotiation in respect of the remaining external borders of the EU's Member States, namely Greece/Albania, Greece/Turkey, Greece/FYROM, Bulgaria/Turkey, Estonia/Russia, Finland/Russia, Poland/Russia, Hungary/Serbia, Hungary/Croatia and Romania/Serbia. In the case of Greece/Turkey, a treaty is hardly likely since Greece is building a wall at its border with Turkey.

It should be noted that in 2009 and 2010, the EU abolished visa requirements for Western Balkan States (leaving aside Kosovo, which does not have a border with a Member State).[26] Border traffic treaties are therefore not now crucial to facilitate travel with these countries. When Croatia joins the EU, there will be two new external borders subject to the local border traffic Regulation (Croatia/Serbia and Croatia/Bosnia), but two existing external borders will become internal borders instead (Hungary/Croatia and Slovenia/Croatia).

The Regulation defines a "border area" to mean an area within 30 kilometres of the border, but this may stretch to 50 kilometres in order to include parts of complete border districts.[27] "Local border traffic" is defined as a crossing for "social, cultural or substantiated economic reasons, or for family reasons" by border residents,[28] who are defined as persons lawfully resident in the border area for more than one year; Member States may reduce this waiting period in "exceptional" and "duly justified" cases.[29]

According to the 2009 report, in several cases Member States signed treaties with a wider scope than the 50 km maximum, or which extended their scope

---

[25] It should be noted that Norway is subject to the local border traffic Regulation as a Schengen associate.

[26] See chapter 7.

[27] Art. 3(2).

[28] Art. 3(3).

[29] Art. 3(6).

to 50 km without meeting the requirements of the Regulation in this regard. On these points, there is clearly no authorisation under the Regulation for Member States to agree a wider scope than 50 km, and the Commission convincingly argued in the 2009 report that only those *parts* of districts falling within 30 km to 50 km from the border can be included within the scope of the rules. However, the Commission offered in its report to keep this issue under review with a view to proposing amendments to the Regulation in future. In the 2011 report, the Commission rejected any amendment to this end, since only Poland had requested it, but it did express a willingness to propose amendments to the legislation, so that the entire Russian region of Kaliningrad would be covered by it. A proposal to this end was subsequently released.[30] In the meantime, the Commission urged Poland and Lithuania to conclude border traffic agreements with Russia.[31]

As for the waiting period, in practice the 2009 and 2011 reports state that all of the treaties concerned set waiting periods of more than one year, and indeed three of them set a three-year waiting period. However, the report also states that the pre-existing Slovenia/Croatia agreement provides for *no* waiting period. It cannot be seriously argued that a reduction of the waiting period below the one-year minimum is "exceptional" if it applies to an *entire* agreement.[32]

Chapter II of the Regulation sets out the main features of an authorised local border traffic regime.[33] An external land border may be crossed by persons who hold a local border permit and possibly also travel documents (depending on agreements between Member States and non-Member States), who have been checked in the SIS and who do not pose a threat to the public policy, public security or public health of any Member State.[34] As compared to the normal rules for crossing borders, there is no requirement to hold a visa (a relevant point, when the Regulation was first adopted, for all bordering non-Member States except Croatia, leaving aside Schengen associates and micro-states),[35] no requirement to show subsistence or the purpose of the visit

---

[30] COM (2011) 461, 27 July 2011.

[31] See also the EU's visa facilitation agreements, discussed in chapter 9. Note that many of these agreements contain declarations regarding local border traffic issues.

[32] Note also point 5 in the preamble to the Reg., which gives a non-exhaustive list of cases which fall within the scope of this exception, "such as those relating to minors, changes in marital status or inheritance of land".

[33] Arts. 4–6.

[34] Art. 4.

[35] As noted already, due to amendments to the EU visa list legislation adopted in 2009 and 2010, most citizens of Western Balkans States (except Kosovo) are now exempt from a visa requirement.

and no absolute requirement to hold a travel document.[36] Border residents may stay up to three months in a border area, depending on bilateral agreements;[37] as the 2009 report points out, this is not subject to the limit of spending three months in *every 180 day period*, as set out in the borders code. Although border residents are subject to entry and exit checks, their travel documents (when they require such documents) are not stamped, by way of derogation from the normal rules.[38] It remains to be seen how the development of an entry-exit system would affect the local border traffic rules.[39]

According to the 2009 and 2011 reports, several Member States impose a health insurance requirement in their bilateral treaties. The Commission convincingly argues that such a requirement is implicitly ruled out by the Regulation, which sets out exhaustive criteria which may be applied for the issue of a local border traffic permit. While the Commission was initially willing to suggest amendments to the Regulation if it transpires that the problems which result from this (ie the costs of providing emergency medical treatment for some persons with a local border traffic permit) could not be resolved by bilateral agreement between the health services of the States concerned, in 2011 it ruled out amendments to this end, in particular because the Member States which did not impose a health insurance requirement had in practice not suffered from "medical tourism".

The reports also notes that most Member States' treaties impose a time limit of 90 days per 180 days (ie, matching the borders code), and one even imposes a 30-day time limit. The Commission also notes that in any case, the absence of a stamping obligation makes it difficult to check on whether the time limits are being complied with.

Chapter III of the Regulation sets out the basic rules governing the special border traffic permit.[40] The permit is limited in validity to the border area of the issuing Member State.[41] It must bear a photograph of the holder and other basic information as specified in the Regulation.[42] There is no standard EU-wide format for the permit, but its security features and technical specifications must comply with the EU legislation establishing a standard format for

---

[36] Compare to the entry conditions in Art. 5 of the Schengen Borders Code (as discussed in chapter 3).

[37] Art. 5.

[38] Art. 6; compare with Art. 10 of the Schengen Borders Code (n. 3 above).

[39] See further section 6 below.

[40] Arts. 7–12.

[41] Art. 7(2).

[42] Art. 7(3).

residence permits.[43] Since the subsequent amendment of that EU legislation, this means that the permit will have to contain biometric information as from 2011 (photographs) and 2012 (fingerprints).[44]

A permit can only be issued if four conditions are met: possession of a valid travel document; proof of status as a border resident and of grounds to cross the external border frequently; a check in the SIS; and lack of any threat to the public policy, public security, or public health of any Member State.[45] The permits are valid for a period of between one and five years, and the fees charged cannot exceed those for issuing short-term visas; Member States may issue the permits free of charge.[46] In practice, according to the 2009 and 2011 reports, all but one of the Member States' treaties provides for a five-year period of validity, and all (according to the 2011 report) provide for a fee of 20 to 35 euros.

The permits can be issued by national authorities or consulates, and Member States must keep a permanent record of them.[47] There are no other standardised conditions, so although the border traffic permit can be compared to a visa, the visa code (and previously the Common Consular Instructions) does not govern its issue, and the Visa Information System will not apply. On the other hand, there are no express provisions conferring procedural rights on persons applying for or holding a border traffic permit, although it is arguable that implied rights exist nonetheless pursuant to the general principles of EU law, and now also the EU's Charter of Fundamental Rights.

Chapter IV of the Regulation concerns the implementation of the local border traffic regime.[48] The only means to introduce or maintain a local border

---

[43] Art. 8.
[44] Reg. 1030/2002 (OJ 2002 L 157/1) was amended by Reg. 380/2008 (OJ 2008 L 115/1) to provide for the introduction of biometric data (fingerprints and photographs) into residence permits. Biometric data must be integrated into the permits two years (as regards photographs) and three years (as regards fingerprints) from the adoption of the relevant implementing measures (Art. 9 of Reg. 1030/2002, as amended by Reg. 380/2008). These measures were adopted in May 2009. On this legislation, see further volume 2 of this book (chapter 1).
[45] Art. 9.
[46] Arts. 10 and 11. Note that the visa code does not permit the issue of visas free of charge for persons in local border zones, so holding a local border traffic permit significantly simplifies the position (Art. 16 of the visa code, Reg 810/2009, OJ 2009 L 243/1; see chapter 8). Then again, many of the third countries in question are now on the EU visa whitelist (see chapter 7), and/or have visa facilitation treaties with the EU, which reduce the fees for visa applications (see chapter 9).
[47] Art. 12.
[48] Arts. 13–15.

traffic regime is by means of bilateral agreements between Member States and neighbouring third countries. Any new bilateral agreement must be compatible with the Regulation, and any existing agreements must be amended to conform to it.[49] In either case, Member States must allow the Commission to screen draft agreements, and make any amendments required by the Commission.[50]

According to the 2009 and 2011 reports, Member States had not always accepted the Commission's demands to renegotiate agreements, although the Commission had not responded (as it could have done) by bringing infringement actions against those States.[51] Presumably, if a Member State disagreed with a Commission decision, it could sue to annul that decision in the EU courts; but in practice, it is clear that in those cases at least some Member States are simply going ahead anyway with their plans for bilateral treaties, and implicitly daring the Commission to sue them. The Commission's reluctance to sue Member States may be due to a desire to avoid complicating the Member States' and the EU's relations with the third countries concerned.

The relevant bilateral agreements must contain provisions on the readmission of persons abusing the border traffic regime, in the event that the EU or the Member State concerned has not concluded a readmission agreement with the relevant country.[52] Since the entry into force of EU readmission agreements with most neighbouring third countries, this provision is only relevant (for now) as regards Belarus and Turkey (until an agreement is negotiated with the former and concluded with the latter).[53] Also, the bilateral agreements must confer reciprocal rights on EU citizens and legally-resident third-country nationals living in the border areas of Member States; the 2009 report objects that the Slovenia/Croatia agreement infringes this requirement. Furthermore, bilateral agreements can "exceptionally" liberalise the normal requirements to cross the borders only at authorised crossing points, on the condition that the Member States concerned still carry out surveillance and random checks along the borders, and ease the requirement that all third-country nationals must be subject to thorough checks at the external borders.[54]

---

[49] Art. 13(1).

[50] Art. 13(2).

[51] On the infringement procedure, see Art. 226 EC (now Art. 258 TFEU).

[52] Art. 13(3).

[53] On the EU's readmission agreements, see volume 2 of this book (chapter 20).

[54] Art. 15; compare with Arts. 4 and 7 of the Schengen Borders Code (n. 3 above).

Lastly, Chapter V of the Regulation sets out final provisions.[55] The Regulation does not affect the specific rules concerning Spanish enclaves in Morocco.[56] Member States must establish penalties for abuse of a permit, and report regularly to the Commission on cases of abuse.[57] The 2011 report refers to only about 40 cases of reported abuse, out of over 110,000 permits issued. More broadly, the 2011 report concludes that "relatively few abuses occur in the practical implementation of the" treaties and that "there is no evidence that [permit] holders would systematically travel to other Member States in violation of the rules."

Member States have to notify all bilateral agreements to the Commission, which must make them public.[58] The Commission has failed to comply with this obligation, except in the context of its 2009 and 2011 reports (and the publication of the 2009 report was a separate obligation). Finally, the Schengen Convention has been amended to refer to this Regulation, rather than national border traffic treaties.[59]

Assessing the local border traffic Regulation, its rules addressed the need to simplify border crossing for the many thousands of visa nationals who have been on the EU's external border following the EU enlargements of 2004 and 2007 (until the visa waivers for the Western Balkan States in 2009 and 2010), and whose economic, cultural and personal links to the new Member States were sundered when visa obligations were applied to these neighbouring countries. So the border traffic legislation in principle makes a useful contribution to enhancing both the EU's political relationship with its neighbours—who are expected to take on many obligations to assist the EU and who suffered substantial disadvantages following enlargement—and the daily life of many individual residents of border regions, including those EU citizens who benefit from maintaining economic, cultural and personal links to the east.

In light of the Commission's assessment of the operation of the border traffic regime in its 2009 and 2011 reports, it would be desirable to amend the Regulation to extend its geographical scope to the extent that the geographical limit as currently drafted undercuts the "spirit" of the rules, in particular

---

[55] Arts. 16–21.
[56] Art. 16.
[57] Art. 17.
[58] Art. 19.
[59] Art. 20, amending Art. 136(3) of the Convention (n. 3 above); see further section 5 below. Note that the Commission has proposed to repeal Art. 136 of the Convention entirely (COM (2011) 118, 10 Mar. 2011).

(as the Commission proposed) as regards Kaliningrad. It would also be reasonable to consider flexibility on the question of whether a health insurance requirement can be imposed for the issue of a local border traffic permit, on the condition that it is not possible in practice to address this issue by means of separate agreements.

4. *Passport Security*

In December 2004, the Council adopted a Regulation harmonising the security features of EU citizens' passports as regards the inclusion of biometric information (fingerprints and digital photographs).[60] This Regulation was subsequently amended in 2009,[61] partly in order to provide for exceptions from the obligation to include biometrics in passports. As discussed elsewhere in this book,[62] the UK sued to annul the original 2004 Regulation because its attempt to opt in to the legislation was refused by the Council, but the UK's challenge was unsuccessful.[63] The Regulation is intended to be consistent with other measures requiring the insertion of photos and fingerprints into residence permits and visas, although ultimately it proved technically impossible to insert biometric information into visas.[64] It should be recalled that there are also Resolutions of Member States which have established other features of the design of a uniform format for EU passports.[65]

The Regulation was largely prompted by American demands for the inclusion of high-security features in the passports of countries subject to the American visa waiver programme.[66] It provides for mandatory inclusion of digital photographs and fingerprints in EU passports, in accordance with the technical standards set out in an Annex to the Regulation.[67] Passports must be issued as individual documents,[68] and the Commission must report by 26 June

---

[60] Reg. 2252/2004, OJ 2004 L 385/1.

[61] Reg. 444/2009, OJ 2009 L 144/1. The Reg has not been codified.

[62] See chapter 2. See also the discussion of the EU's competence to adopt this Reg. in that chapter.

[63] Case C-137/05 *UK v Council* [2007] ECR I-11593.

[64] See chapter 11 and volume 2, chapter 1 of this book as regards Schengen visas and residence permits respectively.

[65] OJ 1981 C 241/1; OJ 1982 C 179/1; OJ 1986 C 185/1; OJ 1995 C 200/1; OJ 2000 C 310/1; and OJ 2004 C 245/1.

[66] See the explanatory memorandum to the proposal (COM (2004) 116, 18 Feb. 2004), p 3. On the issue of visa requirements for EU citizens to visit the USA, see further chapter 7.

[67] Art. 1(1) and (2).

[68] Art. 1(1), second sub-paragraph, as inserted by Reg. 444/2009. This obligation must be implemented by 26 June 2012 (see final sub-paragraph of Art. 6, as inserted by Reg. 444/2009).

2012 on children travelling across the external borders in order to examine whether to adopt a common approach on the protection of children crossing the external borders.[69] Children under 12 years old are exempt from the fingerprinting obligation, although Member States which already fingerprinted children between 6 and 12 years old as of 26 June 2009 can continue to do so for a four-year period after that date, ie until 26 June 2013.[70] The Commission must also report by 26 June 2012 on whether to alter the age limit, based on an independent technical study of the accuracy of fingerprint data taken from children under 12 for "identification and verification purposes" (ie checking the fingerprints on a one-to-one and one-to-many basis respectively).[71] Also, persons are exempt from the obligation if taking their fingerprints is physically impossible.[72]

The Regulation applies to passports and travel documents issued by Member States, but not to identity cards or to temporary passports or travel documents having a validity of under a year.[73] Biometric data must be collected by qualified national officials, who must act in accordance with international human rights law and ensure the dignity of the person concerned if the biometric information cannot be taken.[74] Further security standards can be adopted by the Commission, assisted by a "comitology" committee of Member States' representatives.[75] There are basic data protection rules, and the Regulation specifies that checking the biometric information in the passport is without prejudice to the rules in the Schengen Borders Code concerning checks of EU citizens at the external borders.[76] Member States had to apply the Regulation 18 months after the adoption of technical specifications as regards digital photographs, and 36 months after the adoption of technical

---

[69] Art. 1(1), third sub-paragraph, as inserted by Reg. 444/2009.

[70] Art. 1(2a)(a), as inserted by Reg. 444/2009.

[71] Art. 5a, as inserted by Reg. 444/2009.

[72] Art. 1(2a)(b), as inserted by Reg. 444/2009. There is a special rule if this impossibility is only temporary: see Art. 1(2b), as inserted by Reg. 444/2009.

[73] Art. 1(3).

[74] Art. 1a, as inserted by Reg. 444/2009.

[75] Art. 2, as amended by Reg. 444/2009; see also Arts. 3(1) and 5. For the English translations of two implementing measures, adopted by the Commission in 2005 and 2006, see: <http://ec.europa.eu/justice_home/doc_centre/freetravel/documents/doc_freetravel_documents_en.htm>. On the "comitology" process, see further chapter 2.

[76] Art 4, as amended by Reg. 444/2009, referring to Art. 7(2) of the Borders Code (n. 3 above); see chapter 3. It should be noted that the passports Reg does not amend the Borders Code, so there is no new legal requirement to check passports going beyond the rules in the Borders Code.

specifications as regards fingerprints.[77] In practice, this obligation has applied as from 28 August 2007 as regards facial images, and 28 June 2009 as regards fingerprints.[78]

In the Commission's view, this is only a first step; that institution wishes to see the creation of "[a]t EU level, a centralised, biometrics-based, 'EU passport register', which would contain the fingerprints of passport applicants" with the passport number "and most probably some other, but limited, relevant data".[79] However, the 2009 amendment to the Regulation states that the legislation is not a legal base regarding passport databases, which are "strictly a matter of national law".[80]

5. *Other Measures*

A number of other EU meaures have also been adopted concerning borders issues. Financing for external border control measures through the EU budget is provided for via means of the Decision establishing a European Borders Fund,[81] which replaced in part the previous "ARGO" programme.[82]

A series of transitional measures have addressed the transitional position of, on the one hand, persons transiting though the newer Member States to the States fully applying Schengen rules, and on the other hand, persons holding residence permits from Switzerland and Liechtenstein, before those States' full participation in the Schengen *acquis*.

For the first category of persons, the EU adopted a transitional Decision in 2006 which permitted (but did not require) the 10 newer Member States which had joined the EU in 2004 (but which did not yet participate fully in the Schengen *acquis*) to recognise as equivalent to their national visas, for the purpose of transit, Schengen visas, long-stay visas and residence permits issued by those Member States which were fully applying the Schengen rules.[83] Newer Member States were also permitted to recognise the various "national short-term visas, long-term visas and resident permits" issued by other newer

---

[77] Art. 6, as amended by Reg. 444/2009.
[78] See SEC (2009) 320, 9 Mar. 2009, p. 10.
[79] See points 2 and 8 of its explanatory memorandum (COM (2004) 116, 18 Feb. 2004).
[80] Recital 8 in the preamble, Reg. 444/2009. See also the discussion of competence issues in chapter 2.
[81] OJ 2007 L 144/22.
[82] OJ 2002 L 161/11, amended in 2004 (OJ 2004 L 371/48).
[83] Art. 2, 2006 Decision (OJ 2006 L 167/8).

Member States for the purpose of transit.[84] The transit could only last for a maximum of five days.[85] Eight out of the ten newer Member States applied this transitional Decision.[86] Following the enlargement of the Schengen zone at the end of 2007, this Decision now only applies to Cyprus.[87]

A similar Decision was adopted in June 2008, after Romania and Bulgaria had joined the EU in 2007.[88] These two Member States were given the same choice to recognise, for the purposes of transit, Schengen documents, documents issued by each other, and moreover documents issued by Cyprus; Cyprus in turn has the option to recognise documents issued by Romania and Bulgaria. All three States opted to apply this Decision.[89]

As for Switzerland and Liechtenstein, the EU adopted a separate transitional decision in 2006, which required full Schengen States to recognise residence permits issued by Switzerland and Liechtenstein as equivalent to a visa for the purposes of transit for a five-day period.[90] Member States which had joined the EU in 2004 had an option to apply this Decision, on condition that they also applied the transitional Decision relating to accession countries.[91] This Decision was then amended in 2008, to apply also to Romania and Bulgaria.[92] Since the extension of the Schengen zone to Switzerland at the end of 2008, the Decision applies only to residence permits issued by Liechtenstein.[93]

This legislation was the subject of the judgment of the Court of Justice in *Kqiku*.[94] Mr. Kqiku travelled with his family from Switzerland to Germany to visit family and friends in Cologne and Stuttgart between 4–6 August 2006: a fairly harmless summer holiday break one might think. However, Mr. Kqiku was the subject of criminal proceedings because, although he and his family

---

[84] Art. 3, 2006 Decision (ibid.). The types of documents covered by this rule are listed in an Annex to the Decision.

[85] Art. 4, 2006 Decision.

[86] OJ 2006 C 251/20. The exceptions were Estonia and Lithuania.

[87] Art. 6, 2006 Decision.

[88] OJ 2008 L 161/30. Again, the national documents concerned are listed in an Annex to the Decision.

[89] OJ 2008 C 312/8.

[90] OJ 2006 L 167/8, Arts. 1 and 3. The residence permits in question are listed in an Annex to the Decision.

[91] Art. 3, 2006 Decision (ibid.). Again, eight of ten of the newer Member States applied this Decision (see n. 86 above).

[92] OJ 2008 L 162/27; the amended Decision has not been codified. Romania and Bulgaria both decided to apply this Decision (n. 89 above).

[93] Art. 5, 2006 Decision (n. 90 above).

[94] Case C-139/08 [2009] ECR I-2887.

had residence permits in Switzerland, those permits were only recognised at that time as valid for transit through the Schengen Area not for stays, however short. For a stay, he and his family would have to have visas. The Court of Justice took an astonishingly literal approach to the question. As Mr Kqiku and his family only had Swiss residence permits equivalent to Schengen transit visas and although they had stayed in Germany for less time than would have been permitted if they were actually transiting the country (if they had visas for that purpose) they could properly be the objects of criminal proceedings for illegal entry into Germany as their purpose was a visit for which they did not hold the specific visa.

Next, Directive 2004/82 on the advance transfer of passenger data, which also has a legal base relating to illegal migration as well as border controls, is discussed in volume 2 of this book.[95]

There are also some remaining provisions of the Schengen Convention relating to border controls. Article 136 of the Convention concerns border control treaties between Member States and third countries. It provided, in its original form, as follows:

1. A Contracting Party which envisages conducting negotiations on border checks with a third State shall inform the other Contracting Parties thereof in good time.
2. No Contracting Party shall conclude with one or more third States agreements simplifying or abolishing border checks without the prior agreement of the other Contracting Parties, subject to the right of the Member States of the European Communities to conclude such agreements jointly.
3. Paragraph 2 shall not apply to agreements on local border traffic in so far as those agreements comply with the exceptions and arrangements adopted under Article 3(1).

Article 136(3) was amended by the Regulation on local border traffic to read instead as follows:[96]

3. Paragraph 2 shall not apply to bilateral Agreements on local border traffic as referred to in Article 13 of Regulation (EC) No 1931/2006 of the European Parliament and of the Council of 20 December 2006 laying down rules on local border traffic at the external land borders of the Member States.

---

[95] OJ 2004 L 261/24; see chapter 1 of volume 2.
[96] Art. 20 of Reg. 1931/2006 (n. 18 above).

This issue is further addressed by a Protocol to the Treaties relating to EU external competence over external borders, added at the time of the Treaty of Amsterdam and the subject of purely technical amendments made by the Treaty of Lisbon, which reads (after the entry into force of the latter Treaty) as follows:

THE HIGH CONTRACTING PARTIES,

TAKING INTO ACCOUNT the need of the Member States to ensure effective controls at their external borders, in cooperation with third countries where appropriate,

HAVE AGREED UPON the following provisions, which shall be annexed to the Treaty on European Union and to the Treaty on the Functioning of the European Union:

The provisions on the measures on the crossing of external borders included in Article 77(2)(b) of the Treaty on the Functioning of the European Union shall be without prejudice to the competence of Member States to negotiate or conclude agreements with third countries as long as they respect Union law and other relevant international agreements.

The better view is that the Protocol confirms that the EU's external competence relating to external borders is not *a priori* exclusive, but can become exclusive by exercise. As for Article 136 of the Schengen Convention, following the integration of the Schengen *acquis* into the EU legal order and the conclusion of Schengen association agreements by the EU, a "third state" is presumably now any country which is neither an EU Member State nor a Schengen associate, and the reference to agreements concluded collectively by Member States must now be understood as a reference to treaties concluded by the *EU*.[97]

In March 2011, the Commission proposed the repeal of Article 136 of the Schengen Convention,[98] on the grounds that it was unecessary since EU legislation provided for specific provisions on external borders negotiations between Member States and third States, and conflicted in principle with EU external relations law.[99] However, the Protocol on external competence as borders could only be repealed by way of Treaty amendment.

---

[97] For further elaboration of these points, see Peers, *EU Justice and Home Affairs Law*, 3rd ed. (OUP, 2011), 222–225.

[98] COM (2010) 118, 10 Mar. 2011. On this proposal, which largely concerns amendments to the Borders Code, see further chapters 3 and 11.

[99] In addition to the existing rules in the border traffic Reg., the March 2011 proposal (ibid) would insert specific rules on Member States' bilateral agreements in Art. 4(2) and Annex VI of the Borders Code.

Finally, there are still two decisions of the Schengen Executive Committee concerning border controls which have not been repealed, although they are both in practice obsolete.[100] Three other Executive Committee Decisions which were jointly allocated to legal bases relating to border control and to other matters are also still in force.[101]

6. *Future Measures*

In this area, leaving aside issues relating to the development of the SIS, the Stockholm programme on the future of EU JHA cooperation calls upon the Commission:[102]

— [to] present proposals for an entry/exit system alongside a fast track registered traveller programme with a view to such a system becoming operational as soon as possible,
— to prepare a study on the possibility and usefulness of developing a European system of travel authorisation and, where appropriate, to make the necessary proposals,
— to continue to examine the issue of automated border controls and other issues connected to rendering border management more efficient.

These measures are were due to be presented in 2011,[103] following on from a Commission communication of 2008 on the development of an entry-exit

---

[100] Sch/Com-ex (98) 1 on the activities of a task force (OJ 2000 L 239/191) and SCH/Com-ex (94) 29 Rev 2 (OJ 2000 L 239/130), concerning bringing into force of the Convention.

[101] For the Council's decision on the allocation of the *acquis*, see OJ 1999 L 176/17. The Decisions in question are: SCH/Com-ex (99) 14 (OJ 2000 L 239/298), concerning a manual of documents on which a visa may be affixed, which was allocated to Art. 62 EC (as it then was) generally; SCH/Com-ex (98) 37 def 2 (OJ 2000 L 239/203), an action plan to combat illegal immigration, allocated to Arts. 62 and 63 EC and to the third pillar; and SCH/Com-ex (94) 16 Rev, on the acquisition of common entry and exit stamps (OJ 2000 L 239/166), which was allocated to Art. 62(2) EC generally. For more on the first and third measures, see chapter 11; note that the Commission has proposed to replace the first measure (COM (2010) 662, 12 Nov. 2010), and the Council and European Parliament have agreed in principle to this proposal (Council doc. 12058/11, 27 June 2011). The second measure is obsolete.

[102] OJ 2010 C 115, point 5.1. See also the Commission action plan on the implementation of the programme (COM (2010) 171, 20 Apr. 2010).

[103] See the Commission work programme for 2011 (COM (2010) 623, 27 Oct. 2010).

system, a registered traveller programme and an EU system of travel authorisation.[104] According to this communication, the main purpose of the entry-
exit system will be to identify third-country nationals who have "overstayed"
their period of permitted stay, whether or not they were subject to a visa obligation. Such persons are the biggest category of irregular migrants in the
EU.[105] The system will record data on "the time and place of entry, the length
of stay authorised, and the transmission of automated alerts" to the authorities
on overstayers, once they violate the rules in question and also when they
leave the EU. The system will also update information in case of change of status (justified overstay, or a grant of residence), and will obviously be linked in
some way to the Visa Information System ("VIS").[106]

In order to avoid the implementation of this system creating lengthy queues
at border posts, a new status of "trusted traveller" for certain third-country
nationals will be created. These people will be pre-screened based on common
EU criteria, and will be exempt from some of the conditions of entry at the
border, enjoying "fast-track" entry through automated border gates, which
would keep a record of their movements across the external borders. In the
Commission's view, the entry-exit system and the accompanying trusted traveller programme could be applicable by 2015.

Finally, the possible electronic system of travel authorisation would apply to
non-visa nationals, "who would be requested to make an electronic application supplying, in advance of travelling, data identifying the traveller and
specifying the passport and travel details". This data would be used to verify
that the person concerned fulfilled the entry conditions "before travelling to
the EU, while using a lighter and simpler procedure compared to a visa".

It remains to be seen whether the contribution that such measures might
arguably make to the prevention of irregular migration and the detection of
irregular migrants will be considered by the Council and the EP to justify their
cost and practical consequences, and whether the technical difficulties which
have beset the development of the VIS and SIS II would be avoided.[107]

During the first half of 2011, the Commission showed signs of faltering
on its commitment to propose legislation on this issue, planning instead to
issue a communication on "smart borders" assessing the costs and benefits of

---

[104] Communication on the next steps in border management (COM (2008) 69, 13 Feb. 2008).
[105] See the impact assessment attached to the Commission communication: SEC (2008) 153,
13 Feb. 2008).
[106] On the VIS, see chapter 10.
[107] For further comments, see Peers, n. 97 above, 197–199.

the idea.[108] However, the European Council (EU leaders) still seem committed to the concept.[109]

Other plans for future measures include the development of a mechanism "in order to respond to exceptional circumstances putting the overall functioning of Schengen cooperation at risk", which "[a]s a very last resort" include "a safeguard clause…to allow the exceptional reintroduction of internal border controls in a truly critical situation where a Member State is no longer able to comply with its obligations under the Schengen rules." That step "would be taken on the basis of specified objective criteria and a common assessment, for a strictly limited scope and period of time, taking into account the need to be able to react in urgent cases", and would not affect free movement rights.[110]

Finally, the Commission plans to present by the end of 2011 a proposal for legislation concerning a European Border Surveillance System ("Eurosur"), which is a system for the sharing of information between national border control authorities, along with Frontex.[111]

---

[108] See the Communication on immigration, COM (2011) 248, 4 May 2011, p. 10. The communication on "smart borders" is due in Sep. 2011 (Annex 1, COM (2011) 248).

[109] See para. 24 of the European Council conclusions of June 2011: "an entry/exit system and a registered travellers' programme should be introduced".

[110] See para. 22 of the European Council conclusions of June 2011. The conclusions requested the Commission to make a proposal to this end by Sep. 2011.

[111] This proposal is is due in Sep. 2011 (Annex 1, COM (2011) 248). See also para. 23 of the European Council conclusions of June 2011. On the development of Eurosur, see: COM (2008) 68, 13 Feb. 2008; SEC (2009) 1265, 24 Sep. 2009; and SEC (2011) 145, 28 Jan. 2011.

Chapter 7

EU Visa Lists

1. *Introduction and Overview*

1.1. *Prior to the Treaty of Amsterdam*

The power to adopt a visa list for *all* Member States of the European Union was originally conferred by Article 100c of the EC Treaty, inserted into that Treaty by the original Treaty on European Union (the Maastricht Treaty) as from 1 November 1993. This power was to be exercised until the end of 1995 by a unanimous vote in the Council, on a proposal from the Commission, after consulting the European Parliament (EP). After that date the Council was to vote by qualified majority vote (QMV). The power conferred at this point was a power to "determine the third countries whose nationals must be in possession of a visa when crossing the external borders of the Member States", in other words to determine a visa "black-list". The Treaty was silent as to whether the EC also had powers to determine a visa "white-list".

In practice, the Council used its powers to adopt a visa list Regulation in 1995,[1] although this Regulation set only a visa black-list, leaving it up to Member States to decide on whether to impose a visa requirement for States not on the list. This Regulation was then annulled by the Court of Justice in 1997, on the grounds that the EP had not been reconsulted about the changes made by the Council to the Commission's original proposal.[2] The 1995 Regulation was subsequently replaced in 1999 by a Regulation with essentially the same wording.[3] The Commission published regular updates on the application of these Regulations by Member States.[4] It should also be noted that the Court of Justice ruled during this period that Article 100c EC did not confer

---

[1] Reg. 2317/95 (OJ 1995 L 234/1). For an analysis of this Regulation, see Peers, "The Visa Regulation: Free Movement Blocked Indefinitely", 21 ELRev. (1996) 150. On the Community's powers under the TEU, see Hailbronner, "Visa Regulations and Third Country Nationals in EC law" 31 CMLRev. (1994) 969.

[2] Case C-392/95 *EP v Council* [1997] ECR I-3213.

[3] Reg. 574/1999 (OJ 1999 L 72/2).

[4] See OJ 1996 C 379; OJ 1997 C 180; OJ 1998 C 101; OJ 1999 C 133; and OJ 2000 C 272.

competence upon the EC to harmonise the list of States whose nationals would require airport transit visas.[5]

In the meantime, the Member States participating in the Schengen *acquis* were increasingly harmonising the visa list which applied to those countries, by way of Decisions of the Schengen Executive Committee,[6] pursuant to the general obligation to harmonise visa policy set out in the 1990 Schengen Convention.[7]

1.2. *The Treaty of Amsterdam*

Following the entry into force of the Treaty of Amsterdam on 1 May 1999, the EC had powers to decide on "the list of third countries whose nationals must be in possession of visas when crossing the external borders and those whose nationals are exempt from that requirement", according to Article 62(2)(b)(i) EC.[8] So the Treaty now expressly conferred the power to adopt a white-list, as well as a black-list. The decision-making rules (QMV in Council with consultation of the EP) remained the same, but the jurisdiction of the Court of Justice was cut back, so that only final national courts could send references to the Court on visa matters (as well as other issues related to borders, immigration, asylum and civil law).[9] Another important change was that the UK and Ireland could opt out of visa list legislation from this point. They have consistently done so, and indeed the case law of the Court of Justice could even be interpreted to mean that they *must* do so.[10] On the other hand, the special rules on Denmark's position mean that it is bound by the visa list legislation as normal EC (now EU) law. New Member States had to apply the visa list rules as of the date of accession, while Norway, Iceland, Switzerland and (in future) Liechtenstein also apply these rules as Schengen associates.[11]

---

[5] Case C-170/96 *Commission* v *Council* [1998] ECR I-2763. The Court ruled that a "Joint Action" adopted pursuant to the original rules establishing the so-called "third pillar" of EU law (OJ 1996 L 63/8) was therefore valid. The issue of airport transit visas is now regulated by the EU's visa code: see chapter 8.

[6] SCH/Com-ex(97)32 and SCH/Com-ex(98)53, rev. 2, respectively OJ 2000 L 239/186 and 206.

[7] Art. 9(1) of the Convention (OJ 2000 L 239/19). See also the "standstill" on national visa lists set out in Art. 9(2) of that Convention.

[8] The prior Art. 100c EC was repealed by the Treaty of Amsterdam.

[9] Art. 68 EC.

[10] Cases C-77/05 *UK* v *Council* [2007] ECR I-11459 and C-137/05 *UK* v *Council* [2007] ECR I-11593; see also Case C-482/08 *UK* v *Council*, judgment of 26 Oct. 2010, not yet reported. For discussion, see chapter 2.

[11] For more on all these issues of territorial scope, see further chapter 2.

The EC's visa list powers were used first of all after the entry into force of the Treaty of Amsterdam to adopt Regulation 539/2001, which established full harmonisation of the list of third countries whose nationals do, or do not, need a visa to cross the external borders of the Member States.[12] This Regulation, which repealed the prior Regulation and the Schengen Executive Committee Decisions on the subject,[13] was amended five times before the entry into force of the Treaty of Lisbon, in: December 2001;[14] March 2003;[15] July 2005;[16] December 2006;[17] and November 2009.[18] The visa list Regulation was also amended following the 2003 and 2005 accessions of new Member States to the EU, in each case deleting the names of the new Member States from the legislation.[19] In 2008, the Commission proposed the adoption of a codified version of the Regulation (as it stood then), but this proposal has not been adopted.[20] An informal codification appears as an Annex to this chapter.

Finally, it should also be noted that the EU has visa waiver treaties with several small island States and with Brazil,[21] and that the EU's visa facilitation treaties abolish visa requirements for one category of persons (holders of diplomatic passports).[22] Denmark and the Schengen associates are encouraged to negotiate parallel treaties to the EU's visa waiver treaties, while the UK and Ireland have opted out of them.

1.3. *The Treaty of Lisbon*

Since the entry into force of the Treaty of Lisbon, the issue of visas is now addressed by Article 77 of the Treaty on the Functioning of the European Union (TFEU). Article 77(2)(a) TFEU simply provides for the adoption of measures concerning "the common policy on visas and other short-stay

---

[12] OJ 2001 L 81/1.

[13] Art. 7(1) and (3). Art 7(2) amended the Common Consular Instructions and the Common Manual, which have since been replaced by the visa code and the borders code (see chapters 8 and 3).

[14] Reg. 2414/2001 (OJ 2001 L 327/1).

[15] Reg. 453/2003 (OJ 2003 L 69/10).

[16] Reg. 851/2005 (OJ 2005 L 141/3).

[17] Reg. 1932/2006 (OJ 2006 L 405/23).

[18] Reg. 1244/2009 (OJ 2009 L 336/1).

[19] Annex II, part 18, to the 2003 Accession Treaty (OJ 2003 L 236) and Reg. 1791/2006 (OJ 2006 L 363/1), part 11.B (Romania and Bulgaria).

[20] COM (2008) 761, 28 Nov. 2008.

[21] See discussion in section 2.1 below.

[22] For details of the visa facilitation treaties, see chapter 9.

residence permits", without mentioning visa lists specifically. But it is obvious that a "common policy on visas" must include rules on a common visa list. The Treaty of Lisbon also changed the decision-making procedure as regards visa lists; legislation in this area must now be adopted by means of the ordinary legislative procedure, which entails QMV in the Council with the joint decision-making power of the EP (previously known as co-decision). The position of Denmark, the UK and Ireland is unchanged.

So far, there have been three proposals to amend the visa list legislation since the entry into force of the Treaty of Lisbon.[23] Two were adopted late in 2010, and the third was released in May 2011 (the "2011 proposal"); it was still under discussion as of 1 August 2011.[24] Also, the proposal to codify the visa list legislation, first proposed in 2008, is still outstanding; it is now also subject to the ordinary legislative procedure.[25]

2. *The Visa List Regulation*

First of all, a "visa" for the purpose of the Regulation is defined in Article 2. The Regulation governs short-stay visas for entry into one or more Member States (for periods of less than three months in total), or visas for the purposes of transit, but does not govern visas "for transit at an airport". As noted above, such visas are now regulated by the visa code.[26] The Regulation is without prejudice to Member States' competence regarding recognition of states and other entities, and travel and identity documents issued by their authorities.[27] The 2011 proposal would amend the definition of "visa" to take account of the revised wording in the visa code, plus the Court of Justice case law on freedom to travel.[28]

---

[23] COM (2010) 256, 27 May 2010 and COM (2010) 358, 5 July 2010.
[24] Respectively Regs. 1091/2010 and 1211/2010 (OJ 2010 L 329/1 and OJ 2010 L 339/6), and COM (2011) 290, 24 May 2011.
[25] See COM (2009) 665, 2 Dec. 2009.
[26] See chapter 8.
[27] Art. 6.
[28] The revised Art. 2 would define a "visa" as "an authorisation issued by a Member State with a view to transit through or an intended stay in the territory of the Member States of a duration of no more than three months in any six-month period from the date of first entry in the territory of the Member States". While this definition no longer expressly excludes airport transit visas, the explanatory memorandum to the 2011 proposal (at p. 6) makes clear that the definition is not intended to apply to them. On the relevant Court of Justice case law (Case C-241/05 *Bot* [2006] ECR I-9627), see chapter 11.

2.1. *The White-List and Black-List*

Article 1(1) of the Regulation, first sub-paragraph, specifies that Annex I sets out a definitive list of those third countries whose nationals must have visas to cross the external borders (the black-list), while Article 1(2), first sub-paragraph, specifies that Annex II sets out the list of third countries whose nationals do not need visas to cross the external borders of the Member States (the white-list).[29] Both the black-list and white-list in the initial version of Regulation 539/2001 were almost entirely simply taken over from those applied by the Schengen states, who had, as noted above, largely harmonised their visa list policies by the end of 1998. The only country left on the so-called "grey list" by that time (ie, whose nationals were subject to visa requirements in some Schengen states but not others), was Colombia. As compared to the Schengen rules, the initial version of Regulation 539/2001 moved Colombia to the black-list and shifted Romania, Bulgaria, Hong Kong and Macao to the white-list.

However, as regards Romania, Article 8(2) of the visa list Regulation initially specified that the abolition of visas provided for in Article 1(2) would not apply to nationals of countries listed in Annex II and designated with an asterisk, until the Council took a further legislative decision following a report from the Commission on "the undertakings [that country] is prepared to enter into on illegal immigration and illegal residence, including repatriation of persons from that country who are illegally resident". In fact, the only country in Annex II designated by an asterisk was Romania. Romania was then later placed on the white-list by means of the 2001 amendment to the Regulation,[30] and the 2005 Accession treaty then removed all reference to that country from the Regulation as from its membership in the EU.

The black-list consisted initially of 130 countries and three "entities and territorial authorities" which at least one Member State does not recognise (East Timor, the Palestinian Authority and Taiwan). The white-list consisted initially of 44 countries and two "Special Adminstrative Regions" of China (Hong Kong and Macao). In addition, nationals of Norway, Iceland and Liechtenstein are exempt from a visa requirement when crossing the external borders of the Member States, but the Regulation does not include them in the white-list,

---

[29] The 2011 proposal would amend the first sub-paragraph of Art. 1(2), again to take account of the Court of Justice ruling in *Bot* (see ibid).

[30] Reg. 2414/2001, n. 14 above. This Reg. amended Art. 1(2) of the visa list Reg., and deleted Art. 8(2).

because the visa exemption for these three countries flows from the agreement on the European Economic Area.[31]

Geographically, the original white-list included every state in Western Europe and all twelve states in Central, Eastern and Southern Europe which were in 2001 negotiating membership of the European Union.[32] Elsewhere in Europe, the white-list originally included only Croatia, which left Albania, Turkey, the rest of the former Yugoslavia[33] and the remaining European successor states of the former Soviet Union on the black-list.[34] Subsequently, the 2003 amendment to the Regulation removed Switzerland from the Regulation entirely, on the grounds that, like Norway, Iceland and Liechtenstein, visa abolition for Swiss nationals now flows from a treaty requirement of the EU.[35] As noted already, the 2003 and 2005 accession treaties removed the names of the new Member States from the legislation. The 2006 amendment replaced the reference to the "Federal Republic of Yugoslavia" with separate references to Serbia and Montenegro, due to the break-up of that country. Most significantly, the 2009 amendment to the Regulation moved Serbia, Montenegro and the Former Yugoslav Republic of Macedonia (FYROM) to the whitelist,[36] and the first amendment of 2010 moved Albania and Bosnia-Herzegovina to the white-list also. However, the visa exemption for nationals of these countries only applies to persons who hold biometric passports. Also, the visa exemption excludes holders of Serbian passports issued by the "Serbian Coordination Directorate", ie the holders of Serbian passports residing in Kosovo, because of the perceived risk of illegal immigration.[37]

As for the future agenda of visa liberalisation with European countries, the EU has started a "visa dialogue" with "Eastern partnership" countries (Ukraine, Belarus, Moldova, Armenia, Azerbaijan and Georgia), which include the possibility of the EU removing visa requirements on the basis of a "roadmap" addressing issues such as: "document security; fight against irregular migration, including readmission; public order issues; and external relation

---

[31] OJ 1994 L 1/1. See recital 6 in the preamble.
[32] Bulgaria, Cyprus, Czech Republic, Estonia, Hungary, Latvia, Lithuania, Malta, Poland, Romania, Slovakia and Slovenia.
[33] Initially, Bosnia-Hercegovina, the Federal Republic of Yugoslavia and the Former Yugoslav Republic of Macedonia.
[34] Russia, Ukraine, Belarus, Moldova, Armenia, Azerbaijan and Georgia.
[35] See the EU-Swiss treaty on free movement of persons (OJ 2002 L 114).
[36] The same Reg. moved Kosovo to the black-list, although this was "without prejudice to the status of Kosovo" (recital 5 in the preamble, Reg. 1244/2009, n. 18 above).
[37] See recital 4 in the preamble to Reg. 1244/2009, ibid).

issues, including human rights of migrants and other vulnerable groups". The EU also has a visa dialogue with Russia.[38]

Outside Europe, the white-list originally included most Latin American states: Argentina, Bolivia, Brazil, Chile, Ecuador (initially), Paraguay, Uruguay and Venezuela in South America, and Costa Rica, Guatemala, Honduras, Mexico, Nicaragua, Panama and Salvador in Central America. Only Peru, Surinam, Guyana, Belize and Colombia were on the black-list initially. However, the 2003 amendment to the Regulation added Ecuador to the black-list, and the 2006 amendment added Bolivia to the black-list. So among States in the northern Andes, only Venezuela remains on the white-list.

As noted above, the EU has two visa waiver treaties with Brazil, one of them covering holders of diplomatic, service and official passports,[39] and one of them concerning ordinary passport holders.[40] The latter treaty waives the visa requirement for tourists and businesspeople (as defined in the treaty), but not for other categories of ordinary visa holders. Bilateral visa waiver agreements, where they exist, will continue to apply to the excluded categories as regards visits of EU citizens to Brazil, while Brazilians falling within the excluded categories visiting the EU will still not be subject to a visa requirement, pursuant to the EU's visa list Regulation.

The white-list also includes the USA and Canada in North America, but all Caribbean states were initially on the black-list. However, the 2006 amendment moved four small Caribbean island States (Antigua and Barbuda, the Bahamas, Barbados and Saint Kitts and Nevis) onto the white-list, subject to agreeing visa waiver treaties with the EU. These treaties were applied provisionally from 28 May 2009.[41]

Every state in Africa, without exception, was on the original black-list. However, the 2006 amendment to the Regulation placed two Indian Ocean

---

[38] See COM (2008) 823, 2 Dec. 2008 (Eastern partnership), and the St Petersburg statement on EU–Russia relations: <http://www.delrus.ec.europa.eu/en/p_234.htm>. It should be recalled that for now, the EU has—or plans to have—visa facilitation treaties with all of these countries: see chapter 9. See also the conclusions of the Foreign Affairs Council on relations with the South Caucasus, 14 June 2010.

[39] OJ 2011 L 66/1. The EU concluded this treaty in Feb. 2011, and Brazil had already ratified it as well, so it has applied from 1 April 2011 (OJ 2011 L 63/1).

[40] COM (2010) 419 and 420, 6 Aug 2010. The EU decided to conclude this treaty also in Feb. 2011, but Brazil has not yet concluded it at time of writing.

[41] OJ 2009 L 169 (text of treaties); OJ 2009 L 321/38 to 43 (Council decisions on conclusion and provisional application). The treaties formally entered into force on 1 Mar. 2010 (Barbados), 1 Apr. 2010 (Bahamas) and 1 May 2010 (Antigua): see OJ 2010 L 56/1. The treaty with St. Kitts is not yet formally in force.

island States (Mauritius and the Seychelles) onto the white-list, again subject to agreeing visa waiver treaties with the EU.[42]

The majority of Asian states are also on the black-list, but there are important exceptions: Japan and South Korea in North-East Asia, Israel in West Asia, and Brunei, Malaysia and Singapore in South-East Asia (along with the Chinese regions of Hong Kong and Macao). Furthermore, the second amendment to the visa list in 2010 moved Taiwan to the white-list. The 2003 amendments to the Regulation reclassified East Timor as a country rather than a territorial entity in light of that country's independence and recognition as a state, and the 2006 amendments renamed that country "Timor-Leste". The 2006 amendments also changed the name of "Brunei" to "Brunei Darussalam".

Finally, Australia and New Zealand are on the white-list, but all the "microstates" in the Pacific are on the black-list. The 2006 amendments to the Regulation changed the name of "Western Samoa" to "Samoa", while the second amendment of 2010 deleted reference to citizens of the Northern Mariana Islands from the black-list, on the grounds that the citizens of that entity have US passports and are generally governed by US law.

Article 1(3) sets out rules which apply in the event that the third countries listed in the two Annexes break apart. The successor states will automatically be subject to the same list which applied to their predecessor state, unless the Council decides otherwise by means of the legislative procedure to amend the Regulation. Following the entry into force of the Treaty of Lisbon, the EP has joint power with the Council as regards this process.

It should also be noted that since the 2006 amendment, there are uniform rules on the visa status of what might be called "quasi-British citizens". In particular, a visa waiver applies to all "British Nationals (Overseas)", while a visa requirement applies to "British Overseas Territories Citizens who do not have the right of abode in the United Kingdom", "British Overseas Citizens", "British Subjects who do not have the right of abode in the United Kingdom" and "British Protected Persons".

The EU has consistently required third countries to make unilateral commitments or enter into treaty obligations with the EU before it will exempt them from visa obligations. In particular, Hong Kong and Macao had to agree to negotiate readmission treaties before the EU placed them on the white-list in 2001,[43] while Romania and Bulgaria had to commit themselves to changes in national immigration law (to prevent illegal residence of their nationals in

---

[42] Ibid; these treaties also applied provisionally from 28 May 2009, and formally entered into force on 1 Jan. 2010 (Seychelles) and 1 Mar. 2010 (Mauritius).

[43] On readmission treaties, see further volume 2 of this book, chapter 20.

the Member States and accept their readmission),[44] and the island micro-states had to sign visa waiver agreements with the EU, as discussed above.

While Article 9 of the 1990 Schengen Convention permitted emergency unilateral reimposition of visa requirements by a Member State,[45] and Article 64(2) EC permitted emergency measures to be taken to benefit multiple Member States in the event of a mass influx, neither provision was ever invoked in practice.[46] Following the entry into force of the visa code (which repealed Article 9 of the Schengen Convention) and the Treaty of Lisbon (which repealed Article 64(2) EC),[47] there is no express provision of EU law which permits Member States to make unilateral changes to the visa lists, even in an emergency.[48]

However, in light of concerns about the possible impact of waiving the visa requirements for Western Balkan States in 2009 and 2010, the Commission agreed to establish a monitoring system. The first report under this procedure was issued in May 2011.[49] Furthermore, the 2011 proposal to amend the visa list would entrench a "safeguard clause" in the Regulation, which would allow one or more Member States to request the Commission to re-impose visa requirements on an emergency basis.[50] The grounds for invoking this clause would be an increase of over 50% in a six month period of persons illegally staying; or an identical increase over the same period in the number of asylum applications, if the success rate of such applications was under 3%; or an identical increase in the number of rejected readmission applications. The Commission would have to make a decision, taking account of all available data, within three months, to re-impose visas for six months. It could take a further such decision for a nine-month period, if it proposed to re-impose visas permanently.[51]

---

[44] See the initial Commission report on Bulgarian and Romanian commitments (COM (2001) 61, 2 Feb. 2001) and the follow-up report on Romania, following the deferral of the visa waiver for that State (COM (2001) 361, 29 June 2001).

[45] OJ 2000 L 239/19.

[46] The previous EC Treaty clause (Art. 100c(2)) allowing reimposition of visas for six months on a non-EU country where there was an "emergency" leading to a "threat of a sudden inflow" from that country was never applied either.

[47] The replacement Treaty clause (Art. 78(3) TFEU) appears to apply only to asylum matters.

[48] It is arguable, however, that Art. 347 TFEU, which permits Member States to derogate from EU law generally as regards a war, threat of war or serious internal conflict, could justify the unilateral imposition of a visa obligation.

[49] SEC (2011) 695, 30 May 2011.

[50] Proposed new Art. 1a of the Reg.

[51] The procedural rules would be set out in a new Art. 4a of the Reg. On the comitology process, see chapter 2.

2.2. *Categories of Persons*

While the visa list Regulation sets out an exhaustive list of the third States and non-State entities whose nationals must be subjected to, or exempted from, a visa requirement, it leaves Member States a degree of flexibility as regards whether to impose a visa or not on certain *categories* of persons. However, this flexibility has been reduced over time, particularly by the 2006 amendment to the Regulation.

First of all, there are mandatory rules as regards certain categories of persons. Article 3 of the original version of the visa list Regulation required Member States to impose a visa requirement on stateless persons and recognised refugees, as defined by the relevant international conventions, if the third country where they reside and which issued their travel document is a black-list country. The 2006 amendment simply moved this rule to Article 1(1) of the Regulation.[52] This provision is without prejudice to the 1959 Council of Europe Convention on the abolition of visas for refugees,[53] which gives lawfully resident refugees with a travel document issued by one of the Contracting Parties the right to travel to other Countracting Parties without a visa for stays of up to three months.

On the other hand, as from the 2006 amendment, Member States are required to exempt three categories of persons from the visa requirement: those covered by the EU's local border traffic legislation, school pupils residing in a Member State which applies the EU Joint Action on liberalising school trips and recognised refugees and stateless persons who reside in a Member State and hold a travel document issued by that State.[54] Previously, a visa exemption had been optional for the final category of persons.[55] The 2011 proposal would add mandatory exemptions for civilian air crew members and civilian sea crew members, in case of shore leave.[56] At present Member States have an option whether to waive or impose visa requirements for these groups.[57]

---

[52] Art. 3 of the visa list Reg. was repealed by the 2006 amendment.

[53] ETS 31.

[54] Art. 1(2) of the visa list Reg., as amended by the 2006 amendment. On the border traffic legislation, see further chapter 6.

[55] See Arts. 3 and 4(2) of the original visa list Reg. The first category of persons had not existed prior to the 2006 amendment, since the EU's border traffic legislation (Reg. 1931/2006, OJ 2006 L 405/1) was adopted at the same time as the 2006 amendment to the visa list legislation. The second category of persons had not been referred to in the visa list rules prior to the 2006 amendment.

[56] Proposed amendments to Art. 1(2).

[57] See the present Art. 4(1)(b).

Secondly, as for the optional visa exemptions or visa requirements for certain categories of persons, there are three possible exemptions, which in turn permit Member States to derogate from either list, from the black-list only or from the white-list only.

As for derogations from either list, Article 4(1) currently lists five categories of persons (essentially transport, emergency and diplomatic personnel, including holders of service/official passports or special passports) who may be either exempted from a visa requirement or subject to it, irrespective of whether they have the nationality of a state or entity on the white-list or the black-list.[58] The 2011 proposal would amend this list in four respects. First of all, as noted already, it would require Member States to exempt civilian air crews, as well as civilian sea crews on shore leave, from the visa requirements.[59] Next, it would remove any discretion to waive or require visas for sea crew in transit, or emergency rescue crews.[60] Thirdly, it would amend the discretion regarding persons holding laissez-passers issued by "some intergovernmental international organisations" to refer also to the issue of "diplomatic or service passports" and to documents issued by "other entities subject to international law".[61] Finally, it would amend the rule regarding the possible visa waiver for diplomats, et al, by deleting a reference to legislation which has since been repealed.[62]

Next, derogations from the black-list are permitted by Article 4(2), which allows Member States to exempt three categories of persons from a visa requirement: school pupils from a visa requirement if they are travelling in a school party from a white-list country, or from Switzerland or Liechtenstein; refugees or stateless persons who reside in any have a travel document from a white-list country; and members of the armed forces of NATO members or of countries linked to NATO.[63] The 2011 proposal would permit Member States

---

[58] Art. 4(1)(a) was amended by the 2006 amendment, to align the reference to holders of "diplomatic passports, service/official passports or special passports" with other EU legislation. On the position of holders of diplomatic and service passports, see Guild, "When Even Machiavelli's Prince Needs a Visa Migration, Euro-Mediterranean Relations and Intercultural Dialogue" 15 EFARev. (2010) 367.

[59] The current Art. 4(1)(b) would be repealed.

[60] The current Art. 4(1)(c) would be repealed.

[61] Proposed new Art. 4(1)(c), which would replace the current Art. 4(1)(e).

[62] Proposed amendment to Art. 4(1)(a).

[63] The final category was added by the 2006 amendment. The same amendment clarified that the first category of persons included those residing in Switzerland or Liechtenstein; this was a necessary change given that the countries concerned were no longer listed in the Reg. following the 2003 amendment. The category of refugees and stateless persons with travel documents issued by white-list countries was previously set out in Art. 3 of the Reg., but was

also to waive visa requirements for refugees and stateless persons in the UK or Ireland who have a travel document issued by one of those countries.[64]

Finally, Article 4(3) allows Member States to impose visa requirements on persons from white-list countries if they are carrying out a paid activity during their stay. The 2011 proposal would add a new Article 4(4), which would permit Member States to exempt Turkish nationals from visa requirements to the extent required by the EU/Turkey association agreement.[65]

According to Article 5, information on the options which Member States choose must be communicated to the Commission and published in the *Official Journal*.[66]

There are also special rules set out in other EU legislation concerning visa exemptions for persons holding a long-stay visa, and for persons covered by EU rules on transit through Cyprus, Romania, Bulgaria and Liechtenstein.[67]

2.3. *Visa Reciprocity*

Article 1(4) of the Regulation originally set out a complex procedure in the event that any state on the white-list imposed a visa requirement upon any Member State. In that case, a Member State could inform the Commission and the Council of this fact, with the result that a visa requirement would automatically have been imposed upon nationals of that third state 30 days after notification unless the Council decided otherwise by a qualified majority. This planned re-introduction would have been published in the EU's *Official Journal*. Also, the Commission had to consider a request from a Member State or the Council that it propose an amendment to the Regulation to move the third state in question to Annex I from Annex II. If the third state waived the visa requirement on EU nationals before the adoption of amendments to the Annexes by this procedure, the Member State concerned had to inform the Commission and Council, with such notification published in the *Official Journal*. As a result, the provisional re-introduction of visas would have been repealed seven days after publication of this notice. However, these rules were never applied in practice.

---

moved to Art. 4(2) by the 2006 amendment, which did not change the substance of this option.

[64] Proposed new Art. 4(2)(d).

[65] The relevant rules are discussed in chapter 2. See particularly Case C-221/11 *Demirkan*, pending.

[66] These reports were published in OJ 2001 C 363/21, OJ 2003 C 68/2, OJ 2006 C 311/16 and OJ 2008 C 74/40.

[67] See chapters 6 and 11.

The 2003 amendment to the Regulation required the Commission to submit a report on the "reciprocity" principle by 30 June 2003.[68] Following the Commission's report, which argued that the original reciprocity rules in the Regulation were too blunt and needed to be more diplomatically nuanced,[69] the Regulation was amended in 2005 to adjust the visa reciprocity procedure, by amending Article 1(4) and adding a new Article 1(5).[70]

Following this amendment, the issue of visa reciprocity is addressed by a more diplomatic procedure. In place of a semi-automatic imposition of an EU visa requirement against a third State not applying reciprocity, the Commission must enter into discussions with the third State with a view to ensuring visa-free travel. The Commission must subsequently report to the Council, possibly proposing re-imposition of the visa requirement. In a series of reports on the application of these rules, the Commission has described some success in encouraging third States to drop visa requirements for all EU Member States, with greater difficulties (but some gradual success) as regards Canada, Australia and the US.[71] In fact, Canada *re-imposed* visa controls on Czech citizens in 2009, due to concerns about asylum applications by Czech Roma, and the EU is considering possible counter-measures.[72] But the threat of such action was not yet, at time of writing, sufficient to change the Canadian position. The 2011 proposal would make a minor change to these rules, to clarify that the ordinary legislative procedure would have to be used to re-impose visa requirements; the Commission expressly rejected the argument that the procedure should again become more automatic.[73]

3. *Comments*

While there is no formal legal requirement to review the visa list regularly, a review of the rules takes place in practice approximately every 18 months on average, as evidenced by the seven amendments to the rules in the eleven years since the visa Regulation was initially adopted. Such reviews are

---

[68] N. 15 above. Note also that reciprocity is guaranteed in some cases by EU visa waiver treaties (discussed above).

[69] Document JAI-B-1 (2004) 1372, Rev, 18 Feb. 2004.

[70] N. 16 above. See also the Council and Commission statement (OJ 2005 C 172/1).

[71] There have been six reports on the application of the reciprocity rules: COM (2006) 3, 10 Jan. 2006; COM (2006) 568, 3 Oct. 2006; COM (2007) 533, 13 Sep. 2007; COM (2008) 486, 23 July 2008; COM (2009) 560, 19 Oct. 2009; and COM (2010) 620, 5 Nov. 2010.

[72] See the special Commission report on this issue: COM (2009) 562, 19 Oct. 2009.

[73] Proposed amendment to Art. 1(4)(c).

welcome, but it would be preferable to have formal procedures for these reviews, in the interests of transparency.

More fundamentally, there is a need for binding substantive rules governing the review of the visa lists.[74] The proposals for amendments to the lists have never substantiated in detail the arguments that various third countries should be moved to the white list or the black list on grounds of illegal immigration or public security. In fact, it has been questioned whether the application of the current criteria in practice complies with non-discrimination obligations imposed by international human rights law.[75]

A sound suggestion for a more rigorous approach to the visa waiver issue was suggested by the EP, in its draft report on the EU's visa code:[76]

> When a third country fulfils conditions such as low rejection rates, application of a readmission agreement, a low percentage of nationals overstaying their visas and a small number of individuals deported for illegal employment, the Commission shall consider whether or not to propose lifting the visa obligation for nationals of that third country in accordance with the relevant provisions of Council Regulation (EC) No 539/2001.

Furthermore, in some cases the EU's demands on third States as a condition for exempting them from visa requirements are clearly disproportionate. While it is legitimate and proportionate for the EU to insist on reciprocity from the countries concerned, to insist that they readmit their own citizens in the event of breach of EU or national immigration law and to consider whether they take effective measures to prevent counterfeiting of their passports and fraudulent means of passport acquisition, demands relating to broader aspects of the immigration policy of the States concerned, including the control or readmission of non-nationals of the relevant State, cannot be justified. There is simply no rational connection between such policies and the admission of the nationals of the States concerned to EU territory. In such cases, the EU is using visa exemption as a bargaining chip as part of its broader external relations strategy.[77]

Next, it is unfortunate that the Member States cannot bring themselves to accept the abolition of visa requirements for refugees with Geneva Convention travel documents issued by *any* State on the white-list. The reference to the Council of Europe Agreement of 1959 on the abolition of visas for refugees is

---

[74] For detailed criticism of the criteria for the black-list and the list itself, see Guild, "The Border Abroad: Visas and Border Controls" in Groenendijk, Guild and Minderhoud, eds., *In Search of Europe's Borders* (Kluwer, 2003) 87 at 98–103.

[75] See Cholewinski, *Borders and Discrimination in the European Union* (ILPA, 2002), s. 1.3.1.

[76] Art. 42d in the proposed amendments set out in the Lax report (A6-0081/2008).

[77] See further chapter 9, as regards visa facilitation agreements.

now irrelevant, given that the twenty-three parties to this agreement consist of nineteen Member States and four Schengen associates, but no other countries.[78] These countries already ensure the movement of lawfully resident refugees without visas, either because they are party to the Schengen rules on freedom to travel for persons with residence permits,[79] or (as regards non-Schengen States which are EU Member States) because the visa Regulation already requires the abolition of visas for the visits of refugees and stateless persons from any Member State.

There are no convincing reasons for refusing to accept visa-free travel of refugees where their readmission is guaranteed by the State which issues them travel documents.[80] In particular, it is hard to see how a large number of such persons could successfully claim asylum in the EU, given the "safe country of asylum" provisions of the Directive on asylum procedures.[81] If there is a concern that white-list countries will be unwilling to readmit such persons, this could be addressed by agreeing on a list of white-list countries where there is *not* such a threat,[82] by encouraging more states to ratify the Council of Europe Agreement (including opening signature of that Agreement up to non-European States)[83] and by considering bilateral or multilateral agreements to agree similar obligations with non-European States and to adopt equivalent rules for stateless persons.

---

[78] ETS 31. The eight Member States which have not ratified the Agreement are: Austria; Greece; Bulgaria; Cyprus; Estonia; Latvia; Lithuania; and Slovenia. Furthermore, the UK and France have denounced it.

[79] See chapter 11, although it should be noted that Liechtenstein does not yet apply the Schengen rules in practice. It should be recalled that Art. 24 of Directive 2004/83 (the qualification Directive, OJ 2004 L 304/12) requires residence permits to be issued to refugees, although this Directive does not apply to Schengen associates.

[80] See Art. 5 of the Council of Europe Agreement.

[81] Directive 2005/85, OJ 2005 L 326/13. See *EU Asylum Law: Text and Commentary* (forthcoming).

[82] In particular, it should be recalled that the Western Balkan States, Hong Kong and Macao have readmission treaties with the EU which require them to readmit any third-country nationals who are irregularly resident in the EU, which those States or entities have issued a residence permit to. See further volume 2 of this book. It is also notable that the EU has unilaterally agreed to waive the airport transit visa requirement for persons holding particular residence permits from Japan, Canada, the USA, Andorra and San Marino, where those permits guarantee the "unconditional readmission" of the person concerned (Art. 3(5)(b) of the visa code, Reg. 810/2009, OJ 2009 L 243/1). This approach could be applied by analogy to a visa waiver as regards refugees holding the relevant residence permits as well as travel documents from those countries.

[83] Art. 10 of that Agreement expressly provides for this possibility.

Annex

Council Regulation 539/2001
of 15 March 2001
listing the third countries whose nationals must be in possession of visas
when crossing the external borders and those whose nationals are exempt
from that requirement

[informal codification, as of 1 August 2011]
[original footnotes omitted]

THE COUNCIL OF THE EUROPEAN UNION,

Having regard to the Treaty establishing the European Community, and in particular Article 62, point (2)(b)(i) thereof,

Having regard to the proposal from the Commission,

Having regard to the opinion of the European Parliament,

Whereas:

(1) Under Article 62, point (2)(b) of the Treaty, the Council is to adopt rules relating to visas for intended stays of no more than three months, and in that context it is required to determine the list of those third countries whose nationals must be in possession of visas when crossing the external borders and those whose nationals are exempt from that requirement. Article 61 cites those lists among the flanking measures which are directly linked to the free movement of persons in an area of freedom, security and justice.

(2) This Regulation follows on from the Schengen acquis in accordance with the Protocol integrating it into the framework of the European Union, hereinafter referred to as the 'Schengen Protocol'. It does not affect Member States' obligations deriving from the acquis as defined in Annex A to Decision 1999/435/EC of 20 May 1999 concerning the definition of the Schengen acquis for the purpose of determining, in conformity with the relevant provisions of the Treaty establishing the European Community and the Treaty on European Union, the legal basis for each of the provisions or decisions which constitute the acquis.

(3) This Regulation constitutes the further development of those provisions in respect of which closer cooperation has been authorised under the Schengen Protocol and falls within the area referred to in Article 1, point B, of Decision 1999/437/EC of 17 May 1999 on certain arrangements for the application of the Agreement concluded by the Council of the European Union and the Republic of Iceland and the Kingdom of Norway

concerning the association of those two States with the implementation, application and development of the Schengen acquis.

(4) Pursuant to Article 1 of the Protocol on the position of the United Kingdom and Ireland annexed to the Treaty on European Union and to the Treaty establishing the European Community, Ireland and the United Kingdom are not participating in the adoption of this Regulation. Consequently and without prejudice to Article 4 of the aforementioned Protocol, the provisions of this Regulation apply neither to Ireland nor to the United Kingdom.

(5) The determination of those third countries whose nationals are subject to the visa requirement, and those exempt from it, is governed by a considered, case-by-case assessment of a variety of criteria relating *inter alia* to illegal immigration, public policy and security, and to the European Union's external relations with third countries, consideration also being given to the implications of regional coherence and reciprocity. Provision should be made for a Community mechanism enabling this principle of reciprocity to be implemented if one of the third countries included in Annex II to this Regulation decides to make the nationals of one or more Member States subject to the visa obligation.

(6) As the Agreement on the European Economic Area exempts nationals of Iceland, Liechtenstein and Norway from the visa requirement, these countries are not included in the list in Annex II hereto.

(7) As regards stateless persons and recognised refugees, without prejudice to obligations under international agreements signed by the Member States and in particular the European Agreement on the Abolition of Visas for Refugees, signed at Strasbourg on 20 April 1959, the decision as to the visa requirement or exemption should be based on the third country in which these persons reside and which issued their travel documents. However, given the differences in the national legislation applicable to stateless persons and to recognised refugees, Member States may decide whether these categories of persons shall be subject to the visa requirement, where the third country in which these persons reside and which issued their travel documents is a third country whose nationals are exempt from the visa requirement.

(8) In specific cases where special visa rules are warranted, Member States may exempt certain categories of persons from the visa requirement or impose it on them in accordance with public international law or custom.

(9) With a view to ensuring that the system is administered openly and that the persons concerned are informed, Member States should communicate

to the other Member States and to the Commission the measures which they take pursuant to this Regulation. For the same reasons, that information should also be published in the *Official Journal of the European Communities.*

(10) The conditions governing entry into the territory of the Member States or the issue of visas do not affect the rules currently governing recognition of the validity of travel documents.

(11) In accordance with the principle of proportionality stated in Article 5 of the Treaty, enacting a Regulation listing the third countries whose nationals must be in possession of visas when crossing the external borders, and those whose nationals are exempt from that requirement, is both a necessary and an appropriate means of ensuring that the common visa rules operate efficiently.

(12) This Regulation provides for full harmonisation as regards the third countries whose nationals are subject to the visa requirement for the crossing of Member States' external borders and those whose nationals are exempt from that requirement.[84]

HAS ADOPTED THIS REGULATION:

Article 1

1. Nationals of third countries on the list in Annex I shall be required to be in possession of a visa when crossing the external borders of the Member States.

   Without prejudice to the requirements stemming from the European Agreement on the Abolition of Visas for Refugees signed at Strasbourg on 20 April 1959, recognised refugees and stateless persons shall be required to be in possession of a visa when crossing the external borders of the Member States if the third country in which they are resident and which has issued them with their travel document is a third country listed in Annex I to this Regulation.[85]

2. Nationals of third countries on the list in Annex II shall be exempt from the requirement set out in paragraph 1 for stays of no more than three months in all.[86]

---

[84] This recital was amended by Reg. 2424/2001, to delete two further sentences.

[85] The second sub-paragraph of Art. 1(1) was added by Reg. 1932/2006.

[86] The first sub-paragraph of Art. 1(2) was amended by Reg. 2424/2001, to delete a reference to Art. 8(2). The second sub-paragraph of Art. 1(2) was added by Reg. 1932/2006.

The following shall also be exempt from the visa requirement:

- the nationals of third countries listed in Annex I to this Regulation who are holders of a local border traffic card issued by the Member States pursuant to Regulation (EC) No 1931/2006 of the European Parliament and of the Council of 20 December 2006 laying down rules on local border traffic at the external land borders of the Member States and amending the provisions of the Schengen Convention* when these holders exercise their right within the context of the Local Border Traffic regime;
- school pupils who are nationals of a third country listed in Annex I and who reside in a Member State applying Council Decision 94/795/ JHA of 30 November 1994 on a joint action adopted by the Council on the basis of Article K.3.2.b of the Treaty on European Union concerning travel facilities for school pupils from third countries resident in a Member State** and are travelling in the context of a school excursion as members of a group of school pupils accompanied by a teacher from the school in question;
- recognised refugees and stateless persons and other persons who do not hold the nationality of any country who reside in a Member State and are holders of a travel document issued by that Member State.

3. Nationals of new third countries formerly part of countries on the lists in Annexes I and II shall be subject respectively to the provisions of paragraphs 1 and 2 unless and until the Council decides otherwise under the procedure laid down in the relevant provision of the Treaty.

4. Where a third country listed in Annex II introduces a visa requirement for nationals of a Member State, the following provisions shall apply:[87]

   (a) within 90 days of such introduction, or its announcement, the Member State concerned shall notify the Council and the Commission in writing; the notification shall be published in the C series of the *Official Journal of the European Union*. The notification shall specify the date of implementation of the measure and the type of travel documents and visas concerned.

   If the third country decides to lift the visa obligation before the expiry of this deadline, the notification becomes superfluous;

   (b) the Commission shall immediately after publication of that notification and in consultation with the Member State concerned, take steps with the authorities of the third country in order to restore visa-free travel;

   (c) within 90 days after publication of that notification, the Commission, in consultation with the Member State concerned, shall report to the

---

[87] Art. 1(4) was replaced by Reg. 851/2005.

Council. The report may be accompanied by a proposal providing for the temporary restoration of the visa requirement for nationals of the third country in question. The Commission may also present this proposal after deliberations in Council on its report. The Council shall act on such proposal by a qualified majority within three months;

(d) if it considers it necessary, the Commission may present a proposal for the temporary restoration of the visa requirement for nationals of the third country referred to in subparagraph (c) without a prior report. The procedure provided for in subparagraph (c) shall apply to that proposal. The Member State concerned may state whether it wishes the Commission to refrain from the temporary restoration of such visa requirement without a prior report;

(e) the procedure referred to in subparagraphs (c) and (d) does not affect the Commission's right to present a proposal amending this Regulation in order to transfer the third country concerned to Annex I. Where a temporary measure as referred to in subparagraphs (c) and (d) has been decided, the proposal amending this Regulation shall be presented by the Commission at the latest nine months after the entry into force of the temporary measure. Such a proposal shall also include provisions for lifting of temporary measures, which may have been introduced pursuant to the procedures referred to in subparagraphs (c) and (d). In the meantime the Commission will continue its efforts in order to induce the authorities of the third country in question to reinstall visa-free travel for the nationals of the Member State concerned;

(f) where the third country in question abolishes the visa requirement, the Member State shall immediately notify the Council and the Commission to that effect. The notification shall be published in the C series of the *Official Journal of the European Union*. Any temporary measure decided upon under subparagraph (d) shall terminate seven days after the publication in the Official Journal. In case the third country in question has introduced a visa requirement for nationals of two or more Member States the termination of the temporary measure will only terminate after the last publication.

5. As long as visa exemption reciprocity continues not to exist with any third country listed in Annex II in relation to any of the Member States, the Commission shall report to the European Parliament and the Council before the 1 July of every even-numbered year on the situation of non-reciprocity and shall, if necessary, submit appropriate proposals.[88]

---

[88] Art. 1(5) was added by Reg. 851/2005.

Article 2

For the purposes of this Regulation, 'visa' shall mean an authorisation issued by a Member State or a decision taken by such State which is required with a view to:
— entry for an intended stay in that Member State or in several Member States of no more than three months in total,
— entry for transit through the territory of that Member State or several Member States, except for transit at an airport.

Article 3[89]

Article 4

1. A Member State may provide for exceptions from the visa requirement provided for by Article 1(1) or from the exemption from the visa requirement provided for by Article 1(2) as regards:
   (a) holders of diplomatic passports, service/official passports or special passports in accordance with one of the procedures laid down in Articles 1(1) and 2(1) of Regulation (EC) No 789/2001 of 24 April 2001 reserving to the Council implementing powers with regard to certain detailed provisions and practical procedures for examining visa applications*.[90]
   (b) civilian air and sea crew;
   (c) the flight crew and attendants on emergency or rescue flights and other helpers in the event of disaster or accident;
   (d) the civilian crew of ships navigating in international waters;
   (e) the holders of laissez-passer issued by some intergovernmental international organisations to their officials.
2. A Member State may exempt from the visa requirement:[91]
   (a) a school pupil having the nationality of a third country listed in Annex I who resides in a third country listed in Annex II or in Switzerland and Liechtenstein and is travelling in the context of a school excursion as a member of a group of school pupils accompanied by a teacher from the school in question;

---

[89] Art. 3 was deleted by Reg. 1932/2006.
[90] Art. 4(1)(a) was replaced by Reg. 1932/2006.
[91] Art. 4(2) was replaced by Reg. 1932/2006.

(b) recognised refugees and stateless persons if the third country where they reside and which issued their travel document is one of the third countries listed in Annex II;

(c) members of the armed forces travelling on NATO or Partnership for Peace business and holders of identification and movement orders provided for by the Agreement of 19 June 1951 between the Parties to the North Atlantic Treaty Organisation regarding the status of their forces.

3. A Member State may provide for exceptions from the exemption from the visa requirement provided for in Article 1(2) as regards persons carrying out a paid activity during their stay.

Article 5

1. Within 10 working days of the entry into force of this Regulation, Member States shall communicate to the other Member States and the Commission the measures they have taken pursuant to Article 3, second indent and Article 4. Any further changes to those measures shall be similarly communicated within five working days.

2. The Commission shall publish the measures communicated pursuant to paragraph 1 in the *Official Journal of the European Communities* for information.

Article 6

This Regulation shall not affect the competence of Member States with regard to the recognition of States and territorial units and passports, travel and identity documents issued by their authorities.

Article 7

1. Council Regulation (EC) No 574/1999 shall be replaced by this Regulation.

2. The final versions of the Common Consular Instruction (CCI) and of the Common Manual (CM), as they result from the Decision of the Schengen Executive Committee of 28 April 1999 (SCH/Com-ex(99) 13) shall be amended as follows:

1. the heading of Annex 1, part I of the CCI and of Annex 5, part I of the CM, shall be replaced by the following: 'Common list of third countries the nationals of which are subject to the visa requirement imposed by Regulation (EC) No 539/2001';

2. the list in Annex 1, part I of the CCI and in Annex 5, part I of the CM shall be replaced by the list in Annex I to this Regulation;

3. the heading of Annex 1, part II of the CCI and of Annex 5, part II of the CM shall be replaced by the following: 'Common list of third countries the nationals of which are exempted from the visa requirement by Regulation (EC) No 539/2001';

4. the list in Annex 1, part II of the CCI and in Annex 5, part II of the CM shall be replaced by the list in Annex II to this Regulation;

5. part III of Annex 1 to the CCI and part III of Annex 5 of the CM shall be deleted.

3. The decisions of the Schengen Executive Committee of 15 December 1997 (SCH/Com-ex(97)32) and of 16 December 1998 (SCH/Com-ex(98)53, rev.2) shall be repealed.

Article 8

This Regulation shall enter into force on the 20th day following that of its publication in the *Official Journal of the European Communities*.[92]

This Regulation shall be binding in its entirety and directly applicable in the Member States in accordance with the Treaty establishing the European Community.

Done at Brussels, 15 March 2001.

ANNEX I
Common list referred to in Article 1(1)

1. STATES[93]

Afghanistan	Angola
Albania	Armenia
Algeria	Azerbaijan

---

[92] Reg. 2424/2001 amended Art. 8, to delete a transitional rule relating to Romania.

[93] Reg. 453/2003 added East Timor to Part 1 of Annex I, and Ecuador from Annex II to Annex I. Reg. 1932/2006 moved Bolivia to Annex I from Annex II and moved six micro-States to Annex II. It also changed the name of East Timor and Samoa, and replaced the reference to the "Federal Republic of Yugoslavia" with references to "Serbia" and "Montenegro". Reg. 1244/2009 moved Serbia, Montenegro and FYROM from Annex I to Annex II. Reg. 1091/2010 moved Albania and Bosnia Annex I to Annex II. Finally, Reg. 1211/2010 removed all reference to "Northern Mariana".

Bahrain
Bangladesh
Belarus
Belize
Benin
Bhutan
Bolivia
Bosnia and Herzegovina
Botswana
Burkina Faso
Burma/Myanmar
Burundi
Cambodia
Cameroon
Cape Verde
Central African Republic
Chad
China
Colombia
Congo
Côte d'Ivoire
Cuba
Democratic Republic
    of the Congo
Djijbouti
Dominica
Dominican Republic
Ecuador
Egypt
Equatorial Guinea
Eritrea
Ethiopia
Fiji
Gabon
Gambia
Georgia
Ghana
Grenada
Guinea
Guinea-Bissau

Guyana
Haiti
India
Indonesia
Iran
Iraq
Jamaica
Jordan
Kazakhstan
Kenya
Kiribati
Kuwait
Kyrgyzstan
Laos
Lebanon
Lesotho
Liberia
Libya
Madagascar
Malawi
Maldives
Mali
Marshall Islands
Mauritania
Micronesia
Moldova
Mongolia
Morocco
Mozambique
Namibia
Nauru
Nepal
Niger
Nigeria
North Korea
Oman
Pakistan
Palau
Papua New Guinea
Peru

Philippines	Tanzania
Qatar	Thailand
Russia	The Comoros
Rwanda	Timor-Leste
Saint Lucia	Togo
Saint Vincent and the Grenadines	Tonga
Samoa	Trinidad and Tobago
São Tomé and Príncipe	Tunisia
Saudi Arabia	Turkey
Senegal	Turkmenistan
Sierra Leone	Tuvalu
Solomon Islands	Uganda
Somalia	Ukraine
South Africa	United Arab Emirates
Sri Lanka	Uzbekistan
Sudan	Vanuatu
Surinam	Vietnam
Swaziland	Yemen
Syria	Zambia
Tajikistan	Zimbabwe

2. ENTITIES AND TERRITORIAL AUTHORITIES THAT ARE NOT RECOGNISED AS STATES BY AT LEAST ONE MEMBER STATE[94]

Kosovo as defined by the United Nations Security Council Resolution 1244 of 10 June 1999
Palestinian Authority

3. BRITISH CITIZENS WHO ARE NOT NATIONALS OF THE UNITED KINGDOM OF GREAT BRITAIN AND NORTHERN IRELAND FOR THE PURPOSES OF COMMUNITY LAW:[95]

British Overseas Territories Citizens who do not have the right of abode in the United Kingdom
British Overseas Citizens
British Subjects who do not have the right of abode in the United Kingdom
British Protected Persons

---

[94] Reg. 453/2003 moved East Timor to Part 1 of Annex I. The reference to Kosovo was added by Reg. 1244/2009. Reg. 1211/2010 moved Taiwan from Annex I to Annex II.
[95] Part 3 was added by Reg. 1932/2006.

ANNEX II[96]
Common list referred to in Article 1(2)

1. STATES
Albania(*)
Andorra
Antigua and Barbuda*
Argentina
Australia
Bahamas*
Barbados*
Bosnia and Herzegovina(*)
Brazil
Brunei Darussalam
Canada
Chile
Costa Rica
Croatia
Ecuador
Former Yugoslav Republic of Macedonia(*)
Guatemala
Holy See
Honduras
Israel
Japan
Malaysia
Mauritius*
Mexico
Monaco
Montenegro(*)
New Zealand
Nicaragua
Panama

---

[96] Reg. 2424/2001 deleted an asterisk and a footnote relating to Romania. The 2003 and 2005 accession treaties deleted all reference to the 12 countries which joined the EU at that point. Reg. 453/2003 moved Ecuador (to Annex I) and deleted all reference to Switzerland. Reg. 1932/2006 changed the name of Brunei, and moved the six micro-States from Annex I, with the attached footnote. It also moved Bolivia to Annex I. Reg. 1244/2009 moved Serbia, Montenegro and FYROM from Annex I to Annex II, and added the relevant footnote. Reg. 1091/2010 moved Albania and Bosnia Annex I to Annex II, with the same footnote.

Paraguay
Saint Kitts and Nevis*
Salvador
San Marino
Serbia (excluding holders of Serbian passports issued by the Serbian Coordination Directorate (in Serbian: *Koordinaciona uprava*)) (*)
Seychelles*
Singapore
South Korea
United States of America
Uruguay
Venezuela

* The exemption from the visa requirement will apply from the date of entry into force of an agreement on visa exemption to be concluded with the European Community.

(*) The visa requirement exemption applies only to holders of biometric passports.

2. SPECIAL ADMINISTRATIVE REGIONS OF THE PEOPLE'S REPUBLIC OF CHINA

Hong Kong SAR (1)
Macao SAR (2)

   (1) The visa requirement exemption applies only to holders of a 'Hong Kong Special Administrative Region' passport.
   (2) The visa requirement exemption applies only to holders of a 'Região Administrativa Especial de Macau' passport.

3. BRITISH CITIZENS WHO ARE NOT NATIONALS OF THE UNITED KINGDOM OF GREAT BRITAIN AND NORTHERN IRELAND FOR THE PURPOSES OF COMMUNITY LAW:[97]
   British Nationals (Overseas)

4. ENTITIES AND TERRITORIAL AUTHORITIES THAT ARE NOT RECOGNISED AS STATES BY AT LEAST ONE MEMBER STATE:[98]
   Taiwan (*)

(*) The exemption from the visa requirement applies only to holders of passports issued by Taiwan which include an identity card number.

---

[97] Part 3 was added by Reg. 1932/2006.
[98] Part 4 was added by Reg. 1211/2010.

Chapter 8

The Visa Code

1. *Introduction and Overview*

The Commission originally proposed the Regulation establishing the visa code in July 2006,[1] and the code (formally Regulation 810/2009) was officially adopted in July 2009.[2] The code has applied from 5 April 2010, except for the rules on appeals, which have applied from 5 April 2011.[3]

In common with most measures discussed in this book, the code does not apply to the UK and Ireland, and applies to Denmark in the form of international law. It also applies to the Schengen associates: Norway, Iceland, Switzerland and (in future) Liechtenstein.[4]

The code replaced a myriad of prior rules governing the issue of visas by EU Member States.[5] In particular, it replaced the original source of the basic rules governing Schengen visas: Articles 9–17 of the Schengen Convention,[6] supplemented by the Common Consular Instructions (CCI) adopted by the Schengen Executive Committee.[7] After the incorporation of the Schengen *acquis* into the EC and EU legal order, in accordance with the Treaty of Amsterdam, the CCI had been amended on a number of occasions by the Council, pursuant to a Regulation, adopted in 2001,[8] which conferred powers to amend the CCI, along with four other Schengen measures concerning

---

[1] COM (2006) 403, 19 July 2006.

[2] OJ 2009 L 243/1. For further discussion of the code, see Meloni, "The Community Code on Visas: Harmonisation at last?", 34 ELRev. (2009) 671.

[3] Art. 58(2) and (5). All references in this chapter are to the visa code, unless otherwise specified.

[4] See chapter 2.

[5] Art. 56. Annex XIII to the code sets out a correlation table comparing the visa code and the prior measures.

[6] OJ 2000 L 239.

[7] The consolidated text of the CCI as of 1 May 1999, as integrated into the EC legal order, was set out in SCH/Com-ex (99) 13, OJ 2000 L 239/307.

[8] Reg. 789/2001, OJ 2001 L 116/2.

visas,[9] in part upon itself, and in part upon individual Member States. The Commission brought a legal challenge to this Regulation, on the grounds that the Regulation did not adequately explain why implementing powers had not been conferred on the Commission (which is the normal legal rule), but the Court of Justice dismissed the challenge.[10]

The various amendments to the CCI adopted by the Council,[11] which were also replaced by the visa code, had addressed issues such as: the obligation of applicants to pay a fee for a visa *application*, not just when the visa is issued;[12] the use of a standard form for Schengen visa applications;[13] out harmonised rules on the use of travel agents in the visa process;[14] establishing a standard fee of €35 for Schengen visa applications;[15] strengthening the normal obligation to interview visa applicants in consulates;[16] liberalising the rules on the representation of one Member State by another, as regards visa applications;[17] imposing an obligation in principle for visa applicants to have medical insurance;[18] and increasing the standard fee for an application to €60 as from the start of 2007, in order to fund the Visa Information System (VIS).[19]

---

[9] The other four measures were: Executive Committee Decisions SCH/Com-ex (98) 56 and SCH/Com-ex (99) 14 (OJ 2000 L 239/207 and 298), which both concerned a manual of travel documents to which a visa could be affixed; a manual concerning the issuance of Schengen visas in third States where not all the Schengen States are represented (Document SCH/II (95) 16, 19th revision, referred to in point III of the Decision consolidating the text of the CCI (ibid.), but not published in the OJ); and document SCH/II-Vision (99) 5 ("Schengen Consultation Network (Technical Specifications)"), referred to in Executive Committee Decision SCH/Com-ex (94) 15 rev (OJ 2000 L 239/165, as corrected by a later Council Decision (OJ 2000 L 272/24)), which concerns a computerised procedure for consulting the central authorities of other Member States on visa applications. The latter measure was initially confidential, but then was largely declassified by the Council (OJ 2003 L 116/22).

[10] Case C-257/01 *Commission v Council* [2005] ECR I–345.

[11] The amendments made by Member States to the CCI (see Art. 2, Reg 789/2001) were not published in the OJ.

[12] OJ 2002 L 20/5.

[13] OJ 2002 L 123/50.

[14] OJ 2002 L 187/44.

[15] OJ 2003 L 152/82.

[16] OJ 2004 L 5/74.

[17] OJ 2004 L 5/76. This Decision also replaced the manual on the issuance of Schengen visas in third States where not all the Schengen States are represented (Document SCH/II (95) 16, 19th revision, n. 9 above) with an Annex to the CCI.

[18] OJ 2004 L 5/79.

[19] OJ 2006 L 175/77.

It was also still possible to amend the CCI by means of legislation, and indeed several legislative acts amended the Instructions.[20] In particular, a major amendment to the CCI adopted in 2009 (Regulation 390/2009), which was also replaced by the visa code, regulated the process of taking biometric data from visa applicants, pursuant to the planned operation of the VIS.[21] Due to all these changes, the CCI were frequently consolidated informally.[22]

The visa code also replaced a number of other EU measures and Decisions of the Schengen Executive Committee relating to visas, namely: five Schengen Executive Committee Decisions, concerning a harmonised form for sponsorship of visa applicants, extending or shortening the validity of a visa and the exchange of statistics;[23] a Joint Action adopted in 2006 concerning airport transit visas;[24] the 2001 Regulation conferring power on the Council to amend the CCI (except as regards the Schengen Consultation Network);[25] another 2001 Regulation concerning freedom to travel with a long-stay visa;[26] and a 2003 Regulation concerning visas issued at the border.[27] Despite this legislative simplification, a number of specific EU measures and Schengen Executive Committee Decisions relating to visas remain in force; these measures are discussed in chapter 11 of this book.

It should also be recalled that there are also visa facilitation treaties between the EU and a number of third States, which differ from the general rules in the visa code as regards issues such as standardised supporting documents for applications, a lower standard visa fee and further exemptions from visa fees. These treaties are discussed in the next chapter.

Finally, the visa code can be implemented by the Commission, which has the power to amend nine of the thirteen Annexes to the Code, by means (at the moment) of the "regulatory procedure with scrutiny" (involving a form of

---

[20] Art. 7(2) of Reg. 539/2001 (OJ 2001 L 81/1); Art. 2 of Reg. 1091/2001 (OJ 2001 L 150/4); Art. 2 of Reg. 334/2002 (OJ 2002 L 53/7); Art. 5(4) of Reg. 415/2003 (OJ 2003 L 64/1); Art. 11(1) of Reg. 693/2003 (OJ 2003 L 99/8); and Art. 39(2)(c) of the Schengen Borders code (Reg. 562/2006, OJ 2006 L 105/1).

[21] OJ 2009 L 131/1.

[22] The consolidated CCI were published in OJ 2002 C 313/1, OJ 2003 C 310/1 and OJ 2005 C 326/1.

[23] SCH/Com-ex (93) 21 (OJ 2000 L 239/151); SCH/Com-ex (93) 24 (OJ 2000 L 239/154); SCH/Com-ex (94) 25 (OJ 2000 L 239/173); SCH/Com-ex (98) 12 (OJ 2000 L 239/196); and SCH/Com-ex (98) 57 (OJ 2000 L 239/299).

[24] OJ 1996 L 63/8.

[25] Reg. 789/2001 (n. 8 above).

[26] Reg. 1091/2001 (n. 20 above).

[27] Reg. 415/2003 (ibid.).

control by the European Parliament (EP)),[28] as well as the power to adopt operational instructions for consular authorities, by means of the "regulatory procedure" (until 1 March 2011) and the "examination procedure" (after that date).[29] As of 1 August 2011, the Commission had adopted two measures implementing the Code, setting out operational instructions for consular authorities.[30] Member States are also obliged to notify a number of national decisions to the Commission, which is obliged to publish them.[31] However, as of 1 August 2011, the Commission had only briefly made this information available, and then withdrawn it.

2. *Text and Analysis*

Title I of the visas code concerns respectively the objective and scope of the code, and the relevant definitions.[32] The code is "without prejudice" to the position of third-country nationals as regards EU free movement law and agreements extending EU free movement law to non-EU states.[33]

2.1. *Title II: Airport Transit Visas (Article 3)*

Title II of the code concerns airport transit visas (ATVs).[34] First of all, it refers to a standard list of countries (set out in Annex IV to the code) whose nationals require airport transit visas to cross through the international transit areas of airports.[35] This list replaces the (identical) list previously attached to the

---

[28] Arts. 50 and 52. For a list of the Annexes, see below. As discussed further in chapter 2, the regulatory procedure with scrutiny will be replaced in future with the delegated acts procedure, although the visa code will first have to be amended to give effect to that change.

[29] Arts. 51–52. For more on the change in comitology rules as from 1 Mar. 2011, see further chapter 2.

[30] These measures are the Handbook for the processing of visa applications and the modification of issued visas (C(2010) 1620 final, 19 Mar. 2010) and the Handbook for the organisation of visa sections and local Schengen cooperation (C(2010) 3667 final, 11 June 2010). For the text of both Decisions, see: <http://ec.europa.eu/home-affairs/policies/borders/borders_visa_en.htm>.

[31] Art 53.

[32] Arts. 1 and 2.

[33] Art. 1(2). See also Art. 3(5)(d) of the Code, which exempts family members of EU citizens from any airport transit visa requirement, and also Art. 24(2)(a) and Annex XI, Art. 4.

[34] For the definition of "airport transit visa", see Art 2(5); see also Art. 1(3) on the scope of the code.

[35] Art. 3(1). This list consists of twelve states: Afghanistan, Sri Lanka, Iran, Iraq, Ethiopia, Eritrea, Somalia, Nigeria, Ghana, Pakistan, Bangladesh and Congo.

CCI,[36] as well as a similar list of states attached to the Joint Action of 1996 (now repealed).[37]

Member States may decide that the nationals of additional States will require ATVs (ie a purely national list) in the event of "urgent cases of massive inflow of illegal immigrants", subject to prior notification of the Commission before introducing or withdrawing such a national requirement.[38] These national lists are subject to annual review in the "comitology committee" established by the visa code Regulation, in order to decide whether to add the countries concerned to the uniform EU list of states requiring ATVs.[39] Any decision to amend the common list must be taken by the Commission, subject to control by the Member States, the Council and the EP pursuant (for now) to the "regulatory procedure with scrutiny".[40] If the countries concerned are not added to the uniform EU list, the Member State which listed them can either keep those countries on its national list (if the criteria for listing them are still met) or withdraw the ATV requirement.[41] There could presumably be a judicial review of whether the criteria are met for a national decision to place (or retain) a country on an ATV list in light of the criteria in the visa code. However, it should be noted that there are no criteria governing the addition or removal of countries to the common EU list.[42]

In any event, neither the EU common list nor any national list can apply an ATV requirement to six categories of persons:[43] those holding a Schengen visa, national long-stay visa or residence permit issued by a Member State; those holding a valid residence permit issued by the USA, Japan, Canada, San Marino or Andorra, if the permit is listed in Annex V to the visa code and

---

[36] Annex 3 to the CCI, Part 1.

[37] The Joint Action list (n 24 above) comprised ten of the twelve countries which were on the CCI list (the exceptions were Pakistan and Bangladesh).

[38] Art. 3(2). These decisions have to be notified to the Commission: see Art. 53(1)(b).

[39] Art. 3(3).

[40] See Arts. 50 and 52(3).

[41] Art. 3(4).

[42] The preamble to the code (point 5) states only that airport transit rules, including an ATV requirement, are "necessary...in order to combat illegal immigration". It might be arguable that, in conjunction with the principle of proportionality, a decision to add a country to the common ATV list could be challenged if there is insufficient evidence that nationals of that state present a risk of irregular migration.

[43] Although the code is not explicit on this point, it is assumed that this list is exhaustive, given the underlying intention of harmonising national policies in order to create a common policy (see, for instance, point 3 of the preamble, and previously Arts. 9(1) and 10(1) of the Schengen Convention).

guarantees unqualified readmission;[44] those holding a visa issued by a Member State, an EEA state, or by the USA, Canada or Japan, or when they return from those countries having used the visa; family members of EU citizens who have exercised free movement rights; holders of diplomatic passports; and flight crew members who are nationals of States which are party to the Chicago Convention on civil aviation.[45]

Compared to the Commission's original proposal, the same countries appear in the common ATV list, but a fundamental change suggested by the Commission – the complete abolition of national lists of ATV requirements – was rejected by the Council.[46] Compared to the rules in the CCI, again the same twelve countries are still subject in the visa code to a common ATV requirement (as noted above), while the CCI (before its repeal) provided that the nationals of no fewer than thirty-one other states were subject to an ATV requirement in at least one, but not all, Schengen States.[47] There were no substantive criteria in the CCI for these unilateral national decisions.[48] It remains to be seen, after the application of the visa code, whether the new criteria for Member States to maintain national lists of ATV requirements will in fact lead to less divergence in ATV requirements across the EU. In principle, the criteria should lead to a reduction in divergence, since "urgent cases of mass influx" *prima facie* sets a high threshold to justify the imposition of an ATV requirement. Moreover, the power to maintain national lists should be interpreted narrowly, as it is an exception to the general rule.

In any event, the exceptions from the ATV requirement in the code are more uniform than under the CCI. The CCI specified that, for the common list, the ATV requirement was waived if the person concerned holds a listed residence permit issued by an EEA Member State.[49] But it was up to each

---

[44] Annex V can also be amended by the Commission, pursuant (for now) to the regulatory procedure with scrutiny (Arts. 50 and 52(3)).

[45] Art. 3(5).

[46] See Art. 22 and Annexes VI and VII of the original proposal.

[47] Annex 3, Part II of the CCI. This does not take account of changes which took place after the last consolidation of the CCI in 2005.

[48] According to the *chapeau* to Annex 3 to the CCI, a Member State changing its national list "undertakes to inform its partners and to take account of their interests". See also the open-ended Art. 5 of the 1996 Joint Action on ATVs.

[49] The lists in question were set out in Part III of Annex 3 to the CCI. The 1996 Joint Action was less precise, since it permitted Member States to decide whether or not to exempt a non-exhaustive list of categories of persons from the ATV requirement (Art. 4, Joint Action). However, the Joint Action gave Member States discretion as to whether to impose an ATV requirement on stateless persons and refugees (Art. 6), whereas the visa code implicitly requires Member States to insist on an ATV (unless the persons concerned fall within one of the categories listed in Art 3(5) of the visa code).

Member State to determine whether there was an exemption from the ATV requirement for holders of diplomatic, service or official passports. As for the States whose nationals were subject to an ATV requirement in fewer than all Member States, there were widely differing categories of exceptions from the requirement. So it is clear that the code must have brought about further harmonisation as regards exceptions from the ATV requirement, even if it has not led to further harmonisation as regards the list of countries whose nationals are subject to that requirement in the first place.

2.2. *Title III: Conditions and Procedures for Issuing Visas (Articles 4–36)*

Chapter I of Title III of the visa code defines the authorities taking part in the application procedure.[50] As a general rule, subject to limited exceptions, visa applications must be decided upon by consulates.[51] The visa code then specifies which Member State is responsible for considering applications for different types of visa;[52] Member States are obliged to cooperate to prevent situations in which an application cannot be processed because the Member State responsible does not have a consulate or representation from another Member State in the third State concerned.[53] Applicants should normally apply to the relevant consulate in the State in which they are legally resident (ie Algerian citizens legally resident in the USA and wishing to visit France should apply for a Schengen visa at a French consulate in the USA, not a French consulate in Algeria), unless they provide a justification for applying instead to a consulate in a State in which they are legally present.[54] The general rules also apply to visa applicants legally residing in Member States.[55]

There are detailed rules on one Member State's representation of (an)other Member State(s) for the purpose of processing visa applications or for taking biometric information for applicants.[56] These rules, *inter alia*, encourage Member States to conclude representation arrangements with each other in countries or regions where some Member States lack consulates.[57] There is, however, no guarantee that a nearby consulate which is able to process applications will be available for all visa applications; the radical solution of a move toward common EU consulates, perhaps constituting part of the EU External

---

[50] Arts. 4–8.
[51] Art. 4
[52] Art. 5(1) to (3).
[53] Art. 5(4).
[54] Art. 6.
[55] Art. 7.
[56] Art. 8. These arrangements have to be notified to the Commission: see Art. 53(1)(a).
[57] Art. 8(5) and (6).

Action Service which has been established pursuant to the Treaty of Lisbon,[58] is not mentioned in the visa code.

Chapter II of Title III of the visa code concerns the application process.[59] Visa applications cannot be made more than three months before the date of travel, except as regards multiple-entry visas, where the application can be made up to six months before the date of travel.[60] Applicants normally have to appear in person to apply for a visa, but this is subject to a number of exceptions.[61] Each applicant must fill out the standard application form, even children who are listed on their parent's passport.[62] Applicants must also present a valid travel document.[63]

Applicants must also present biometric data (a photograph and ten fingerprints);[64] this issue was agreed separately when Regulation 390/2009 was negotiated.[65] Fingerprints can be taken by honorary consuls or private service providers.[66] There are uniform exemptions from the fingerprinting requirement: children under twelve; persons for whom fingerprinting is physically impossible; heads of state, senior politicians and their spouses and delegations on official visits; and senior royal family members on official visits.[67]

The code then details the rules concerning supporting documents to be submitted by applicants,[68] the requirement of medical insurance,[69] the fee for visa applicants[70] and the service fee for the use of private companies to collect biometric data (see further below).[71] The application fee remained €60, and the maximum service fee is half that amount.[72] However, the application fee

---

[58] See Art. 24(2), revised TEU. For the Decision establishing the service, see OJ 2010 L 201/30.

[59] Arts. 9–17.

[60] Art. 9.

[61] Art. 10(1) and (2). See also the statement of the German delegation when the code was adopted, as regards personal interviews with applicants (Council doc. 11110/09, 24 June 2009).

[62] Art. 11. The standard application form is set out in Annex I to the Code.

[63] Art. 12.

[64] Art. 13. However, fingerprints normally only need to be taken once every five years (Art. 13(3)).

[65] N. 21 above.

[66] Art. 13(6), referring to Arts. 42 and 43.

[67] Art. 13(7).

[68] Art. 14 and Annex II. As compared to the previous rules, the standard Schengen sponsorship form no longer applies.

[69] Art. 15.

[70] Art. 16. It should also be noted that since the rules on fees now appear in the main text of the code, they can only be amended by the legislative process, not as an implementing measure.

[71] Art. 17.

[72] Arts. 16(1) and 17(4).

must be reduced to €35 for children between six and twelve years old.[73] The fee must be waived for: children under six years old; students, pupils and teachers on study trips; researchers as defined by an EU recommendation; and representatives of non-profit organisations attending seminars and similar events.[74] Also, the fee *may* be waived for children between six and twelve, holders of diplomatic and service passports and participants in non-profit seminars and similar events who are under 25 years old.[75] The fee may furthermore be waived or reduced in individual cases, if this "serves to promote cultural or sporting interests as well as interests in the field of foreign policy, development policy and other areas of vital public interest or for humanitarian reasons".[76] There is no longer an express provision for waiving fee for family members of EU or EEA citizens,[77] but of course the exemption of such persons from visa fees follows from the general priority of EU free movement law recognised by the visa code.[78]

Chapter III of Title III of the visa code concerns the examination of and decisions taken upon applications.[79] This includes rules on verification of consular competence,[80] admissibility of applications[81] and the stamping of applicants' travel documents.[82]

The key issue is of course the substantive grounds for deciding on the application for a visa. The visa code specifies that consulates are to apply the criteria for admission set out in the Schengen Borders Code: possession of a valid travel document; justification of the purpose and conditions of the visit, and sufficient subsistence; non-listing in the Schengen Information System (SIS); and not posing a "threat to public policy, internal security, public health or the international relations of any of the Member States".[83] In this context, "particular consideration shall be given to assessing whether the applicant presents a

---

[73] Art. 16(2).

[74] Art. 16(4).

[75] Art. 16(5). There could be further harmonisation of these optional exceptions, pursuant to the rules on local consular cooperation (see discussion of Art. 48 below).

[76] Art. 16(6).

[77] See previously Part VII of the CCI, point 4, second paragraph.

[78] Art. 1(2); the exemption from the visa fee for such persons is set out in Art. 5(2), second subparagraph, of Directive 2004/38 (OJ 2004 L 229/35).

[79] Arts. 18–23.

[80] Art. 18.

[81] Art. 19. There was no equivalent provision in the CCI.

[82] Art. 20, referring also to Annex III. Note that this Article will be irrelevant once the VIS has been fully rolled out (Art. 20(3)).

[83] Art. 21(1), referring to Art. 5 of the Borders Code (n. 20 above). On these rules in the Borders Code, see further chapter 3.

risk of illegal immigration or a risk to the security of the Member States and whether the applicant intends to leave the territory of the Member States before the expiry of the visa applied for."[84]

Also, the VIS (when fully operational) must be checked for each application,[85] and (fleshing out the provisions of the Schengen Borders code) consulates must also check for the veracity of documents, the intentions of the applicant, sufficient means of the applicant for subsistence, a listing for refusal of entry in the SIS, that the applicant is not "a threat to public policy, internal security or public health" as defined in the Borders Code and (an additional criterion) that the applicant has sufficient medical insurance.[86] The consulate must also assess whether the applicant has overstayed the permitted length of stay on the territory at present, or in the past.[87] There are separate criteria relating to applications for airport transit visas.[88] Decisions on each application have to be based on the "authenticity and reliability" of the documents submitted, and the "veracity and reliability" of the applicant.[89] If necessary, further documents or a personal interview can be requested.[90] Finally, the visa code specifies that a previous refusal of a visa application will not automatically mean a refusal of a new application; rather, a new application "shall be assessed on the basis of all available information".[91] However, it remains to be seen whether the introduction of the VIS will in practice nonetheless lead to an increased tendency to reject applications due to prior refusals, because information on prior refusals will be more readily available to consulates.

The visa code then sets out rules for the controversial system of "prior consultation", according to which one Member State may require the authorities of all other Member States to inform them of all visa applications from nationals of particular third countries or from particular categories of such nationals.[92] The consulted State's authorities must reply within seven days of

---

[84] Art. 21(1).

[85] Art. 21(2). On the VIS, see further chapter 10.

[86] Art. 21(3). These are the same grounds set out in Art. 5(1) of the Borders Code, with the addition of the medical insurance requirement. Art. 21(5) sets out more rules relating to subsistence, including a further cross-reference to the Schengen Borders Code as regards subsistence criteria set by Member States.

[87] Art. 21(4).

[88] Art. 21(6).

[89] Art. 21(7).

[90] Art. 21(8).

[91] Art. 21(9).

[92] Art. 22(1). Note that the procedure does not apply to ATVs. Compare to the CCI provisions (Part V, point 2.3).

the consultation, or they are deemed to have no objections to the application.[93] If they do have objections, this is not a ground as such for refusing a visa application,[94] but obviously in practice the authorities deciding on the application are far more likely to reject it if the consulted Member State objects.[95] However, it should be noted that even if the consulted Member State objects to the application, the consulting Member State can still decide "exceptionally" to issue a visa with limited territorial validity (an "LTV visa").[96] The visa code does not explicitly specify that *only* an LTV visa (ie not a uniform visa) can be issued in the event of objections to the application by the consulted Member State; although that is a possible interpretation of the code, this interpretation should be rejected in the absence of an express and unambiguous provision to this end, because it would in effect constitute both an additional ground for refusal of an application and a new rule on decision-making competence, neither of which are mentioned in the relevant Articles of the Code.[97]

The code does not specify whether the applicant (or indeed the consulting Member State) must be told of the consulted Member State's reasons for objecting to an application. However, an obligation for the consulted Member State to give reasons for its objection is necessarily implied for the visa code, for in the absence of such reasons it would be impossible for the consulting Member State (if it decides to reject the application on the basis of objections by the consulted State) to satisfy its obligation to give reasons for its rejection of the application, and for the applicant to exercise effectively his or her right of appeal against this rejection in the absence of knowing the reasons for the rejection (see further discussion of these procedural rights below).

In practice, the consultation process is carried out in accordance with the "Schengen Consultation Network" established by previous Schengen Executive

---

[93] Art. 22(2). The seven-day deadline was previously in the CCI, but the possibilities for extending the deadline (Part V, point 2.3(e) of the CCI) were dropped in the code.

[94] This is not a ground for refusal set out in Art. 32(1) or Annex VI, and it is assumed that the grounds for refusal set out there are exhaustive (see further discussion below). Nor is there any provision in Arts. 5–8 (see further discussion above) that transfers responsibility for decision-making in these cases to the consulted Member State.

[95] Presumably the consulted Member State, if it objects to the application and gives its reasons, will give one or more of the reasons listed in Art. 32(1).

[96] Art. 25(1)(a)(ii); an LTV visa can also be issued without the required consultation in the case of urgency (Art. 25(1)(a)(iii). See further discussion of LTV visas below.

[97] It might be objected that there is no "refusal" of an application if an LTV visa is issued. However, in light of the obvious differences between LTV and uniform visas, the better view is that refusing an application for a uniform visa and issuing an LTV visa instead amounts to a refusal of the original application for the purposes of the code. This means that the obligation to notify the refusal and the reasons for it, and the right to appeal, are still applicable.

Committee Decisions; this Network will be phased out as the VIS is phased in, for the VIS will integrate a new system for such consultations.[98] Member States shall inform the Commission of any new consultation requirements, or any withdrawal of existing requirements; the Commission shall inform other Member States and the public.[99] The requirement to inform the public of the consultation requirement is a major change from the position under the CCI, when such arrangements were kept secret.[100]

Another change from the prior rules is the possibility to replace the consultation requirement with a less onerous information requirement, which is identical to the consultation requirement except for the lack of any facility for the informed Member State to comment on the visa application.[101]

A decision (whether positive or negative) on visa applications must be made within fifteen days, although extensions of this period to thirty or sixty days are permissible under certain conditions.[102]

Chapter IV of Title III of the visa code concerns issuing a visa.[103] It specifies that visas can be valid for one entry, two entries or multiple entries, with a maximum validity of five years and (normally) a period of grace of 15 days.[104] Multiple-entry visas "shall" be issued where there is both a proven need to travel frequently and the applicant has proven his or her "integrity and reliability".[105]

Next, there are rules on visas with limited territorial validity ("LTV" visas), ie visas which are valid only for one or possibly more, but less than all, of the Schengen States.[106] LTV visas are issued "exceptionally", either where a Member State "considers it necessary on humanitarian grounds, for reasons of national interest or because of international obligations", to derogate from the criteria for entry set out in the Schengen Borders Code, to issue a visa despite the objections of a Member State which had to be consulted in accordance with the consultation procedure (see above), or to issue a visa "for reasons of urgency" even though such a consultation has not been carried out;[107] or

---

[98] Art. 22(5). See further chapter 10.

[99] Art. 22(3) and (4), and Art. 53(1)(d) and (2). Previously the relevant list was also set out in an Annex to the CCI (Annex 5), which was amended at the behest of each Member State.

[100] See Annex 5 to the consolidated CCI (n. 22 above).

[101] Arts. 31 and 53(1)(e) and (2).

[102] Art. 23. There was no equivalent provision in the CCI.

[103] Arts. 24–32.

[104] Art. 24(1). The CCI rules did not contain a provision on grace periods (Part V, point 2.3).

[105] Art. 24(2).

[106] On the territorial scope of LTV visas, see Art. 25(2).

[107] Art. 25(1)(a). There is a requirement to inform other Member States in such cases: see Art. 25(4).

where a new visa is to be issued to a person who has already used a visa within the same six-month period.[108] There is also a special rule for cases where a travel document is not recognized by all Member States.[109]

There are comparable specific rules on the issue of airport transit visas,[110] as well as detailed technical rules on filling in, invalidating and fixing visa stickers.[111] The visa code confirms that simple possession of a visa "shall not confer an automatic right of entry".[112]

The visa code also contains key provisions on the grounds for refusing a visa and the procedural rights for visa applicants in the case of refusal.[113] An application "shall" be refused: if the applicant does not meet the conditions for obtaining a visa;[114] if the applicant has already stayed for three of the last six months on the basis of a visa;[115] or if there are "reasonable doubts" about the authenticity, veracity or reliability of the applicant's documents or statements.[116] The visa code is silent as to whether Member States may also invoke other grounds for refusing an application, but given the uniform nature of Schengen visas and the lack of any space for "other" grounds for refusal on the standard notification form, it should be concluded that they cannot. It must therefore follow as a corollary that there is an obligation to issue a visa if the criteria for its issue are satisfied.

Following a refusal of an application, in a major change from the rules in the CCI, the applicant must informed of the refusal and the grounds for it (by use of a standard form),[117] and applicants whose applicants are refused have the "right to appeal" in accordance with the national law of the Member State which refused their application.[118] The rules on notification and appeal also

---

[108] Art. 25(1)(b). Compare to the rules on extending visas, as set out in Art. 33 (see below).

[109] Art. 25(3).

[110] Art. 26.

[111] Arts. 27–29 and Annexes VII and VIII.

[112] Art. 30.

[113] Art. 32. These rules are "without prejudice" to the possibility of issuing an LTV visa (see above).

[114] Art. 32(1)(a)(i) to (iii) and (v) to (vi); these mirror the conditions for obtaining a visa set out in Art 21(3) (see above).

[115] Art. 32(1)(a)(iv).

[116] Art. 32(1)(b).

[117] Art. 32(2). The standard form is set out in Annex VI.

[118] Art. 32(3). The provisions on notification and appeal can be compared to the similar provisions in the Schengen Borders Code (see chapter 3) and to the right of access to information in the VIS (see chapter 10), considering that in the first case, the grounds for refusal of entry and refusal of a visa are nearly the same, and in the second case that information on refusals of visa applications, etc will be inserted into the VIS (see Arts. 32(5) and 34(8)) and therefore subject to the right of access to VIS data anyway.

apply to visa applications at the border, and to decisions on annulment and revocation of visas.[119] However, as noted above, the provisions on notification and appeal rights applied later than the rest of the Code (from 5 April 2011).[120]

Chapter V of Title III of the visa code concerns modification of an issued visa.[121] First, a visa "shall" be extended (free of charge) where there is "proof of *force majeure* or humanitarian reasons preventing [the visa holder] from leaving the territory of the Member States" (as regards *force majeure*, see for instance the Icelandic volcano of 2010);[122] a visa *may* be extended (for a fee of €30) where there is "proof of serious personal reasons" justifying this.[123] This differs from the prior rules in that there was previously no case where there was an obligation to extend a visa.[124]

On the other hand, a visa shall be annulled (presumably with retroactive effect) "where it becomes evident that the conditions for issuing it were not met at the time when it was issued, in particular if there are serious grounds for believing that the visa was fraudulently obtained",[125] and a visa shall be revoked "where it becomes evident that the conditions for issuing it are no

---

[119] Arts. 34(6) and (7) and 35(7).

[120] Art. 58(5).

[121] Arts. 33–34.

[122] Art. 33(1).

[123] Art. 33(2). Note that in either case, there is no explicit reference in the code to the right of appeal if an application for an extension is refused.

[124] See Sch/com-ex (93) 21 (n. 23 above). Also, the code differs from the prior rules in that there is no longer a reference to extension for occupational reasons; there is no longer a ban on changing the purpose of the visa if extended; there is no longer a 90-day limit on the stay; Member States must inform the Commission of the relevant authorities which decide on extensions (whereas such authorities were previously listed in the Executive Committee Decision); the extension must take the form of a visa sticker, not a stamp (which was previously an option); the extension of visas for persons subject to the consultation process is no longer limited to "exceptional" cases; extensions must be listed in the VIS; there is no longer a reference to national procedures applying to the extension; and there are now rules on the fees for an extension (free where extension is mandatory, €30 where it is not).

[125] Art. 34(1). Compare to the previous rules SCH/Com-ex (93)24 (ibid), which referred to "cancellation" rather than annulment. The new rules now specify that the visa should in principle be annulled by the State which issued it, whereas the old rules applied only to cancellation at the border. The right of appeal and notification of the decision is also added, along with more precise rules on marking the visa sticker to indicate the annulment, and a requirement to enter the annulment decision in the VIS.

longer met".[126] Visas can also be annulled or revoked on the same grounds pursuant to the borders code.[127]

Chapter VI of Title III of the visa code concerns the issue of a visa at the border.[128] Visas can only be issued at the border in "exceptional" cases, where the applicant meets the conditions for entry in the Schengen Borders Code, is certain to return to the country of origin or transit and "has not been in a position to apply for a visa in advance and submits, if required, supporting documents substantiating unforeseeable and imperative reasons for entry".[129] The medical insurance requirement may be waived in certain cases for such visas,[130] but visas issued at the border can only be issued for a maximum of fifteen days.[131] Where the conditions for entry at the border are not met, or the applicant is part of a category of persons whose application should be subject to prior consultation, an LTV visa can be issued.[132] There are special rules relating to the issue of visas to seafarers at the border.[133]

2.3. *Title IV: Member States' Consulates (Articles 37–47)*

The rules in the visa code concerning the organisation and management of visa sections include basic rules on security and confidentiality at consulates,[134] the resources of consulates[135] and the conduct of staff.[136] Member States

---

[126] Art. 34(2). Compare to the previous rules SCH/Com-ex (93)24 (ibid,), which referred to "rescission", rather than revocation. The possibility of merely shortening the validity of a visa has been dropped. The rules now specify that the visa should in principle be revoked by the State which issued it, and provide for the visa holder to request the revocation of the visa. As with annulment of visas, there are provisions on the right of appeal and notification of decisions, marking the visa sticker to indicate the revocation (there was no prior rule on this point at all), and entering the decision in the VIS.

[127] See the amendment to the borders code (n. 20 above) made by Art. 55 of the visa code.

[128] Arts. 35–36.

[129] Art. 35(1).

[130] Art. 35(2).

[131] Art. 35(3).

[132] Art. 35(4) and (5).

[133] Art. 36 and Annex IX.

[134] Art. 37; compare to CCI Part VII, points 1–3. The provision on retaining information will in practice presumably be replaced by the relevant provisions of the VIS Regulation as the VIS is fully rolled out.

[135] Art. 38. There were no provisions in the CCI on this issue.

[136] Art. 39. These rules are identical to those set out in Art. 6 of the Schengen Borders Code (n. 20 above), with the addition of a requirement to treat applicants courteously (Art. 39(1)).

are encouraged to cooperate via various means, in particular as regards collection of biometric information, in the form either of representation (see further above), co-location, Common Application Centres, honorary consuls or, as a last resort, the use of external service providers (ie private companies) to collect biometric information.[137]

Finally, the visa code also sets out detailed rules on the collection of annual statistics,[138] and the provision of information to the general public.[139]

2.4. *Title V: Local Consular Cooperation (Article 48)*

Local consulates and the Commission must consult as to whether there should be harmonised rules on the local level as regards certain issues,[140] which will then be drawn up in accordance with a "comitology" procedure, without any special involvement of the EP.[141] Local consular cooperation must also lead to the drawing up of common information sheets for applicants, the exchange of local information and statistics and discussion of operational issues.[142] Local reports shall be drawn up, followed by an annual report by the Commission regarding each jurisdiction.[143] Interestingly, Member States not applying the Schengen *acquis* may be invited to participate in local consular cooperation.[144]

There were no provisions in the CCI on this issue, until Reg. 390/2009 (n. 21 above) added point 5 to Part III of the CCI, which is identical to Art. 39 of the code.

[137] Arts. 40–45. For explanation of the concepts of co-location and Common Application Centres, see Art. 41(1) and (2).

[138] Art. 46 (and Art. 53(1)(i)), referring also to the table in Annex XII. This provision of the Code replaces SCH/Com-ex (94) 25 (n. 23 above), which differed from the Annex in the Code in particular as regards the categories of information to be provided and the frequency of supplying information.

[139] Art. 47. This is a more detailed provision than Part VII of the CCI, point 1.8, which was added by Reg. 390/2009 (n. 21 above).

[140] These issues are a harmonised list of supporting documents, a common approach to the optional exemptions from the visa fee as regards specified categories of persons, common translations of the application form and an exhaustive list of travel documents issued by the host country. Compare also to Part VIII of the CCI, points 1 to 4, and SCH/Com-ex (98) 12 (n. 23 above) as regards the exchange of statistics at local level.

[141] Art. 48(1), referring to Art. 52(2).

[142] Art. 48(2) to (4).

[143] Art. 48(5).

[144] Art. 48(6).

2.5. *Title VI: Final Provisions (Articles 49–58)*

The final provisions of the code concern: the standard special rules applicable to participants in the Olympic Games;[145] the procedure for amending most of the Annexes to the Regulation;[146] the procedure for drawing up operational instructions regarding the code;[147] the different procedures for adopting implementing measures;[148] notifications to the Commission by Member States;[149] amendments to the VIS Regulation and the Schengen Borders Code;[150] repeal of prior measures;[151] monitoring and evaluation of the visa Code;[152] and the entry into force of the Code.[153]

There are thirteen Annexes attached to the Code, concerning in turn:
a) the harmonised visa application form (Annex I);
b) a non-exhaustive list of documents supporting a visa application (Annex II);
c) a uniform format and use of the stamp indicating that an application is admissible (Annex III);
d) a list of the countries subject to a common EU ATV requirement (Annex IV);
e) a list of the non-Member State residence permits that, if held, will waive the ATV requirement (Annex V);
f) the standard form for notifying and giving reasons for refusing a visa application (Annex VI);
g) rules on filling in the visa sticker (Annex VII);
h) rules on affixing the visa sticker (Annex VIII);
i) rules on issuing visas to seafarers (Annex IX);
j) a list of minimum requirements to apply to external service providers (Annex X);

---

[145] Art. 49, referring to Annex XI.

[146] Art. 50, referring to Art. 52(3), which confers power on the Commission to adopt implementing measures subject to the "regulatory procedure with scrutiny". For a list of the Annexes, see below.

[147] Art. 51, referring to Art. 52(2), which confers power on the Commission to adopt implementing measures subject initially (until 1 Mar. 2011) to a regulatory committee procedure, and since then to an "examination" procedure, following changes to the rules on "comitology" procedures (see chapter 2).

[148] Art. 52.

[149] Art. 53.

[150] Arts. 54 and 55.

[151] Art. 56.

[152] Art. 57.

[153] Art. 58.

k)   specific procedures relating to Olympic participants (Annex XI);
l)   the requirements relating to annual statistics to be send to the Commission (Annex XII); and
m) a correlation table comparing the code to the previous measures in force (Annex XIII).

Nine of the Annexes can be amended at present by the specific comitology process giving fuller powers to the EP (the "regulatory procedure with scrutiny"), until the visa code is amended to provide for a "delegated acts" procedure.[154] The exceptions are Annexes IX, X, XI and XIII, which can only be amended by the full legislative process, although this point is moot for Annex XIII, since it consists only of a correlation table.

3. Comments

In general, the code is welcome from a variety of perspectives. Most strikingly, the creation of rights of appeal against refusal of an application, coupled with the necessary corollary right to be informed of a refusal for an application and the reasons for that refusal, provides an essential basic guarantee for applicants.

Also, the code is especially necessary in the context of VIS, given the prospect that consulates' expedited access to records of prior refusals in the VIS will in practice mean that prior refusals will be used to justify refusals of fresh applications to visit any Schengen State by the same applicants for up to five years after the original refusal.[155] The widespread access to such data and its use for such purposes cannot be justified unless applicants have the right to know whether and why their application has been refused, and have the opportunity to challenge the refusal (and subsequently rectify the data in the VIS if their challenge is successful). In that light, the code should have been negotiated and adopted before or at the same time as the VIS Regulation, but ultimately the delay in adopting the code does not matter too much, since the VIS is not due to start operations fully until October 2011. So even the appeal provisions of the visa code were in force before the VIS will begin operations.

Other welcome provisions in the visa code include the precise definition of inadmissible applications, which will ensure that rejections of applications not based on the merits of the application are listed separately in the VIS and so should not be used against applicants when they make subsequent

---

[154] Art. 50, referring to Art. 52(3). On the "comitology" process, see chapter 2.
[155] See further chapter 10.

applications. The provisions on multiple-entry visas and the further provisions for reduction or waiver of visa fees (although limited) provide for further useful facilitation of the issue of visas, and the abolition of the secrecy relating to the rules on consultations was long overdue. Finally, the visa code has resulted in a significant simplification of the legislative framework as compared to the prior rules, which can only be welcomed from the point of view of clarity, transparency and legal certainty. However, it is simply outrageous that the important information which Member States were obliged to send to the Commission by October 2009 was still not (permanently) public nearly two years later.[156]

---

[156] Arts. 53 and 58(3).

REGULATION (EC) No 810/2009 OF THE EUROPEAN PARLIAMENT AND OF THE COUNCIL

of 13 July 2009

establishing a Community Code on Visas (Visa Code)

[original footnotes omitted]

THE EUROPEAN PARLIAMENT AND THE COUNCIL OF THE EUROPEAN UNION,

Having regard to the Treaty establishing the European Community, and in particular Article 62(2)(a) and (b)(ii) thereof,

Having regard to the proposal from the Commission,

Acting in accordance with the procedure laid down in Article 251 of the Treaty,

Whereas:

(1) In accordance with Article 61 of the Treaty, the creation of an area in which persons may move freely should be accompanied by measures with respect to external border controls, asylum and immigration.

(2) Pursuant to Article 62(2) of the Treaty, measures on the crossing of the external borders of the Member States shall establish rules on visas for intended stays of no more than three months, including the procedures and conditions for issuing visas by Member States.

(3) As regards visa policy, the establishment of a 'common corpus' of legislation, particularly via the consolidation and development of the *acquis* (the relevant provisions of the Convention implementing the Schengen Agreement of 14 June 1985 and the Common Consular Instructions, is one of the fundamental components of 'further development of the common visa policy as part of a multi-layer system aimed at facilitating legitimate travel and tackling illegal immigration through further harmonisation of national legislation and handling practices at local consular missions', as defined in the Hague Programme: strengthening freedom, security and justice in the European Union.

(4) Member States should be present or represented for visa purposes in all third countries whose nationals are subject to visa requirements. Member States lacking their own consulate in a given third country or in a certain part of a given third country should endeavour to conclude representation arrangements in order to avoid a disproportionate effort on the part of visa applicants to have access to consulates.

(5) It is necessary to set out rules on the transit through international areas of airports in order to combat illegal immigration. Thus nationals from a

common list of third countries should be required to hold airport transit visas. Nevertheless, in urgent cases of mass influx of illegal immigrants, Member States should be allowed to impose such a requirement on nationals of third countries other than those listed in the common list. Member States' individual decisions should be reviewed on an annual basis.

(6) The reception arrangements for applicants should be made with due respect for human dignity. Processing of visa applications should be conducted in a professional and respectful manner and be proportionate to the objectives pursued.

(7) Member States should ensure that the quality of the service offered to the public is of a high standard and follows good administrative practices. They should allocate appropriate numbers of trained staff as well as sufficient resources in order to facilitate as much as possible the visa application process. Member States should ensure that a 'one-stop' principle is applied to all applicants.

(8) Provided that certain conditions are fulfilled, multiple-entry visas should be issued in order to lessen the administrative burden of Member States' consulates and to facilitate smooth travel for frequent or regular travellers. Applicants known to the consulate for their integrity and reliability should as far as possible benefit from a simplified procedure.

(9) Because of the registration of biometric identifiers in the Visa Information System (VIS) as established by Regulation (EC) No 767/2008 of the European Parliament and of the Council of 9 July 2008 concerning Visa Information System (VIS) and the exchange of data between Member States on short-stay visas (VIS Regulation), the appearance of the applicant in person—at least for the first application—should be one of the basic requirements for the application for a visa.

(10) In order to facilitate the visa application procedure of any subsequent application, it should be possible to copy fingerprints from the first entry into the VIS within a period of 59 months. Once this period of time has elapsed, the fingerprints should be collected again.

(11) Any document, data or biometric identifier received by a Member State in the course of the visa application process shall be considered a consular document under the Vienna Convention on Consular Relations of 24 April 1963 and shall be treated in an appropriate manner.

(12) Directive 95/46/EC of the European Parliament and of the Council of 24 October 1995 on the protection of individuals with regard to the processing of personal data and on the free movement of such data applies to the Member States with regard to the processing of personal data pursuant to this Regulation.

(13) In order to facilitate the procedure, several forms of cooperation should be envisaged, such as limited representation, co-location, common application centres, recourse to honorary consuls and cooperation with external service providers, taking into account in particular data protection requirements set out in Directive 95/46/EC. Member States should, in accordance with the conditions laid down in this Regulation, determine the type of organisational structure which they will use in each third country.

(14) It is necessary to make provision for situations in which a Member State decides to cooperate with an external service provider for the collection of applications. Such a decision may be taken if, in particular circumstances or for reasons relating to the local situation, cooperation with other Member States in the form of representation, limited representation, co-location or a Common Application Centre proves not to be appropriate for the Member State concerned. Such arrangements should be established in compliance with the general principles for issuing visas and with the data protection requirements set out in Directive 95/46/EC. In addition, the need to avoid visa shopping should be taken into consideration when establishing and implementing such arrangements.

(15) Where a Member State has decided to cooperate with an external service provider, it should maintain the possibility for all applicants to lodge applications directly at its diplomatic missions or consular posts.

(16) A Member State should cooperate with an external service provider on the basis of a legal instrument which should contain provisions on its exact responsibilities, on direct and total access to its premises, information for applicants, confidentiality and on the circumstances, conditions and procedures for suspending or terminating the cooperation.

(17) This Regulation, by allowing Member States to cooperate with external service providers for the collection of applications while establishing the 'one-stop' principle for the lodging of applications, creates a derogation from the general rule that an applicant must appear in person at a diplomatic mission or consular post. This is without prejudice to the possibility of calling the applicant for a personal interview.

(18) Local Schengen cooperation is crucial for the harmonised application of the common visa policy and for proper assessment of migratory and/or security risks. Given the differences in local circumstances, the operational application of particular legislative provisions should be assessed among Member States' diplomatic missions and consular posts in individual locations in order to ensure a harmonised application of the legislative provisions to prevent visa shopping and different treatment of visa applicants.

(19) Statistical data are an important means of monitoring migratory movements and can serve as an efficient management tool. Therefore, such data should be compiled regularly in a common format.

(20) The measures necessary for the implementation of this Regulation should be adopted in accordance with Council Decision 1999/468/EC of 28 June 1999 laying down the procedures for the exercise of implementing powers conferred on the Commission.

(21) In particular, the Commission should be empowered to adopt amendments to the Annexes to this Regulation. Since those measures are of general scope and are designed to amend non-essential elements of this Regulation, inter alia, by supplementing it with new non-essential elements, they must be adopted in accordance with the regulatory procedure with scrutiny provided for in Article 5a of Decision 1999/468/EC.

(22) In order to ensure the harmonised application of this Regulation at operational level, instructions should be drawn up on the practice and procedures to be followed by Member States when processing visa applications.

(23) A common Schengen visa Internet site is to be established to improve the visibility and a uniform image of the common visa policy. Such a site will serve as a means to provide the general public with all relevant information in relation to the application for a visa.

(24) Appropriate measures should be adopted for the monitoring and evaluation of this Regulation.

(25) The VIS Regulation and Regulation (EC) No 562/2006 of the European Parliament and of the Council of 15 March 2006 establishing a Community Code on the rules governing the movement of persons across borders (Schengen Borders Code) should be amended in order to take account of the provisions of this Regulation.

(26) Bilateral agreements concluded between the Community and third countries aiming at facilitating the processing of applications for visas may derogate from the provisions of this Regulation.

(27) When a Member State hosts the Olympic Games and the Paralympic Games, a particular scheme facilitating the issuing of visas to members of the Olympic family should apply.

(28) Since the objective of this Regulation, namely the establishment of the procedures and conditions for issuing visas for transit through or intended stays in the territory of the Member States not exceeding three months in any six-month period, cannot be sufficiently achieved by the Member States and can therefore be better achieved at Community level, the Community may adopt measures, in accordance with the

principle of subsidiarity as set out in Article 5 of the Treaty. In accordance with the principle of proportionality, as set out in that Article, this Regulation does not go beyond what is necessary in order to achieve that objective.

(29) This Regulation respects fundamental rights and observes the principles recognised in particular by the Council of Europe's Convention for the Protection of Human Rights and Fundamental Freedoms and by the Charter of Fundamental Rights of the European Union.

(30) The conditions governing entry into the territory of the Member States or the issue of visas do not affect the rules currently governing recognition of the validity of travel documents.

(31) In accordance with Articles 1 and 2 of the Protocol on the Position of Denmark annexed to the Treaty on European Union and to the Treaty establishing the European Community, Denmark does not take part in the adoption of this Regulation and is not bound by it, or subject to its application. Given that this Regulation builds on the Schengen *acquis* under the provisions of Title IV of Part Three of the Treaty establishing the European Community, Denmark shall, in accordance with Article 5 of that Protocol, decide within a period of six months after the date of adoption of this Regulation whether it will implement it in its national law.

(32) As regards Iceland and Norway, this Regulation constitutes a development of provisions of the Schengen *acquis* within the meaning of the Agreement concluded between the Council of the European Union and the Republic of Iceland and the Kingdom of Norway concerning the association of those two States with the implementation, application and development of the Schengen *acquis* which fall within the area referred to in Article 1, point B of Council Decision 1999/437/EC on certain arrangements for the application of that Agreement.

(33) An arrangement should be made to allow representatives of Iceland and Norway to be associated with the work of committees assisting the Commission in the exercise of its implementing powers under this Regulation. Such an arrangement has been contemplated in the Exchange of Letters between the Council of the European Union and Iceland and Norway concerning committees which assist the European Commission in the exercise of its executive powers, annexed to the abovementioned Agreement. The Commission has submitted to the Council a draft recommendation with a view to negotiating this arrangement.

(34) As regards Switzerland, this Regulation constitutes a development of the provisions of the Schengen *acquis* within the meaning of the Agreement between the European Union, the European Community and the Swiss Confederation on the Swiss Confederation's association with the implementation, application and development of the Schengen *acquis*, which fall within the area referred to in Article 1, point B, of Decision 1999/437/EC read in conjunction with Article 3 of Council Decision 2008/146/EC on the conclusion of that Agreement.

(35) As regards Liechtenstein, this Regulation constitutes a development of provisions of the Schengen *acquis* within the meaning of the Protocol signed between the European Union, the European Community, the Swiss Confederation and the Principality of Liechtenstein on the accession of the Principality of Liechtenstein to the Agreement concluded between the European Union, the European Community and the Swiss Confederation on the Swiss Confederation's association with the implementation, application and development of the Schengen *acquis*, which fall within the area referred to in Article 1, point B, of Decision 1999/437/EC read in conjunction with Article 3 of Council Decision 2008/261/EC on the signing of that Protocol.

(36) This Regulation constitutes a development of the provisions of the Schengen *acquis* in which the United Kingdom does not take part, in accordance with Council Decision 2000/365/EC of 29 May 2000 concerning the request of the United Kingdom of Great Britain and Northern Ireland to take part in some of the provisions of the Schengen *acquis*. The United Kingdom is therefore not taking part in its adoption and is not bound by it or subject to its application.

(37) This Regulation constitutes a development of the provisions of the Schengen *acquis* in which Ireland does not take part, in accordance with Council Decision 2002/192/EC of 28 February 2002 concerning Ireland's request to take part in some of the provisions of the Schengen *acquis*. Ireland is therefore not taking part in the adoption of the Regulation and is not bound by it or subject to its application.

(38) This Regulation, with the exception of Article 3, constitutes provisions building on the Schengen *acquis* or otherwise relating to it within the meaning of Article 3(2) of the 2003 Act of Accession and within the meaning of Article 4(2) of the 2005 Act of Accession,

HAVE ADOPTED THIS REGULATION:

TITLE I
GENERAL PROVISIONS

Article 1
Objective and scope

1. This Regulation establishes the procedures and conditions for issuing visas for transit through or intended stays in the territory of the Member States not exceeding three months in any six-month period.
2. The provisions of this Regulation shall apply to any third-country national who must be in possession of a visa when crossing the external borders of the Member States pursuant to Council Regulation (EC) No 539/2001 of 15 March 2001 listing the third countries whose nationals must be in possession of visas when crossing the external borders and those whose nationals are exempt from that requirement, without prejudice to:
   (a) the rights of free movement enjoyed by third-country nationals who are family members of citizens of the Union;
   (b) the equivalent rights enjoyed by third-country nationals and their family members, who, under agreements between the Community and its Member States, on the one hand, and these third countries, on the other, enjoy rights of free movement equivalent to those of Union citizens and members of their families.
3. This Regulation also lists the third countries whose nationals are required to hold an airport transit visa by way of exception from the principle of free transit laid down in Annex 9 to the Chicago Convention on International Civil Aviation, and establishes the procedures and conditions for issuing visas for the purpose of transit through the international transit areas of Member States' airports.

Article 2
Definitions

For the purpose of this Regulation the following definitions shall apply:
1. 'third-country national' means any person who is not a citizen of the Union within the meaning of Article 17(1) of the Treaty;
2. 'visa' means an authorisation issued by a Member State with a view to:
   (a) transit through or an intended stay in the territory of the Member States of a duration of no more than three months in any six-month period from the date of first entry in the territory of the Member States;
   (b) transit through the international transit areas of airports of the Member States;

3. 'uniform visa' means a visa valid for the entire territory of the Member States;
4. 'visa with limited territorial validity' means a visa valid for the territory of one or more Member States but not all Member States;
5. 'airport transit visa' means a visa valid for transit through the international transit areas of one or more airports of the Member States;
6. 'visa sticker' means the uniform format for visas as defined by Council Regulation (EC) No 1683/95 of 29 May 1995 laying down a uniform format for visas;
7. 'recognised travel document' means a travel document recognised by one or more Member States for the purpose of affixing visas;
8. 'separate sheet for affixing a visa' means the uniform format for forms for affixing the visa issued by Member States to persons holding travel documents not recognised by the Member State drawing up the form as defined by Council Regulation (EC) No 333/2002 of 18 February 2002 on a uniform format for forms for affixing the visa issued by Member States to persons holding travel documents not recognised by the Member State drawing up the form;
9. 'consulate' means a Member State's diplomatic mission or a Member State's consular post authorised to issue visas and headed by a career consular officer as defined by the Vienna Convention on Consular Relations of 24 April 1963;
10. 'application' means an application for a visa;
11. 'commercial intermediary' means a private administrative agency, transport company or travel agency (tour operator or retailer).

TITLE II
AIRPORT TRANSIT VISA

Article 3
Third-country nationals required to hold an airport transit visa

1. Nationals of the third countries listed in Annex IV shall be required to hold an airport transit visa when passing through the international transit areas of airports situated on the territory of the Member States.
2. In urgent cases of mass influx of illegal immigrants, individual Member States may require nationals of third countries other than those referred to in paragraph 1 to hold an airport transit visa when passing through the international transit areas of airports situated on their territory. Member States shall notify the Commission of such decisions before their entry into force and of withdrawals of such an airport transit visa requirement.

3. Within the framework of the Committee referred to in Article 52(1), those notifications shall be reviewed on an annual basis for the purpose of transferring the third country concerned to the list set out in Annex IV.

4. If the third country is not transferred to the list set out in Annex IV, the Member State concerned may maintain, provided that the conditions in paragraph 2 are met, or withdraw the airport transit visa requirement.

5. The following categories of persons shall be exempt from the requirement to hold an airport transit visa provided for in paragraphs 1 and 2:

   (a) holders of a valid uniform visa, national long-stay visa or residence permit issued by a Member State;

   (b) third-country nationals holding the valid residence permits listed in Annex V issued by Andorra, Canada, Japan, San Marino or the United States of America guaranteeing the holder's unconditional readmission;

   (c) third-country nationals holding a valid visa for a Member State or for a State party to the Agreement on the European Economic Area of 2 May 1992, Canada, Japan or the United States of America, or when they return from those countries after having used the visa;

   (d) family members of citizens of the Union as referred to in Article 1(2) (a);

   (e) holders of diplomatic passports;

   (f) flight crew members who are nationals of a contracting Party to the Chicago Convention on International Civil Aviation.

TITLE III
PROCEDURES AND CONDITIONS FOR ISSUING VISAS

CHAPTER I
Authorities taking part in the procedures relating to applications

Article 4
Authorities competent for taking part in the procedures relating to applications

1. Applications shall be examined and decided on by consulates.

2. By way of derogation from paragraph 1, applications may be examined and decided on at the external borders of the Member States by the authorities responsible for checks on persons, in accordance with Articles 35 and 36.

3. In the non-European overseas territories of Member States, applications may be examined and decided on by the authorities designated by the Member State concerned.

4. A Member State may require the involvement of authorities other than the ones designated in paragraphs 1 and 2 in the examination of and decision on applications.

5. A Member State may require to be consulted or informed by another Member State in accordance with Articles 22 and 31.

Article 5
Member State competent for examining and deciding on an application

1. The Member State competent for examining and deciding on an application for a uniform visa shall be:
   (a) the Member State whose territory constitutes the sole destination of the visit(s);
   (b) if the visit includes more than one destination, the Member State whose territory constitutes the main destination of the visit(s) in terms of the length or purpose of stay; or
   (c) if no main destination can be determined, the Member State whose external border the applicant intends to cross in order to enter the territory of the Member States.

2. The Member State competent for examining and deciding on an application for a uniform visa for the purpose of transit shall be:
   (a) in the case of transit through only one Member State, the Member State concerned; or
   (b) in the case of transit through several Member States, the Member State whose external border the applicant intends to cross to start the transit.

3. The Member State competent for examining and deciding on an application for an airport transit visa shall be:
   (a) in the case of a single airport transit, the Member State on whose territory the transit airport is situated; or
   (b) in the case of double or multiple airport transit, the Member State on whose territory the first transit airport is situated.

4. Member States shall cooperate to prevent a situation in which an application cannot be examined and decided on because the Member State that is competent in accordance with paragraphs 1 to 3 is neither present nor represented in the third country where the applicant lodges the application in accordance with Article 6.

Article 6
Consular territorial competence

1. An application shall be examined and decided on by the consulate of the competent Member State in whose jurisdiction the applicant legally resides.
2. A consulate of the competent Member State shall examine and decide on an application lodged by a third-country national legally present but not residing in its jurisdiction, if the applicant has provided justification for lodging the application at that consulate.

Article 7
Competence to issue visas to third-country nationals legally present within the territory of a Member State

Third-country nationals who are legally present in the territory of a Member State and who are required to hold a visa to enter the territory of one or more other Member States shall apply for a visa at the consulate of the Member State that is competent in accordance with Article 5(1) or (2).

Article 8
Representation arrangements

1. A Member State may agree to represent another Member State that is competent in accordance with Article 5 for the purpose of examining applications and issuing visas on behalf of that Member State. A Member State may also represent another Member State in a limited manner solely for the collection of applications and the enrolment of biometric identifiers.
2. The consulate of the representing Member State shall, when contemplating refusing a visa, submit the application to the relevant authorities of the represented Member State in order for them to take the final decision on the application within the time limits set out in Article 23(1), (2) or (3).
3. The collection and transmission of files and data to the represented Member State shall be carried out in compliance with the relevant data protection and security rules.
4. A bilateral arrangement shall be established between the representing Member State and the represented Member State containing the following elements:
   (a) it shall specify the duration of such representation, if only temporary, and procedures for its termination;
   (b) it may, in particular when the represented Member State has a consulate in the third country concerned, provide for the provision of premises, staff and payments by the represented Member State;

(c) it may stipulate that applications from certain categories of third-country nationals are to be transmitted by the representing Member State to the central authorities of the represented Member State for prior consultation as provided for in Article 22;

(d) by way of derogation from paragraph 2, it may authorise the consulate of the representing Member State to refuse to issue a visa after examination of the application.

5. Member States lacking their own consulate in a third country shall endeavour to conclude representation arrangements with Member States that have consulates in that country.

6. With a view to ensuring that a poor transport infrastructure or long distances in a specific region or geographical area does not require a disproportionate effort on the part of applicants to have access to a consulate, Member States lacking their own consulate in that region or area shall endeavour to conclude representation arrangements with Member States that have consulates in that region or area.

7. The represented Member State shall notify the representation arrangements or the termination of such arrangements to the Commission before they enter into force or are terminated.

8. Simultaneously, the consulate of the representing Member State shall inform both the consulates of other Member States and the delegation of the Commission in the jurisdiction concerned about representation arrangements or the termination of such arrangements before they enter into force or are terminated.

9. If the consulate of the representing Member State decides to cooperate with an external service provider in accordance with Article 43, or with accredited commercial intermediaries as provided for in Article 45, such cooperation shall include applications covered by representation arrangements. The central authorities of the represented Member State shall be informed in advance of the terms of such cooperation.

CHAPTER II
Application

Article 9
Practical modalities for lodging an application

1. Applications shall be lodged no more than three months before the start of the intended visit. Holders of a multiple-entry visa may lodge the application before the expiry of the visa valid for a period of at least six months.

2. Applicants may be required to obtain an appointment for the lodging of an application. The appointment shall, as a rule, take place within a period of two weeks from the date when the appointment was requested.
3. In justified cases of urgency, the consulate may allow applicants to lodge their applications either without appointment, or an appointment shall be given immediately. 4. Applications may be lodged at the consulate by the applicant or by accredited commercial intermediaries, as provided for in Article 45(1), without prejudice to Article 13, or in accordance with Article 42 or 43.

Article 10
General rules for lodging an application

1. Without prejudice to the provisions of Articles 13, 42, 43 and 45, applicants shall appear in person when lodging an application.
2. Consulates may waive the requirement referred to in paragraph 1 when the applicant is known to them for his integrity and reliability.
3. When lodging the application, the applicant shall:
    (a) present an application form in accordance with Article 11;
    (b) present a travel document in accordance with Article 12;
    (c) present a photograph in accordance with the standards set out in Regulation (EC) No 1683/95 or, where the VIS is operational pursuant to Article 48 of the VIS Regulation, in accordance with the standards set out in Article 13 of this Regulation;
    (d) allow the collection of his fingerprints in accordance with Article 13, where applicable;
    (e) pay the visa fee in accordance with Article 16;
    (f) provide supporting documents in accordance with Article 14 and Annex II;
    (g) where applicable, produce proof of possession of adequate and valid travel medical insurance in accordance with Article 15.

Article 11
Application form

1. Each applicant shall submit a completed and signed application form, as set out in Annex I. Persons included in the applicant's travel document shall submit a separate application form. Minors shall submit an application form signed by a person exercising permanent or temporary parental authority or legal guardianship.
2. Consulates shall make the application form widely available and easily accessible to applicants free of charge.

3. The form shall be available in the following languages:
   (a) the official language(s) of the Member State for which a visa is requested;
   (b) the official language(s) of the host country;
   (c) the official language(s) of the host country and the official language(s) of the Member State for which a visa is requested; or
   (d) in case of representation, the official language(s) of the representing Member State.

   In addition to the language(s) referred to in point (a), the form may be made available in another official language of the institutions of the European Union.
4. If the application form is not available in the official language(s) of the host country, a translation of it into that/those language(s) shall be made available separately to applicants.
5. A translation of the application form into the official language(s) of the host country shall be produced under local Schengen cooperation provided for in Article 48.
6. The consulate shall inform applicants of the language(s) which may be used when filling in the application form.

Article 12
Travel document

The applicant shall present a valid travel document satisfying the following criteria:
(a) its validity shall extend at least three months after the intended date of departure from the territory of the Member States or, in the case of several visits, after the last intended date of departure from the territory of the Member States. However, in a justified case of emergency, this obligation may be waived;
(b) it shall contain at least two blank pages;
(c) it shall have been issued within the previous 10 years.

Article 13
Biometric identifiers

1. Member States shall collect biometric identifiers of the applicant comprising a photograph of him and his 10 fingerprints in accordance with the safeguards laid down in the Council of Europe's Convention for the Protection of Human Rights and Fundamental Freedoms, in the Charter of Fundamental Rights of the European Union and in the United Nations Convention on the Rights of the Child.

2. At the time of submission of the first application, the applicant shall be required to appear in person. At that time, the following biometric identifiers of the applicant shall be collected:—a photograph, scanned or taken at the time of application, and—his 10 fingerprints taken flat and collected digitally.

3. Where fingerprints collected from the applicant as part of an earlier application were entered in the VIS for the first time less than 59 months before the date of the new application, they shall be copied to the subsequent application.

   However, where there is reasonable doubt regarding the identity of the applicant, the consulate shall collect fingerprints within the period specified in the first subparagraph.

   Furthermore, if at the time when the application is lodged, it cannot be immediately confirmed that the fingerprints were collected within the period specified in the first subparagraph, the applicant may request that they be collected.

4. In accordance with Article 9(5) of the VIS Regulation, the photograph attached to each application shall be entered in the VIS. The applicant shall not be required to appear in person for this purpose.

   The technical requirements for the photograph shall be in accordance with the international standards as set out in the International Civil Aviation Organization (ICAO) document 9303 Part 1, 6th edition.

5. Fingerprints shall be taken in accordance with ICAO standards and Commission Decision 2006/648/EC of 22 September 2006 laying down the technical specifications on the standards for biometric features related to the development of the Visa Information System.

6. The biometric identifiers shall be collected by qualified and duly authorised staff of the authorities competent in accordance with Article 4(1), (2) and (3). Under the supervision of the consulates, the biometric identifiers may also be collected by qualified and duly authorised staff of an honorary consul as referred to in Article 42 or of an external service provider as referred to in Article 43. The Member State(s) concerned shall, where there is any doubt, provide for the possibility of verifying at the consulate fingerprints which have been taken by the external service provider.

7. The following applicants shall be exempt from the requirement to give fingerprints:
   (a) children under the age of 12;
   (b) persons for whom fingerprinting is physically impossible. If the fingerprinting of fewer than 10 fingers is possible, the maximum number of fingerprints shall be taken. However, should the impossibility be

temporary, the applicant shall be required to give the fingerprints at the following application. The authorities competent in accordance with Article 4(1), (2) and (3) shall be entitled to ask for further clarification of the grounds for the temporary impossibility. Member States shall ensure that appropriate procedures guaranteeing the dignity of the applicant are in place in the event of there being difficulties in enrolling;

(c) heads of State or government and members of a national government with accompanying spouses, and the members of their official delegation when they are invited by Member States' governments or by international organisations for an official purpose;

(d) sovereigns and other senior members of a royal family, when they are invited by Member States' governments or by international organisations for an official purpose. 8. In the cases referred to in paragraph 7, the entry 'not applicable' shall be introduced in the VIS in accordance with Article 8(5) of the VIS Regulation.

Article 14
Supporting documents

1. When applying for a uniform visa, the applicant shall present:
   (a) documents indicating the purpose of the journey;
   (b) documents in relation to accommodation, or proof of sufficient means to cover his accommodation;
   (c) documents indicating that the applicant possesses sufficient means of subsistence both for the duration of the intended stay and for the return to his country of origin or residence, or for the transit to a third country into which he is certain to be admitted, or that he is in a position to acquire such means lawfully, in accordance with Article 5(1)(c) and (3) of the Schengen Borders Code;
   (d) information enabling an assessment of the applicant's intention to leave the territory of the Member States before the expiry of the visa applied for.
2. When applying for an airport transit visa, the applicant shall present:
   (a) documents in relation to the onward journey to the final destination after the intended airport transit;
   (b) information enabling an assessment of the applicant's intention not to enter the territory of the Member States.
3. A non-exhaustive list of supporting documents which the consulate may request from the applicant in order to verify the fulfilment of the conditions listed in paragraphs 1 and 2 is set out in Annex II.

4. Member States may require applicants to present a proof of sponsorship and/or private accommodation by completing a form drawn up by each Member State. That form shall indicate in particular:
   (a) whether its purpose is proof of sponsorship and/or of accommodation;
   (b) whether the host is an individual, a company or an organisation;
   (c) the host's identity and contact details; (d) the invited applicant(s);
   (e) the address of the accommodation;
   (f) the length and purpose of the stay;
   (g) possible family ties with the host.
   In addition to the Member State's official language(s), the form shall be drawn up in at least one other official language of the institutions of the European Union. The form shall provide the person signing it with the information required pursuant to Article 37(1) of the VIS Regulation. A specimen of the form shall be notified to the Commission.
5. Within local Schengen cooperation the need to complete and harmonise the lists of supporting documents shall be assessed in each jurisdiction in order to take account of local circumstances.
6. Consulates may waive one or more of the requirements of paragraph 1 in the case of an applicant known to them for his integrity and reliability, in particular the lawful use of previous visas, if there is no doubt that he will fulfil the requirements of Article 5(1) of the Schengen Borders Code at the time of the crossing of the external borders of the Member States.

Article 15
Travel medical insurance

1. Applicants for a uniform visa for one or two entries shall prove that they are in possession of adequate and valid travel medical insurance to cover any expenses which might arise in connection with repatriation for medical reasons, urgent medical attention and/or emergency hospital treatment or death, during their stay(s) on the territory of the Member States.
2. Applicants for a uniform visa for more than two entries (multiple entries) shall prove that they are in possession of adequate and valid travel medical insurance covering the period of their first intended visit.
   In addition, such applicants shall sign the statement, set out in the application form, declaring that they are aware of the need to be in possession of travel medical insurance for subsequent stays.
3. The insurance shall be valid throughout the territory of the Member States and cover the entire period of the person's intended stay or transit. The minimum coverage shall be EUR 30 000.

When a visa with limited territorial validity covering the territory of more than one Member State is issued, the insurance cover shall be valid at least in the Member States concerned.

4. Applicants shall, in principle, take out insurance in their country of residence. Where this is not possible, they shall seek to obtain insurance in any other country.

    When another person takes out insurance in the name of the applicant, the conditions set out in paragraph 3 shall apply.

5. When assessing whether the insurance cover is adequate, consulates shall ascertain whether claims against the insurance company would be recoverable in a Member State.

6. The insurance requirement may be considered to have been met where it is established that an adequate level of insurance may be presumed in the light of the applicant's professional situation. The exemption from presenting proof of travel medical insurance may concern particular professional groups, such as seafarers, who are already covered by travel medical insurance as a result of their professional activities.

7. Holders of diplomatic passports shall be exempt from the requirement to hold travel medical insurance.

Article 16
Visa fee

1. Applicants shall pay a visa fee of EUR 60.
2. Children from the age of six years and below the age of 12 years shall pay a visa fee of EUR 35.
3. The visa fee shall be revised regularly in order to reflect the administrative costs.
4. The visa fee shall be waived for applicants belonging to one of the following categories:
    (a) children under six years;
    (b) school pupils, students, postgraduate students and accompanying teachers who undertake stays for the purpose of study or educational training;
    (c) researchers from third countries travelling for the purpose of carrying out scientific research as defined in Recommendation No 2005/761/ EC of the European Parliament and of the Council of 28 September 2005 to facilitate the issue by the Member States of uniform short-stay visas for researchers from third countries travelling within the Community for the purpose of carrying out scientific research;

(d) representatives of non-profit organisations aged 25 years or less participating in seminars, conferences, sports, cultural or educational events organised by non-profit organisations.

5. The visa fee may be waived for:
   (a) children from the age of six years and below the age of 12 years;
   (b) holders of diplomatic and service passports;
   (c) participants aged 25 years or less in seminars, conferences, sports, cultural or educational events, organised by non-profit organisations.
   Within local Schengen cooperation, Members States shall aim to harmonise the application of these exemptions.

6. In individual cases, the amount of the visa fee to be charged may be waived or reduced when to do so serves to promote cultural or sporting interests as well as interests in the field of foreign policy, development policy and other areas of vital public interest or for humanitarian reasons.

7. The visa fee shall be charged in euro, in the national currency of the third country or in the currency usually used in the third country where the application is lodged, and shall not be refundable except in the cases referred to in Articles 18(2) and 19(3).

   When charged in a currency other than euro, the amount of the visa fee charged in that currency shall be determined and regularly reviewed in application of the euro foreign exchange reference rate set by the European Central Bank. The amount charged may be rounded up and consulates shall ensure under local Schengen cooperation that they charge similar fees.

8. The applicant shall be given a receipt for the visa fee paid.

Article 17
Service fee

1. An additional service fee may be charged by an external service provider referred to in Article 43. The service fee shall be proportionate to the costs incurred by the external service provider while performing one or more of the tasks referred to in Article 43(6).

2. The service fee shall be specified in the legal instrument referred to in Article 43(2).

3. Within the framework of local Schengen cooperation, Member States shall ensure that the service fee charged to an applicant duly reflects the services offered by the external service provider and is adapted to local circumstances. Furthermore, they shall aim to harmonise the service fee applied.

4. The service fee shall not exceed half of the amount of the visa fee set out in Article 16(1), irrespective of the possible reductions in or exemptions from the visa fee as provided for in Article 16(2), (4), (5) and (6).

5. The Member State(s) concerned shall maintain the possibility for all applicants to lodge their applications directly at its/their consulates.

CHAPTER III
Examination of and decision on an application

Article 18
Verification of consular competence

1. When an application has been lodged, the consulate shall verify whether it is competent to examine and decide on it in accordance with the provisions of Articles 5 and 6. 2. If the consulate is not competent, it shall, without delay, return the application form and any documents submitted by the applicant, reimburse the visa fee, and indicate which consulate is competent.

Article 19
Admissibility

1. The competent consulate shall verify whether:
   — the application has been lodged within the period referred to in Article 9(1),
   — the application contains the items referred to in Article 10(3)(a) to (c),
   — the biometric data of the applicant have been collected, and
   — the visa fee has been collected.
2. Where the competent consulate finds that the conditions referred to in paragraph 1 have been fulfilled, the application shall be admissible and the consulate shall:
   — follow the procedures described in Article 8 of the VIS Regulation, and
   — further examine the application.
   Data shall be entered in the VIS only by duly authorised consular staff in accordance with Articles 6(1), 7, 9(5) and 9(6) of the VIS Regulation.
3. Where the competent consulate finds that the conditions referred to in paragraph 1 have not been fulfilled, the application shall be inadmissible and the consulate shall without delay:
   — return the application form and any documents submitted by the applicant,
   — destroy the collected biometric data,
   — reimburse the visa fee, and
   — not examine the application.

4. By way of derogation, an application that does not meet the requirements set out in paragraph 1 may be considered admissible on humanitarian grounds or for reasons of national interest.

Article 20
Stamp indicating that an application is admissible

1. When an application is admissible, the competent consulate shall stamp the applicant's travel document. The stamp shall be as set out in the model in Annex III and shall be affixed in accordance with the provisions of that Annex.
2. Diplomatic, service/official and special passports shall not be stamped.
3. The provisions of this Article shall apply to the consulates of the Member States until the date when the VIS becomes fully operational in all regions, in accordance with Article 48 of the VIS Regulation.

Article 21
Verification of entry conditions and risk assessment

1. In the examination of an application for a uniform visa, it shall be ascertained whether the applicant fulfils the entry conditions set out in Article 5(1)(a), (c), (d) and (e) of the Schengen Borders Code, and particular consideration shall be given to assessing whether the applicant presents a risk of illegal immigration or a risk to the security of the Member States and whether the applicant intends to leave the territory of the Member States before the expiry of the visa applied for.
2. In respect of each application, the VIS shall be consulted in accordance with Articles 8(2) and 15 of the VIS Regulation. Member States shall ensure that full use is made of all search criteria pursuant to Article 15 of the VIS Regulation in order to avoid false rejections and identifications.
3. While checking whether the applicant fulfils the entry conditions, the consulate shall verify:
   (a) that the travel document presented is not false, counterfeit or forged;
   (b) the applicant's justification for the purpose and conditions of the intended stay, and that he has sufficient means of subsistence, both for the duration of the intended stay and for the return to his country of origin or residence, or for the transit to a third country into which he is certain to be admitted, or is in a position to acquire such means lawfully;
   (c) whether the applicant is a person for whom an alert has been issued in the Schengen Information System (SIS) for the purpose of refusing entry;

(d) that the applicant is not considered to be a threat to public policy, internal security or public health as defined in Article 2(19) of the Schengen Borders Code or to the international relations of any of the Member States, in particular where no alert has been issued in Member States' national databases for the purpose of refusing entry on the same grounds;

(e) that the applicant is in possession of adequate and valid travel medical insurance, where applicable.

4. The consulate shall, where applicable, verify the length of previous and intended stays in order to verify that the applicant has not exceeded the maximum duration of authorised stay in the territory of the Member States, irrespective of possible stays authorised under a national long-stay visa or a residence permit issued by another Member State.

5. The means of subsistence for the intended stay shall be assessed in accordance with the duration and the purpose of the stay and by reference to average prices in the Member State(s) concerned for board and lodging in budget accommodation, multiplied by the number of days stayed, on the basis of the reference amounts set by the Member States in accordance with Article 34(1)(c) of the Schengen Borders Code. Proof of sponsorship and/ or private accommodation may also constitute evidence of sufficient means of subsistence.

6. In the examination of an application for an airport transit visa, the consulate shall in particular verify:

(a) that the travel document presented is not false, counterfeit or forged;

(b) the points of departure and destination of the third-country national concerned and the coherence of the intended itinerary and airport transit;

(c) proof of the onward journey to the final destination.

7. The examination of an application shall be based notably on the authenticity and reliability of the documents submitted and on the veracity and reliability of the statements made by the applicant.

8. During the examination of an application, consulates may in justified cases call the applicant for an interview and request additional documents.

9. A previous visa refusal shall not lead to an automatic refusal of a new application. A new application shall be assessed on the basis of all available information.

Article 22
Prior consultation of central authorities of other Member States

1. A Member State may require the central authorities of other Member States to consult its central authorities during the examination of applications

lodged by nationals of specific third countries or specific categories of such nationals. Such consultation shall not apply to applications for airport transit visas.

2. The central authorities consulted shall reply definitively within seven calendar days after being consulted. The absence of a reply within this deadline shall mean that they have no grounds for objecting to the issuing of the visa.

3. Member States shall notify the Commission of the introduction or withdrawal of the requirement of prior consultation before it becomes applicable. This information shall also be given within local Schengen cooperation in the jurisdiction concerned.

4. The Commission shall inform Member States of such notifications.

5. From the date of the replacement of the Schengen Consultation Network, as referred to in Article 46 of the VIS Regulation, prior consultation shall be carried out in accordance with Article 16(2) of that Regulation.

Article 23
Decision on the application

1. Applications shall be decided on within 15 calendar days of the date of the lodging of an application which is admissible in accordance with Article 19.

2. That period may be extended up to a maximum of 30 calendar days in individual cases, notably when further scrutiny of the application is needed or in cases of representation where the authorities of the represented Member State are consulted.

3. Exceptionally, when additional documentation is needed in specific cases, the period may be extended up to a maximum of 60 calendar days.

4. Unless the application has been withdrawn, a decision shall be taken to:
   (a) issue a uniform visa in accordance with Article 24;
   (b) issue a visa with limited territorial validity in accordance with Article 25;
   (c) refuse a visa in accordance with Article 32; or
   (d) discontinue the examination of the application and transfer it to the relevant authorities of the represented Member State in accordance with Article 8(2).

   The fact that fingerprinting is physically impossible, in accordance with Article 13(7)(b), shall not influence the issuing or refusal of a visa.

CHAPTER IV
Issuing of the visa

Article 24
Issuing of a uniform visa

1. The period of validity of a visa and the length of the authorised stay shall be based on the examination conducted in accordance with Article 21.

    A visa may be issued for one, two or multiple entries. The period of validity shall not exceed five years.

    In the case of transit, the length of the authorised stay shall correspond to the time necessary for the purpose of the transit.

    Without prejudice to Article 12(a), the period of validity of the visa shall include an additional 'period of grace' of 15 days.

    Member States may decide not to grant such a period of grace for reasons of public policy or because of the international relations of any of the Member States.

2. Without prejudice to Article 12(a), multiple-entry visas shall be issued with a period of validity between six months and five years, where the following conditions are met:

    (a) the applicant proves the need or justifies the intention to travel frequently and/or regularly, in particular due to his occupational or family status, such as business persons, civil servants engaged in regular official contacts with Member States and EU institutions, representatives of civil society organisations travelling for the purpose of educational training, seminars and conferences, family members of citizens of the Union, family members of third-country nationals legally residing in Member States and seafarers; and

    (b) the applicant proves his integrity and reliability, in particular the lawful use of previous uniform visas or visas with limited territorial validity, his economic situation in the country of origin and his genuine intention to leave the territory of the Member States before the expiry of the visa applied for.

3. The data set out in Article 10(1) of the VIS Regulation shall be entered into the VIS when a decision on issuing such a visa has been taken.

Article 25
Issuing of a visa with limited territorial validity

1. A visa with limited territorial validity shall be issued exceptionally, in the following cases:

(a) when the Member State concerned considers it necessary on humanitarian grounds, for reasons of national interest or because of international obligations,

    (i) to derogate from the principle that the entry conditions laid down in Article 5(1)(a), (c), (d) and (e) of the Schengen Borders Code must be fulfilled;

    (ii) to issue a visa despite an objection by the Member State consulted in accordance with Article 22 to the issuing of a uniform visa; or

    (iii) to issue a visa for reasons of urgency, although the prior consultation in accordance with Article 22 has not been carried out;

or

(b) when for reasons deemed justified by the consulate, a new visa is issued for a stay during the same six-month period to an applicant who, over this six-month period, has already used a uniform visa or a visa with limited territorial validity allowing for a stay of three months.

2. A visa with limited territorial validity shall be valid for the territory of the issuing Member State. It may exceptionally be valid for the territory of more than one Member State, subject to the consent of each such Member State.

3. If the applicant holds a travel document that is not recognised by one or more, but not all Member States, a visa valid for the territory of the Member States recognising the travel document shall be issued. If the issuing Member State does not recognise the applicant's travel document, the visa issued shall only be valid for that Member State.

4. When a visa with limited territorial validity has been issued in the cases described in paragraph 1(a), the central authorities of the issuing Member State shall circulate the relevant information to the central authorities of the other Member States without delay, by means of the procedure referred to in Article 16(3) of the VIS Regulation.

5. The data set out in Article 10(1) of the VIS Regulation shall be entered into the VIS when a decision on issuing such a visa has been taken.

Article 26
Issuing of an airport transit visa

1. An airport transit visa shall be valid for transiting through the international transit areas of the airports situated on the territory of Member States.

2. Without prejudice to Article 12(a), the period of validity of the visa shall include an additional 'period of grace' of 15 days.

Member States may decide not to grant such a period of grace for reasons of public policy or because of the international relations of any of the Member States.

3. Without prejudice to Article 12(a), multiple airport transit visas may be issued with a period of validity of a maximum six months.
4. The following criteria in particular are relevant for taking the decision to issue multiple airport transit visas:
   (a) the applicant's need to transit frequently and/or regularly; and
   (b) the integrity and reliability of the applicant, in particular the lawful use of previous uniform visas, visas with limited territorial validity or airport transit visas, his economic situation in his country of origin and his genuine intention to pursue his onward journey.
5. If the applicant is required to hold an airport transit visa in accordance with the provisions of Article 3(2), the airport transit visa shall be valid only for transiting through the international transit areas of the airports situated on the territory of the Member State(s) concerned. 6. The data set out in Article 10(1) of the VIS Regulation shall be entered into the VIS when a decision on issuing such a visa has been taken.

Article 27
Filling in the visa sticker

1. When the visa sticker is filled in, the mandatory entries set out in Annex VII shall be inserted and the machine-readable zone filled in, as provided for in ICAO document 9303, Part 2.
2. Member States may add national entries in the 'comments' section of the visa sticker, which shall not duplicate the mandatory entries in Annex VII.
3. All entries on the visa sticker shall be printed, and no manual changes shall be made to a printed visa sticker.
4. Visa stickers may be filled in manually only in case of technical force majeure. No changes shall be made to a manually filled in visa sticker.
5. When a visa sticker is filled in manually in accordance with paragraph 4 of this Article, this information shall be entered into the VIS in accordance with Article 10(1)(k) of the VIS Regulation.

Article 28
Invalidation of a completed visa sticker

1. If an error is detected on a visa sticker which has not yet been affixed to the travel document, the visa sticker shall be invalidated.
2. If an error is detected after the visa sticker has been affixed to the travel document, the visa sticker shall be invalidated by drawing a cross with

indelible ink on the visa sticker and a new visa sticker shall be affixed to a different page.

3. If an error is detected after the relevant data have been introduced into the VIS in accordance with Article 10(1) of the VIS Regulation, the error shall be corrected in accordance with Article 24(1) of that Regulation.

Article 29
Affixing a visa sticker

1. The printed visa sticker containing the data provided for in Article 27 and Annex VII shall be affixed to the travel document in accordance with the provisions set out in Annex VIII.
2. Where the issuing Member State does not recognise the applicant's travel document, the separate sheet for affixing a visa shall be used.
3. When a visa sticker has been affixed to the separate sheet for affixing a visa, this information shall be entered into the VIS in accordance with Article 10(1)(j) of the VIS Regulation.
4. Individual visas issued to persons who are included in the travel document of the applicant shall be affixed to that travel document.
5. Where the travel document in which such persons are included is not recognised by the issuing Member State, the individual stickers shall be affixed to the separate sheets for affixing a visa.

Article 30
Rights derived from an issued visa

Mere possession of a uniform visa or a visa with limited territorial validity shall not confer an automatic right of entry.

Article 31
Information of central authorities of other Member States

1. A Member State may require that its central authorities be informed of visas issued by consulates of other Member States to nationals of specific third countries or to specific categories of such nationals, except in the case of airport transit visas.
2. Member States shall notify the Commission of the introduction or withdrawal of the requirement for such information before it becomes applicable. This information shall also be given within local Schengen cooperation in the jurisdiction concerned.
3. The Commission shall inform Member States of such notifications.
4. From the date referred to in Article 46 of the VIS Regulation, information shall be transmitted in accordance with Article 16(3) of that Regulation.

Article 32
Refusal of a visa

1. Without prejudice to Article 25(1), a visa shall be refused:
   (a) if the applicant:
      (i) presents a travel document which is false, counterfeit or forged;
      (ii) does not provide justification for the purpose and conditions of the intended stay;
      (iii) does not provide proof of sufficient means of subsistence, both for the duration of the intended stay and for the return to his country of origin or residence, or for the transit to a third country into which he is certain to be admitted, or is not in a position to acquire such means lawfully;
      (iv) has already stayed for three months during the current six-month period on the territory of the Member States on the basis of a uniform visa or a visa with limited territorial validity;
      (v) is a person for whom an alert has been issued in the SIS for the purpose of refusing entry;
      (vi) is considered to be a threat to public policy, internal security or public health as defined in Article 2(19) of the Schengen Borders Code or to the international relations of any of the Member States, in particular where an alert has been issued in Member States' national databases for the purpose of refusing entry on the same grounds; or
      (vii) does not provide proof of holding adequate and valid travel medical insurance, where applicable;

   or
   (b) if there are reasonable doubts as to the authenticity of the supporting documents submitted by the applicant or the veracity of their contents, the reliability of the statements made by the applicant or his intention to leave the territory of the Member States before the expiry of the visa applied for.

2. A decision on refusal and the reasons on which it is based shall be notified to the applicant by means of the standard form set out in Annex VI.

3. Applicants who have been refused a visa shall have the right to appeal. Appeals shall be conducted against the Member State that has taken the final decision on the application and in accordance with the national law of that Member State. Member States shall provide applicants with information regarding the procedure to be followed in the event of an appeal, as specified in Annex VI.

4. In the cases referred to in Article 8(2), the consulate of the representing Member State shall inform the applicant of the decision taken by the represented Member State.
5. Information on a refused visa shall be entered into the VIS in accordance with Article 12 of the VIS Regulation.

CHAPTER V
Modification of an issued visa

Article 33
Extension

1. The period of validity and/or the duration of stay of an issued visa shall be extended where the competent authority of a Member State considers that a visa holder has provided proof of force majeure or humanitarian reasons preventing him from leaving the territory of the Member States before the expiry of the period of validity of or the duration of stay authorised by the visa. Such an extension shall be granted free of charge.
2. The period of validity and/or the duration of stay of an issued visa may be extended if the visa holder provides proof of serious personal reasons justifying the extension of the period of validity or the duration of stay. A fee of EUR 30 shall be charged for such an extension.
3. Unless otherwise decided by the authority extending the visa, the territorial validity of the extended visa shall remain the same as that of the original visa.
4. The authority competent to extend the visa shall be that of the Member State on whose territory the third-country national is present at the moment of applying for an extension.
5. Member States shall notify to the Commission the authorities competent for extending visas.
6. Extension of visas shall take the form of a visa sticker.
7. Information on an extended visa shall be entered into the VIS in accordance with Article 14 of the VIS Regulation.

Article 34
Annulment and revocation

1. A visa shall be annulled where it becomes evident that the conditions for issuing it were not met at the time when it was issued, in particular if there are serious grounds for believing that the visa was fraudulently obtained. A visa shall in principle be annulled by the competent authorities of the Member State which issued it. A visa may be annulled by the competent

authorities of another Member State, in which case the authorities of the Member State that issued the visa shall be informed of such annulment.

2. A visa shall be revoked where it becomes evident that the conditions for issuing it are no longer met. A visa shall in principle be revoked by the competent authorities of the Member State which issued it. A visa may be revoked by the competent authorities of another Member State, in which case the authorities of the Member State that issued the visa shall be informed of such revocation.

3. A visa may be revoked at the request of the visa holder. The competent authorities of the Member States that issued the visa shall be informed of such revocation.

4. Failure of the visa holder to produce, at the border, one or more of the supporting documents referred to in Article 14(3), shall not automatically lead to a decision to annul or revoke the visa.

5. If a visa is annulled or revoked, a stamp stating 'ANNULLED' or 'REVOKED' shall be affixed to it and the optically variable feature of the visa sticker, the security feature 'latent image effect' as well as the term 'visa' shall be invalidated by being crossed out.

6. A decision on annulment or revocation of a visa and the reasons on which it is based shall be notified to the applicant by means of the standard form set out in Annex VI.

7. A visa holder whose visa has been annulled or revoked shall have the right to appeal, unless the visa was revoked at his request in accordance with paragraph 3. Appeals shall be conducted against the Member State that has taken the decision on the annulment or revocation and in accordance with the national law of that Member State. Member States shall provide applicants with information regarding the procedure to be followed in the event of an appeal, as specified in Annex VI.

8. Information on an annulled or a revoked visa shall be entered into the VIS in accordance with Article 13 of the VIS Regulation.

CHAPTER VI
Visas issued at the external borders

Article 35
Visas applied for at the external border

1. In exceptional cases, visas may be issued at border crossing points if the following conditions are satisfied:

   (a) the applicant fulfils the conditions laid down in Article 5(1)(a), (c), (d) and (e) of the Schengen Borders Code;

(b) the applicant has not been in a position to apply for a visa in advance and submits, if required, supporting documents substantiating unforeseeable and imperative reasons for entry; and

(c) the applicant's return to his country of origin or residence or transit through States other than Member States fully implementing the Schengen *acquis* is assessed as certain.

2. Where a visa is applied for at the external border, the requirement that the applicant be in possession of travel medical insurance may be waived when such travel medical insurance is not available at that border crossing point or for humanitarian reasons.

3. A visa issued at the external border shall be a uniform visa, entitling the holder to stay for a maximum duration of 15 days, depending on the purpose and conditions of the intended stay. In the case of transit, the length of the authorised stay shall correspond to the time necessary for the purpose of the transit.

4. Where the conditions laid down in Article 5(1)(a), (c), (d) and (e) of the Schengen Borders Code are not fulfilled, the authorities responsible for issuing the visa at the border may issue a visa with limited territorial validity, in accordance with Article 25(1)(a) of this Regulation, for the territory of the issuing Member State only.

5. A third-country national falling within a category of persons for whom prior consultation is required in accordance with Article 22 shall, in principle, not be issued a visa at the external border.

    However, a visa with limited territorial validity for the territory of the issuing Member State may be issued at the external border for such persons in exceptional cases, in accordance with Article 25(1)(a).

6. In addition to the reasons for refusing a visa as provided for in Article 32(1) a visa shall be refused at the border crossing point if the conditions referred to in paragraph 1(b) of this Article are not met.

7. The provisions on justification and notification of refusals and the right of appeal set out in Article 32(3) and Annex VI shall apply.

Article 36
Visas issued to seafarers in transit at the external border

1. A seafarer who is required to be in possession of a visa when crossing the external borders of the Member States may be issued with a visa for the purpose of transit at the border where:

    (a) he fulfils the conditions set out in Article 35(1); and

    (b) he is crossing the border in question in order to embark on, re-embark on or disembark from a ship on which he will work or has worked as a seafarer.

2. Before issuing a visa at the border to a seafarer in transit, the competent national authorities shall comply with the rules set out in Annex IX, Part 1, and make sure that the necessary information concerning the seafarer in question has been exchanged by means of a duly completed form for seafarers in transit, as set out in Annex IX, Part 2.
3. This Article shall apply without prejudice to Article 35(3), (4) and (5).

TITLE IV
ADMINISTRATIVE MANAGEMENT AND ORGANISATION

Article 37
Organisation of visa sections

1. Member States shall be responsible for organising the visa sections of their consulates.

   In order to prevent any decline in the level of vigilance and to protect staff from being exposed to pressure at local level, rotation schemes for staff dealing directly with applicants shall be set up, where appropriate. Particular attention shall be paid to clear work structures and a distinct allocation/division of responsibilities in relation to the taking of final decisions on applications. Access to consultation of the VIS and the SIS and other confidential information shall be restricted to a limited number of duly authorised staff. Appropriate measures shall be taken to prevent unauthorised access to such databases.
2. The storage and handling of visa stickers shall be subject to adequate security measures to avoid fraud or loss. Each consulate shall keep an account of its stock of visa stickers and register how each visa sticker has been used.
3. Member States' consulates shall keep archives of applications. Each individual file shall contain the application form, copies of relevant supporting documents, a record of checks made and the reference number of the visa issued, in order for staff to be able to reconstruct, if need be, the background for the decision taken on the application.

   Individual application files shall be kept for a minimum of two years from the date of the decision on the application as referred to in Article 23(1).

Article 38
Resources for examining applications and monitoring of consulates

1. Member States shall deploy appropriate staff in sufficient numbers to carry out the tasks relating to the examining of applications, in such a way as to ensure reasonable and harmonised quality of service to the public.
2. Premises shall meet appropriate functional requirements of adequacy and allow for appropriate security measures.

3. Member States' central authorities shall provide adequate training to both expatriate staff and locally employed staff and shall be responsible for providing them with complete, precise and up-to-date information on the relevant Community and national law.
4. Member States' central authorities shall ensure frequent and adequate monitoring of the conduct of examination of applications and take corrective measures when deviations from the provisions of this Regulation are detected.

Article 39
Conduct of staff

1. Member States' consulates shall ensure that applicants are received courteously.
2. Consular staff shall, in the performance of their duties, fully respect human dignity. Any measures taken shall be proportionate to the objectives pursued by such measures.
3. While performing their tasks, consular staff shall not discriminate against persons on grounds of sex, racial or ethnic origin, religion or belief, disability, age or sexual orientation.

Article 40
Forms of cooperation

1. Each Member State shall be responsible for organising the procedures relating to applications. In principle, applications shall be lodged at a consulate of a Member State.
2. Member States shall:
   (a) equip their consulates and authorities responsible for issuing visas at the borders with the required material for the collection of biometric identifiers, as well as the offices of their honorary consuls, whenever they make use of them, to collect biometric identifiers in accordance with Article 42; and/or
   (b) cooperate with one or more other Member States, within the framework of local Schengen cooperation or by other appropriate contacts, in the form of limited representation, co-location, or a Common Application Centre in accordance with Article 41.
3. In particular circumstances or for reasons relating to the local situation, such as where:
   (a) the high number of applicants does not allow the collection of applications and of data to be organised in a timely manner and in decent conditions; or

(b) it is not possible to ensure a good territorial coverage of the third country concerned in any other way; and where the forms of cooperation referred to in paragraph 2(b) prove not to be appropriate for the Member State concerned, a Member State may, as a last resort, cooperate with an external service provider in accordance with Article 43.

4. Without prejudice to the right to call the applicant for a personal interview, as provided for in Article 21(8), the selection of a form of organisation shall not lead to the applicant being required to appear in person at more than one location in order to lodge an application.

5. Member States shall notify to the Commission how they intend to organise the procedures relating to applications in each consular location.

Article 41
Cooperation between Member States

1. Where 'co-location' is chosen, staff of the consulates of one or more Member States shall carry out the procedures relating to applications (including the collection of biometric identifiers) addressed to them at the consulate of another Member State and share the equipment of that Member State. The Member States concerned shall agree on the duration of and conditions for the termination of the co-location as well as the proportion of the visa fee to be received by the Member State whose consulate is being used.

2. Where 'Common Application Centres' are established, staff of the consulates of two or more Member States shall be pooled in one building in order for applicants to lodge applications (including biometric identifiers). Applicants shall be directed to the Member State competent for examining and deciding on the application. Member States shall agree on the duration of and conditions for the termination of such cooperation as well as the cost-sharing among the participating Member States. One Member State shall be responsible for contracts in relation to logistics and diplomatic relations with the host country.

3. In the event of termination of cooperation with other Member States, Member States shall assure the continuity of full service.

Article 42
Recourse to honorary consuls

1. Honorary consuls may also be authorised to perform some or all of the tasks referred to in Article 43(6). Adequate measures shall be taken to ensure security and data protection.

2. Where the honorary consul is not a civil servant of a Member State, the performance of those tasks shall comply with the requirements set out in Annex X, except for the provisions in point D(c) of that Annex.

3. Where the honorary consul is a civil servant of a Member State, the Member State concerned shall ensure that requirements comparable to those which would apply if the tasks were performed by its consulate are applied.

Article 43

Cooperation with external service providers

1. Member States shall endeavour to cooperate with an external service provider together with one or more Member States, without prejudice to public procurement and competition rules.

2. Cooperation with an external service provider shall be based on a legal instrument that shall comply with the requirements set out in Annex X.

3. Member States shall, within the framework of local Schengen cooperation, exchange information about the selection of external service providers and the establishment of the terms and conditions of their respective legal instruments.

4. The examination of applications, interviews (where appropriate), the decision on applications and the printing and affixing of visa stickers shall be carried out only by the consulate.

5. External service providers shall not have access to the VIS under any circumstances. Access to the VIS shall be reserved exclusively to duly authorised staff of consulates.

6. An external service provider may be entrusted with the performance of one or more of the following tasks:
   (a) providing general information on visa requirements and application forms;
   (b) informing the applicant of the required supporting documents, on the basis of a checklist;
   (c) collecting data and applications (including collection of biometric identifiers) and transmitting the application to the consulate;
   (d) collecting the visa fee;
   (e) managing the appointments for appearance in person at the consulate or at the external service provider;
   (f) collecting the travel documents, including a refusal notification if applicable, from the consulate and returning them to the applicant.

7. When selecting an external service provider, the Member State(s) concerned shall scrutinise the solvency and reliability of the company, including the necessary licences, commercial registration, company statutes, bank contracts, and ensure that there is no conflict of interests.

8. The Member State(s) concerned shall ensure that the external service provider selected complies with the terms and conditions assigned to it in the legal instrument referred to in paragraph 2.

9. The Member State(s) concerned shall remain responsible for compliance with data protection rules for the processing of data and shall be supervised in accordance with Article 28 of Directive 95/46/EC.

   Cooperation with an external service provider shall not limit or exclude any liability arising under the national law of the Member State(s) concerned for breaches of obligations with regard to the personal data of applicants or the performance of one or more of the tasks referred to in paragraph 6. This provision is without prejudice to any action which may be taken directly against the external service provider under the national law of the third country concerned.

10. The Member State(s) concerned shall provide training to the external service provider, corresponding to the knowledge needed to offer an appropriate service and sufficient information to applicants.

11. The Member State(s) concerned shall closely monitor the implementation of the legal instrument referred to in paragraph 2, including:
    (a) the general information on visa requirements and application forms provided by the external service provider to applicants;
    (b) all the technical and organisational security measures required to protect personal data against accidental or unlawful destruction or accidental loss, alteration, unauthorised disclosure or access, in particular where the cooperation involves the transmission of files and data to the consulate of the Member State(s) concerned, and all other unlawful forms of processing personal data;
    (c) the collection and transmission of biometric identifiers;
    (d) the measures taken to ensure compliance with data protection provisions.

    To this end, the consulate(s) of the Member State(s) concerned shall, on a regular basis, carry out spot checks on the premises of the external service provider.

12. In the event of termination of cooperation with an external service provider, Member States shall ensure the continuity of full service.

13. Member States shall provide the Commission with a copy of the legal instrument referred to in paragraph 2.

Article 44
Encryption and secure transfer of data

1. In the case of representation arrangements between Member States and cooperation of Member States with an external service provider and recourse to honorary consuls, the represented Member State(s) or the Member State(s) concerned shall ensure that the data are fully encrypted, whether electronically transferred or physically transferred on an electronic storage medium from the authorities of the representing Member State to the authorities of the represented Member State(s) or from the external service provider or from the honorary consul to the authorities of the Member State(s) concerned.

2. In third countries which prohibit encryption of data to be electronically transferred from the authorities of the representing Member State to the authorities of the represented Member State(s) or from the external service provider or from the honorary consul to the authorities of the Member State(s) concerned, the represented Members State(s) or the Member State(s) concerned shall not allow the representing Member State or the external service provider or the honorary consul to transfer data electronically.

   In such a case, the represented Member State(s) or the Member State(s) concerned shall ensure that the electronic data are transferred physically in fully encrypted form on an electronic storage medium from the authorities of the representing Member State to the authorities of the represented Member State(s) or from the external service provider or from the honorary consul to the authorities of the Member State(s) concerned by a consular officer of a Member State or, where such a transfer would require disproportionate or unreasonable measures to be taken, in another safe and secure way, for example by using established operators experienced in transporting sensitive documents and data in the third country concerned.

3. In all cases the level of security for the transfer shall be adapted to the sensitive nature of the data.

4. The Member States or the Community shall endeavour to reach agreement with the third countries concerned with the aim of lifting the prohibition against encryption of data to be electronically transferred from the authorities of the representing Member State to the authorities of the represented Member State(s) or from the external service provider or from the honorary consul to the authorities of the Member State(s) concerned.

Article 45
Member States' cooperation with commercial intermediaries

1. Member States may cooperate with commercial intermediaries for the lodging of applications, except for the collection of biometric identifiers.
2. Such cooperation shall be based on the granting of an accreditation by Member States' relevant authorities. The accreditation shall, in particular, be based on the verification of the following aspects:
   (a) the current status of the commercial intermediary: current licence, the commercial register, contracts with banks;
   (b) existing contracts with commercial partners based in the Member States offering accommodation and other package tour services;
   (c) contracts with transport companies, which must include an outward journey, as well as a guaranteed and fixed return journey.
3. Accredited commercial intermediaries shall be monitored regularly by spot checks involving personal or telephone interviews with applicants, verification of trips and accommodation, verification that the travel medical insurance provided is adequate and covers individual travellers, and wherever deemed necessary, verification of the documents relating to group return.
4. Within local Schengen cooperation, information shall be exchanged on the performance of the accredited commercial intermediaries concerning irregularities detected and refusal of applications submitted by commercial intermediaries, and on detected forms of travel document fraud and failure to carry out scheduled trips.
5. Within local Schengen cooperation, lists shall be exchanged of commercial intermediaries to which accreditation has been given by each consulate and from which accreditation has been withdrawn, together with the reasons for any such withdrawal. Each consulate shall make sure that the public is informed about the list of accredited commercial intermediaries with which it cooperates.

Article 46
Compilation of statistics

Member States shall compile annual statistics on visas, in accordance with the table set out in Annex XII. These statistics shall be submitted by 1 March for the preceding calendar year.

Article 47
Information to the general public

1. Member States' central authorities and consulates shall provide the general public with all relevant information in relation to the application for a visa, in particular:
   (a) the criteria, conditions and procedures for applying for a visa;
   (b) the means of obtaining an appointment, if applicable;
   (c) where the application may be submitted (competent consulate, Common Application Centre or external service provider);
   (d) accredited commercial intermediaries;
   (e) the fact that the stamp as provided for in Article 20 has no legal implications;
   (f) the time limits for examining applications provided for in Article 23(1), (2) and (3);
   (g) the third countries whose nationals or specific categories of whose nationals are subject to prior consultation or information;
   (h) that negative decisions on applications must be notified to the applicant, that such decisions must state the reasons on which they are based and that applicants whose applications are refused have a right to appeal, with information regarding the procedure to be followed in the event of an appeal, including the competent authority, as well as the time limit for lodging an appeal;
   (i) that mere possession of a visa does not confer an automatic right of entry and that the holders of visa are requested to present proof that they fulfil the entry conditions at the external border, as provided for in Article 5 of the Schengen Borders Code.
2. The representing and represented Member State shall inform the general public about representation arrangements as referred to in Article 8 before such arrangements enter into force.

TITLE V
LOCAL SCHENGEN COOPERATION

Article 48
Local Schengen cooperation between Member States' consulates

1. In order to ensure a harmonised application of the common visa policy taking into account, where appropriate, local circumstances, Member States' consulates and the Commission shall cooperate within each jurisdiction and assess the need to establish in particular:

(a) a harmonised list of supporting documents to be submitted by applicants, taking into account Article 14 and Annex II;

(b) common criteria for examining applications in relation to exemptions from paying the visa fee in accordance with Article 16(5) and matters relating to the translation of the application form in accordance with Article 11(5);

(c) an exhaustive list of travel documents issued by the host country, which shall be updated regularly.

If in relation to one or more of the points (a) to (c), the assessment within local Schengen cooperation confirms the need for a local harmonised approach, measures on such an approach shall be adopted pursuant to the procedure referred to in Article 52(2).

2. Within local Schengen cooperation a common information sheet shall be established on uniform visas and visas with limited territorial validity and airport transit visas, namely, the rights that the visa implies and the conditions for applying for it, including, where applicable, the list of supporting documents as referred to in paragraph 1(a).

3. The following information shall be exchanged within local Schengen cooperation:

(a) monthly statistics on uniform visas, visas with limited territorial validity, and airport transit visas issued, as well as the number of visas refused;

(b) with regard to the assessment of migratory and/or security risks, information on:
   (i) the socioeconomic structure of the host country;
   (ii) sources of information at local level, including social security, health insurance, fiscal registers and entry-exit registrations;
   (iii) the use of false, counterfeit or forged documents;
   (iv) illegal immigration routes;
   (v) refusals;

(c) information on cooperation with transport companies;

(d) information on insurance companies providing adequate travel medical insurance, including verification of the type of coverage and possible excess amount.

4. Local Schengen cooperation meetings to deal specifically with operational issues in relation to the application of the common visa policy shall be organised regularly among Member States and the Commission. These meetings shall be convened within the jurisdiction by the Commission, unless otherwise agreed at the request of the Commission. Single-topic meetings may be organised and sub-groups set up to study specific issues within local Schengen cooperation.

5. Summary reports of local Schengen cooperation meetings shall be drawn up systematically and circulated locally. The Commission may delegate the drawing up of the reports to a Member State. The consulates of each Member State shall forward the reports to their central authorities. On the basis of these reports, the Commission shall draw up an annual report within each jurisdiction to be submitted to the European Parliament and the Council.

6. Representatives of the consulates of Member States not applying the Community *acquis* in relation to visas, or of third countries, may on an ad hoc basis be invited to participate in meetings for the exchange of information on issues relating to visas.

TITLE VI
FINAL PROVISIONS

Article 49
Arrangements in relation to the Olympic Games and Paralympic Games

Member States hosting the Olympic Games and Paralympic Games shall apply the specific procedures and conditions facilitating the issuing of visas set out in Annex XI.

Article 50
Amendments to the Annexes

Measures designed to amend non-essential elements of this Regulation and amending Annexes I, II, III, IV, V, VI, VII, VIII and XII shall be adopted in accordance with the regulatory procedure with scrutiny referred to in Article 52(3).

Article 51
Instructions on the practical application of the Visa Code

Operational instructions on the practical application of the provisions of this Regulation shall be drawn up in accordance with the procedure referred to in Article 52(2).

Article 52
Committee procedure

1. The Commission shall be assisted by a committee (the Visa Committee).
2. Where reference is made to this paragraph, Articles 5 and 7 of Decision 1999/468/EC shall apply, having regard to the provisions of Article 8

thereof and provided that the implementing measures adopted in accordance with this procedure do not modify the essential provisions of this Regulation.

The period laid down in Article 5(6) of Decision 1999/468/EC shall be three months.

3. Where reference is made to this paragraph, Articles 5a(1) to (4) and 7 of Decision 1999/468/EC shall apply, having regard to the provisions of Article 8 thereof.

Article 53
Notification

1. Member States shall notify the Commission of:
   (a) representation arrangements referred to in Article 8;
   (b) third countries whose nationals are required by individual Member States to hold an airport transit visa when passing through the international transit areas of airports situated on their territory, as referred to in Article 3;
   (c) the national form for proof of sponsorship and/or private accommodation referred to in Article 14(4), if applicable;
   (d) the list of third countries for which prior consultation referred to in Article 22(1) is required;
   (e) the list of third countries for which information referred to in Article 31(1) is required;
   (f) the additional national entries in the 'comments' section of the visa sticker, as referred to in Article 27(2);
   (g) authorities competent for extending visas, as referred to in Article 33(5);
   (h) the forms of cooperation chosen as referred to in Article 40;
   (i) statistics compiled in accordance with Article 46 and Annex XII.
2. The Commission shall make the information notified pursuant to paragraph 1 available to the Member States and the public via a constantly updated electronic publication.

Article 54
Amendments to Regulation (EC) No 767/2008

Omitted (see text of VIS Regulation in chapter 10)

Article 55
Amendments to Regulation (EC) No 562/2006

Annex V, Part A of Regulation (EC) No 562/2006 is hereby amended as follows:

(a) point 1(c), shall be replaced by the following:

'(c) annul or revoke the visas, as appropriate, in accordance with the conditions laid down in Article 34 of Regulation (EC) No 810/2009 of the European Parliament and of the Council of 13 July 2009 establishing a Community code on visas (Visa Code) (*); _____ (*) OJ L 243, 15.9.2009, p. 1.';

(b) point 2 shall be deleted.

Article 56
Repeals

1. Articles 9 to 17 of the Convention implementing the Schengen Agreement of 14 June 1985 shall be repealed.
2. The following shall be repealed:
   (a) Decision of the Schengen Executive Committee of 28 April 1999 on the definitive versions of the Common Manual and the Common Consular Instructions (SCH/Com-ex (99) 13 (the Common Consular Instructions, including the Annexes);
   (b) Decisions of the Schengen Executive Committee of 14 December 1993 extending the uniform visa (SCH/Com-ex (93) 21) and on the common principles for cancelling, rescinding or shortening the length of validity of the uniform visa (SCH/Com-ex (93) 24), Decision of the Schengen Executive Committee of 22 December 1994 on the exchange of statistical information on the issuing of uniform visas (SCH/Com-ex (94) 25), Decision of the Schengen Executive Committee of 21 April 1998 on the exchange of statistics on issued visas (SCH/Com-ex (98) 12) and Decision of the Schengen Executive Committee of 16 December 1998 on the introduction of a harmonised form providing proof of invitation, sponsorship and accommodation (SCH/Com-ex (98) 57);
   (c) Joint Action 96/197/JHA of 4 March 1996 on airport transit arrangements;
   (d) Council Regulation (EC) No 789/2001 of 24 April 2001 reserving to the Council implementing powers with regard to certain detailed provisions and practical procedures for examining visa applications;
   (e) Council Regulation (EC) No 1091/2001 of 28 May 2001 on freedom of movement with a long-stay visa;
   (f) Council Regulation (EC) No 415/2003 of 27 February 2003 on the issue of visas at the border, including the issue of such visas to seamen in transit;
   (g) Article 2 of Regulation (EC) No 390/2009 of the European Parliament and of the Council of 23 April 2009 amending the Common Consular

Instructions on visas for diplomatic and consular posts in relation to the introduction of biometrics including provisions on the organisation of the reception and processing of visa applications.

3. References to repealed instruments shall be construed as references to this Regulation and read in accordance with the correlation table in Annex XIII.

Article 57
Monitoring and evaluation

1. Two years after all the provisions of this Regulation have become applicable, the Commission shall produce an evaluation of its application. This overall evaluation shall include an examination of the results achieved against objectives and of the implementation of the provisions of this Regulation, without prejudice to the reports referred to in paragraph 3.

2. The Commission shall transmit the evaluation referred to in paragraph 1 to the European Parliament and the Council. On the basis of the evaluation, the Commission shall submit, if necessary, appropriate proposals with a view to amending this Regulation.

3. The Commission shall present, three years after the VIS is brought into operation and every four years thereafter, a report to the European Parliament and to the Council on the implementation of Articles 13, 17, 40 to 44 of this Regulation, including the implementation of the collection and use of biometric identifiers, the suitability of the ICAO standard chosen, compliance with data protection rules, experience with external service providers with specific reference to the collection of biometric data, the implementation of the 59-month rule for the copying of fingerprints and the organisation of the procedures relating to applications. The report shall also include, on the basis of Article 17(12), (13) and (14) and of Article 50(4) of the VIS Regulation, the cases in which fingerprints could factually not be provided or were not required to be provided for legal reasons, compared with the number of cases in which fingerprints were taken. The report shall include information on cases in which a person who could factually not provide fingerprints was refused a visa. The report shall be accompanied, where necessary, by appropriate proposals to amend this Regulation.

4. The first of the reports referred to in paragraph 3 shall also address the issue of the sufficient reliability for identification and verification purposes of fingerprints of children under the age of 12 and, in particular, how fingerprints evolve with age, on the basis of the results of a study carried out under the responsibility of the Commission.

Article 58
Entry into force

1. This Regulation shall enter into force on the 20th day following its publication in the *Official Journal of the European Union.*
2. It shall apply from 5 April 2010.
3. Article 52 and Article 53(1)(a) to (h) and (2) shall apply from 5 October 2009.
4. As far as the Schengen Consultation Network (Technical Specifications) is concerned, Article 56(2)(d) shall apply from the date referred to in Article 46 of the VIS Regulation.
5. Article 32(2) and (3), Article 34(6) and (7) and Article 35(7) shall apply from 5 April 2011.

This Regulation shall be binding in its entirety and directly applicable in the Member States in accordance with the Treaty establishing the European Community.

Chapter 9

Visa Facilitation

1. *Introduction*

Starting in 2007, the EU has negotiated and concluded a series of visa facilitation agreements with third States, always in conjunction with readmission agreements.[1] More such treaties are under negotiation or planned. This chapter examines these agreements in detail.

Visa facilitation treaties are in force with Russia,[2] Ukraine,[3] Western Balkans states (except for Croatia),[4] Moldova[5] and (as from 1 March 2011) Georgia.[6] However, the treaties with the Western Balkans states of course now have little relevance since the abolition of visa requirements for those countries, except for those cases where the person concerned is exceptionally required to obtain a visa, for instance because they reside in Kosovo or do not hold a biometric passport.[7] Negotiations for another such agreement are underway with Cape Verde, and in February 2011, the Council gave the Commission authority to begin negotiations with Belarus. The EU has also committed itself in principle to negotiate visa facilitation agreements with the other "Eastern partnership" States (Armenia and Azerbaijan), provided that there is sufficient commitment by these countries to the values and principles espoused by the EU.[8] It remains to be seen whether visa facilitation treaties might be negotiated with

---

[1] On readmission treaties, see volume 2 of this book (chapter 20). The negotiations for the readmission and visa facilitation agreements always took place in parallel, except as regards Albania, where the readmission agreement was negotiated several years before the visa facilitation agreement, and Russia and Ukraine, where negotiations for a readmission agreement got underway first and negotiations on visa facilitation agreements started later.

[2] OJ 2007 L 129.

[3] OJ 2007 L 332. As an example, the text of the EU/Ukraine visa facilitation agreement is annexed to this chapter.

[4] OJ 2007 L 334.

[5] OJ 2007 L 334.

[6] COM (2010) 197 and 198, 5 May 2010. The treaty was signed in June 2010 (OJ 2010 L 308/1) and concluded by the EU in Jan. 2011 (OJ 2011 L 44/1).

[7] See further chapter 7. Presumably this explains why these treaties have not been abrogated.

[8] See the declaration annexed to the European Council conclusions of March 2009.

North African and Middle Eastern countries, following the major political changes in those States beginning early in 2011.[9]

2. *Background*

Since the negotiation of readmission treaties with Russia and Ukraine had stalled, the EU sought to offer those countries incentives to sign such treaties which would fall short of full visa liberalisation. Negotiation of visa facilitation treaties with these States began in 2004 and 2005, but the Council also decided to adopt a "common approach on visa facilitation", which was agreed at the end of 2005.[10] The common approach states that negotiations on such treaties should be considered, on a "case by case assessment of third countries, while bearing in mind the EU's overall relationship with…candidate countries, countries with a European perspective and countries covered by the European Neighbourhood Policy as well as strategic partners". While visa facilitation agreements are linked to readmission agreements, the former (unlike the latter) are not to be offered "proactively" to non-EU states. Moreover, "the existence of a readmission agreement, or the willingness of a third-country to negotiate one, does not automatically nor routinely lead to the opening of negotiations on a visa facilitation agreement"; the EU will instead seek other instruments in order to secure a readmission agreement, including "development policy" measures.

The factors to consider when authorising a mandate to negotiate a visa facilitation agreement are: "whether a readmission agreement is in place or under active negotiation; external relations objectives; implementation record of existing bilateral agreements and progress on related issues in the area of justice, freedom and security (e.g. border management, document security, migration and asylum, fight against terrorism,…organised crime and corruption); and security concerns, migratory movements and the impact of the visa facilitation agreement." As to the substance of the agreements, they are likely to differ between countries, depending on the "visa policy of the country concerned, the introduction of biometric passports and the existing practical problems." Finally, these agreements are to be based on reciprocity, take precedence over national visa facilitation treaties in cases of overlap, and must include a monitoring or a suspension clause.

---

[9] The Commission has explicitly endorsed the idea of the negotiation and conclusion of such treaties, in its Communication on the Southern Neighbourhood – COM (2011) 292, 24 May 2011. So far, the Council has not responded to this idea.

[10] Council doc. 16030/05, 21 Dec. 2005.

The next development was the adoption of a new Decision in 2006 raising the standard fee for visa applications from €35 to €60, in order to cover the cost of introduction of biometric visas and the Visa Information System.[11] As part of the overall compromise on this issue, it was agreed that the increase in fees would be frozen at the lower level for an extra year (until the start of 2008) for the nationals of any country for which the Council had granted the Commission a negotiating mandate for a visa facilitation agreement by the end of 2006. The Commission was also requested to propose mandates for negotiations for visa facilitation agreements, "starting with" Western Balkans countries. Since the visa facilitation treaties were linked to readmission treaties, this approach gave Russia, Ukraine and (subsequently) Western Balkan States and Moldova a limited time period to negotiate readmission treaties with the EU, if they wished to avoid a large increase in the visa fees applicable to their citizens (considering that the newer Member States were also about to raise visa application fees when they joined Schengen fully). This strategy worked, inducing all of the third States to negotiate readmission treaties by the end-2007 deadline.

3. *Content of the Agreements*

The visa facilitation agreements are broadly similar, except that the agreement with Russia is less generous than the others, and the most recent agreement (with Georgia) takes account of the points raised in the Commission's assessment of the implementation of the earlier agreements.[12] The following summary takes the EU/Ukraine visa facilitation agreement as a model, but indicates where other visa facilitation treaties diverge from that model.

The agreements apply to visas for a stay of three months within a six-month period, ie the standard period applicable to Schengen visas.[13] The agreements are in principle reciprocal,[14] although this point is largely moot for the time being as the EU's partners do not impose a visa obligation on EU citizens, with the exception of Russia.

For a number of categories of persons, the agreements simplify the process of supplying supporting documents for a visa application, by listing the single

---

[11] OJ 2006 L 175/77. On the negotiation of this decision, see further Peers, "Key Legislative Developments on Migration in the European Union", 8 EJML (2006) 321 at 351–356.

[12] See section 4 below.

[13] Arts. 1(1) and 3(d).

[14] Note that the treaties do not require the EU's partners to waive the visa requirement. Art. 1(2) specifies that if the EU's partners do decide to apply a visa requirement, the agreement would then apply as regards the issue of visas to EU citizens.

specific document necessary to support the application.[15] These rules apply to: members of official delegations; business people; professional drivers; train crews; journalists; participants in scientific, cultural and artistic activities, including university exchange programmes; pupils, students and teachers on educational trips; participants in sports events; participants in twin cities programmes; close relatives (parents, grandparents, children) visiting nationals of the partner State legally resident in a Member State;[16] relatives visiting for burial ceremonies; visits to burial grounds; and medical visits.[17] This compares to the rules in the EU's visa code regarding supporting documents, which are less precise.[18]

It should be noted that the visa facilitation agreements do not exempt applicants from the EU's general rules applying to visa applications, including the rules on lodging an application form, supplying biometric data (once the Visa Information System, or "VIS", is operational in the States concerned), holding a travel document of possessing medical insurance.[19] Nor do they exempt visa applications from the substantive rules applying to the examination of visa applications (subsistence requirement, checks in the Schengen Information System, and requirements as regards threats to public policy, internal security, public health and international relations.[20]

Multiple-entry visas with a term of validity of up to five years must be issued to: members of governments, parliaments and the highest courts; permanent members of official delegations who regularly participate in meetings, etc in the EU; and specified close family members visiting nationals of the EU's partners who are legally resident in the EU.[21] This can be compared to the less

---

[15] Art. 4.

[16] For the definition of legal residence, see Art. 3(e).

[17] The relevant provision in the agreement with Russia does not apply to burial grounds or medical visits. The relevant provisions in the agreements with Western Balkan States, Georgia and Moldova also apply to professionals and civil society, and most agreements with Western Balkan States also contain provisions on religious and tourist visits. The agreement with Montenegro also includes rules on supporting documents for judges' visits, while the agreement with Albania includes a special rule on politically persecuted people. The agreement with Moldova includes a wider definition of medical visitors. Finally, the agreement with Georgia does not contain specific rules on burial grounds or train crew, but contains wider definitions of journalists and medical visitors (ie, including accompanying people).

[18] Art. 14 of the code (Reg. 810/2009, OJ 2009 L 243/1). For more on the visa code, see chapter 8.

[19] See Arts. 9–13 and 15 of the visa code (ibid). On the VIS, see further chapter 10.

[20] Art. 21(3) of the visa code (ibid).

[21] Art. 5(1). The agreements with Ukraine, Moldova and the Former Yugoslav Republic of Macedonia also include journalists and business people in this category, while the agreement with Russia does not include members of official delegations and the agreement with Bosnia

precise provisions in the visa code, which provide for the issue of a multiple-entry visa valid between six months and five years to a wider list of persons, subject to the conditions (which do not appear in the visa facilitation agreement) that "the applicant proves the need or justifies the intention to travel frequently and/or regularly, in particular due to his occupational or family status," and that "the applicant proves his integrity and reliability, in particular the lawful use of previous uniform visas or visas with limited territorial validity, his economic situation in the country of origin and his genuine intention to leave the territory of the Member States before the expiry of the visa applied for."[22]

Multiple-entry visas with a term of validity of up to one year must be issued, subject to certain conditions,[23] to: business people and journalists; professional drivers; train crews; participants in "scientific, cultural and artistic activities"; participants in sports events and professionals accompanying them; and participants in twin cities' exchange programmes. Subsequently the latter categories of persons can obtain a multiple-entry visa valid for between two and five years.[24]

The fee for a visa application is fixed at €35,[25] and is waived altogether for a long list of categories of persons, namely: close relatives; members of official

---

does not include politicians. The agreement with the Former Yugoslav Republic of Macedonia also includes members of religious communities.

[22] Art. 24(2) of the code (n. 18 above).

[23] Art. 5(2). The persons concerned must have obtained a visa in the previous year and used it legally, and have "reasons" for requesting a multiple-entry visa. Arguably this requirement is not as stringent as the requirements in the visa code.

[24] Art. 5(3). This is subject to the condition that the persons concerned must have made use in the previous two years of the one-year multiple-entry visas and used them legally, and that the "reasons for requesting a multiple-entry visa are still valid". Information on prior use of visas will be subject in future to storage in the Visa Information System (see chapter 10) as well as the planned entry-exit system (see chapter 6). The agreements with Ukraine, Moldova and the Former Yugoslav Republic of Macedonia do not include journalists and business people in this category, since these persons are covered by Art. 5(1) instead. The agreement with Russia applies Art. 5(2) and (3) to members of official delegations. The agreements with the Western Balkans and Georgia also apply Art. 5(2) and (3) to other official delegations, professionals, students, medical visitors, civil society and (for the Western Balkans) religious visitors, while the agreement with Moldova applies Art. 5(2) and (3) to official delegations, professionals, students and civil society. The agreement with Montenegro also applies these rules to judges, and the agreement with the Former Yugoslav Republic of Macedonia applies them to mayors. The agreement with Georgia does not apply the rules to train crews.

[25] Art. 6(1). A higher fee of €70 applies to urgent applications in the treaties with Ukraine and Russia (but not the other treaties). This fee is either waived entirely or set at €35 only for the various special categories (Art. 6(3)).

delegations; members of governments, parliaments and higher courts; pupils, students and teachers on educational visits; disabled persons and those accompanying them; persons travelling on humanitarian grounds; participants in sports events; participants in scientific, cultural and exchange activities; participants in official exchange programmes; journalists; pensioners; professional drivers; train crews; and children under 18 and dependent children under 21.[26] The agreement with Georgia expressly permits a service fee to be charged for the collection of biometric data.[27]

This compares to rules in the visa code, which provide for a usual fee of €60, with a mandatory reduction only for children between six and twelve years old (reduced fee of €35),[28] and a mandatory waiver for: children under six years old; students, pupils and teachers on study trips; researchers as defined by an EU recommendation; and representatives of non-profit organisations attending seminars and similar events. While the visa code also permits (but does not require) the application fee to be waived for children between six and twelve, holders of diplomatic and service passports and participants in non-profit seminars and similar events who are under 25 years old, and on a case-by-case basis on policy grounds, this falls well short of the fee waivers required by visa facilitation treaties.

Each treaty requires visa decisions to be taken within ten days, with a reduction to two or three days in urgent cases and a possible extension to thirty days in individual cases, in particular if further scrutiny of the application is necessary.[29] In contrast, the visa code provides for a decision within fifteen days, with a possible extension to thirty days or even sixty days.[30]

In the event of lost or stolen travel documents, visitors can leave the territory on the basis of valid replacement documents without the requirement to obtain a visa.[31] If a visitor cannot leave within the period of validity of the visa

---

[26] Art. 6(4). The agreement with Russia does not waive fees for the final four categories of persons. The agreements with Western Balkan states only waive fees for children under 6, but also waive fees for religious visitors, civil society and professionals, although the agreement with Bosnia does not waive fees for politicians, the agreement with the Former Yugoslav Republic of Macedonia also waives fees for mayors and the agreement with Albania waives fees for politically persecuted persons. The agreement with Moldova waives fees for professionals. Finally, the agreement with Georgia waives fees for civil society, but not drivers or train crews, and only for children under 12.

[27] Art. 6(2) of that agreement. Compare to Art. 17 of the visa code (n. 18 above).

[28] Art. 16 of the visa code (ibid).

[29] Art 7. The consequence of a failure to decide within these time limits is not specified.

[30] Art. 23(1) to (3) of the code (n. 18 above).

[31] Art. 8.

due to *force majeure*, the visa must be extended free of charge.[32] For persons with valid diplomatic passports, the visa requirement is waived altogether.[33] There is a special rule in the agreement with Russia as regards the simplification of registration procedures.[34]

Nationals of partner States can travel within the territory of the Member States on an equal footing with EU citizens, subject to Member States' national rules on "national security" and the EU rules on the limited territorial validity of visas.[35] There is a joint committee for the management of each agreement, and each agreement takes precedence over any Member State's national treaties falling within the same scope.[36] However, the agreements with Western Balkan states provide for the continuation for five years of pre-existing treaties with Member States which waive visa requirements for service passport holders.[37] Issues outside the scope of the agreements, such as "the refusal to issue a visa, recognition of travel documents, proof of sufficient means of subsistence and the refusal of entry and expulsion measures", are addressed by the national law of the partner State or the Member States, or by EU law.[38]

Finally, there are Protocols to each agreement on the position of the Member States not yet fully applying the Schengen *acquis*,[39] and joint declarations to each agreement as regards the position of the UK, Ireland, Denmark and Schengen associates, encouraging the negotiation of separate visa facilitation treaties with such States.[40] There are also sundry declarations to various agreements as follows: an EU declaration on the issues of visits to burial grounds;[41] a Commission declaration on the reasons for refusing a visa;[42] an

---

[32] Art. 9. These rules are broader in the agreements with the Former Yugoslav Republic of Macedonia and Georgia. These provisions do not differ from the visa code (Art. 33(1), n. 18 above).

[33] Art. 10. This applies for the standard period of ninety days within a 180-day period.

[34] Art. 10 of that agreement.

[35] Art. 11. The EU rules concerned are set out in Art. 25 of the visa code.

[36] Arts. 12 and 13.

[37] Art. 13 of each agreement.

[38] Art. 2(2).

[39] The agreements apply to those Member States as regards the purely national visas they issue, pending their participation in the Schengen *acquis*. On the territorial scope of EU law in this area, see chapter 2.

[40] Again, see chapter 2.

[41] This only applies to the treaties with Russia and Ukraine. The declaration states that the standard period of validity for visas in this case will only be "up to 14 days".

[42] Only the agreement with Ukraine includes this declaration, which refers to the proposal for the EU visa code, then under discussion. See now Art. 32 of the code (n. 18 above).

EU declaration on access and information for visa applicants;[43] the review of visa processing fees;[44] a joint declaration on the possible suspension of the agreement if the diplomatic exception is abused;[45] an EU declaration as regards the suspension of the agreement if visa requirements are introduced against some Member States only;[46] a Commission declaration on representation for issuing visas in the third State concerned;[47] a declaration regarding visas for seamen;[48] joint declarations on a future visa-free regime and on avoiding repeated fees when a second visa application has to be made;[49] an EU declaration as regards a broader definition of family members;[50] a joint declaration as regards travel documents;[51] and a declaration by some Member States on a their willingness to negotiate treaties on facilitation of local border traffic in accordance with the EU's border traffic legislation.[52]

4. *Implementation of the Agreements*

The Commission released a report on the implementation of visa facilitation agreements in 2009.[53] This report pointed out that the visa facilitation treaties applied to over half of visa applicants,[54] and noted that visa applications

---

[43] Again, the declarations (except to the agreements with Russia and Georgia) refer to the proposal for the EU visa code, but also state some elements of what an information policy should entail. See now Art. 47 of the code (ibid). The declarations in the treaties with Russia and Georgia refer only to information issues, and the declaration in the treaty with Russia is a joint declaration.

[44] Only the agreement with Russia has a declaration on this point.

[45] Only the agreements with Russia and Georgia have a declaration on this point.

[46] Only the agreement with Georgia has a declaration on this point.

[47] Only the agreement with Moldova has a declaration on this point.

[48] Only the agreement with Montenegro has a declaration on this point.

[49] Only the agreement with the Former Yugoslav Republic of Macedonia has declarations on these points. The latter point refers implicitly to the Greek practice of issuing only visas with limited territorial validity and refusing to accept the validity of Schengen visas issued by other Member States to nationals of the State concerned.

[50] The agreements with the Western Balkans and Georgia include this declaration.

[51] Only the agreement with Georgia has a declaration on this point.

[52] On that legislation, and on the negotiation and application of such treaties in practice, see chapter 6. As regards Ukraine, there are declarations by Poland, Hungary, Slovakia and Romania; as regards Moldova, there are reciprocal declarations by Moldova and Romania; as regards the Former Yugoslav Republic of Macedonia, there is a declaration by Bulgaria; and as regards Serbia, there are declarations by Bulgaria, Hungary and Romania.

[53] SEC (2009) 1401, 15 Oct. 2009.

[54] This percentage will have dropped since, due to the subsequent waiver of visa requirements for five of the third States with visa facilitation agreements (ie the Western Balkan States); see chapter 7.

increased in some of the countries concerned, but decreased in others; it should be recalled that the application of most of these treaties broadly coincided with the extension of the Schengen zone.

There were small drops in the refusal rate of applications, and there appeared to be a large increase in the numbers of visas issued free of charge and of multiple-entry visas. While the EU's neighbours continued to complain about a number of aspects of the visa- issuing process, the Commission argued that many of these complaints would be addressed by the (then) forthcoming application of the visa code. However, the Commission did suggest the renegotiation of the relevant treaties, to address the specific issues of the simplification of supporting documents (as regards persons connected to journalists and medical visitors), broader fee waivers, the possibility for external service providers to charge a service fee, the abolition of the "urgency fee" applying to the agreements with Russia and the Ukraine and a ban on the discriminatory introduction of a visa obligation on citizens of only one EU Member State (in light of experience with Moldova).

The Commission proposed mandates to renegotiate the treaties with Russia, Ukraine and Moldova in 2010, presumably to take account of the suggestions in its review of the application of the treaties. The Council had agreed to give the Commission a renegotiation mandate in April 2011, but the renegotiations have not yet finished. But the issues raised by the Commission were addressed in the treaty with Georgia, which was signed and concluded subsequently. Presumably the negotiating mandates for visa facilitation treaties with Cape Verde and Belarus (which are not public) similarly take account of the Commission's assessment of the initial agreements.

5. *Comments*

It is clear that visa facilitation agreements represent a compromise between the desire of newer Member States for visa-free travel with neighbouring third countries and the desire of the first fifteen Member States to maintain a more restrictive visa regime in the interests of reducing irregular immigration.[55] More broadly, the EU's visa facilitation treaties form part of its developing policy with neighbouring States and part of its policy designed to induce nearby States to negotiate readmission treaties.[56] The Commission has recently

---

[55] The same can be said of the development of EU rules on border traffic, on which see chapter 6.

[56] On both points, see further Trauner and Kruse, "EC Visa Facilitation and Readmission Agreements: A New Standard EU Foreign Policy Tool?", 10 EJML (2008) 411.

suggested that the visa facilitation route needs to be more widely used to this end.[57] Any extension of visa facilitation agreements would be welcome, given the reasonable balance which they represent between simplifying travel for nationals of third countries and meeting the concerns about security and irregular migration of some Member States. In practice, visa facilitation agreements appear to play a transitional role in the short-term or longer-term development of visa liberalisation as regards the third States concerned – and to that extent, they should be even further welcomed.

---

[57] See the communication on evaluation of readmission agreements (COM (2011) 76, 23 Feb. 2011).

Annex

EU/Ukraine Visa Facilitation Agreement

THE EUROPEAN COMMUNITY,

hereinafter referred to as 'the Community', and

UKRAINE,

hereinafter referred to as 'the Parties',

WITH A VIEW to further developing friendly relations between the Contracting Parties and desiring to facilitate people to people contacts as an important condition for a steady development of economic, humanitarian, cultural, scientific and other ties, by facilitating the issuing of visas to Ukrainian citizens,

DESIRING to regulate the regime of mutual travel of citizens of Ukraine and Member States of the European Union,

BEARING IN MIND that, as from 1 May 2005, EU citizens are exempted from the visa requirement when travelling to Ukraine for a period of time not exceeding 90 days or transiting through the territory of Ukraine,

RECOGNISING that if Ukraine would reintroduce the visa requirement for EU citizens, the same facilitations granted under this agreement to the Ukrainian citizens would automatically, on the basis of reciprocity, apply to EU citizens,

HAVING REGARD to the EU Ukraine Policy Action Plan, which noted that a constructive dialogue on visa facilitation between the EU and Ukraine would be established, with a view to preparing for negotiations on a visa facilitation agreement, taking account of the need for progress on the ongoing negotiations for an EC-Ukraine readmission agreement,

RECOGNISING that visa facilitation should not lead to illegal migration and paying special attention to security and readmission,

RECOGNISING the introduction of a visa free travel regime for the citizens of Ukraine as a long term perspective,

TAKING INTO ACCOUNT the Protocol on the position of the United Kingdom and Ireland and the Protocol integrating the Schengen *acquis* into the framework of the European Union, annexed to the Treaty on European Union and the Treaty establishing the European Community and confirming that the provisions of this agreement do not apply to the United Kingdom and Ireland,

TAKING INTO ACCOUNT the Protocol on the position of Denmark annexed to the Treaty on European Union and the Treaty establishing the European Community and confirming that the provisions of this agreement do not apply to the Kingdom of Denmark,

HAVE AGREED AS FOLLOWS:

Article 1
Purpose and scope of application

1. The purpose of this Agreement is to facilitate the issuance of visas for an intended stay of no more than 90 days per period of 180 days to the citizens of Ukraine.
2. If Ukraine would reintroduce the visa requirement for EU citizens or certain categories of EU citizens, the same facilitations granted under this agreement to the Ukrainian citizens would automatically, on the basis of reciprocity, apply to EU citizens concerned.

Article 2
General clause

1. The visa facilitations provided in this Agreement shall apply to citizens of Ukraine only insofar as they are not exempted from the visa requirement by the laws and regulations of the Community or the Member States, the present agreement or other international agreements.
2. The national law of Ukraine, or of the Member States or Community law shall apply to issues not covered by the provisions of this Agreement, such as the refusal to issue a visa, recognition of travel documents, proof of sufficient means of subsistence and the refusal of entry and expulsion measures.

Article 3
Definitions

For the purpose of this Agreement:

(a) 'Member State' shall mean any Member State of the European Union, with the exception of the Kingdom of Denmark, the Republic of Ireland and the United Kingdom;
(b) 'citizen of the European Union' shall mean a national of a Member State as defined in point (a);
(c) 'citizen of Ukraine' shall mean any person who holds the citizenship of Ukraine;

(d) 'visa' shall mean an authorisation issued by a Member State or a decision taken by such State which is required with a view to:
— entry for an intended stay in that Member State or in several Member States of no more than 90 days in total,
— entry for transit through the territory of that Member State or several Member States;
(e) 'legally residing person' shall mean a citizen of Ukraine authorised or entitled to stay for more than 90 days in the territory of a Member State, on the basis of Community or national legislation.

Article 4
Supporting documents regarding the purpose of the journey

1. For the following categories of citizens of Ukraine, the following documents are sufficient for justifying the purpose of the journey to the other Party:
(a) for members of official delegations who, following an official invitation addressed to Ukraine, shall participate in meetings, consultations, negotiations or exchange programmes, as well as in events held in the territory of one of the Member States by intergovernmental organisations:
— a letter issued by an Ukrainian authority confirming that the applicant is a member of its delegation travelling to the other Party to participate at the aforementioned events, accompanied by a copy of the official invitation;
(b) for business people and representatives of business organisations:
— a written request from a host legal person or company, or an office or a branch of such legal person or company, State and local authorities of the Member States or organising committees of trade and industrial exhibitions, conferences and symposia held in the territories of the Member States;
(c) for drivers conducting international cargo and passenger transportation services to the territories of the Member States in vehicles registered in Ukraine:
— a written request from the national association of carriers of Ukraine providing for international road transportation, stating the purpose, duration and frequency of the trips;
(d) for members of train, refrigerator and locomotive crews in international trains, travelling to the territories of the Member States:
— a written request from the competent railway company of Ukraine stating the purpose, duration and frequency of the trips;

(e) for journalists:
 — a certificate or other document issued by a professional organisation proving that the person concerned is a qualified journalist and a document issued by his/her employer stating that the purpose of the journey is to carry out journalistic work;

(f) for persons participating in scientific, cultural and artistic activities, including university and other exchange programmes:
 — a written request from the host organisation to participate in those activities;

(g) for pupils, students, post-graduate students and accompanying teachers who undertake trips for the purposes of study or educational training, including in the framework of exchange programmes as well as other school related activities:
 — a written request or a certificate of enrolment from the host university, college or school or student cards or certificates of the courses to be attended;

(h) for participants in international sports events and persons accompanying them in a professional capacity:
 — a written request from the host organisation: competent authorities, national sport Federations and National Olympic Committees of the Member States;

(i) for participants in official exchange programmes organised by twin cities: a written request of the Head of Administration/Mayor of these cities;

(j) for close relatives — spouse, children (including adopted), parents (including custodians), grandparents and grandchildren
 — visiting citizens of Ukraine legally residing in the territory of the Member States:
 — a written request from the host person;

(k) relatives visiting for burial ceremonies:
 — an official document confirming the fact of death as well as confirmation of the family or other relationship between the applicant and the buried;

(l) for visiting military and civil burial grounds:
 — an official document confirming the existence and preservation of the grave as well as family or other relationship between the applicant and the buried;

(m) for visiting for medical reasons:
 — an official document of the medical institution confirming necessity of medical care in this institution and proof of sufficient financial means to pay the medical treatment.

2. The written request mentioned in paragraph 1 of this Article shall contain the following items:
   (a) for the invited person: name and surname, date of birth, sex, citizenship, number of the identity document, time and purpose of the journey, number of entries and name of minor children accompanying the invited person;
   (b) for the inviting person: name and surname and address; or
   (c) for the inviting legal person, company or organisation: full name and address and
   — if the request is issued by an organisation, the name and position of the person who signs the request;
   — if the inviting person is a legal person or company or an office or a branch of such legal person or company established in the territory of a Member State, the registration number as required by the national law of the Member State concerned.
3. For the categories of persons mentioned in paragraph 1 of this article, all categories of visas are issued according to the simplified procedure without requiring any other justification, invitation or validation concerning the purpose of the journey, provided for by the legislation of the Member States.

Article 5
Issuance of multiple-entry visas

1. Diplomatic missions and consular posts of the Member States shall issue multiple-entry visas with the term of validity of up to five years to the following categories of persons:
   (a) members of national and regional Governments and Parliaments, Constitutional Courts and Supreme Courts if they are not exempted from the visa requirement by the present Agreement, in the exercise of their duties, with a term of validity limited to their term of office if this is less than 5 years;
   (b) permanent members of official delegations who, following official invitations addressed to Ukraine, shall regularly participate in meetings, consultations, negotiations or exchange programmes, as well as in events held in the territory of the Member States by intergovernmental organisations;
   (c) spouses and children (including adopted), who are under the age of 21 or are dependant, and parents (including custodians) visiting citizens of Ukraine legally residing in the territory of the Member States with the term of validity limited to the duration of the validity of their authorisation for legal residence.

(d) business people and representatives of business organisations who regularly travel to the Member States;

(e) journalists.

2. Diplomatic missions and consular posts of the Member States shall issue multiple-entry visas with the term of validity of up to one year to the following categories of persons, provided that during the previous year they have obtained at least one visa, have made use of it in accordance with the laws on entry and stay of the visited State and that there are reasons for requesting a multiple-entry visa:

(a) drivers conducting international cargo and passenger transportation services to the territories of the Member States in vehicles registered in Ukraine;

(b) members of train, refrigerator and locomotive crews in international trains, travelling to the territories of the Member States;

(c) persons participating in scientific, cultural and artistic activities, including university and other exchange programmes, who regularly travel to the Member States;

(d) participants in international sports events and persons accompanying them in a professional capacity;

(e) participants in official exchange programmes organised by twin cities.

3. Diplomatic missions and consular posts of the Member States shall issue multiple-entry visas with the term of validity of a minimum of two years and a maximum of five years to the categories of persons referred to in paragraph 2 of this Article, provided that during the previous two years they have made use of the one year multiple-entry visas in accordance with the laws on entry and stay of the visited State and that the reasons for requesting a multiple-entry visa are still valid.

4. The total period of stay of persons referred to in paragraphs 1 to 3 of this Article shall not exceed 90 days per period of 180 days in the territory of the Member States.

Article 6
Fees for processing visa applications

1. The fee for processing visa applications of Ukrainian citizens shall amount to EUR 35. The aforementioned amount may be reviewed in accordance with the procedure provided for in Article 14(4).

2. If Ukraine would reintroduce the visa requirement for EU citizens, the visa fee to be charged by Ukraine shall not be higher than EUR 35 or the amount agreed if the fee is reviewed in accordance with the procedure provided for in Article 14(4).

3. The Member States shall charge a fee of EUR 70 for processing visas in cases where the visa application and the supporting documents have been submitted by the visa applicant within three days before his/her envisaged date of departure. This will not apply to cases pursuant to Article 6(4)(b), (c), (e), (f), (j), (k) and Article 7(3). For categories mentioned in Article 6(4)(a), (d), (g), (h), (i), (l) to (n), the fee in urgent cases is the same as provided for in Article 6(1).
4. Fees for processing the visa application are waived for the following categories of persons:
    (a) for close relatives—spouses, children (including adopted) parents (including custodians), grandparents and grandchildren—of citizens of Ukraine legally residing in the territory of the Member States;
    (b) for members of official delegations who, following an official invitation addressed to Ukraine, shall participate in meetings, consultations, egotiations or exchange programmes, as well as in events held in the territory of one of the Member States by intergovernmental organisations;
    (c) members of national and regional Governments and Parliaments, Constitutional Courts and Supreme Courts, in case they are not exempted from the visa requirement by the present Agreement;
    (d) pupils, students, post-graduate students and accompanying teachers who undertake trips for the purpose of study or educational training;
    (e) disabled persons and the person accompanying them, if necessary;
    (f) persons who have presented documents proving the necessity of their travel on humanitarian grounds, including to receive urgent medical treatment and the person accompanying such person, or to attend a funeral of a close relative, or to visit a close relative seriously ill;
    (g) participants in international sports events and persons accompanying them;
    (h) persons participating in scientific, cultural and artistic activities including university and other exchange programmes;
    (i) participants in official exchange programmes organised by twin cities;
    (j) journalists;
    (k) pensioners;
    (l) drivers conducting international cargo and passenger transportation services to the territories of the Member States in vehicles registered in Ukraine;
    (m) members of train, refrigerator and locomotive crews in international trains, travelling to the territories of the Member States;
    (n) children under the age of 18 and dependant children under the age of 21.

Article 7
Length of procedures for processing visa applications

1. Diplomatic missions and consular posts of the Member States shall take a decision on the request to issue a visa within 10 calendar days of the date of the receipt of the application and documents required for issuing the visa.
2. The period of time for taking a decision on a visa application may be extended up to 30 calendar days in individual cases, notably when further scrutiny of the application is needed.
3. The period of time for taking a decision on a visa application may be reduced to two working days or less in urgent cases.

Article 8
Departure in case of lost or stolen documents

Citizens of the European Union and of Ukraine who have lost their identity documents, or from whom these documents have been stolen while staying in the territory of Ukraine or the Member States, may leave that territory on the grounds of valid identity documents entitling to cross the border issued by diplomatic missions or consular posts of the Member States or of the Ukraine without any visa or other authorisation.

Article 9
Extension of visa in exceptional circumstances

The citizens of Ukraine who do not have the possibility to leave the territory of the Member States by the time stated in their visas for reasons of *force majeure* shall have the term of their visas extended free of charge in accordance with the legislation applied by the receiving State for the period required for their return to the State of their residence.

Article 10
Diplomatic passports

1. Citizens of Ukraine, holders of valid diplomatic passports can enter, leave and transit through the territories of the Member States without visas.
2. Persons mentioned in paragraph 1 of this Article may stay in the territories of the Member States for a period not exceeding 90 days per period of 180 days.

Article 11
Territorial validity of visas

Subject to the national rules and regulations concerning national security of the Member States and subject to EU rules on visas with limited territorial validity, the citizens of Ukraine shall be entitled to travel within the territory of the Member States on equal basis with European Union citizens.

Article 12
Joint Committee for management of the Agreement

1. The Parties shall set up a joint committee of experts (hereinafter referred to as 'the Committee'), composed by representatives of the European Community and of Ukraine. The Community shall be represented by the Commission of the European Communities, assisted by experts from the Member States.
2. The Committee shall, in particular, have the following tasks:
    (a) monitoring the implementation of the present Agreement;
    (b) suggesting amendments or additions to the present Agreement;
    (c) settling disputes arising out of the interpretation or application of the provisions in this Agreement.
3. The Committee shall meet whenever necessary at the request of one of the Parties and at least once a year.
4. The Committee shall establish its rules of procedure.

Article 13
Relation of this Agreement with bilateral Agreements between Member States and Ukraine

As from its entry into force, this Agreement shall take precedence over provisions of any bilateral or multilateral agreements or arrangements concluded between individual Member States and Ukraine, insofar as the provisions of the latter agreements or arrangements cover issues dealt with by the present Agreement.

Article 14
Final clauses

1. This Agreement shall be ratified or approved by the Parties in accordance with their respective procedures and shall enter into force on the first day of the second month following the date on which the Parties notify each other that the procedures referred to above have been completed.
2. By way of derogation to paragraph 1 of this Article, the present agreement shall only enter into force at the date of the entry into force of the Agreement between the European Community and Ukraine on readmission of persons if this date is after the date provided for in paragraph 1 of this Article.
3. This Agreement is concluded for an indefinite period of time, unless terminated in accordance with paragraph 6 of this Article.

4. This Agreement may be amended by written agreement of the Parties. Amendments shall enter into force after the Parties have notified each other of the completion of their internal procedures necessary for this purpose.

5. Each Party may suspend in whole or in part this Agreement for reasons of public order, protection of national security or protection of public health. The decision on suspension shall be notified to the other Party not later than 48 hours before its entry into force. The Party that has suspended the application of this Agreement shall immediately inform the other Party once the reasons for the suspension no longer apply.

6. Each Party may terminate this Agreement by giving written notice to the other Party. This Agreement shall cease to be in force 90 days after the date of such notification.

Done at Luxembourg on the eighteenth day of June in the year two thousand and seven, in duplicate each in the Bulgarian, Czech, Danish, Dutch, English, Estonian, Finnish, French, German, Greek, Hungarian, Italian, Latvian, Lithuanian, Maltese, Polish, Portuguese, Romanian, Slovak, Slovenian, Spanish, Swedish and Ukrainian languages, each of these texts being equally authentic.

PROTOCOL TO THE AGREEMENT ON THE MEMBER STATES THAT DO NOT FULLY APPLY THE SCHENGEN *ACQUIS*

Those Member States which are bound by the Schengen *acquis* but which do not issue yet Schengen visas, while awaiting the relevant decision of the Council to that end, shall issue national visas the validity of which is limited to their own territory.

These Member States may unilaterally recognise Schengen visas and residence permits for the purpose of transit through their territory, in accordance with Council Decision No 895/2006/EC.

EUROPEAN COMMUNITY DECLARATION ON ISSUANCE OF SHORT-STAY VISAS FOR VISITS OF MILITARY AND CIVIL BURIAL GROUNDS

Diplomatic missions and consular posts of the Member States, shall as a general rule, issue short-stay visas for a period of up to 14 days for persons visiting military and civil burial grounds.

JOINT DECLARATION CONCERNING DENMARK

The Parties take note that the present Agreement does not apply to the procedures for issuing visas by the diplomatic missions and consular posts of the Kingdom of Denmark.

In such circumstances, it is desirable that the authorities of Denmark and of Ukraine conclude, without delay, a bilateral agreement on the facilitation of the issuance of visas in similar terms as the Agreement between the European Community and Ukraine.

JOINT DECLARATION CONCERNING THE UNITED KINGDOM AND IRELAND

The Parties take note that the present Agreement does not apply to the territory of the United Kingdom and Ireland.

In such circumstances, it is desirable that the authorities of the United Kingdom, Ireland and Ukraine, conclude bilateral agreements on the facilitation of the issuance of visas.

JOINT DECLARATION CONCERNING ICELAND AND NORWAY

The Parties take note of the close relationship between the European Community and Norway and Iceland, particularly by virtue of the Agreement of 18 May 1999 concerning the association of these countries with the implementation, application and development of the Schengen *acquis*.

In such circumstances, it is desirable that the authorities of Norway, Iceland and Ukraine conclude, without delay, bilateral agreements on the facilitation of the issuance of visas in similar terms as the Agreement between the European Community and Ukraine.

COMMISSION DECLARATION ON THE MOTIVATION OF THE DECISION TO REFUSE A VISA

Recognising the importance of transparency for visa applicants, the European Commission recalls that the legislative proposal on the recast of the Common Consular Instructions on visas for the diplomatic missions and consular posts has been adopted on 19 July 2006 and addresses the issue of the motivation of visa refusals and appeal possibilities.

EUROPEAN COMMUNITY DECLARATION ON ACCESS OF VISA APPLICANTS AND HARMONISATION OF INFORMATION ON PROCEDURES FOR ISSUING SHORT-STAY VISAS AND DOCUMENTS TO BE SUBMITTED WHEN APPLYING FOR SHORT-STAY VISAS

Recognising the importance of transparency for visa applicants, the European Community recalls that the legislative proposal on the recast of the Common Consular Instructions on visas for the diplomatic missions and consular posts has been adopted on 19 July 2006 by the European Commission and addresses the issue of conditions of access of visa applicants to diplomatic missions and consular posts of the Member States.

Regarding the information to be provided to visa applicants the European Community considers that appropriate measures should be taken:

— in general, to draw up basic information for applicants on the procedures and conditions for applying for visas and on their validity,
— the European Community will draw up a list of minimum requirements in order to ensure that Ukrainian applicants are given coherent and uniform basic information and are required to submit, in principle, the same supporting documents.

The information mentioned above is to be disseminated widely (on the notice boards of consulates, in leaflets, on websites, etc.).

The diplomatic missions and consular posts of the Member States shall provide information about existing possibilities under the Schengen *acquis* for facilitation of the issuing of short-stay visas on a case-by-case basis.

DRAFT POLITICAL DECLARATION ON LOCAL BORDER TRAFFIC DECLARATION FROM POLAND, HUNGARY, SLOVAK REPUBLIC AND ROMANIA

The Republic of Hungary, the Republic of Poland, the Slovak Republic, as well as Romania as from the date of joining the EU, declare their willingness to enter into negotiations of bilateral agreements with Ukraine for the purpose of implementing the local border traffic regime established by the EC Regulation adopted on 5 October 2006 laying down rules on local border traffic at the external land borders of the Member States and amending the Schengen Convention.

Chapter 10

Visa Information System

1. *Introduction*

The Visa Information System (the "VIS") has been established by two measures. The first measure, adopted in 2004, was a Council Decision which established the system in principle and authorised the Commission to manage the development of the VIS project, with funding from the EU budget.[1] A second, more detailed, measure which sets out the precise functioning of the system was adopted in June 2008: Regulation 767/2008 (the "VIS Regulation").[2]

The VIS has also been the subject of a number of other EU measures. First of all, at the same time as adopting the VIS Regulation, the Council also adopted a third-pillar (ie policing and criminal law) measure giving police access to the VIS (the 'third-pillar VIS Decision').[3] This latter measure was challenged unsuccessfully by the UK in the EU's Court of Justice, on the grounds that the UK should have been given fuller access to VIS data for policing purposes.[4] The Council also subsequently adopted measures amending the visa format rules, the Common Consular Instructions (CCI) and the Schengen borders code in order to take account of the VIS.[5] The VIS Regulation

---

[1] OJ 2004 L 213/5. The Commission has adopted several implementing measures on the basis of this Decision: see OJ 2006 L 267/41 (laying down technical specifications for standards for biometric features), OJ 2006 L 305/13 (establishing VIS sites during the development phase) and OJ 2008 L 194/3 (on interfaces with national systems).

[2] OJ 2008 L 218/60. The Commission has adopted five measures implementing the VIS Reg., as regards: the consultation mechanism in the VIS (on which, see below: OJ 2009 L 117/3); the specifications for the use of fingerprints in the VIS (OJ 2009 L 270/14); data processing (OJ 2009 L 315/30); the regional roll-out of the VIS (OJ 2010 L 23/62); and security (OJ 2010 L 112/25).

[3] OJ 2008 L 218/129. On the distinction between third pillar measures and other EU acts, see chapter 2.

[4] Case C-482/08 *UK v Council*, judgment of 26 Oct. 2010, not yet reported. See further chapter 2.

[5] See respectively Regs. 856/2008 (OJ 2008 L 235/1), 390/2009 (OJ 2009 L 131/1) and 81/2009 (OJ 2009 L 35/56). Reg. 390/2009 has since been subsumed into the visa code (Reg. 810/2009 (OJ 2009 L 243/1). See chapters 3 and 8 as regards the borders and visa code respectively. Relevant amendments were also made to the rules establishing the Schengen consultation network (OJ 2009 L 353/49).

itself has already been amended by the Regulation establishing the visa code, in order to ensure consistency between the two measures.[6] Finally, the Commission has proposed to set up an agency to manage the VIS, the second-generation Schengen Information II ("SIS II"), and Eurodac, the EU system for comparison of asylum-seekers' fingerprints, and the legislation to establish this agency has been agreed in principle.[7] If the EU establishes an entry-exit system, a registered traveller system and (possibly) an electronic traveller authorisation system, this will likely have a further impact on the VIS.[8]

According to the VIS Regulation, the VIS will become operational following a decision adopted by the Commission, once the Commission has adopted all of the necessary implementing measures and tested the system successfully (along with Member States), and the Member States have notified the Commission that they are ready to transmit the necessary data from the first region in which the VIS is to become applicable.[9] The first three regions will be North Africa, the Near East and the (Persian) Gulf, along with the external borders of the EU; they were decided by the Commission[10] by means of a "comitology" process,[11] applying the criteria of the risk of illegal immigration, threats to internal security and the feasibility of collecting biometrics.[12]

The roll-out to subsequent regions will be decided by the same process and the same criteria,[13] subject to the possibility of individual Member States

---

[6] Art 54 of the code (ibid). The amended VIS Reg. has not been codified formally; but see the informal codification in the annex to this chapter. All references in this chapter are to the VIS Reg. as amended, unless otherwise indicated.

[7] COM (2009) 293, 24 June 2009; revised: COM (2010) 93, 19 Mar. 2010. The Regulation establishing the agency had not yet been formally adopted as of 1 August 2011. For the text as agreed in principle between the Council and the European Parliament, see Council doc. 10827/1/1/11, 6 June 2011. The agency is likely to become operational in 2012.

[8] See chapter 6, section 5.

[9] Arts 51(2) and 48(1).

[10] OJ 2010 L 23/62. The North Africa region consists of Algeria, Egypt, Libya, Mauritania, Morocco and Tunisia. The Near East region consists of Israel, Jordan, the Lebanon and Syria. The Gulf region consists of Afghanistan, Bahrain, Iran, Iraq, Kuwait, Oman, Qatar, Saudi Arabia, the United Arab Emirates and Yemen. It might be noted that Afghanistan is a long way from the Gulf, and that Palestine is not covered; for the reasons for this, see recital 5 in the preamble to the Decision.

[11] See generally chapter 2.

[12] Art 48(4). See also the JHA Council conclusions of 1–2 Dec. 2005.

[13] See also the JHA Council conclusions of 1–2 Dec. 2005, which call for the "roll-out" of the VIS worldwide within two years from the start of operations. The EU immigration and asylum pact, adopted by the European Council in October 2008, refers to generalising the issue of biometric visas by 1 Jan. 2012 at the latest (point III of the pact, in Council doc. 13440/08,

applying the VIS to those further regions in advance, if they are capable of transmitting "at least" the alphanumeric data and photograph data connected to applications.[14] The VIS was intended to become operational as of 24 June 2011, and to "go live" in October 2011,[15] but it was unclear at time of writing whether the first deadline had been met (or whether the second deadline would be).

2. Details of the VIS Regulation

2.1. General Provisions

Chapter I of the VIS Regulation (Articles 1-7) sets out its general provisions. These comprise a brief description of the subject-matter and scope of the VIS Regulation,[16] as well as a longer description of its purpose.[17] The VIS "has the purpose of improving the implementation of the common visa policy, consular cooperation and consultation between" Member States' visa authorities by facilitating the exchange of data in order to achieve seven purposes: to facilitate the application procedure; to avoid bypassing the rules concerning the responsible Member State for considering the application; to facilitate the fight against fraud; to facilitate checks at external borders and within the territory; to assist in identifying irregular migrants; to facilitate application of the "Dublin" rules on responsibility for asylum applications;[18] and to contribute to preventing "threats to internal security" of any Member States.

Next, the VIS Regulation contains a "bridging" clause linking it to the parallel third pillar VIS Decision, giving the police authorities access to VIS data.[19] Those authorities can access VIS data in individual cases following a

---

24 Sep. 2008). The Commission must publish the date of the full roll-out to each region (Art 48(5)), but there is no obligation to publish the details of any advance application of the VIS by "early adopters". The Commission has proposed publishing the latter information as an Annex to the Border Guards' Handbook (see COM (2008) 101, 22 Feb. 2008, p. 5).

[14] Art 48(3). It follows that transmission of fingerprint data will be an option for those Member States who are "early adopters" of the VIS in additional regions, until the full roll-out of the VIS to those regions.

[15] See the conclusions of the JHA Council, 7–8 Oct. 2010. On the development of the VIS, see the Commission reports: SEC (2005) 439, 4 Mar. 2005; SEC (2006) 610, 10 May 2006; SEC (2007) 833, 13 June 2007; COM (2008) 714, 10 Nov. 2008; COM (2009) 473, 15 Sep. 2009; COM (2010) 588, 22 Oct. 2010; and COM (2011) 346, 14 June 2011.

[16] Art. 1.

[17] Art. 2.

[18] On these rules, see further *EU Asylum Law: Text and Commentary* (forthcoming).

[19] Art. 3; for the Decision, see n. 3 above.

specific request "if there are reasonable grounds to consider that access to VIS data will substantially contribute to the prevention, detection or investigation of terrorist offences and of other serious criminal offences". Europol may also access VIS data "within the limits of its mandate and when necessary for the performance of its tasks".[20] Access by police authorities can only be obtained through central access points, which will check first whether the criteria for access are satisfied,[21] and VIS data accessed by this procedure cannot be made available to third countries or international organisations, other than in "an exceptional case of urgency" as provided for in the third pillar VIS Decision.[22] The VIS Regulation is also "without prejudice" to the obligation under national law for visa authorities to inform national police or prosecution authorities about suspected criminal offences.[23]

The VIS Regulation includes a definition of eleven terms.[24] In particular, a "visa" for the purposes of the Regulation comprises a "short-stay visa", a "transit visa", an "airport transit visa", a limited territorial validity ("LTV") visa, and a long-stay visa valid concurrently as a short-stay visa, as defined in various Schengen measures.[25] A "verification" of identity entails a one-to-one check (ie checking the applicant's data against the data contained in *one* other VIS file, while an "identification" entails a one-to-many check (ie checking the applicant's data against *multiple* VIS files, and perhaps even all VIS files).[26]

There is an exhaustive list of the categories of data which can be recorded in the VIS:[27] alphanumeric data (e.g., letters and numbers) on the applicant and on visas requested, issued, refused, annulled, revoked or extended;[28] photographs; fingerprints; and links to other visa applications by the applicant or persons who will be travelling with the applicant.[29] Only visa authorities can enter, delete or amend data,[30] but other authorities (as well as visa authorities) can access the data for the purposes provided for in the VIS Regulation

---

[20] Art. 3(1).

[21] Art. 3(2). In "an exceptional case of urgency", the access can take place without a prior check.

[22] Art. 3(3); on the position where VIS data is accessed by other authorities, see section 2.3 below.

[23] Art. 3(4).

[24] Art. 4.

[25] Art. 4(1).

[26] Arts. 4(9) and (10).

[27] Art. 5(1).

[28] See definition in Art. 4(11).

[29] See Arts. 8(3) and 8(4), which refers to group applications and applications by the applicant's spouse and children. A "group" application is defined in Art. 4(6) as a group of persons who are required for legal reasons to travel together.

[30] Art. 6(1).

(see below).[31] A list of all authorities with powers to alter or access data must be published and regularly updated.[32] Finally, there are obligations to ensure that use of the VIS is "necessary, appropriate and proportionate",[33] that there is no discrimination when using the VIS on grounds of "sex, racial or ethnic origin, religion or belief, disability, age or sexual orientation", and that VIS use "fully respects the human dignity and the integrity" of the applicant or visa holder.[34]

It is striking that the VIS Regulation does not include any express special rule for the position of EU citizens' third-country national family members,[35] who are potentially subject to visa requirements if their State of nationality is subject to visa requirements in the first place, either a) to enter the Schengen area,[36] if they are resident in a non-Schengen EU Member State but do not hold a "residence card" as specified in EU free movement law;[37] or if b) if they are resident in a Schengen State but do not qualify for freedom to travel within the Schengen area because they do not hold a specified national residence permit or provisional residence permit.[38] However, it must be presumed that in the event of any conflict, the EU free movement rules will take precedence over the VIS Regulation as a higher rule of law, and because the underlying substantive rules on visas are expressly subject to EU free movement law.[39]

2.2. *Use of the VIS by Visa Authorities*

Chapter II of the VIS Regulation (Articles 8-17) sets out rules on use of the VIS by visa authorities. A national visa authority must create a file in the VIS

---

[31] Art. 6(2).

[32] Art. 6(3).

[33] Art. 7(1).

[34] Art. 7(2). The list of prohibited grounds for discrimination matches the list in Art. 19 of the Treaty on the Functioning of the European Union (TFEU).

[35] Compare with Arts. 3(a) and 2(5) of the Schengen Borders Code (Reg. 562/2006, OJ 2006 L 105/1), Art. 25 of the SIS II Regulation (Reg. 1987/2006, OJ 2006 L 381/4) and (as regards the current SIS) Case C-503/03 *Commission v Spain* [2006] ECR I-1097. However, as regards the use of the VIS at external borders, the Borders Code provides for an implicit exception for such family members (Art. 7(3) of the Code, read with Art. 2(5) and 2(6)).

[36] See Art. 5(1)(a), Schengen Borders Code (ibid).

[37] Art. 5(2), Directive 2004/38 (OJ 2004 L 229/35). Such family members would also be subject to visa requirements if they were resident in a (non-Schengen) non-EU State.

[38] See Art. 21 of the Schengen Convention and, as regards return across the external borders, Art 5(1)(a), Schengen Borders Code (ibid). The list of relevant national documents is communicated to the Commission in accordance with Art. 34(1)(a) of the Schengen Borders Code, and published in the Official Journal.

[39] Art. 1(2) of the visa code (n. 5 above).

without delay following a visa application.[40] The authority has to check whether that applicant has made a previous visa application which is registered in the VIS,[41] and if so, to link the new application with the previous application(s).[42] Applications must also be linked to parallel applications by family members and members of a group.[43] The system must indicate whether particular data categories are inapplicable; as regards fingerprint data, there must be a distinction indicated in the VIS between legal reasons for not including such data and physical reasons for not including it.[44]

The following six Articles of the VIS Regulation then set out the data that must be entered in different circumstances: when a visa application is first lodged; if a visa is issued; if a visa application is discontinued; if a visa application is refused; if a visa is annulled or revoked, or has its validity shortened; or if a visa is extended.[45] For example, when a visa application is first lodged,[46] the data entered must comprise: the application number; the status information (the fact that a visa has been requested); the authority with which the application was lodged; thirteen items of data from the application form (concerning name, nationality,[47] travel document information, date of the application, the type of visa requested, information on the sponsor,[48] destination and duration of the stay, the purpose of the stay, date of arrival and departure, border of first entry, residence, occupation and employer or school and the names of minors' parents); photographs; and fingerprints.[49]

Where a visa is refused, the authority concerned must enter data as to the reasons why, which must be one of the seven following reasons: a lack of valid travel documents; a false, counterfeit or forged travel document; a failure to justify the purpose and conditions of stay, and in particular representing "a specific risk of illegal immigration"; a previous stay of three months during a six month period on Member States' territory; a lack of sufficient subsistence; an alert in the SIS or a national watchlist; or "a threat to public policy, internal security or the international relations of any" Member State, or to "public

---

[40] Art. 8(1).
[41] Art. 8(2). Obviously visa applications made before the VIS becomes operational will not be registered in the VIS.
[42] Art 8(3).
[43] Art 8(4).
[44] Art. 8(5).
[45] Respectively Arts. 9–14.
[46] Art. 9.
[47] This includes both current nationality and nationality at birth.
[48] This is restricted to the name and address of natural persons, and to the name and address of legal persons, plus the name of a contact person at the legal person.
[49] On the issue of fingerprints, see further chapter 8.

health" as defined in the Schengen Borders Code.[50] It should be noted that there is no ban on processing of "sensitive" categories of personal data.[51]

During the negotiation of the proposal, the Council considered adding the possibility of entering information concerning the "misuse of a visa" where a visa holder had stayed on the territory of a Member State "without authorisation…following expiry of the visa" or "has unlawfully taken up employment", or "there are other grounds which would have justified refusal of the visa, or if a person's liability to pay the costs of living during the stay…was not complied with".[52] This followed an agreement among the "G6" interior ministers (ie, at an informal meeting of the interior ministers from the six biggest Member States) that such a measure would be desirable.[53] However, this idea was rejected due to European Parliament (EP) opposition.[54] Instead, the EP and the Council adopted a joint declaration on this issue, agreeing to examine it in the context of negotiations on the Visa Code, with the Commission invited if necessary to propose amendments to the VIS Regulation after adoption of the Code. Ultimately, the visa code did not address this topic.[55] Furthermore, the EP and the Council "invite[d] the Commission to report not later than three years after the start of operations of the VIS on the situation as regards misuse by persons issuing invitations, and to present, if necessary, suitable proposals for amendments".[56] In practice, this report will be due in 2014, if the VIS becomes fully operational as planned in 2011.

Of course, this issue will in future fall in part within the scope of the EU's plans to develop an "entry-exit" system, which would generate information automatically (assuming it works as planned) on any visa holder's failure to leave the territory of the Member States on time.[57]

---

[50] Art. 12(2). See also Art. 13(2), which requires the grounds for annulling, withdrawing or shortening the validity of a visa to be entered in the VIS.

[51] Compare with Art. 40, SIS II Regulation, referring to Art. 8(1) of the data protection Directive (OJ 1995 L 281/31).

[52] Art. 11a in Council doc. 11632/06. An earlier draft also referred to cases where an asylum application had been finally refused (Council doc. 9083/06, 8 May 2006).

[53] See Council doc. 9130/06, 8 May 2006, which also makes clear that the G6 meeting had agreed to the extension of information held on sponsors in the VIS. Note that G6 meetings include the UK, which did not even participate in the VIS negotiations.

[54] However, a breach of conditions that leads to an annulment, withdrawal or the shortening of validity of a visa would lead to a VIS entry in accordance with Art. 13.

[55] See generally chapter 8.

[56] Joint Statement in the summary of Council acts for June 2008 (Council doc. 12750/2/08, 13 Mar. 2009).

[57] See chapter 6, section 5.

As for the use of the VIS by visa authorities after information is entered, the VIS must be used when examining visa applications, including when taking decisions on whether to withdraw, annul or extend or shorten the validity of a visa.[58] Access to the VIS for this purpose must initially concern only specified data;[59] in the event of a "hit", then the entire file of the applicant and all linked files can be examined for the purpose of deciding on the visa application.[60] The VIS shall also be used by visa authorities when applying the "consultation" procedure (where the consulate of the Member State receiving an application for a visa must consult the authorities of another Member State),[61] and may also be used to transmit information and messages related to consular cooperation, to send requests for documents relating to visa applications, and to transmit such documents.[62] Finally, visa authorities can consult specified data in the VIS for the purposes of reporting and statistics, without identifying individual applicants.[63]

2.3. *Use of VIS by Other Authorities*

Chapter III of the VIS Regulation (Articles 18-22) sets out rules on use of the VIS by other authorities, in five circumstances. First of all, the VIS can be used by external border authorities, using the visa sticker number and fingerprints, for the purposes of checking the authenticity of the visa, verifying the identity of the visa holder (a "one-to-one" search) and confirming that the conditions for entry are satisfied.[64] However, fingerprints cannot be used for these purposes for a three-year period after the VIS begins operations, although this waiting period can be reduced to one year by the Commission as regards air borders.[65]

Before the end of these one-year and three-year periods, the Regulation provides for the Commission to report on "technical progress" regarding the use of fingerprints at external borders, including the question of whether the use of fingerprints for searches at external borders would entail "excessive waiting time at border crossing points". This evaluation must be transmitted to

---

[58] Art. 15(1).

[59] Art. 15(2).

[60] Art. 15(3).

[61] See the relevant implementing measure (OJ 2009 L 117/30).

[62] Art. 16.

[63] Art. 17.

[64] Art. 18(1).

[65] Art. 18(2). The Commission could also reduce the waiting period to an intermediate date between one and three years.

the EP and the Council, either of which may then request the Commission to make a proposal to amend the Regulation.[66]

When the Regulation was finally adopted, Poland and Slovenia made a joint declaration on this provision, suggesting that there might be "technical difficulties" applying the VIS at external borders, that "this type of border control will probably result in serious disturbances for international traffic at border-crossing points", and objecting that the provision did not provide for exceptions.[67] They supported instead the idea that border guards should only have to check people with the number of the visa sticker, and then have discretion to decide which further criteria to check.

The detailed rules relating to the use of the VIS at external borders were subsequently set out in separate amendments to the Schengen Borders Code.[68]

Second, immigration authorities may have access to VIS data *within* the territory of a Member State, in order to verify the identity of a person, to check the authenticity of the visa or to confirm that the conditions for entry are satisfied, either by using the visa sticker number in combination with fingerprints, or by using the visa sticker number alone.[69] Third, in order to *identify* a person (a "one-to-many" search) who may be an irregular migrant, national immigration authorities or border guards may search the VIS using fingerprints.[70]

Fourth, in order to apply the rules on responsibility for asylum applications, a national asylum authority can search the VIS using fingerprint data.[71] Finally, national asylum authorities can search the VIS using fingerprint data in order to assist them with examining the merits of an asylum application.[72]

In each of these cases, in the event of a "hit", the relevant national authorities will be given access to more data from the VIS, for the specific purposes referred to in each case.[73] In the latter three cases, if fingerprints cannot be used or if a search using fingerprints fails, national authorities can search the VIS using other specified data.

---

[66] Art. 50(5).
[67] See the summary of Council documents for June 2008 (n. 56 above).
[68] Reg. 81/2009, n. 5 above. For a detailed discussion, see chapter 3.
[69] Art. 19.
[70] Art. 20. This Article also applies if an attempt to verify identity at the borders or on the territory by means of a one-to-one search has failed, or if there are otherwise doubts about, *inter alia*, the identity of the person concerned: see Arts. 18(5) and 19(3).
[71] Art. 21.
[72] Art. 22.
[73] Arts. 18(4), 19(2), 20(2), 21(2) and 22(2). In the event of a search regarding responsibility for asylum applications, further data can only be accessed if additional conditions are met, corresponding to the criteria for responsibility under the Dublin rules: see Art. 21(2).

2.4. *Retention and Amendment of VIS Data*

Chapter IV of the Regulation (Articles 23-25) sets out rules on retention and amendment of VIS data. Each file must be kept for a period of five years from a specified date, for example the expiry date of a visa, if one has been issued.[74] After that point, the file is deleted automatically. Only the Member State responsible for entering the data may delete or alter it, although another Member State may bring apparent errors to the attention of the responsible Member State.[75] Data shall be deleted in advance if a person gains the nationality of a Member State, or (as regards data on refusal of a visa) if the refusal is overturned.[76]

2.5. *Operation of the VIS and Use of the System*

Chapter V of the Regulation (Articles 26-36) sets out rules on the operation of the VIS and responsibilities for operation and use of the system. Many of the relevant provisions here and in Chapter VI (concerning data protection) were modelled on the SIS II Regulation, which was agreed between the EP and the Council during negotiations on the VIS Regulation.[77] In particular, the VIS is to be managed by a management authority after a transitional period; but in the meantime, the VIS will be managed by the Commission, which may delegate its powers to one or two Member States.[78] This was the same solution agreed as regards SIS II,[79] and a similar solution has been proposed as regards Eurodac.[80] The intention is that the Commission will delegate its powers to France and Austria; this is consistent with the decision to locate the central VIS in France with a back-up system in Austria.[81]

---

[74] Art. 23. Compare to the less precise provisions of Art. 29, SIS II Regulation.

[75] Art. 24. Compare to Art. 34(2) to (4) of the SIS II Regulation, which usefully contains both a deadline to send such information and a dispute-settlement mechanism in the event of a dispute between the Member States concerned. Unfortunately, neither Regulation provides for an express role for the data subject in this context.

[76] Art. 25. Compare to Art. 30 of the SIS II Regulation, which only concerns deletion of data in the event of acquisition of citizenship.

[77] See generally chapter 4.

[78] Art. 26. See the Joint Statement of the EP, Council and Commission on the creation of the management authority (in the summary of Council documents for June 2008, n. 56 above). See now the agreed text of the legislation establishing the agency (n. 7 above).

[79] Arts. 15 and 17(1) of the SIS II Regulation.

[80] See the proposed new Eurodac Regulation (COM (2010) 555, 11 Oct. 2010). The difference is that there is no provision for the Commission to delegate its management of Eurodac to Member States in the meantime.

[81] Art. 27; Art. 4(3), SIS II Regulation.

Next, the VIS Regulation describes the relationship between the central VIS and the national systems,[82] and allocates responsibility as between the management authority and the national authorities.[83] It should be emphasised that the Member States, not the management authority, have the key responsibility of ensuring that data is collected, processed and transmitted lawfully, and that the data are accurate and up-to-date when transmitted; the management authority is responsible for ensuring data security at its end as well as control of its staff.

VIS data can be kept in national files if necessary in specific cases, or where the data was entered by that Member State.[84] In principle data from the VIS cannot be transferred to third countries or international organisations,[85] but "by way of derogation",[86] certain data can be transferred to third countries or international organisations listed in the Annex to the Regulation,[87] "if necessary in individual cases for the purpose of proving the identity of third-country nationals, including for the purpose of return", "only" where a list of four conditions is fulfilled. First of all, one of the following three situations must exist: the Commission has decided on the adequacy of personal data protection in the relevant third state, in accordance with the data protection directive,[88] or an EU readmission agreement is in place,[89] or a the transfer of data "is necessary or legally required on important public interest grounds, or for the establishment, exercise of defence of legal claims", again in accordance with the data protection Directive.[90] Secondly, the third country or international organisation must have agreed only to use the data for the purpose for

---

[82] Art. 28. The provision on staff training (Art. 28(5)) is identical to Art. 14, SIS II Regulation.

[83] Art. 29. Compare Art. 29(1) to Art. 34(1), SIS II Regulation.

[84] Art. 30; compare to Art. 32, SIS II Regulation.

[85] Art. 31(1). The status of non-Schengen EU Member States is not clear.

[86] Art. 31(2). By way of comparison, the ban on transferring SIS II immigration data to third countries or international organisations is absolute: see Art. 39, SIS II Regulation.

[87] These are UN organisations (such as the UNHCR), the International Organisation for Migration and the International Committee of the Red Cross.

[88] Such adequacy decisions have been adopted as of August 2011 as regards Canada, certain private bodies in the USA, Switzerland (which is a Schengen state in any event), Andorra, Israel and Argentina. See: <http://ec.europa.eu/justice_home/fsj/privacy/thridcountries/index_en.htm>.

[89] As of 1 August 2011, EU readmission agreements were in force in thirteen states: Hong Kong, Macao, Sri Lanka, Albania, Serbia, Montenegro, Bosnia and Herzegovina, the Former Yugoslav Republic of Macedonia, Russia, Ukraine, Moldova, Pakistan and Georgia. Negotiations with several other states had been authorised (Algeria, Morocco, China, Turkey and Cape Verde), and a deal with Turkey was announced in Jan. 2011. See further volume 2 of this book (chapter 20).

[90] Art. 26(1)(d) of the data protection Directive.

which they were transmitted. Thirdly, the data must have been transferred in accordance with the relevant provisions of EU and national law.[91] Finally, the Member State which entered the data in the VIS must have given its consent.

The Regulation also provides that such transfers of data "shall not prejudice the rights of refugees and persons requesting international protection, in particular as regards non-refoulement",[92] but it is not clear in concrete terms how this principle will be observed when data is transferred. It should be noted that only data concerning names, nationality, residence, travel documents, and (for minors) parents' names can be transferred – not photographs, fingerprints or any other category of alpha-numeric data.[93]

Chapter V also contains rules on data security,[94] liability for breach of the Regulation,[95] the keeping of records,[96] self-monitoring[97] and penalties for the misuse of data.[98]

2.6. *Data Protection*

Chapter VI of the Regulation (Articles 37-44) sets out data protection rights and rules on data protection supervision of the VIS. Applicants and sponsors have the right to information about the processing of their data.[99] They also have the right of access, correction and deletion of their data;[100] Member States must cooperate as regards the enforcement of these rights.[101] There is a right of action before national courts to enforce the rights of access, correction and deletion.[102] As for the collective enforcement of rights, the Regulation contains

---

[91] Art. 26(1) of the data protection directive gives Member States an option not to apply (*inter alia*) Art. 26(1)(d) of the Directive if provided for by 'domestic law governing particular cases'.

[92] Art. 31(3).

[93] The *chapeau* of Art. 31(2) refers only to the data in Arts. 9(4)(a), (b), (c), (k) and (m).

[94] Art. 32; Art. 32(2) is nearly identical to Art. 10(1), SIS II Regulation. Compare Art. 32(3) to Art. 16, SIS II Regulation.

[95] Art. 33. Compare to Art. 48, SIS II Regulation.

[96] Art. 34. Compare to Arts. 12 and 18 of the SIS II Regulation.

[97] Art. 35, which is identical to Art. 13, SIS II Regulation. This Article was added at the behest of the EP.

[98] Art. 36. This provision is nearly identical to Art. 49, SIS II Regulation.

[99] Art. 37. Compare to the rather unclear Art. 42 of the SIS II Regulation.

[100] Art. 38. Compare to the less precise Art. 41 of the SIS II Regulation.

[101] Art. 39.

[102] Art. 40. Compare to Art. 43 of the SIS II Regulation, which is broader in scope, applying also to compensation in relation to alerts and the right to obtain information. The SIS II provision also contains a review clause and a useful rule on the mutual recognition of national court decisions.

rules on supervision of national authorities by national supervisory bodies,[103] on supervision of the Management Authority by the European Data Protection Supervisor (EDPS),[104] on cooperation between national supervisory bodies and the EDPS[105] and on data protection during the transitional period.[106]

2.7. Final Provisions

Chapter VII of the Regulation (Articles 45-51) sets out final provisions. These concern: implementing powers for the Commission;[107] the integration of the 'Schengen Consultation Network' into the VIS;[108] notification of readiness to transmit data;[109] the start of operations of the VIS (summarised above);[110] the comitology process;[111] rules on monitoring and evaluation;[112] and the entry into force of the Regulation.[113]

3. Assessment

The VIS, once operational, will probably be the largest biometric database in the world. One can only hope that it works accurately and that there is no human error in its application, otherwise the existence of the VIS will be seriously problematic.

As for police access to the VIS, it might be doubted that the VIS data will be of much use to police except possibly identifying fingerprints left a crime scene or providing further information about a suspect for the purpose of

---

[103] Art. 41. Compare to the shorter Art. 44 of the SIS II Regulation.
[104] Art. 42. Compare to the shorter Art. 45 of the SIS II Regulation.
[105] Art. 43. Compare to the shorter Art. 46 of the SIS II Regulation.
[106] Art. 44. Art. 47 of the SIS II Regulation is identical.
[107] Art. 45.
[108] Art. 46. This network concerns the process, referred to above, by which a Member State which receives a visa application from the nationals of a specified country is obliged to consult the authorities of a second Member State before making a decision on the visa application.
[109] Art. 47.
[110] Art. 48.
[111] Art. 49.
[112] Art. 50. Compare to Art. 50 of the SIS II Regulation. The VIS Regulation is unfortunately missing the SIS II provision (Art. 50(3), SIS II Regulation) requiring the publication of annual statistics on use of the system, but it does include a requirement to report regularly on the use of the external transfer provisions (Art. 50(4)), and on a review of the issue of using fingerprints at external borders (Art. 50(5)); see further the discussion above.
[113] Art. 51.

tracing him or her. The VIS Regulation and the parallel third-pillar Decision leave lots of discretion to give extensive access to the police services, but at least a prior check will apply in principle before access is granted. But it might be doubted whether this procedure will be independent or critical of police requests. At least it is certainly welcome that access for the police is limited to specific cases, with no general power to search the entire database to produce "risk assessments". The transfer of VIS data to third states for policing purposes appears to be acceptable in principle under the conditions set out in the Regulation and the Decision, except for the lack of a requirement to ensure the adequacy of third states' data protection standards and the proper application of those rules in practice.

As for the VIS Regulation itself, it would have been useful to have a specific provision on the family members of EU citizens, but for the reasons set out above this principle is in any event protected by other measures. The lack of rules regarding a sponsors' database and provisions on the "misuse" of visas are welcome, in the absence of an impact assessment which would demonstrate the need and properly examine the practical implications of entering such data into the VIS.

It is useful that the Regulation sets out an exhaustive list of grounds to be entered following the refusal and revocation, etc of visas, but the procedural rights in relation to visas needed to be addressed earlier or at the same time, to ensure that a record of refusal or revocation of visas is not unduly taken into account when a later application is made, and that an appeal against such decisions is possible. Although the visa code now guarantees these rights, it remains to be seen how effective these provisions will be in practice.[114]

The external borders provisions may prove to be impractical. It is striking that there was no impact assessment either of the proposal to amend the Schengen Borders Code as regards VIS use or of the practical implications of this particular issue when the Commission assessed the impact of the original proposal for the VIS Regulation.[115] The derogation from use of the VIS upon entry set out in the Schengen Borders Code is drafted quite narrowly, and it may prove impractical to spend time assessing the impact of granting a

---

[114] See further chapter 8.

[115] See SEC (2004) 1628, 28 Dec. 2004. This impact assessment simply states (at p. 17) that "time will be lost at entry and exit points by providing and checking biometric data", without assessing the feasibility of checking such data in all cases of entry. On the same page, the Commission estimates the "very significant" financial costs of the VIS at EU level and for national visa authorities, but this does "not include the costs for the border crossing points as these costs cannot be estimated at the present time".

derogation when a quick decision has to be made to address traffic flows.[116] However, since the visa requirement has now largely been abolished for the Western Balkans,[117] the rules on the full use of the VIS at borders may be more realistic in practice, by the time they are applied. It is also possible that visa facilitation treaties might be amended to address this issue in future.[118] Of course if an entry-exit system is by then operation and applies to all non-visa-nationals at the Commission intends, then the issue will present itself again – all the more so given that an entry-exit system would require non-EU citizens to be checked upon exit as well as entry.[119]

Next, the idea that VIS information might be used to determine the merits of asylum applications is highly questionable. A record of refused visa applications, even on *prima facie* serious grounds like the use of a forged passport, could arguably show that a person is intent on entering and staying in the EU without authorisation – but it could equally arguably prove the genuineness of that person's desperation to flee persecution.[120] The risk is that an asylum authority that sees such a record in the VIS will assume the former, not the latter, and that procedural standards could be curtailed as a result, leaving it difficult for an asylum seeker to rebut the authority's conclusion effectively. This provision should be deleted altogether from the VIS Regulation, at least until the asylum procedures Directive has been amended in order to address such issues fairly.[121]

As compared to SIS II, the VIS Regulation is certainly much clearer as regards the grounds for including data in the system, and as regards who can access the data for which purpose. There are also better provisions in the VIS Regulation as regards the right of information. But the SIS II Regulation has a provision regarding an information campaign for the public, and better provisions regarding the publication of annual statistics, the notification of inaccurate data in the system and remedies (as the SIS II rules apply also to compensation and the right to obtain information, and contain a mutual

---

[116] It should also be kept in mind that, as mentioned above, there is an absolute obligation in the Borders Code to stamp the passports of third-country nationals, even when border controls are relaxed. This existing obligation will already slow down any attempt to clear a backlog at the border crossing.

[117] See chapter 7.

[118] See generally chapter 9.

[119] It should be recalled that, for practical reasons, the USA has not yet been able to introduce a full system of control at exit points.

[120] Cf. the recognition in Art. 31 of the Geneva Convention on refugee status that unauthorised or clandestine means of entry and stay might be necessary for genuine refugees.

[121] On that Directive, see *EU Asylum Law: Text and Commentary* (forthcoming).

recognition obligation and a review clause). In fact, it is the VIS Regulation rules on remedies that need to be reviewed, not the SIS II rules.

On other points, it is unfortunate that data subjects are not informed when one Member State informs another that data in the VIS appears to be inaccurate. The requirement that data on a visa refusal must be removed if that visa refusal is overturned is very welcome. The key issue regarding the planned management authority will be the accountability of that body; it remains to be seen whether the legislation on this issue, and the operation of that body in practice, will satisfy the necessary standard.

As for external transfers of VIS data, one of the conditions allows transfers on grounds of the general public interest; this could obviously be interpreted broadly by Member States. Again, it is unfortunately that there is no general requirement of adequate data standards applicable to all external transfers of VIS data. And, as noted above, how exactly will the provision on non-refoulement work on this context? The one undeniably useful limit on the external transfer of VIS data is that only certain categories of data are covered.

Next, as regards data protection issues, the penalties clause in the Regulation could be better. It should also have applied to data security (as considered during negotiations) and to breaches of all data protection rules (as first proposed), and there should have been criminal penalties not only for serious infringements but also perhaps for serious stupidity – such as posting CD-Roms containing the VIS database or drunkenly leaving a computer containing a copy of the VIS on a train.[122] The data security rules in the VIS Regulation are good, but can only work fully if we assume that the humans who use the VIS will be infallible. The rules on collective enforcement of the data protection rules are also good on paper, but in practice the resources of supervisory authorities are a crucial issue.

The monitoring provisions of the VIS Regulation have useful provisions as regards reviews on external transfers and the use of fingerprints, as well as data security. But it is unfortunate that there is no obligation to publish annual statistics or to review to what extent the VIS is being used lawfully.

In general it can be expected that the VIS Regulation, if it works as planned, will be practically useful in identifying (or deterring) a significant number of persons who make multiple or fraudulent visa applications or who present a fraudulent visa at an external border. But the consequence of this might of course be a greater use of irregular methods of entry across the external borders. Conversely the greater ease of identifying persons making fraudulent

---

[122] Both these examples are taken from the practice of the British civil service.

applications could likely lead in practice to facilitation of the visa applications of *bona fide* travellers, since authorities will have available a full record of the "clean sheets" maintained by such travellers. The more problematic use of the VIS will be for the "in-between" cases – where applications were refused on more questionable (or non-existent) grounds, or where circumstances have changed (ie an applicant was unemployed before, but now has a job), but the record of prior refusal or revocation in the VIS is used to justify subsequent refusals of applications indefinitely.[123] As noted above, it remains to be seen whether the visa code will in practice effectively address these problems.

---

[123] Although there is a five-year retention period for information on each visa application, that retention period will apply individually for each new refusal. An applicant would have to leave five years between any applications for Schengen visas to make sure that his or her record in the VIS was fully purged of refusals. But by then a *blank* record in the VIS could be used against applicants, with consulates preferring to give preferential treatment to those applicants who already have a "clean" record (cf credit records), and even presuming that applicants with a blank record are likely to have waited five years since their last (refused) application.

Annex

Regulation (EC) No 767/2008 of the European
Parliament and of the Council

of 9 July 2008

concerning the Visa Information System (VIS) and the exchange
of data between Member States on short-stay visas (VIS Regulation)

[original footnotes omitted]

THE EUROPEAN PARLIAMENT AND THE COUNCIL OF THE EUROPEAN UNION,

Having regard to the Treaty establishing the European Community, and in particular Article 62(2)(b)(ii) and Article 66 thereof,

Having regard to the proposal from the Commission,

Acting in accordance with the procedure laid down in Article 251 of the Treaty,

Whereas:

(1) Building upon the conclusions of the Council of 20 September 2001, and the conclusions of the European Council in Laeken in December 2001, in Seville in June 2002, in Thessaloniki in June 2003 and in Brussels in March 2004, the establishment of the Visa Information System (VIS) represents one of the key initiatives within the policies of the European Union aimed at establishing an area of freedom, security and justice.

(2) Council Decision 2004/512/EC of 8 June 2004 establishing the Visa Information System (VIS) established the VIS as a system for the exchange of visa data between Member States.

(3) It is now necessary to define the purpose, the functionalities and responsibilities for the VIS, and to establish the conditions and procedures for the exchange of visa data between Member States to facilitate the examination of visa applications and related decisions, taking into account the orientations for the development of the VIS adopted by the Council on 19 February 2004 and to give the Commission the mandate to set up the VIS.

(4) For a transitional period, the Commission should be responsible for the operational management of the central VIS, of the national interfaces and of certain aspects of the communication infrastructure between the central VIS and the national interfaces.

In the long term, and following an impact assessment containing a substantive analysis of alternatives from a financial, operational and organisational perspective, and legislative proposals from the Commission, a permanent Management Authority with responsibility for these tasks should be established. The transitional period should last for no more than five years from the date of entry into force of this Regulation.

(5) The VIS should have the purpose of improving the implementation of the common visa policy, consular cooperation and consultation between central visa authorities by facilitating the exchange of data between Member States on applications and on the decisions relating thereto, in order to facilitate the visa application procedure, to prevent 'visa shopping', to facilitate the fight against fraud and to facilitate checks at external border crossing points and within the territory of the Member States. The VIS should also assist in the identification of any person who may not, or may no longer, fulfil the conditions for entry to, stay or residence on the territory of the Member States, and facilitate the application of Council Regulation (EC) No 343/2003 of 18 February 2003 establishing the criteria and mechanism for determining the Member State responsible for examining an asylum application lodged in one of the Member States by a third-country national, and contribute to the prevention of threats to the internal security of any of the Member States.

(6) This Regulation is based on the acquis of the common visa policy. The data to be processed by the VIS should be determined on the basis of the data provided by the common form for visa applications as introduced by Council Decision 2002/354/EC of 25 April 2002 on the adaptation of Part III of, and the creation of an Annex 16 to, the Common Consular Instructions [4], and the information on the visa sticker provided for in Council Regulation (EC) No 1683/95 of 29 May 1995 laying down a uniform format for visas.

(7) The VIS should be connected to the national systems of the Member States to enable the competent authorities of the Member States to process data on visa applications and on visas issued, refused, annulled, revoked or extended.

(8) The conditions and procedures for entering, amending, deleting and consulting the data in the VIS should take into account the procedures laid down in the Common Consular Instructions on visas for the diplomatic missions and consular posts (the Common Consular Instructions).

(9) The technical functionalities of the network for consulting the central visa authorities as laid down in Article 17(2) of the Convention implementing the Schengen Agreement of 14 June 1985 between the Governments of the States of the Benelux Economic Union, the Federal Republic of Germany and the French Republic on the gradual abolition of checks at their common borders (the Schengen Convention) should be integrated into the VIS.

(10) To ensure reliable verification and identification of visa applicants, it is necessary to process biometric data in the VIS.

(11) It is necessary to define the competent authorities of the Member States, the duly authorised staff of which are to have access to enter, amend, delete or consult data for the specific purposes of the VIS in accordance with this Regulation to the extent necessary for the performance of their tasks.

(12) Any processing of VIS data should be proportionate to the objectives pursued and necessary for the performance of the tasks of the competent authorities. When using the VIS, the competent authorities should ensure that the human dignity and integrity of the persons whose data are requested are respected and should not discriminate against persons on grounds of sex, racial or ethnic origin, religion or belief, disability, age or sexual orientation.

(13) This Regulation should be complemented by a separate legal instrument adopted under Title VI of the Treaty on European Union concerning access for the consultation of the VIS by authorities responsible for internal security.

(14) The personal data stored in the VIS should be kept for no longer than is necessary for the purposes of the VIS. It is appropriate to keep the data for a maximum period of five years, in order to enable data on previous applications to be taken into account for the assessment of visa applications, including the applicants' good faith, and for the documentation of illegal immigrants who may, at some stage, have applied for a visa. A shorter period would not be sufficient for those purposes. The data should be deleted after a period of five years, unless there are grounds to delete them earlier.

(15) Precise rules should be laid down as regards the responsibilities for the establishment and operation of the VIS, and the responsibilities of the Member States for the national systems and the access to data by the national authorities.

(16) Rules on the liability of the Member States in respect of damage arising from any breach of this Regulation should be laid down. The liability of the Commission in respect of such damage is governed by the second paragraph of Article 288 of the Treaty.

(17) Directive 95/46/EC of the European Parliament and of the Council of 24 October 1995 on the protection of individuals with regard to the processing of personal data and on the free movement of such data applies to the processing of personal data by the Member States in application of this Regulation. However, certain points should be clarified in respect of

the responsibility for the processing of data, of safeguarding the rights of the data subjects and of the supervision on data protection.

(18) Regulation (EC) No 45/2001 of the European Parliament and the Council of 18 December 2000 on the protection of individuals with regard to the processing of personal data by the Community institutions and bodies and on the free movement of such data applies to the activities of the Community institutions or bodies when carrying out their tasks as responsible for the operational management of the VIS. However, certain points should be clarified in respect of the responsibility for the processing of data and of the supervision of data protection.

(19) The National Supervisory Authorities established in accordance with Article 28 of Directive 95/46/EC should monitor the lawfulness of the processing of personal data by the Member States, while the European Data Protection Supervisor as established by Regulation (EC) No 45/2001 should monitor the activities of the Community institutions and bodies in relation to the processing of personal data, taking into account the limited tasks of the Community institutions and bodies with regard to the data themselves.

(20) The European Data Protection Supervisor and the National Supervisory Authorities should cooperate actively with each other.

(21) The effective monitoring of the application of this Regulation requires evaluation at regular intervals.

(22) The Member States should lay down rules on penalties applicable to infringements of the provisions of this Regulation and ensure that they are implemented.

(23) The measures necessary for the implementation of this Regulation should be adopted in accordance with Council Decision 1999/468/EC of 28 June 1999 laying down the procedures for the exercise of implementing powers conferred on the Commission.

(24) This Regulation respects the fundamental rights and observes the principles recognised in particular by the Charter of Fundamental Rights of the European Union.

(25) Since the objectives of this Regulation, namely the establishment of a common Visa Information System and the creation of common obligations, conditions and procedures for the exchange of visa data between Member States, cannot be sufficiently achieved by the Member States and can therefore, by reason of the scale and impact of the action, be better achieved at Community level, the Community may adopt measures, in accordance with the principle of subsidiarity as set out in Article 5 of the Treaty. In accordance with the principle of proportionality, as set out

in that Article, this Regulation does not go beyond what is necessary in order to achieve those objectives.

(26) In accordance with Articles 1 and 2 of the Protocol on the position of Denmark, annexed to the Treaty on European Union and the Treaty establishing the European Community, Denmark does not take part in the adoption of this Regulation and is therefore not bound by it or subject to its application. Given that this Regulation builds upon the Schengen acquis under the provisions of Title IV of Part Three of the Treaty establishing the European Community, Denmark should, in accordance with Article 5 of that Protocol, decide within a period of six months after the adoption of this Regulation whether it will implement it in its national law.

(27) As regards Iceland and Norway, this Regulation constitutes a development of provisions of the Schengen acquis within the meaning of the Agreement concluded by the Council of the European Union and the Republic of Iceland and the Kingdom of Norway concerning the association of those two States with the implementation, application and development of the Schengen acquis, which falls within the area referred to in Article 1, point B of Council Decision 1999/437/EC of 17 May 1999 on certain arrangements for the application of that Agreement.

(28) An arrangement should be made to allow representatives of Iceland and Norway to be associated with the work of committees assisting the Commission in the exercise of its implementing powers. Such an arrangement has been contemplated in the Agreement in the form of Exchange of Letters between the Council of the European Union and the Republic of Iceland and the Kingdom of Norway concerning committees which assist the European Commission in the exercise of its executive powers, annexed to the Agreement referred to in Recital 27.

(29) This Regulation constitutes a development of provisions of the Schengen acquis in which the United Kingdom does not take part, in accordance with Council Decision 2000/365/EC of 29 May 2000 concerning the request of the United Kingdom of Great Britain and Northern Ireland to take part in some of the provisions of the Schengen acquis, and subsequent Council Decision 2004/926/EC of 22 December 2004 on the putting into effect of parts of the Schengen acquis by the United Kingdom of Great Britain and Northern Ireland. The United Kingdom is therefore not taking part in its adoption and is not bound by it or subject to its application.

(30) This Regulation constitutes a development of provisions of the Schengen acquis in which Ireland does not take part, in accordance with Council Decision 2002/192/EC of 28 February 2002 concerning Ireland's request

to take part in some of the provisions of the Schengen acquis. Ireland is therefore not taking part in its adoption and is not bound by it or subject to its application.

(31) As regards Switzerland, this Regulation constitutes a development of the provisions of the Schengen acquis within the meaning of the Agreement signed by the European Union, the European Community and the Swiss Confederation on the association of the Swiss Confederation with the implementation, application and development of the Schengen acquis which falls within the area referred to in Article 1, point B of Decision 1999/437/EC read in conjunction with Article 4(1) of Council Decision 2004/860/EC.

(32) An arrangement should be made to allow representatives of Switzerland to be associated with the work of committees assisting the Commission in the exercise of its implementing powers. Such an arrangement has been contemplated in the Exchange of Letters between the Community and Switzerland, annexed to the Agreement referred to in Recital 31.

(33) This Regulation constitutes an act building on the Schengen acquis or otherwise related to it within the meaning of Article 3(2) of the 2003 Act of Accession and Article 4(2) of the 2005 Act of Accession,

HAVE ADOPTED THIS REGULATION:

CHAPTER I
GENERAL PROVISIONS

Article 1
Subject matter and scope

This Regulation defines the purpose of, the functionalities of and the responsibilities for the Visa Information System (VIS), as established by Article 1 of Decision 2004/512/EC. It sets up the conditions and procedures for the exchange of data between Member States on applications for short-stay visas and on the decisions taken in relation thereto, including the decision whether to annul, revoke or extend the visa, to facilitate the examination of such applications and the related decisions.

Article 2
Purpose

The VIS shall have the purpose of improving the implementation of the common visa policy, consular cooperation and consultation between central visa authorities by facilitating the exchange of data between Member States on applications and on the decisions relating thereto, in order:

(a) to facilitate the visa application procedure;
(b) to prevent the bypassing of the criteria for the determination of the Member State responsible for examining the application;
(c) to facilitate the fight against fraud;
(d) to facilitate checks at external border crossing points and within the territory of the Member States;
(e) to assist in the identification of any person who may not, or may no longer, fulfil the conditions for entry to, stay or residence on the territory of the Member States;
(f) to facilitate the application of Regulation (EC) No 343/2003;
(g) to contribute to the prevention of threats to the internal security of any of the Member States.

Article 3
Availability of data for the prevention, detection and investigation of terrorist offences and other serious criminal offences

1. The designated authorities of the Member States may in a specific case and following a reasoned written or electronic request access the data kept in the VIS referred to in Articles 9 to 14 if there are reasonable grounds to consider that consultation of VIS data will substantially contribute to the prevention, detection or investigation of terrorist offences and of other serious criminal offences. Europol may access the VIS within the limits of its mandate and when necessary for the performance of its tasks.

2. The consultation referred to in paragraph 1 shall be carried out through central access point(s) which shall be responsible for ensuring strict compliance with the conditions for access and the procedures established in Council Decision 2008/633/JHA of 23 June 2008 concerning access for consultation of the Visa Information System (VIS) by the designated authorities of Member States and by Europol for the purposes of the prevention, detection and investigation of terrorist offences and of other serious criminal offences. Member States may designate more than one central access point to reflect their organisational and administrative structure in fulfilment of their constitutional or legal requirements. In an exceptional case of urgency, the central access point(s) may receive written, electronic or oral requests and only verify ex-post whether all the conditions for access are fulfilled, including whether an exceptional case of urgency existed. The ex-post verification shall take place without undue delay after the processing of the request.

3. Data obtained from the VIS pursuant to the Decision referred to in paragraph 2 shall not be transferred or made available to a third country or to an international organisation. However, in an exceptional case of urgency, such data may be transferred or made available to a third country or an international organisation exclusively for the purposes of the prevention and detection of terrorist offences and of other serious criminal offences and under the conditions set out in that Decision. In accordance with national law, Member States shall ensure that records on such transfers are kept and make them available to national data protection authorities on request. The transfer of data by the Member State which entered the data in the VIS shall be subject to the national law of that Member State.

4. This Regulation is without prejudice to any obligations under applicable national law for the communication of information on any criminal activity detected by the authorities referred to in Article 6 in the course of their duties to the responsible authorities for the purposes of preventing, investigating and prosecuting the related criminal offences.

Article 4
Definitions

For the purposes of this Regulation, the following definitions shall apply:
1. 'visa' means:
   (a) "uniform visa" as defined in Article 2(3) of Regulation (EC) No 810/2009 of the European Parliament and of the Council of 13 July 2009 establishing a Community code on Visas (Visa Code);[124]
   (c) "airport transit visa" as defined in Article 2(5) of Regulation (EC) No 810/2009;[125]
   (d) "visa with limited territorial validity" as defined in Article 2(4) of Regulation (EC) No 810/2009;[126]

---

[124] The revised text of Art. 4(1)(a) was inserted by the visa code. Art. 4(1)(a) previously read: '(a)'short-stay visa' as defined in Article 11(1)(a) of the Schengen Convention'. The visa code also deleted Art. 4(1)(b), which had read: '(b) "transit visa" as defined in Article 11(1)(b) of the Schengen Convention'.

[125] The revised text of Art. 4(1)(c) was inserted by the visa code. Art. 4(1)(c) previously read: '(c) "airport transit visa" as defined in part I, point 2.1.1, of the Common Consular Instructions'.

[126] The revised text of Art. 4(1)(d) was inserted by the visa code. Art. 4(1)(d) previously read: '(d) "visa with limited territorial validity" as defined in Articles 11(2), 14 and 16 of the Schengen Convention'. The visa code also deleted Art. 4(1)(e), which had read: '(e) "national long-stay visa valid concurrently as a short-stay visa" as defined in Article 18 of the Schengen Convention'.

2. 'visa sticker' means the uniform format for visas as defined by Regulation (EC) No 1683/95;
3. 'visa authorities' means the authorities which in each Member State are responsible for examining and for taking decisions on visa applications or for decisions whether to annul, revoke or extend visas, including the central visa authorities and the authorities responsible for issuing visas at the border in accordance with Council Regulation (EC) No 415/2003 of 27 February 2003 on the issue of visas at the border, including the issue of such visas to seamen in transit;
4. 'application form' means the uniform application form for visas in Annex 16 to the Common Consular Instructions;
5. 'applicant' means any person subject to the visa requirement pursuant to Council Regulation (EC) No 539/2001 of 15 March 2001 listing the third countries whose nationals must be in possession of visas when crossing the external borders and those whose nationals are exempt from that requirement, who has lodged an application for a visa;
6. 'group members' means applicants who are obliged for legal reasons to enter and leave the territory of the Member States together;
7. 'travel document' means a passport or other equivalent document entitling the holder to cross the external borders and to which a visa may be affixed;
8. 'Member State responsible' means the Member State which has entered the data in the VIS;
9. 'verification' means the process of comparison of sets of data to establish the validity of a claimed identity (one-to-one check);
10. 'identification' means the process of determining a person's identity through a database search against multiple sets of data (one-to-many check);
11. 'alphanumeric data' means data represented by letters, digits, special characters, spaces and punctuation marks.

Article 5
Categories of data

1. Only the following categories of data shall be recorded in the VIS:
   (a) alphanumeric data on the applicant and on visas requested, issued, refused, annulled, revoked or extended referred to in Articles 9(1) to (4) and Articles 10 to 14;
   (b) photographs referred to in Article 9(5);
   (c) fingerprint data referred to in Article 9(6);
   (d) links to other applications referred to in Article 8(3) and (4).

2. The messages transmitted by the infrastructure of the VIS, referred to in Article 16, Article 24(2) and Article 25(2), shall not be recorded in the VIS, without prejudice to the recording of data processing operations pursuant to Article 34.

Article 6
Access for entering, amending, deleting and consulting data

1. Access to the VIS for entering, amending or deleting the data referred to in Article 5(1) in accordance with this Regulation shall be reserved exclusively to the duly authorised staff of the visa authorities.
2. Access to the VIS for consulting the data shall be reserved exclusively to the duly authorised staff of the authorities of each Member State which are competent for the purposes laid down in Articles 15 to 22, limited to the extent that the data are required for the performance of their tasks in accordance with those purposes, and proportionate to the objectives pursued.
3. Each Member State shall designate the competent authorities, the duly authorised staff of which shall have access to enter, amend, delete or consult data in the VIS. Each Member State shall without delay communicate to the Commission a list of these authorities, including those referred to in Article 41(4), and any amendments thereto. That list shall specify for what purpose each authority may process data in the VIS.

Within 3 months after the VIS has become operational in accordance with Article 48(1), the Commission shall publish a consolidated list in the Official Journal of the European Union. Where there are amendments thereto, the Commission shall publish once a year an updated consolidated list.

Article 7
General principles

1. Each competent authority authorised to access the VIS in accordance with this Regulation shall ensure that the use of the VIS is necessary, appropriate and proportionate to the performance of the tasks of the competent authorities.
2. Each competent authority shall ensure that in using the VIS, it does not discriminate against applicants and visa holders on grounds of sex, racial or ethnic origin, religion or belief, disability, age or sexual orientation and that it fully respects the human dignity and the integrity of the applicant or of the visa holder.

CHAPTER II
ENTRY AND USE OF DATA BY VISA AUTHORITIES

Article 8
Procedures for entering data upon the application

1. When the application is admissible according to Article 19 of Regulation (EC) No 810/2009, the visa authority shall create without delay the application file, by entering the data referred to in Article 9 in the VIS, as far as these data are required to be provided by the applicant.[127]
2. When creating the application file, the visa authority shall check in the VIS, in accordance with Article 15, whether a previous application of the individual applicant has been registered in the VIS by any of the Member States.
3. If a previous application has been registered, the visa authority shall link each new application file to the previous application file on that applicant.
4. If the applicant is travelling in a group or with his spouse and/or children, the visa authority shall create an application file for each applicant and link the application files of the persons travelling together.
5. Where particular data are not required to be provided for legal reasons or factually cannot be provided, the specific data field(s) shall be marked as 'not applicable'. In the case of fingerprints, the system shall for the purposes of Article 17 permit a distinction to be made between the cases where fingerprints are not required to be provided for legal reasons and the cases where they cannot be provided factually; after a period of four years this functionality shall expire unless it is confirmed by a Commission decision on the basis of the evaluation referred to in Article 50(4).

Article 9
Data to be entered on application[128]

The visa authority shall enter the following data in the application file:
1. the application number;
2. status information, indicating that a visa has been requested;

---

[127] The visa code amended the first part of Art. 8(1), which had previously read: 'On receipt of an application'.
[128] The visa code amended the heading of Art. 9, which previously read: 'Data upon lodging the application'.

3. the authority with which the application has been lodged, including its location, and whether the application has been lodged with that authority representing another Member State;
4. the following data to be taken from the application form:
   (a) surname (family name), surname at birth (former family name(s)), first name(s) (given name(s)); date of birth, place of birth, country of birth, sex;[129]
   (b) current nationality and nationality at birth;
   (c) type and number of the travel document, the authority which issued it and the date of issue and of expiry;
   (d) place and date of the application;[130]
   (f) details of the person issuing an invitation and/or liable to pay the applicant's subsistence costs during the stay, being:
      (i) in the case of a natural person, the surname and first name and address of the person;
      (ii) in the case of a company or other organisation, the name and address of the company/other organisation, surname and first name of the contact person in that company/organisation;
   (g) Member State(s) of destination and duration of the intended stay or transit;[131]
   (h) main purpose(s) of the journey;[132]
   (i) intended date of arrival in the Schengen area and intended date of departure from the Schengen area;[133]
   (j) Member State of first entry;[134]
   (k) the applicant's home address;[135]

---

[129] Art. 9(4)(a) was replaced by the visa code. It previously read: '(a) surname, surname at birth (former surname(s)); first name(s); sex; date, place and country of birth'.

[130] Art. 9(4)(e) was repealed by the visa code. It had read: '(e) type of visa requested'.

[131] Art. 9(4)(g) was replaced by the visa code. It previously read: '(g) main destination and duration of the intended stay'.

[132] Art. 9(4)(h) was replaced by the visa code. It previously read: '(h) purpose of travel'.

[133] Art. 9(4)(i) was replaced by the visa code. It previously read: '(i) intended date of arrival and departure'.

[134] Art. 9(4)(j) was replaced by the visa code. It previously read: '(j) intended border of first entry or transit route'.

[135] Art. 9(4)(k) was replaced by the visa code. It previously read: '(k) residence'.

(l) current occupation and employer; for students: name of educational establishment;[136]

(m) in the case of minors, surname and first name(s) of the applicant's parental authority or legal guardian;[137]

5. a photograph of the applicant, in accordance with Regulation (EC) No 1683/95;

6. fingerprints of the applicant, in accordance with the relevant provisions of the Common Consular Instructions.

Article 10
Data to be added for a visa issued

1. Where a decision has been taken to issue a visa, the visa authority that issued the visa shall add the following data to the application file:

(a) status information indicating that the visa has been issued;

(b) the authority that issued the visa, including its location, and whether that authority issued it on behalf of another Member State;

(c) place and date of the decision to issue the visa;

(d) the type of visa;

(e) the number of the visa sticker;

(f) the territory in which the visa holder is entitled to travel, in accordance with the relevant provisions of the Common Consular Instructions;

(g) the commencement and expiry dates of the validity period of the visa;

(h) the number of entries authorised by the visa in the territory for which the visa is valid;

(i) the duration of the stay as authorised by the visa;

(j) if applicable, the information indicating that the visa has been issued on a separate sheet in accordance with Council Regulation (EC) No 333/2002 of 18 February 2002 on a uniform format for forms for affixing the visa issued by Member States to persons holding travel documents not recognised by the Member State drawing up the form.

(k) if applicable, the information indicating that the visa sticker has been filled in manually.[138]

2. If an application is withdrawn or not pursued further by the applicant before a decision has been taken whether to issue a visa, the visa authority

---

[136] The visa code replaced the word 'school' with 'educational establishment'.

[137] The visa code replaced the words 'father and mother' with 'parental authority or legal guardian'.

[138] Art. 10(1)(k) was added by the visa code.

with which the application was lodged shall indicate that the application has been closed for these reasons and the date when the application was closed.

Article 11
Data to be added where the examination of the application is discontinued

Where the visa authority representing another Member State discontinues the examination of the application, it shall add the following data to the application file:[139]

1. status information indicating that the examination of the application has been discontinued;
2. the authority that discontinued the examination of the application, including its location;
3. place and date of the decision to discontinue the examination;
4. the Member State competent to examine the application.

Article 12
Data to be added for a visa refusal

1. Where a decision has been taken to refuse a visa, the visa authority which refused the visa shall add the following data to the application file:
   (a) status information indicating that the visa has been refused and whether that authority refused it on behalf of another Member State;[140]
   (b) the authority that refused the visa, including its location;
   (c) place and date of the decision to refuse the visa.
2. The application file shall also indicate the ground(s) for refusal of the visa, which shall be one or more of the following:
   (a) the applicant:
      (i) presents a travel document which is false, counterfeit or forged;
      (ii) does not provide justification for the purpose and conditions of the intended stay;
      (iii) does not provide proof of sufficient means of subsistence, both for the duration of the intended stay and for the return to his country of origin or residence, or for the transit to a third country into

---

[139] This first paragraph was amended by the visa code. It had previously referred to cases where the representing authority was 'forced to discontinue' the examination.

[140] The visa code amended Art. 12(1)(a), which had previously referred only to 'status information indicating that the visa has been refused'.

which he is certain to be admitted, or is not in a position to acquire such means lawfully;

(iv) has already stayed for three months during the current six-month period on the territory of the Member States on a basis of a uniform visa or a visa with limited territorial validity;

(v) is a person for whom an alert has been issued in the SIS for the purpose of refusing entry;

(vi) is considered to be a threat to public policy, internal security or public health as defined in Article 2(19) of the Schengen Borders Code or to the international relations of any of the Member States, in particular where an alert has been issued in Member States' national databases for the purpose of refusing entry on the same grounds;

(vii) does not provide proof of holding adequate and valid travel medical insurance, where applicable;

(b) the information submitted regarding the justification for the purpose and conditions of the intended stay was not reliable;

(c) the applicant's intention to leave the territory of the Member States before the expiry of the visa could not be ascertained;

(d) sufficient proof that the applicant has not been in a position to apply for a visa in advance justifying application for a visa at the border was not provided.[141]

Article 13
Data to be added for a visa annulled or revoked[142]

1. Where a decision has been taken to annul or to revoke a visa, the visa authority that has taken the decision shall add the following data to the application file:

   (a) status information indicating that the visa has been annulled or revoked;

   (b) authority that annulled or revoked the visa, including its location;

   (c) place and date of the decision.

2. The application file shall also indicate the ground(s) for annulment or revocation, which shall be:

   (a) one or more of the ground(s) listed in Article 12(2);

   (b) the request of the visa holder to revoke the visa.

---

[141] Art. 12(2) was replaced by the visa code.
[142] Art. 13 was replaced by the visa code.

Article 14
Data to be added for a visa extended

1. Where a decision has been taken to extend the period of validity and/or the duration of stay of an issued visa, the visa authority which extended the visa shall add the following data to the application file:[143]
   (a) status information indicating that the visa has been extended;
   (b) the authority that extended the visa, including its location;
   (c) place and date of the decision;
   (d) the number of the visa sticker of the extended visa;[144]
   (e) the commencement and expiry dates of the extended period;
   (f) period of the extension of the authorised duration of the stay;
   (g) the territory in which the visa holder is entitled to travel, if the territorial validity of the extended visa differs from that of the original visa; [145]
   (h) the type of the visa extended.
2. The application file shall also indicate the grounds for extending the visa, which shall be one or more of the following:
   (a) force majeure;
   (b) humanitarian reasons;
   (d) serious personal reasons.[146]

Article 15
Use of the VIS for examining applications

1. The competent visa authority shall consult the VIS for the purposes of the examination of applications and the decisions relating to those applications, including the decision whether to annul, revoke, or extend the visa in accordance with the relevant provisions.[147]
2. For the purposes referred to in paragraph 1, the competent visa authority shall be given access to search with one or several of the following data:
   (a) the application number;
   (b) the data referred to in Article 9(4)(a);
   (c) the data on the travel document, referred to in Article 9(4)(c);

---

[143] This opening paragraph was replaced by the visa code.
[144] Art. 14(1)(d) was amended by the visa code.
[145] Art. 14(1)(g) was amended by the visa code.
[146] The visa code deleted Art. 14(2)(c), which had read: '(c) serious occupational reasons.'
[147] The visa code deleted a reference to shortening the validity of the visa in Art. 15(1).

(d) the surname, first name and address of the natural person or the name and address of the company/other organisation, referred to in Article 9(4)(f);

(e) fingerprints;

(f) the number of the visa sticker and date of issue of any previous visa.

3. If the search with one or several of the data listed in paragraph 2 indicates that data on the applicant are recorded in the VIS, the competent visa authority shall be given access to the application file(s) and the linked application file(s) pursuant to Article 8(3) and (4), solely for the purposes referred to in paragraph 1.

Article 16
Use of the VIS for consultation and requests for documents

1. For the purposes of consultation between central visa authorities on applications according to Article 17(2) of the Schengen Convention, the consultation request and the responses thereto shall be transmitted in accordance with paragraph 2 of this Article.

2. The Member State which is responsible for examining the application shall transmit the consultation request with the application number to the VIS, indicating the Member State or the Member States to be consulted.

   The VIS shall transmit the request to the Member State or the Member States indicated.

   The Member State or the Member States consulted shall transmit their response to the VIS, which shall transmit that response to the Member State which initiated the request.

3. The procedure set out in paragraph 2 may also apply to the transmission of information on the issue of visas with limited territorial validity and other messages related to consular cooperation as well as to the transmission of requests to the competent visa authority to forward copies of travel documents and other documents supporting the application and to the transmission of electronic copies of those documents. The competent visa authorities shall respond to the request without delay.

4. The personal data transmitted pursuant to this Article shall be used solely for the consultation of central visa authorities and consular cooperation.

Article 17
Use of data for reporting and statistics

The competent visa authorities shall have access to consult the following data, solely for the purposes of reporting and statistics without allowing the identification of individual applicants:

1. status information;
2. the competent visa authority, including its location;
3. current nationality of the applicant;
4. Member State of first entry;[148]
5. date and place of the application or the decision concerning the visa;
6. the type of visa issued;[149]
7. the type of the travel document;
8. the grounds indicated for any decision concerning the visa or visa application;
9. the competent visa authority, including its location, which refused the visa application and the date of the refusal;
10. the cases in which the same applicant applied for a visa from more than one visa authority, indicating these visa authorities, their location and the dates of refusals;
11. main purpose(s) of the journey;[150]
12. the cases in which the data referred to in Article 9(6) could factually not be provided, in accordance with the second sentence of Article 8(5);
13. the cases in which the data referred to in Article 9(6) was not required to be provided for legal reasons, in accordance with the second sentence of Article 8(5);
14. the cases in which a person who could factually not provide the data referred to in Article 9(6) was refused a visa, in accordance with the second sentence of Article 8(5).

CHAPTER III
ACCESS TO DATA BY OTHER AUTHORITIES

Article 18
Access to data for verification at external border crossing points

1. For the sole purpose of verifying the identity of the visa holder and/or the authenticity of the visa and/or whether the conditions for entry to the territory of the Member States in accordance with Article 5 of the Schengen Borders Code are fulfilled, the competent authorities for carrying out checks at external border crossing points in accordance with the Schengen Borders Code shall, subject to paragraphs 2 and 3, have access to search

---

[148] The visa code amended this provision, which had referred to 'border of first entry'.
[149] The visa code amended this provision, which had also referred to the type of visa 'requested'.
[150] The visa code amended this provision, which had referred to 'purpose of travel'.

using the number of the visa sticker in combination with verification of fingerprints of the visa holder.

2. For a maximum period of three years after the VIS has started operations, the search may be carried out using only the number of the visa sticker. As from one year after the start of operations, the period of three years may be reduced in the case of air borders in accordance with the procedure referred to in Article 49(3).

3. For visa holders whose fingerprints cannot be used, the search shall be carried out only with the number of the visa sticker.

4. If the search with the data listed in paragraph 1 indicates that data on the visa holder are recorded in the VIS, the competent border control authority shall be given access to consult the following data of the application file as well as of linked application file(s) pursuant to Article 8(4), solely for the purposes referred to in paragraph 1:
    (a) the status information and the data taken from the application form, referred to in Article 9(2) and (4);
    (b) photographs;
    (c) the data entered in respect of the visa(s) issued, annulled, revoked or whose validity is extended, referred to in Articles 10, 13 and 14.[151]

5. In circumstances where verification of the visa holder or of the visa fails or where there are doubts as to the identity of the visa holder, the authenticity of the visa and/or the travel document, the duly authorised staff of those competent authorities shall have access to data in accordance with Article 20(1) and (2).

Article 19
**Access to data for verification within the territory
of the Member States**

1. For the sole purpose of verifying the identity of the visa holder and/or the authenticity of the visa and/or whether the conditions for entry to, stay or residence on the territory of the Member States are fulfilled, the authorities competent for carrying out checks within the territory of the Member States as to whether the conditions for entry to, stay or residence on the territory of the Member States are fulfilled, shall have access to search with the number of the visa sticker in combination with verification of fingerprints of the visa holder, or the number of the visa sticker.

---

[151] The visa code dropped a reference to shortening the validity of visas.

For visa holders whose fingerprints cannot be used, the search shall be carried out only with the number of the visa sticker.

2. If the search with the data listed in paragraph 1 indicates that data on the visa holder are recorded in the VIS, the competent authority shall be given access to consult the following data of the application file as well as of linked application file(s) pursuant to Article 8(4), solely for the purposes referred to in paragraph 1:

   (a) the status information and the data taken from the application form, referred to in Article 9(2) and (4);

   (b) photographs;

   (c) the data entered in respect of the visa(s) issued, annulled, revoked or whose validity is extended, referred to in Articles 10, 13 and 14.[152]

3. In circumstances where verification of the visa holder or of the visa fails or where there are doubts as to the identity of the visa holder, the authenticity of the visa and/or the travel document, the duly authorised staff of the competent authorities shall have access to data in accordance with Article 20(1) and (2).

Article 20
Access to data for identification

1. Solely for the purpose of the identification of any person who may not, or may no longer, fulfil the conditions for the entry to, stay or residence on the territory of the Member States, the authorities competent for carrying out checks at external border crossing points in accordance with the Schengen Borders Code or within the territory of the Member States as to whether the conditions for entry to, stay or residence on the territory of the Member States are fulfilled, shall have access to search with the fingerprints of that person.

   Where the fingerprints of that person cannot be used or the search with the fingerprints fails, the search shall be carried out with the data referred to in Article 9(4)(a) and/or (c); this search may be carried out in combination with the data referred to in Article 9(4)(b).

2. If the search with the data listed in paragraph 1 indicates that data on the applicant are recorded in the VIS, the competent authority shall be given access to consult the following data of the application file and the linked

---

[152] The visa code dropped a reference to shortening the validity of visas.

application file(s), pursuant to Article 8(3) and (4), solely for the purposes referred to in paragraph 1:

(a) the application number, the status information and the authority to which the application was lodged;

(b) the data taken from the application form, referred to in Article 9(4);

(c) photographs;

(d) the data entered in respect of any visa issued, refused, annulled, revoked or whose validity is extended, or of applications where examination has been discontinued, referred to in Articles 10 to 14.[153]

3. Where the person holds a visa, the competent authorities shall access the VIS first in accordance with Articles 18 or 19.

Article 21
Access to data for determining the responsibility
for asylum applications

1. For the sole purpose of determining the Member State responsible for examining an asylum application according to Articles 9 and 21 of Regulation (EC) No 343/2003, the competent asylum authorities shall have access to search with the fingerprints of the asylum seeker.

   Where the fingerprints of the asylum seeker cannot be used or the search with the fingerprints fails, the search shall be carried out with the data referred to in Article 9(4)(a) and/or (c); this search may be carried out in combination with the data referred to in Article 9(4)(b).

2. If the search with the data listed in paragraph 1 indicates that a visa issued with an expiry date of no more than six months before the date of the asylum application, and/or a visa extended to an expiry date of no more than six months before the date of the asylum application, is recorded in the VIS, the competent asylum authority shall be given access to consult the following data of the application file, and as regards the data listed in point (g) of the spouse and children, pursuant to Article 8(4), for the sole purpose referred to in paragraph 1:

   (a) the application number and the authority that issued or extended the visa, and whether the authority issued it on behalf of another Member State;

   (b) the data taken from the application form referred to in Article 9(4)(a) and (b);

---

[153] The visa code dropped a reference to shortening the validity of visas.

(c) the type of visa;

(d) the period of validity of the visa;

(e) the duration of the intended stay;

(f) photographs;

(g) the data referred to in Article 9(4)(a) and (b) of the linked application file(s) on the spouse and children.

3. The consultation of the VIS pursuant to paragraphs 1 and 2 of this Article shall be carried out only by the designated national authorities referred to in Article 21(6) of Regulation (EC) No 343/2003.

Article 22
Access to data for examining the application for asylum

1. For the sole purpose of examining an application for asylum, the competent asylum authorities shall have access in accordance with Article 21 of Regulation (EC) No 343/2003 to search with the fingerprints of the asylum seeker.

   Where the fingerprints of the asylum seeker cannot be used or the search with the fingerprints fails, the search shall be carried out with the data referred to in Article 9(4)(a) and/or (c); this search may be carried out in combination with the data referred to in Article 9(4)(b).

2. If the search with the data listed in paragraph 1 indicates that a visa issued is recorded in the VIS, the competent asylum authority shall have access to consult the following data of the application file and linked application file(s) of the applicant pursuant to Article 8(3), and, as regards the data listed in point (e) of the spouse and children, pursuant to Article 8(4), for the sole purpose referred to in paragraph 1:

   (a) the application number;

   (b) the data taken from the application form, referred to in Article 9(4)(a), (b) and (c);

   (c) photographs;

   (d) the data entered in respect of any visa issued, annulled, revoked, or whose validity is extended, referred to in Articles 10, 13 and 14;[154]

   (e) the data referred to in Article 9(4)(a) and (b) of the linked application file(s) on the spouse and children.

3. The consultation of the VIS pursuant to paragraphs 1 and 2 of this Article shall be carried out only by the designated national authorities referred to in Article 21(6) of Regulation (EC) No 343/2003.

---

[154] The visa code dropped a reference to shortening the validity of visas.

CHAPTER IV
RETENTION AND AMENDMENT OF THE DATA

Article 23
Retention period for data storage

1. Each application file shall be stored in the VIS for a maximum of five years, without prejudice to the deletion referred to in Articles 24 and 25 and to the keeping of records referred to in Article 34.

That period shall start:
   (a) on the expiry date of the visa, if a visa has been issued;
   (b) on the new expiry date of the visa, if a visa has been extended;
   (c) on the date of the creation of the application file in the VIS, if the application has been withdrawn, closed or discontinued;
   (d) on the date of the decision of the visa authority if a visa has been refused, annulled, or revoked.[155]

2. Upon expiry of the period referred to in paragraph 1, the VIS shall automatically delete the application file and the link(s) to this file as referred to in Article 8(3) and (4).

Article 24
Amendment of data

1. Only the Member State responsible shall have the right to amend data which it has transmitted to the VIS, by correcting or deleting such data.
2. If a Member State has evidence to suggest that data processed in the VIS are inaccurate or that data were processed in the VIS contrary to this Regulation, it shall inform the Member State responsible immediately. Such message may be transmitted by the infrastructure of the VIS.
3. The Member State responsible shall check the data concerned and, if necessary, correct or delete them immediately.

Article 25
Advance data deletion

1. Where, before expiry of the period referred to in Article 23(1), an applicant has acquired the nationality of a Member State, the application files and the links referred to in Article 8(3) and (4) relating to him or her shall be

---

[155] The visa code dropped a reference to shortening the validity of visas.

deleted without delay from the VIS by the Member State which created the respective application file(s) and links.

2. Each Member State shall inform the Member State(s) responsible without delay if an applicant has acquired its nationality. Such message may be transmitted by the infrastructure of the VIS.

3. If the refusal of a visa has been annulled by a court or an appeal body, the Member State which refused the visa shall delete the data referred to in Article 12 without delay as soon as the decision to annul the refusal of the visa becomes final.

CHAPTER V
OPERATION AND RESPONSIBILITIES

Article 26
Operational management

1. After a transitional period, a management authority (the Management Authority), funded from the general budget of the European Union, shall be responsible for the operational management of the central VIS and the national interfaces. The Management Authority shall ensure, in cooperation with the Member States, that at all times the best available technology, subject to a cost-benefit analysis, is used for the central VIS and the national interfaces.

2. The Management Authority shall also be responsible for the following tasks relating to the communication infrastructure between the central VIS and the national interfaces:
   (a) supervision;
   (b) security;
   (c) the coordination of relations between the Member States and the provider.

3. The Commission shall be responsible for all other tasks relating to the Communication Infrastructure between the central VIS and the national interfaces, in particular:
   (a) tasks relating to implementation of the budget;
   (b) acquisition and renewal;
   (c) contractual matters.

4. During a transitional period before the Management Authority takes up its responsibilities, the Commission shall be responsible for the operational management of the VIS. The Commission may delegate that task and tasks

relating to implementation of the budget, in accordance with Council Regulation (EC, Euratom) No 1605/2002 of 25 June 2002 on the Financial Regulation applicable to the general budget of the European Communities [23], to national public-sector bodies in two different Member States.

5. Each national public-sector body referred to in paragraph 4 shall meet the following selection criteria:

   (a) it must demonstrate that it has extensive experience in operating a large-scale information system;

   (b) it must have considerable expertise in the service and security requirements of a large-scale information system;

   (c) it must have sufficient and experienced staff with the appropriate professional expertise and linguistic skills to work in an international cooperation environment such as that required by the VIS;

   (d) it must have a secure and custom-built facility infrastructure able, in particular, to back up and guarantee the continuous functioning of large-scale IT systems; and

   (e) its administrative environment must allow it to implement its tasks properly and avoid any conflict of interests.

6. Prior to any delegation as referred to in paragraph 4 and at regular intervals thereafter, the Commission shall inform the European Parliament and the Council of the terms of the delegation, its precise scope, and the bodies to which tasks are delegated.

7. Where the Commission delegates its responsibility during the transitional period pursuant to paragraph 4, it shall ensure that the delegation fully respects the limits set by the institutional system laid out in the Treaty. It shall ensure, in particular, that the delegation does not adversely affect any effective control mechanism under Community law, whether by the Court of Justice, the Court of Auditors or the European Data Protection Supervisor.

8. Operational management of the VIS shall consist of all the tasks necessary to keep the VIS functioning 24 hours a day, seven days a week in accordance with this Regulation, in particular the maintenance work and technical developments necessary to ensure that the system functions at a satisfactory level of operational quality, in particular as regards the time required for interrogation of the central database by consular posts, which should be as short as possible.

9. Without prejudice to Article 17 of the Staff Regulations of officials of the European Communities, laid down in Regulation (EEC, Euratom, ECSC) No 259/68 [24], the Management Authority shall apply appropriate rules of professional secrecy or other equivalent duties of confidentiality to all its

staff required to work with VIS data. This obligation shall also apply after such staff leave office or employment or after the termination of their activities.

Article 27
Location of the central Visa Information System

The principal central VIS, which performs technical supervision and administration functions, shall be located in Strasbourg (France) and a back-up central VIS, capable of ensuring all functionalities of the principal central VIS in the event of failure of the system, shall be located in Sankt Johann im Pongau (Austria).

Article 28
Relation to the national systems

1. The VIS shall be connected to the national system of each Member State via the national interface in the Member State concerned.
2. Each Member State shall designate a national authority, which shall provide the access of the competent authorities referred to in Article 6(1) and (2) to the VIS, and connect that national authority to the national interface.
3. Each Member State shall observe automated procedures for processing the data.
4. Each Member State shall be responsible for:
   (a) the development of the national system and/or its adaptation to the VIS according to Article 2(2) of Decision 2004/512/EC;
   (b) the organisation, management, operation and maintenance of its national system;
   (c) the management and arrangements for access of the duly authorised staff of the competent national authorities to the VIS in accordance with this Regulation and to establish and regularly update a list of such staff and their profiles;
   (d) bearing the costs incurred by the national system and the costs of their connection to the national interface, including the investment and operational costs of the communication infrastructure between the national interface and the national system.
5. Before being authorised to process data stored in the VIS, the staff of the authorities having a right to access the VIS shall receive appropriate training about data security and data protection rules and shall be informed of any relevant criminal offences and penalties.

Article 29
Responsibility for the use of data

1. Each Member State shall ensure that the data are processed lawfully, and in particular that only duly authorised staff have access to data processed in the VIS for the performance of their tasks in accordance with this Regulation. The Member State responsible shall ensure in particular that:
   (a) the data are collected lawfully;
   (b) the data are transmitted lawfully to the VIS;
   (c) the data are accurate and up-to-date when they are transmitted to the VIS.
2. The management authority shall ensure that the VIS is operated in accordance with this Regulation and its implementing rules referred to in Article 45(2). In particular, the management authority shall:
   (a) take the necessary measures to ensure the security of the central VIS and the communication infrastructure between the central VIS and the national interfaces, without prejudice to the responsibilities of each Member State;
   (b) ensure that only duly authorised staff have access to data processed in the VIS for the performance of the tasks of the management authority in accordance with this Regulation.
3. The management authority shall inform the European Parliament, the Council and the Commission of the measures which it takes pursuant to paragraph 2.

Article 30
Keeping of VIS data in national files

1. Data retrieved from the VIS may be kept in national files only when necessary in an individual case, in accordance with the purpose of the VIS and in accordance with the relevant legal provisions, including those concerning data protection, and for no longer than necessary in that individual case.
2. Paragraph 1 shall be without prejudice to the right of a Member State to keep in its national files data which that Member State entered in the VIS.
3. Any use of data which does not comply with paragraphs 1 and 2 shall be considered a misuse under the national law of each Member State.

Article 31
Communication of data to third countries or international organisations

1. Data processed in the VIS pursuant to this Regulation shall not be transferred or made available to a third country or to an international organisation.

2. By way of derogation from paragraph 1, the data referred to in Article 9(4) (a), (b), (c), (k) and (m) may be transferred or made available to a third country or to an international organisation listed in the Annex if necessary in individual cases for the purpose of proving the identity of third-country nationals, including for the purpose of return, only where the following conditions are satisfied:

(a) the Commission has adopted a decision on the adequate protection of personal data in that third country in accordance with Article 25(6) of Directive 95/46/EC, or a readmission agreement is in force between the Community and that third country, or the provisions of Article 26(1)(d) of Directive 95/46/EC apply;

(b) the third country or international organisation agrees to use the data only for the purpose for which they were provided;

(c) the data are transferred or made available in accordance with the relevant provisions of Community law, in particular readmission agreements, and the national law of the Member State which transferred or made the data available, including the legal provisions relevant to data security and data protection; and

(d) the Member State(s) which entered the data in the VIS has given its consent.

3. Such transfers of personal data to third countries or international organisations shall not prejudice the rights of refugees and persons requesting international protection, in particular as regards non-refoulement.

Article 32
Data security

1. The Member State responsible shall ensure the security of the data before and during transmission to the national interface. Each Member State shall ensure the security of the data which it receives from the VIS.

2. Each Member State shall, in relation to its national system, adopt the necessary measures, including a security plan, in order to:

(a) physically protect data, including by making contingency plans for the protection of critical infrastructure;

(b) deny unauthorised persons access to national installations in which the Member State carries out operations in accordance with the purposes of the VIS (checks at entrance to the installation);

(c) prevent the unauthorised reading, copying, modification or removal of data media (data media control);

(d) prevent the unauthorised input of data and the unauthorised inspection, modification or deletion of stored personal data (storage control);

(e) prevent the unauthorised processing of data in the VIS and any unauthorised modification or deletion of data processed in the VIS (control of data entry);

(f) ensure that persons authorised to access the VIS have access only to the data covered by their access authorisation, by means of individual and unique user identities and confidential access modes only (data access control);

(g) ensure that all authorities with a right of access to the VIS create profiles describing the functions and responsibilities of persons who are authorised to access, enter, update, delete and search the data and make these profiles available to the National Supervisory Authorities referred to in Article 41 without delay at their request (personnel profiles);

(h) ensure that it is possible to verify and establish to which bodies personal data may be transmitted using data communication equipment (communication control);

(i) ensure that it is possible to verify and establish what data have been processed in the VIS, when, by whom and for what purpose (control of data recording);

(j) prevent the unauthorised reading, copying, modification or deletion of personal data during the transmission of personal data to or from the VIS or during the transport of data media, in particular by means of appropriate encryption techniques (transport control);

(k) monitor the effectiveness of the security measures referred to in this paragraph and take the necessary organisational measures related to internal monitoring to ensure compliance with this Regulation (self-auditing).

3. The Management Authority shall take the necessary measures in order to achieve the objectives set out in paragraph 2 as regards the operation of the VIS, including the adoption of a security plan.

Article 33
Liability

1. Any person who, or Member State which, has suffered damage as a result of an unlawful processing operation or any act incompatible with this Regulation shall be entitled to receive compensation from the Member State which is responsible for the damage suffered. That Member State shall be exempted from its liability, in whole or in part, if it proves that it is not responsible for the event giving rise to the damage.

2. If any failure of a Member State to comply with its obligations under this Regulation causes damage to the VIS, that Member State shall be held liable for such damage, unless and insofar as the Management Authority or another Member State failed to take reasonable measures to prevent the damage from occurring or to minimise its impact.
3. Claims for compensation against a Member State for the damage referred to in paragraphs 1 and 2 shall be governed by the provisions of national law of the defendant Member State.

Article 34
Keeping of records

1. Each Member State and the Management Authority shall keep records of all data processing operations within the VIS. These records shall show the purpose of access referred to in Article 6(1) and in Articles 15 to 22, the date and time, the type of data transmitted as referred to in Articles 9 to 14, the type of data used for interrogation as referred to in Articles 15(2), 17, 18(1) to (3), 19(1), 20(1), 21(1) and 22(1) and the name of the authority entering or retrieving the data. In addition, each Member State shall keep records of the staff duly authorised to enter or retrieve the data.
2. Such records may be used only for the data-protection monitoring of the admissibility of data processing as well as to ensure data security. The records shall be protected by appropriate measures against unauthorised access and deleted after a period of one year after the retention period referred to in Article 23(1) has expired, if they are not required for monitoring procedures which have already begun.

Article 35
Self-monitoring

Member States shall ensure that each authority entitled to access VIS data takes the measures necessary to comply with this Regulation and cooperates, where necessary, with the National Supervisory Authority.

Article 36
Penalties

Member States shall take the necessary measures to ensure that any misuse of data entered in the VIS is punishable by penalties, including administrative and/or criminal penalties in accordance with national law, that are effective, proportionate and dissuasive.

CHAPTER VI
RIGHTS AND SUPERVISION ON DATA PROTECTION

Article 37
Right of information

1. Applicants and the persons referred to in Article 9(4)(f) shall be informed of the following by the Member State responsible:
   (a) the identity of the controller referred to in Article 41(4), including his contact details;
   (b) the purposes for which the data will be processed within the VIS;
   (c) the categories of recipients of the data, including the authorities referred to in Article 3;
   (d) the data retention period;
   (e) that the collection of the data is mandatory for the examination of the application;
   (f) the existence of the right of access to data relating to them, and the right to request that inaccurate data relating to them be corrected or that unlawfully processed data relating to them be deleted, including the right to receive information on the procedures for exercising those rights and the contact details of the National Supervisory Authorities referred to in Article 41(1), which shall hear claims concerning the protection of personal data.
2. The information referred to in paragraph 1 shall be provided in writing to the applicant when the data from the application form, the photograph and the fingerprint data as referred to in Article 9(4), (5) and (6) are collected.
3. The information referred to in paragraph 1 shall be provided to the persons referred to in Article 9(4)(f) on the forms to be signed by those persons providing proof of invitation, sponsorship and accommodation.

In the absence of such a form signed by those persons, this information shall be provided in accordance with Article 11 of Directive 95/46/EC.

Article 38
Right of access, correction and deletion

1. Without prejudice to the obligation to provide other information in accordance with Article 12(a) of Directive 95/46/EC, any person shall have the right to obtain communication of the data relating to him recorded in the VIS and of the Member State which transmitted them to the VIS. Such access to data may be granted only by a Member State. Each Member State shall record any requests for such access.

2. Any person may request that data relating to him which are inaccurate be corrected and that data recorded unlawfully be deleted. The correction and deletion shall be carried out without delay by the Member State responsible, in accordance with its laws, regulations and procedures.

3. If the request as provided for in paragraph 2 is made to a Member State other than the Member State responsible, the authorities of the Member State with which the request was lodged shall contact the authorities of the Member State responsible within a period of 14 days. The Member State responsible shall check the accuracy of the data and the lawfulness of their processing in the VIS within a period of one month.

4. If it emerges that data recorded in the VIS are inaccurate or have been recorded unlawfully, the Member State responsible shall correct or delete the data in accordance with Article 24(3). The Member State responsible shall confirm in writing to the person concerned without delay that it has taken action to correct or delete data relating to him.

5. If the Member State responsible does not agree that data recorded in the VIS are inaccurate or have been recorded unlawfully, it shall explain in writing to the person concerned without delay why it is not prepared to correct or delete data relating to him.

6. The Member State responsible shall also provide the person concerned with information explaining the steps which he can take if he does not accept the explanation provided. This shall include information on how to bring an action or a complaint before the competent authorities or courts of that Member State and on any assistance, including from the national supervisory authorities referred to in Article 41(1), that is available in accordance with the laws, regulations and procedures of that Member State.

Article 39
Cooperation to ensure the rights on data protection

1. The Member States shall cooperate actively to enforce the rights laid down in Article 38(2), (3) and (4).

2. In each Member State, the national supervisory authority shall, upon request, assist and advise the person concerned in exercising his right to correct or delete data relating to him in accordance with Article 28(4) of Directive 95/46/EC.

3. The National Supervisory Authority of the Member State responsible which transmitted the data and the National Supervisory Authorities of the Member States with which the request was lodged shall cooperate to this end.

Article 40

Remedies

1. In each Member State any person shall have the right to bring an action or a complaint before the competent authorities or courts of that Member State which refused the right of access to or the right of correction or deletion of data relating to him, provided for in Article 38(1) and (2).
2. The assistance of the National Supervisory Authorities referred to in Article 39(2) shall remain available throughout the proceedings.

Article 41

Supervision by the National Supervisory Authority

1. The authority or authorities designated in each Member State and endowed with the powers referred to in Article 28 of Directive 95/46/EC (the National Supervisory Authority) shall monitor independently the lawfulness of the processing of personal data referred to in Article 5(1) by the Member State in question, including their transmission to and from the VIS.
2. The National Supervisory Authority shall ensure that an audit of the data processing operations in the national system is carried out in accordance with relevant international auditing standards at least every four years.
3. Member States shall ensure that their National Supervisory Authority has sufficient resources to fulfil the tasks entrusted to it under this Regulation.
4. In relation to the processing of personal data in the VIS, each Member State shall designate the authority which is to be considered as controller in accordance with Article 2(d) of Directive 95/46/EC and which shall have central responsibility for the processing of data by that Member State. Each Member State shall communicate the details of that authority to the Commission.
5. Each Member State shall supply any information requested by the National Supervisory Authorities and shall, in particular, provide them with information on the activities carried out in accordance with Articles 28 and 29(1), grant them access to the lists referred to in Article 28(4)(c) and to its records as referred to in Article 34 and allow them access at all times to all their premises.

Article 42

Supervision by the European Data Protection Supervisor

1. The European Data Protection Supervisor shall check that the personal data processing activities of the Management Authority are carried out in

accordance with this Regulation. The duties and powers referred to in Articles 46 and 47 of Regulation (EC) No 45/2001 shall apply accordingly.

2. The European Data Protection Supervisor shall ensure that an audit of the Management Authority's personal data processing activities is carried out in accordance with relevant international auditing standards at least every four years. A report of such audit shall be sent to the European Parliament, the Council, the Management Authority, the Commission and the National Supervisory Authorities. The Management Authority shall be given an opportunity to make comments before the report is adopted.

3. The Management Authority shall supply information requested by the European Data Protection Supervisor, give him access to all documents and to its records referred to in Article 34(1) and allow him access to all its premises, at any time.

Article 43
**Cooperation between National Supervisory Authorities
and the European Data Protection Supervisor**

1. The National Supervisory Authorities and the European Data Protection Supervisor, each acting within the scope of their respective competences, shall cooperate actively within the framework of their responsibilities and shall ensure coordinated supervision of the VIS and the national systems.

2. They shall, each acting within the scope of their respective competences, exchange relevant information, assist each other in carrying out audits and inspections, examine difficulties of interpretation or application of this Regulation, study problems with the exercise of independent supervision or with the exercise of the rights of data subjects, draw up harmonised proposals for joint solutions to any problems and promote awareness of data protection rights, as necessary.

3. The National Supervisory Authorities and the European Data Protection Supervisor shall meet for that purpose at least twice a year. The costs and servicing of these meetings shall be b for the account of the European Data Protection Supervisor. Rules of procedure shall be adopted at the first meeting. Further working methods shall be developed jointly as necessary.

4. A joint report of activities shall be sent to the European Parliament, the Council, the Commission and the Management Authority every two years. This report shall include a chapter of each Member State prepared by the National Supervisory Authority of that Member State.

Article 44
Data protection during the transitional period

Where the Commission delegates its responsibilities during the transitional period to another body or bodies, pursuant to Article 26(4) of this Regulation, it shall ensure that the European Data Protection Supervisor has the right and is able to exercise his tasks fully, including the carrying out of on-the-spot checks, and to exercise any other powers conferred on him by Article 47 of Regulation (EC) No 45/2001.

CHAPTER VII
FINAL PROVISIONS

Article 45
Implementation by the Commission

1. The central VIS, the national interface in each Member State and the communication infrastructure between the central VIS and the national interfaces shall be implemented by the Commission as soon as possible after the entry into force of this Regulation, including the functionalities for processing the biometric data referred to in Article 5(1)(c).
2. The measures necessary for the technical implementation of the central VIS, the national interfaces and the communication infrastructure between the central VIS and the national interfaces shall be adopted in accordance with the procedure referred to in Article 49(2), in particular:
   (a) for entering the data and linking applications in accordance with Article 8;
   (b) for accessing the data in accordance with Article 15 and Articles 17 to 22;
   (c) for amending, deleting and advance deleting of data in accordance with Articles 23 to 25;
   (d) for keeping and accessing the records in accordance with Article 34;
   (e) for the consultation mechanism and the procedures referred to in Article 16.

Article 46
Integration of the technical functionalities of the
Schengen Consultation Network

The consultation mechanism referred to in Article 16 shall replace the Schengen Consultation Network from the date determined in accordance with the procedure referred to in Article 49(3) when all those Member States which use the Schengen Consultation Network at the date of entry into force of this Regulation have notified the legal and technical arrangements for the use of the VIS for the purpose of consultation between central visa authorities on visa applications according to Article 17(2) of the Schengen Convention.

Article 47
Start of transmission

Each Member State shall notify the Commission that it has made the necessary technical and legal arrangements to transmit the data referred to in Article 5(1) to the central VIS via the national interface.

Article 48
Start of operations

1. The Commission shall determine the date from which the VIS is to start operations, when:
   (a) the measures referred to in Article 45(2) have been adopted;
   (b) the Commission has declared the successful completion of a comprehensive test of the VIS, which shall be conducted by the Commission together with Member States;
   (c) following validation of technical arrangements, the Member States have notified the Commission that they have made the necessary technical and legal arrangements to collect and transmit the data referred to in Article 5(1) to the VIS for all applications in the first region determined according to paragraph 4, including arrangements for the collection and/or transmission of the data on behalf of another Member State.
2. The Commission shall inform the European Parliament of the results of the test carried out in accordance with paragraph 1(b).
3. In every other region, the Commission shall determine the date from which the transmission of the data in Article 5(1) becomes mandatory when Member States have notified the Commission that they have made the necessary technical and legal arrangements to collect and transmit the data referred to in Article 5(1) to the VIS for all applications in the region concerned, including arrangements for the collection and/or transmission of the data on behalf of another Member State. Before that date, each Member State may start operations in any of these regions, as soon as it has notified to the Commission that it has made the necessary technical and legal arrangements to collect and transmit at least the data referred to in Article 5(1)(a) and (b) to the VIS.

4. The regions referred to in paragraphs 1 and 3 shall be determined in accordance with the procedure referred to in Article 49(3). The criteria for the determination of these regions shall be the risk of illegal immigration, threats to the internal security of the Member States and the feasibility of collecting biometrics from all locations in this region.
5. The Commission shall publish the dates for the start of operations in each region in the Official Journal of the European Union.
6. No Member State shall consult the data transmitted by other Member States to the VIS before it or another Member State representing this Member State starts entering data in accordance with paragraphs 1 and 3.

Article 49
Committee

1. The Commission shall be assisted by the committee set up by Article 51(1) of Regulation (EC) No 1987/2006 of the European Parliament and of the Council of 20 December 2006 on the establishment, operation and use of the second generation Schengen Information System (SIS II) [25].
2. Where reference is made to this paragraph, Articles 4 and 7 of Decision 1999/468/EC shall apply.
    The period laid down in Article 4(3) of Decision 1999/468/EC shall be two months.
3. Where reference is made to this paragraph, Article 5 and 7 of Decision 1999/468/EC shall apply.

The period laid down in Article 5(6) of Decision 1999/468/EC shall be two months.

Article 50
Monitoring and evaluation

1. The Management Authority shall ensure that procedures are in place to monitor the functioning of the VIS against objectives relating to output, cost-effectiveness, security and quality of service.
2. For the purposes of technical maintenance, the Management Authority shall have access to the necessary information relating to the processing operations performed in the VIS.
3. Two years after the VIS is brought into operation and every two years thereafter, the Management Authority shall submit to the European Parliament, the Council and the Commission a report on the technical functioning of the VIS, including the security thereof.
4. Three years after the VIS is brought into operation and every four years thereafter, the Commission shall produce an overall evaluation of the VIS.

This overall evaluation shall include an examination of results achieved against objectives and an assessment of the continuing validity of the underlying rationale, the application of this Regulation in respect of the VIS, the security of the VIS, the use made of the provisions referred to in Article 31 and any implications for future operations. The Commission shall transmit the evaluation to the European Parliament and the Council.

5. Before the end of the periods referred to in Article 18(2) the Commission shall report on the technical progress made regarding the use of fingerprints at external borders and its implications for the duration of searches using the number of the visa sticker in combination with verification of the fingerprints of the visa holder, including whether the expected duration of such a search entails excessive waiting time at border crossing points. The Commission shall transmit the evaluation to the European Parliament and the Council. On the basis of that evaluation, the European Parliament or the Council may invite the Commission to propose, if necessary, appropriate amendments to this Regulation.

6. Member States shall provide the Management Authority and the Commission with the information necessary to draft the reports referred to in paragraph 3, 4 and 5.

7. The Management Authority shall provide the Commission with the information necessary to produce the overall evaluations referred to in paragraph 4.

8. During the transitional period before the Management Authority takes up its responsibilities, the Commission shall be responsible for producing and submitting the reports referred to in paragraph 3.

Article 51
Entry into force and application

1. This Regulation shall enter into force on the 20th day following its publication in the Official Journal of the European Union.

2. It shall apply from the date referred to in Article 48(1).

3. Articles 26, 27, 32, 45, 48(1), (2) and (4) and Article 49 shall apply as from 2 September 2008.

4. During the transitional period referred to in Article 26(4), references in this Regulation to the Management Authority shall be construed as references to the Commission.

This Regulation shall be binding in its entirety and directly applicable in the Member States in accordance with the Treaty establishing the European Community.

Chapter 11

Other Visa Measures

1. *Introduction*

In addition to the visa measures examined in the rest of this book (visa list, visa code, visa facilitation treaties and Visa Information System), the EU has adopted sundry other measures relating to visa issues. This chapter considers in turn legislation on the uniform visa format, measures on the conditions for issuing visas and the EU's rules on freedom to travel (with related provisions of the Schengen Convention).

2. *Visa Format*

The Maastricht Treaty conferred powers on the EC to adopt measures on a uniform format for visas originally by Article 100c EC, which provided for the Council to act by qualified majority voting on a proposal from the Commission and after consulting the European Parliament. No opt-outs were provided for. Following the entry into force of the Treaty of Amsterdam, the power to adopt measures on this issue was conferred by Article 62(2)(b)(iii) EC. The decision-making procedure did not change.[1] Denmark was still covered by measures in this area, but the UK and Ireland now had an opt-out, if they wished to exercise it. After the entry into force of the Treaty of Lisbon, the power to adopt measures on this issue is subsumed within the EU's general power to adopt measures on a common visa policy.[2] The rules on Member States' participation did not change. However, the rules on decision-making changed, so that the "ordinary legislative procedure" (previously known as "co-decision") now applies to the adoption of measures in this area, enhancing the powers of the European Parliament.

The first measure adopted in this area was Regulation 1683/95,[3] adopted in 1995. This Regulation has been amended twice, in 2002 and 2008, by

---

[1] See chapter 2.
[2] See ibid.
[3] OJ 1995 L 163/1.

Regulations 334/2002 and 856/2008 respectively.[4] A 2003 proposal to amend the legislation[5] was not agreed due to technical reasons, and was withdrawn in 2006.[6] There was also a proposal to consolidate this legislation in 2008,[7] but this was not adopted, and was also subsequently withdrawn.[8]

The UK and Ireland opted into the first amendment to the 1995 Regulation, but not the second. The Regulation and both amendments build upon the Schengen *acquis*, so apply to Norway, Iceland, Switzerland and (in future) Liechtenstein.

There is also a separate measure in this area, adopted during the Amsterdam period pursuant also to the power conferred at the time by Article 62(2)(b)(iii) EC. This is Regulation 333/2002, which establishes a common format for attaching a visa sticker for a different category of persons, those who have travel documents from an entity which is not recognised.[9] This Regulation provides for the same system as Regulation 334/2002 for implementing the common format. This measure also builds upon the Schengen *acquis* and applies fully to Denmark; the UK and Ireland opted in.

The Regulation provides that Member States must issue visas for intended stays in that Member State or several Member States of no more than three months or transit through the territory or airport transit zone of that Member State or several Member States in the standard format set out in the Annex to the Regulation.[10] Further technical details making the visa difficult to counterfeit or falsify have been established in (secret) implementing measures adopted by the Commission, assisted by a committee of Member States' representatives (a "comitology" committee).[11] The 2002 amendment to the legislation updated the "comitology" rules, since the general rules governing "comitology" procedures had been amended in 1999; it also extended the scope of the Commission's implementing powers.[12] Visa holders have the right to verify the data on

---

[4] OJ 2002 L 53/7 and OJ 2008 L 235/1.

[5] COM (2003) 558, 24 Sep. 2003.

[6] COM (2006) 110, 10 Mar. 2006. On these technical difficulties, see Council doc. 6492/05, 17 Feb. 2005, online at: <http://www.statewatch.org/news/2005/feb/6492.05.pdf>; and see the Statewatch story with further documentation online at: <http://www.statewatch.org/news/2004/dec/07visas- residence- biometrics.htm>.

[7] COM (2008) 891, 19 Dec. 2008.

[8] COM (2010) 623, 27 Oct. 2010, Annex IV.

[9] OJ 2002 L 53/4.

[10] Arts. 1 and 5 and Annex, Reg. 1683/95.

[11] Arts. 2, 3 and 6, Reg. 1683/95. The implementing measures are set out in Commission Decisions 2/96, 7 Feb. 1996 and COM (2000) 4332, 27 Dec. 2000 (both unpublished; see COM (2001) 157, 23 Mar. 2001, p 2). The standard visa format therefore became applicable on 7 Aug. 1996 (see Art. 8, Reg. 1683/95).

[12] Council Decision 1999/468 (OJ 1999 L 184/23). On "comitology" generally, see chapter 2.

the visa and to ask for any corrections or deletions to be made, and only the data set out in the Annex to the Regulation or mentioned in that person's travel document can be included in machine-readable form on the visa.[13]

As from the 2002 amendment, Member States must include a photograph in visas in order to increase security and to pave the way for the introduction of the Visa Information System ("VIS").[14] Member States have had an obligation to introduce photographs in visas from 3 June 2007.[15] Visa holders' biometric data is not stored on a computer chip integrated into each visa sticker, but rather will be stored in the central computer system which will service the VIS, when the VIS begins operations.[16] The 2008 amendment to the legislation ensures that the standard visa format is consistent with the intended introduction of the VIS, so that visa sticker numbers can in future be searched easily via the VIS.

Similarly, several other EU measures provide for a distinct form of visa format,[17] but on the other hand, a number of measures provide for the application of the standard visa format in other contexts.[18] In particular, a Regulation adopted in 2010 provides for the use of the common visa format for all long-stay visas also.[19]

3. *Conditions for Issuing Visas*

Although the vast majority of rules concerning the conditions for issuing visas are now set out in the visas code, along with (for some countries) visa

---

[13] Art. 4, Reg. 1683/95.

[14] On the VIS generally, see chapter 10.

[15] See Art. 1(3), Reg. 334/2002 and the secret implementing Commission Decision C (2002) 2002, 3 June 2002 (unpublished; see COM (2003) 558, 24 Sep. 2003, p 2).

[16] The process of taking and storing biometric data from visa applicants is therefore regulated by the EU's visa code: see chapter 8.

[17] The Regs. regarding the Kaliningrad visa format (Reg. 694/2003, OJ 2003 L 99/15) and the issue of collective visas to seamen (see originally Reg. 415/2003, OJ 2004 L 64/1, and now Art. 36 and Annex IX to the visa code (Reg. 810/2009, OJ 2009 L 243/1)). The Olympic visa regulations provide instead for insertion of numbers into the Olympic accreditation card as the format of the visa (Art. 6, Reg. 1295/2003, OJ 2003 L 183/1 and Art. 6, Reg 2046/2005, OJ 2005 L 334/1). The same rule will apply to any future Olympics held in the Schengen area (see Art. 49 and Annex XI, Art. 6 of the visa code (idem)). On these measures, see further section 3 below.

[18] The Joint Action on airport transit visas (OJ 1996 L 63/8) provided explicitly for use of the standard format (see Art. 2(3)), although the visa code (ibid), which repealed this Joint Action, no longer contains an express rule to this effect; while the ADS treaty with China (OJ 2004 L 83/12) provides implicitly for the use of the standard visa format.

[19] Art. 18 of the Schengen Convention, as amended by Reg. 265/2010 (OJ 2010 L 85/1). See further section 4 below.

facilitation treaties, a number of sundry separate measures still apply. Some were adopted by the Schengen Executive Committee, and some were adopted by the EU before the entry into force of the Maastricht Treaty, or the EC during the "Amsterdam era".

Starting with the Schengen *acquis*, along with the rules in the Schengen Convention and the main rules on the conditions for issuing visas (the Common Consular Instructions, or "CCI"), and leaving aside measures which were not allocated to the EC legal order, pursuant to the Schengen Protocol, when the Treaty of Amsterdam entered into force, there were thirteen Executive Committee Decisions wholly related to visas and five Decisions partly related to visas. The former comprised Decisions on: extending the uniform visa;[20] procedures for cancelling the uniform visa;[21] issuing uniform visas at the border;[22] introducing a computerised procedure for the consultation provided for in Article 17(2);[23] a common visa policy;[24] representation of other Member States when issuing visas;[25] issuing visas at the borders to seamen in transit;[26] harmonisation of visa policy;[27] exchange of visa statistics at local level;[28] stamping of passports of visa applicants;[29] abolition of the visa "grey list";[30] the manual of documents to which a visa may be affixed;[31] and the introduction of a harmonised form for sponsorship.[32] The latter comprised Decisions on: the acquisition of common entry and exit stamps;[33] exchanges of statistical information on visas;[34] an action plan to combat illegal immigration;[35] the coordinated deployment of document advisors;[36] and a manual of documents to which a visa may be affixed.[37]

---

[20] SCH/Com-ex (93) 21 (OJ 2000 OJ L 239/151).
[21] SCH/Com-ex (93) 24 (OJ 2000 L 239/154).
[22] SCH/Com-ex (94) 2 (OJ 2000 L 239/163).
[23] SCH/Com-ex (94) 15 (OJ 2000 L 239/165), corrected by the Council in 2000 (OJ 2000 L 272/24).
[24] SCH/Com-ex (95) PV 1 rev. (OJ 2000 L 239/175).
[25] SCH/Com-ex (96) 13 rev. 1 (OJ 2000 L 239/180).
[26] SCH/Com-ex (96) 27 (OJ 2000 L 239/182).
[27] SCH/Com-ex (97) 32 (OJ 2000 L 239/186).
[28] SCH/Com-ex (98) 12 (OJ 2000 L 239/196).
[29] SCH/Com-ex (98) 21 (OJ 2000 L 239/200).
[30] SCH/Com-ex (98) 53 rev. 2 (OJ 2000 L 239/206).
[31] SCH/Com-ex (98) 56 (OJ 2000 L 239/207).
[32] SCH/Com-ex (98) 57 (OJ 2000 L 239/299).
[33] SCH/Com-ex (94) 16 rev. (OJ 2000 L 239/166).
[34] SCH/Com-ex (94) 25 (OJ 2000 L 239/173).
[35] SCH/Com-ex (98) 37 def. 2 (OJ 2000 L 239/203).
[36] SCH/Com-ex (98) 59 rev. (OJ 2000 L 239/308).
[37] SCH/Com-ex (99) 14 (OJ 2000 L 239/298).

Of these further eighteen decisions, two related to visa lists, and so were repealed by the EC's visa list Regulation in 2001.[38] Two further Decisions – concerning the issue of visas to seamen, and the issue of visas at the border – were repealed when the EC adopted updated rules on these issues in 2003.[39]

Although the visa code subsequently repealed the visa provisions of the Schengen Convention (Articles 9-17 of the Convention), the CCI and five Executive Committee Decisions related to visas,[40] nine Executive Committee Decisions relating to Schengen visas still remain in force, namely: two Decisions concerning a manual of travel documents (ie passports and equivalent documents) to which a visa can be affixed;[41] a Decision establishing the Schengen Consultation Network;[42] harmonising visa policy as regards Indonesia;[43] the principles for issuing Schengen visas as regards representation;[44] the stamping of passports of visa applicants;[45] an action plan to combat illegal immigration;[46] the coordinated deployment of document advisers;[47] and the acquisition of common entry and exit stamps.[48] It may be questioned how much, if at all, these remnants of the Schengen *acquis* are still relevant in practice.[49]

However, two of these remaining measures would be repealed by a proposed EU Decision regarding the manual of travel documents,[50] while the Decision on the Schengen Consultation Network has been amended by the

---

[38] SCH/Com-ex (97) 32 and SCH/Com-ex (98) 53 rev 2 (ns. 27 and 30 above), repealed by Reg. 539/2001 (OJ 2001 L 81/1).

[39] SCH/Com-ex (94) 2 and SCH/Com-ex (96) 27 (ns. 22 and 26 above), repealed by Reg. 415/2003 (n. 17 above).

[40] See further chapter 8, section 1.

[41] SCH/Com-ex (98)56 and SCH/Com-ex (99)14 (ns. 31 and 37 above).

[42] SCH/Com-ex (94) 15 (n. 23 above).

[43] SCH/Com-ex (95) PV 1 Rev (n. 24 above).

[44] SCH/Com-ex (96) 13 Rev (n. 25 above).

[45] SCH/Com-ex (98) 21 (n. 29 above).

[46] SCH/Com-ex (98) 37 def 2 (n. 35 above).

[47] SCH/Com-ex (98) 59 Rev (n. 36 above).

[48] SCH/Com-ex (94) 16 Rev (n. 33 above).

[49] For instance, the issue of stamping the travel documents of visa applicants is addressed in detail in Art. 20 and Annex III of the visa code – which conflicts in part with the Executive Committee Decision on this issue. As for the Decision on representation (SCH/Com-ex (96) 13 Rev), it is not clear how it relates to Art. 8 of the visa code. On the other hand, the Decision on common entry and exit stamps (SCH/Com-ex (94) 16 Rev) is still referred to in Annex IV of the Schengen Borders Code (Reg. 562/2006, OJ 2006 L 105/1).

[50] COM (2010) 662, 12 Nov. 2010. The Council and European Parliament have agreed in principle on this Decision (see the agreed text in Council doc. 12058/11, 27 June 2011, not yet formally adopted).

Council pursuant to the 2001 Regulation conferring the power upon it to amend the Network,[51] and will be replaced once all consulates issuing Schengen visas implement the VIS.[52]

As for EC (now EU) measures, the legislation concerning updates to the visa rules, airport transit visas and the issue of visas at the border and to seamen, was all repealed by the visa code.[53] A number of measures are still in force however:

a) two special Regulations providing for facilitated transit between Kaliningrad and the rest of Russia,[54] which were adopted to assuage Russian concerns about the transit of Russian citizens between the enclave of Kaliningrad, which became surrounded by EU Member States after enlargement of the EU, and the rest of Russia;

b) two Regulations setting out special rules related to holding the Olympics in the EU, although these measures are now obsolete;[55] and

c) a Recommendation on the issue of short-term visas to researchers.[56]

4. *Freedom to Travel – and Other Schengen Provisions*

4.1. *Introduction*

The freedom of third-country nationals to travel around the European Union is an obvious corollary of the idea of a Union without internal borders and of the creation of an area of "freedom, security and justice". The basic rules on such freedom to travel are set out in Articles 19–22 of the Schengen

---

[51] This power was conferred by Reg. 789/2001 (OJ 2001 L 116/2), and the visa code has retained the power to amend the Schengen Consultation Network pursuant to this Reg. until the Network is fully replaced by the VIS (Arts. 56(2)(d) and 58(4) of the code: Reg. 810/2009, OJ 2009 L 243/1). The amending Decisions have been published in OJ 2007 L 192/26, OJ 2007 L 340/92, OJ 2008 L 328/38, OJ 2009 L 353/49 and OJ 2011 L 166/22.

[52] See Arts. 16 and 46 of the VIS Reg. (Reg. 767/2008, OJ 2008 L 218/60) and the Commission decision implementing the VIS Reg. as regards the consultation mechanism integrated into the VIS (OJ 2009 L 117/3). However, there is no EU measure (yet) which formally repeals the Executive Committee Decision on the consultation network, and the measures amending it, as from that date. The Schengen Consultation System and the VIS will co-exist during the roll-out of the VIS.

[53] Respectively, Reg. 789/2001 (n. 51 above); OJ 1996 L 63; and Reg. 415/2003 (n. 17 above).

[54] Regs. 693/2003 and 694/2003 (OJ 2003 L 99/8 and 15).

[55] Regs. 1295/2003 (OJ 2003 L 183/1) and 2046/2005 (OJ 2005 L 334/1). The two Regs. are essentially identical. These rules are now set out in Annex XII to the visa code (see n. 17 above).

[56] OJ 2005 L 289/23.

Convention. Unlike the rules on borders (Articles 2–8 of the Convention, repealed by the Schengen Borders Code) and visas (Articles 9-17 of the Convention, repealed by the visa code), these rules have never been replaced by EU measures, although they were amended for the first time by an EU Regulation in 2010,[57] and a proposal of March 2011 (the "2011 proposal") would make further amendments, if adopted.[58]

In addition to the rules on freedom to travel, certain other provisions of the Schengen Convention linked to visas and borders still remain in force. There are two categories of such rules: Article 18 of the Convention addresses long-stay visas, and Article 25 concerns checks on persons who have applied to obtain (or renew) a residence permit (and now also a long-stay visa) in the Schengen Information System. Furthermore, while Articles 23 and 24 of the Convention, which concern third-country nationals who are irregular residents, have been repealed by the EU's Returns Directive, they historically formed a part of the Schengen rules on visas and borders. These other provisions have been amended more extensively than the Convention rules on freedom to travel.

A consolidated (and annotated) text of Articles 18-25 of the Convention appears in the Annex to this chapter.

4.2. *Freedom to Travel*

The freedom to travel within the EU for nationals of third countries is governed by the rules of the Schengen Convention, which was integrated into the EU legal system as of 1 May 1999 with the entry into force of the Treaty of Amsterdam. Articles 19–24 of the Convention set out the core rules, addressing in turn movement of persons with a Schengen visa (Article 19), movement of non-visa nationals (Article 20), movement of persons with a residence permit from a Member State (Article 21), the obligation to declare entry (Article 22), the obligation to leave if the conditions for stay are not or are no longer satisfied (Article 23) and financial compensation for the costs of expulsion (Article 24). Travel was only permitted for three months within a six month period, but Article 20(2) specifies that Member States may permit a third-country national to stay for another three months in exceptional circumstances or on the basis of a pre-existing bilateral agreement. A subsequent Decision of the Schengen Executive Committee required the Member States to renegotiate such treaties so that nationals of third states could enjoy only a

---

[57] Reg. 265/2010, OJ 2010 L 85/1, applicable from 5 Apr. 2010.
[58] COM (2011) 118, 10 Mar. 2011.

maximum three-month stay,[59] but when defining the Schengen *acquis* in 1999, the Council took the view that this Decision was not part of the Schengen *acquis* which had to be "allocated" to a legal base in the EC or EU Treaty, on the grounds that the Decision concerned an issue not covered by the EC or EU Treaty.[60]

In practice the free movement of persons with residence permits is dependent upon Member States notifying the relevant permits, pursuant to the EU's Borders Code.[61] In particular, this meant that some persons with subsidiary protection status granted by a Member State were not able to exercise the freedom to travel. There is no convincing reason to deny *any* legally resident third-country national the freedom to travel within the European Union, and there is even less reason now there is a common interpretation of the concept of subsidiary protection.[62]

When the Schengen *acquis* was integrated into the EU legal order in 1999, Article 18 of the Schengen Convention governed the ability of a third-country national with a long-stay visa from one Member State to cross the external border of another Member State without having to obtain a visa, and Article 25 of the Convention governed the issue or renewal of residence permits to persons listed in the Schengen Information System ("SIS") as a person to be denied entry to the EU.

The freedom to travel rules have been examined in the judgment of the EU's Court of Justice in *Bot*,[63] which concerned a Romanian national (before the accession of Romania to the EU) who had entered France, left again via other Member States and returned within six months. He was stopped and order out of France on the basis that his stay was in conformity with the Schengen Convention. The issue which the Court of Justice had to decide was what is the date of first entry into the Schengen territory for the purposes of Article 20(1) of the Schengen Convention, which provides that a third

---

[59] Sch/Com-ex(98) 24, 23 June 1998.

[60] OJ 1999 L 176/1. For analysis of this Decision, see Peers, "*Caveat Emptor*? Integrating the Schengen *Acquis* into the European Union Legal Order", in Ward and Dashwood, eds., *Cambridge Yearbook of European Legal Studies Volume 2* (Hart, 2000) 87 at 95–104.

[61] See chapter 3.

[62] See further the discussion of the EU's qualification Directive, in *EU Asylum Law: Text and Commentary* (forthcoming). Note also that the qualification Directive requires Member States to issue residence permits to persons with subsidiary protection; the agreed 2011 version of the Directive extends this to their family members (Council doc. 12337/1/11, 6 July 2011).

[63] Case C-241/05 [2006] ECR I-9627.

country national not subject to a visa requirement can move freely within the Schengen territory for three months out of every six.[64] The French court asked the Court of Justice to clarify the meaning of first entry into the Schengen area.

The problem which the Court struggled with, and in respect of which it was less than satisfied with the Commission's assistance, was how to count presences and absences from the Schengen Area in such a way that a third country national cannot become effectively resident by coming and going in rapid succession. The Court held that first entry means in addition to the "very first entry" (as the Court called it) into the Schengen area, also the first entry into the area which takes place after the expiry of a period of six months from the "very first entry" and also to any other first entry which takes place after the expiry of any new period of six months following an earlier date of first entry. Needless to say, this is quite a mouthful and less than crystal clear. Basically what the Court is seeking to do is to limit lawful presence in the Schengen Area to three months out of every six, irrespective of how many times the individual pops in and out of the area. This must be the border guard's nightmare – someone who has so many entry and exit stamps in his or her passport as to make it virtually impossible in a short period of time to figure out how many days in total they have been in the Schengen Area.

4.3. *Regulation 1091/2001*[65]

This Regulation, with the "legal base" of Articles 62(2)(b)(ii) and 63(3)(a) EC, extended short-term free movement rights to persons who had been granted a long-stay visa by a Member State but who had not yet received a residence permit. It did this by amending Article 18 of the Schengen Convention and the CCI to permit national long-stay permits to be used for short-term free movement for a period of up to three months following their initial date of validity. A parallel Council Decision made further amendments to the CCI to give full effect to the Regulation.[66] However, in practice it applied to only a small minority of holders of long-stay visas.[67]

---

[64] On the equivalent provisions of the Border Code, see chapter 3.

[65] OJ 2001 L 150/4.

[66] OJ 2001 L 150/47.

[67] Out of over one million D visas (long-stay visas) issued in 2004, only about 21,000 (2.1% of the total) were D+C visas, ie qualifying for the freedom to travel (see COM (2006) 403, 19 July 2006, p 12).

4.4. *Proposals for Amendment*

A Portuguese proposal from 2000 would have given the EC (as it was then) the power to sign treaties with third states permitting the stay of their nationals for an extended period of three months in the EU, with reciprocity for EU nationals on the territory of the other state.[68] The idea for this initiative arose because the US and Canada in particular were concerned about the idea that their nationals would only be limited to one three-month stay in the entire Schengen area.[69] This was despite the provisions of Article 20(2) of the Schengen Convention permitting Member States to continue applying such pre-existing agreements, because the Council legal service argued that the integration of the Schengen acquis into the EU legal system required Member States to renegotiate these treaties to bring them into conformity with EU law.[70] The Council was unable to agree on this proposal,[71] and it lapsed in May 2004 when Member States lost the power to propose EU immigration and asylum measures.

The Commission proposed a Directive on the same issue in July 2001,[72] which would have replaced and to some extent amended the Schengen rules on freedom to travel for third-country nationals, along with Articles 18, 23 and 25 of the Convention and Regulation 1091/2001.[73] It would also have set out harmonised rules at Schengen/EU level for the first time regarding further extensions of stay for up to three months. The "legal bases" proposed were Articles 62(3) and 63(3) EC. However, the Council was unable to agree on this proposal either, and the Commission withdrew it.[74]

---

[68] OJ 2000 C 164/6.

[69] See the outcome of proceedings of the mixed committee on visa matters, 22 Nov. 1999 (Council doc. 14225/99, 11 Jan. 2000) and a discussion paper (Council doc. 12976/99, 18 Nov. 1999).

[70] See Council doc. 12976/99, *ibid.* The Council has refused to release the legal service opinion (Council doc. 11167/99, 21 Sep. 1999).

[71] See the outcome of proceedings of the visa working party on 21 Oct. 2002 (Council doc. 13660/02, 31 Oct. 2002).

[72] See also the earlier Commission proposal for a Directive on freedom to travel as part of the so-called "Monti package" of three directives concerning the abolition of border controls. But the proposal then had the "legal base" of Art. 100 EC (later Art. 94 EC, now Art. 115 TFEU), requiring a unanimous vote in the Council, and the UK's opposition and the doubts of other Member States about EC legal competence prevented adoption of any of the three proposals. Alternative proposals for "third pillar" measures also got nowhere: see Peers, *EU Justice and Home Affairs Law*, 1st ed. (Longman, 2000), 74–75.

[73] COM (2001) 388, 10 July 2001; OJ 2001 C 270E/244.

[74] COM (2005) 462, 27 Sep. 2005 and [2006] OJ C 64/3.

4.5. *Regulation 265/2010*

With the imminent agreement on the EU's visa code, the special type of long-term visa introduced by Regulation 1091/2001 would be withdrawn. The Commission therefore suggested, and the Council and EP agreed, that all holders of long-stay visas would have the freedom to travel within the EU, subject to a check in the SIS. Regulation 265/2010, which applied as from 5 April 2010 (the same date that the visa code applied from), therefore provides for long-stay visa holders to enjoy the freedom to travel from that date, and also sets out rules relating to long-stay visas as such: they must be valid for no more than one year (and then replaced with a residence permit, if the person concerned is allowed to stay on the territory of the Member State concerned), and in the common visa format applicable to short-stay visas.[75] There is no obligation to take biometric data from long-stay visa applicants, but this issue was supposed to be reviewed by July 2011.[76] This Regulation amended Articles 18, 21 and 25 of the Schengen Convention.

Unfortunately, Article 25 of the Convention was not amended further in order to take more account of the rights and interests of the migrant as well of the interests of the Member State that intends to issue or renew the residence permit or long-stay visa. The procedural rights of the migrant should be improved upon and specified in detail. For example, it should be specified that the consultations between Member States if there is a SIS alert for the persons concerned "shall determine the detailed reasons for the alert and shall consider the proportionality of the refusal of a residence permit or long-stay visa in light of the continued interests of the reporting Member State, the present interests of the Member State considering the issue of the permit and the rights and circumstances of the applicant when deciding whether to issue the permit." In these cases, there should be an *obligation* to issue or renew the residence permit or long-stay visa "if there are serious grounds, in particular humanitarian grounds, international commitments or commitments arising from EU law which require it to be issued." Member States should also be required to "inform the person concerned of the information exchanged, and of all rights and remedies available to that person."

4.6. *The 2011 Proposal*

The March 2011 proposal to amend the Schengen Borders Code would also repeal Articles 21(3) and 22 of the Schengen Convention, leaving in place only

---

[75] On the visa format rules, see section 2 of this chapter.
[76] See the Joint Statement in the summary of Council acts for Mar. 2010: Council doc. 8252/10, 13 Apr. 2010.

Articles 18-21, 25 and 26 (as amended or supplemented) out of all the original provisions of that Convention which concerned immigration or asylum issues. The rationale for repealing Article 21(3) is that it repeats an obligation which already appears in the Borders Code, while the argument for repealing Article 22 is that it is an ineffective way of controlling movements of third-country nationals.[77] It remains to be seen if these amendments are adopted.

In any event, the amendments are incomplete from a technical point of view. Articles 19(1) and 20(1) of the Convention still refer to the conditions for crossing external borders in the Schengen Convention, although these provisions of the Convention have been repealed by the Schengen Borders Code, and even though Article 21(1) of the Convention has already been amended to refer to the Borders Code instead of the Convention. Equally, Article 19(2) of the Convention still refers to provisions of the Convention which have been repealed by the visas code. Also, the 2011 proposal would leave in place Articles 19(4), 20(3) and 21(4) of the Convention, even though these provisions refer to an Article (Article 22) which would be repealed by the 2011 proposal.

5. *Conclusions*

While the Schengen Borders Code and Schengen visa code have done much to improve the clarity and transparency of EU rules in this area, there is clearly more to be done. In particular, the number and complexity of the remaining provisions of the Schengen Convention (Articles 18-22 and 25), in light of their frequent amendemnt, and the remaining Schengen secondary measures, along with the "stray" provisions of EU legislation in this area (leaving aside major measures like the legislation establishing the Schengen Information System and the Visa Information System), itself not codified (cf the visa list and the visa format legislation), is not comprehensible or transparent for third-country nationals, EU citizens or Member States' officials.

Furthermore, it is odd that some of the remaining provisions of the Convention in this area still refer to "Contracting Parties", while others refer to "Member States", and it is anomalous that the remaining provisions of the Convention in this area refer to "aliens", while EU legislation and the EU Treaties refer to "third-country nationals" instead.

It would be preferable to codify (and where necessary, amend or repeal) the measures in this area so that a limited number of EU secondary measures are

---

[77] See COM (2011) 118, n. 58 above.

in place, each governing a single main aspect of EU law in this field. There should be a single Regulation codifying the rules on freedom to travel (although this would probably necessitate examining possible amendments to Article 20(2) of the Convention, as regards possible extended stays). Articles 18 and 25 of the Convention could be integrated into the EU's planned future migration code, since these provisions only concern holders of long-stay visas and residence permits. Alternatively these provisions could be codified together with the EU's Regulation on a common residence permit format, since these rules all concern the procedural aspects of long-stay visas and residence permits.[78] Article 26 of the Convention (on carrier sanctions) could be codified with the Directive which supplements it.[79] The visa list and visa format legislation could be integrated into the visa code,[80] along with other "stray" EU and Schengen visa measures, and "stray" EU and Schengen rules on borders could be integrated into the borders code.[81]

The end result would entail (*inter alia*) the final repeal of all the provisions of the Schengen *acquis* relating to immigration and asylum. This could only be celebrated from the perspective of democratic legitimacy and transparency.

---

[78] See Reg. 1030/2002 (OJ 2002 L 157/1), as amended by Reg 380/2008 (OJ 2008 L 115/1), which is itself not yet codified. However, this codification should not mean that long-stay visa applicants or holders are subjected to fingerprinting requirements, unless the Commission can present sufficiently good reasons for this in its report on this issue.

[79] Directive 2001/51, OJ 2001 L 187/45. See further volume 2 of this book, chapter 12.

[80] However, there would be some awkward issues as regards the position of Denmark, the UK and Ireland, given that these Member States participate in aspects of the visa list and visa format legislation, but not (or not fully) in other visa measures.

[81] For instance the rules on border traffic and passport security (see chapter 6) could be integrated into the borders code as annexes.

Annex

Articles 18-25, Schengen Convention - as amended

CHAPTER 3
VISAS

Section 2

Long-stay visas

Article 18[82]

1. Visas for stays exceeding three months (long-stay visas) shall be national visas issued by one of the Member States in accordance with its national law or Union law. Such visas shall be issued in the uniform format for visas as set out in Council Regulation (EC) No 1683/95 with the heading specifying the type of visa with the letter "D". They shall be filled out in accordance with the relevant provisions of Annex VII to Regulation (EC) No 810/2009 of the European Parliament and of the Council of 13 July 2009 establishing a Community Code on Visas (Visa Code).
2. Long-stay visas shall have a period of validity of no more than one year. If a Member State allows an alien to stay for more than one year, the long-stay visa shall be replaced before the expiry of its period of validity by a residence permit.

CHAPTER 4
CONDITIONS GOVERNING THE MOVEMENT OF ALIENS

Article 19

1. Aliens who hold uniform visas and who have legally entered the territory of a Contracting Party may move freely within the territories of all the Contracting Parties during the period of validity of their visas, provided that they fulfil the entry conditions referred to in Article 5(1)(a), (c), (d) and (e).[83]

---

[82] This is the current version of Art. 18 of the Convention, valid from 5 Apr. 2010 pursuant to Reg. 265/2010 (OJ 2010 L 85/1). For the two earlier versions of Art. 18, see the note below. The footnotes (references to the visa format and visa code legislation) have been deleted.

[83] Art. 5 of the Convention, on the entry conditions at the external border, was entirely repealed by the Schengen Borders Code (Art. 39(1) of Reg. 562/2006, OJ 2006 L 105/1). This reference must now be read as a reference to the corresponding provisions of the Borders code (see Art. 39(3) of the code).

2. *Pending the introduction of a uniform visa, aliens who hold visas issued by one of the Contracting Parties and who have legally entered the territory of one Contracting Party may move freely within the territories of all the Contracting Parties during the period of validity of their visas up to a maximum of three months from the date of first entry, provided that they fulfil the entry conditions referred to in Article 5(1)(a), (c), (d) and (e).*[84]

3. Paragraphs 1 and 2 shall not apply to visas whose validity is subject to territorial limitation in accordance with Chapter 3 of this Title.[85]

4. This Article shall apply without prejudice to Article 22.

Article 20

1. Aliens not subject to a visa requirement may move freely within the territories of the Contracting Parties for a maximum period of three months during the six months following the date of first entry, provided that they fulfil the entry conditions referred to in Article 5(1)(a), (c), (d) and (e).[86]

2. Paragraph 1 shall not affect each Contracting Party's right to extend beyond three months an alien's stay in its territory in exceptional circumstances or in accordance with a bilateral agreement concluded before the entry into force of this Convention.

3. This Article shall apply without prejudice to Article 22.

Article 21

1. Aliens who hold valid residence permits issued by one of the Member States may, on the basis of that permit and a valid travel document, move freely for up to three months in any six-month period within the territories of the other Member States, provided that they fulfil the entry conditions referred to in Article 5(1)(a), (c) and (e) of Regulation (EC) No 562/2006

---

[84] Art. 19(2) was not defined as forming part of the Schengen *acquis* for the purposes of integration into the EU legal order: see OJ 1999 L 176/1.

[85] Chapter III of Title II of the Convention, on short-stay visas, has been entirely repealed by the visas code (Art. 56(1) of Reg. 810/2009, OJ 2009 L 243/1), except for Art. 18 of the Convention, which is not relevant in this context. This reference must now be read as a reference to the corresponding provisions of the visa code (see Art. 56(3) and Annex XIII of the code).

[86] Again, Art. 5 of the Convention, on the entry conditions at the external border, was entirely repealed by the Schengen Borders Code (Art. 39(1) of Reg. 562/2006, OJ 2006 L 105/1). This reference must now be read as a reference to the corresponding provisions of the Borders Code (see Art. 39(3) of the Code).

of the European Parliament and of the Council of 15 March 2006 establishing a Community Code on the rules governing the movement of persons across borders (Schengen Borders Code) and are not on the national list of alerts of the Member State concerned.[87]

2. Paragraph 1 shall also apply to aliens who hold provisional residence permits issued by one of the Contracting Parties and travel documents issued by that Contracting Party.

2a. The right of free movement laid down in paragraph 1 shall also apply to aliens who hold a valid long-stay visa issued by one of the Member States as provided for in Article 18.[88]

3. The Contracting Parties shall send the Executive Committee a list of the documents that they issue as valid travel documents, residence permits or provisional residence permits within the meaning of this Article.[89]

4. This Article shall apply without prejudice to Article 22.

Article 22[90]

1. Aliens who have legally entered the territory of one of the Contracting Parties shall be obliged to report, in accordance with the conditions laid down by each Contracting Party, to the competent authorities of the Contracting Party whose territory they enter. Such aliens may report either on entry or within three working days of entry, at the discretion of the Contracting Party whose territory they enter.

2. Aliens resident in the territory of one of the Contracting Parties who enter the territory of another Contracting Party shall be required to report to the authorities, as laid down in paragraph 1.

3. Each Contracting Party shall lay down its exemptions from paragraphs 1 and 2 and shall communicate them to the Executive Committee.

---

[87]   Art. 21(1) was replaced with effect from 5 Apr. 2010, by Reg. 265/2010 (OJ 2010 L 85/1). For the original version of Art. 21(1), see the Note below. The footnote (a reference to legislation) has been omitted.

[88]   Para. 2a was inserted by Reg. 265/2010 (OJ 2010 L 85/1), with effect from 5 Apr. 2010.

[89]   The list of residence permits (see the definition in Art. 1 of the Convention) is now communicated to the Commission and published pursuant to Art. 34 of the Schengen Borders Code (Reg. 562/2006, OJ 2006 L 105/1). The 2011 proposal to amend the Borders Code (COM (2011) 118, 10 Mar. 2011) would repeal Art. 21(3) of the Convention, if adopted.

[90]   The 2011 proposal to amend the Borders Code (ibid.) would repeal Art. 22 of the Convention, if adopted.

Article 23[91]

1. Aliens who do not fulfil or who no longer fulfil the short-stay conditions applicable within the territory of a Contracting Party shall normally be required to leave the territories of the Contracting Parties immediately.
2. Aliens who hold valid residence permits or provisional residence permits issued by another Contracting Party shall be required to go to the territory of that Contracting Party immediately.
3. Where such aliens have not left voluntarily or where it may be assumed that they will not do so or where their immediate departure is required for reasons of national security or public policy, they must be expelled from the territory of the Contracting Party in which they were apprehended, in accordance with the national law of that Contracting Party. If under that law expulsion is not authorised, the Contracting Party concerned may allow the persons concerned to remain within its territory.
4. Such aliens may be expelled from the territory of that Party to their countries of origin or any other State to which they may be admitted, in particular under the relevant provisions of the readmission agreements concluded by the Contracting Parties.
5. Paragraph 4 shall not preclude the application of national provisions on the right of asylum, the Geneva Convention relating to the Status of Refugees of 28 July 1951, as amended by the New York Protocol of 31 January 1967, paragraph 2 of this Article or Article 33(1) of this Convention.

Article 24[92]

Subject to the Executive Committee's definition of the appropriate criteria and practical arrangements, the Contracting Parties shall compensate each other for any financial imbalances which may result from the obligation to expel as provided for in Article 23 where such expulsion cannot be effected at the alien's expense.

---

[91] Art. 23 was replaced as of 24 Dec. 2010, pursuant to Art. 20(1) and 21 of the Returns Directive (Directive 2008/115, OJ 2008 L 348/98).

[92] Art. 24 was replaced as of 24 Dec. 2010, pursuant to Art. 20(1) and 21 of the Returns Directive (ibid).

CHAPTER 5

RESIDENCE PERMITS AND ALERTS FOR THE PURPOSES OF REFUSING ENTRY

Article 25

1. Where a Member State considers issuing a residence permit, it shall systematically carry out a search in the Schengen Information System. Where a Member State considers issuing a residence permit to an alien for whom an alert has been issued for the purposes of refusing entry, it shall first consult the Member State issuing the alert and shall take account of its interests; the residence permit shall be issued for substantive reasons only, notably on humanitarian grounds or by reason of international commitments.

   Where a residence permit is issued, the Member State issuing the alert shall withdraw the alert but may put the alien concerned on its national list of alerts.[93]

1a. Prior to issuing an alert for the purposes of refusing entry within the meaning of Article 96, the Member States shall check their national records of long-stay visas or residence permits issued.[94]

2. Where it emerges that an alert for the purposes of refusing entry has been issued for an alien who holds a valid residence permit issued by one of the Contracting Parties, the Contracting Party issuing the alert shall consult the Party which issued the residence permit in order to determine whether there are sufficient reasons for withdrawing the residence permit.

   If the residence permit is not withdrawn, the Contracting Party issuing the alert shall withdraw the alert but may nevertheless put the alien in question on its national list of alerts.

3. Paragraphs 1 and 2 shall apply also to long-stay visas.[95]

Note on Article 18:

Original text of Article 18, until 7 June 2001:

Visas for stays exceeding three months shall be national visas issued by one of the Contracting Parties in accordance with its national law. Such visas shall enable their holders to transit through the territories of the other Contracting

---

[93] Art. 25(1) was replaced with effect from 5 Apr. 2010, by Reg. 265/2010 (OJ 2010 L 85/1). For the original version of Art. 25(1), see the Note below.
[94] Para. 1a was inserted by Reg. 265/2010 (ibid), as from 5 April 2010.
[95] Para. 3 was inserted by Reg. 265/2010 (ibid), as from 5 April 2010.

Parties in order to reach the territory of the Contracting Party which issued the visa, unless they fail to fulfil the entry conditions referred to in Article 5(1) (a), (d) and (e) or they are on the national list of alerts of the Contracting Party through the territory of which they seek to transit.

Text of Article 18, as inserted by Reg. 1091/2001, from 7 June 2001 to 5 April 2010:

Visas for stays exceeding three months shall be national visas issued by one of the Member States in accordance with its national law. For a period of not more than three months from their initial date of validity such visas shall be valid concurrently as uniform short-stay visas, provided that they were issued in accordance with the common conditions and criteria adopted under or pursuant to the relevant provisions of Chapter 3, section 1 and their holders fulfil the entry conditions referred to in Article 5(1)(a), (c), (d) and (e). Otherwise, such visas shall merely enable their holders to transit through the territories of the other Member States in order to reach the territory of the Member State which issued the visa, unless the holders do not fulfil the entry conditions referred to in Article 5(1)(a), (d) and (e) or are on the national list of alerts of the Member State through whose territory they seek to transit.

Note on Article 21:

Before the entry into force of Reg. 265/2010, Article 21(1) read as follows:

1. Aliens who hold valid residence permits issued by one of the Contracting Parties may, on the basis of that permit and a valid travel document, move freely for up to three months within the territories of the other Contracting Parties, provided that they fulfil the entry conditions referred to in Article 5(1)(a), (c) and (e) and are not on the national list of alerts of the Contracting Party concerned.

Note on Article 25:

Before the entry into force of Reg. 265/2010, Article 25(1) read as follows:

1. Where a Contracting Party considers issuing a residence permit to an alien for whom an alert has been issued for the purposes of refusing entry, it shall first consult the Contracting Party issuing the alert and shall take account of its interests; the residence permit shall be issued for substantive reasons only, notably on humanitarian grounds or by reason of international commitments.

If a residence permit is issued, the Contracting Party issuing the alert shall withdraw the alert but may put the alien concerned on its national list of alerts.